IN/VISIBLE WAR

War Culture

Edited by Daniel Leonard Bernardi

Books in this series address the myriad ways in which warfare informs diverse cultural practices, as well as the way cultural practices—from cinema to social media—inform the practice of warfare. They illuminate the insights and limitations of critical theories that describe, explain, and politicize the phenomena of war culture. Traversing both national and intellectual borders, authors from a wide range of fields and disciplines collectively examine the articulation of war, its everyday practices, and its impact on individuals and societies throughout modern history.

Brenda M. Boyle and Jeehyun Lim, eds., *Looking Back on the Vietnam War: Twenty-First-Century Perspectives*

Aaron Michael Kerner, *Torture Porn in the Wake of 9/11: Horror, Exploitation, and the Cinema of Sensation*

Delia Malia Caparoso Konzett, *Hollywood's Hawaii: Race, Nation, and War*

Nan Levinson, *War Is Not a Game: The New Antiwar Soldiers and the Movement They Built*

Matt Sienkiewicz, *The Other Air Force: U.S. Efforts to Reshape Middle Eastern Media Since 9/11*

Jon Simons and John Louis Lucaites, eds., *In/visible War: The Culture of War in Twenty-First-Century America*

IN/VISIBLE WAR

The Culture of War in Twenty-First-Century America

EDITED BY

JON SIMONS AND JOHN LOUIS LUCAITES

RUTGERS UNIVERSITY PRESS
New Brunswick, Camden, and Newark, New Jersey, and London

Library of Congress Cataloging-in-Publication Data
Names: Lucaites, John Louis, editor of compilation. | Simons, Jon, 1961– editor of compilation.
Title: In/visible war : the culture of war in twenty-first-century America /edited by Jon Simons and John Louis Lucaites.
Other titles: Invisible war
Description: New Brunswick, NJ : Rutgers University Press, [2017] | Series: War culture | Includes bibliographical references and index.
Identifiers: LCCN 2016038032| ISBN 9780813585383 (hardcover : alk. paper) | ISBN 9780813585376 (pbk. : alk. paper) | ISBN 9780813585390 (e-book : epub) | ISBN 9780813585406 (e-book : web pdf)
Subjects: LCSH: War in mass media. | Mass media and war—United States. | War and society—United States—History—21st century.
Classification: LCC P96.W352 U553 2017 | DDC 070.4/49355020973—dc23
LC record available at https://lccn.loc.gov/2016038032

A British Cataloging-in-Publication record for this book is available from the British Library.

For photo credits, see page 271.

∞ The paper used in this publication meets the requirements of the American National Standard for Information Sciences—Permanence of Paper for Printed Library Materials, ANSI Z39.48–1992.

www.rutgersuniversitypress.org

Manufactured in the United States of America

CONTENTS

IN/VISIBLE WAR

INTRODUCTION

The Paradox of War's In/visibility

JOHN LOUIS LUCAITES AND JON SIMONS

Those born in the United States in the twenty-first century—or at least subsequent to September 11, 2001—have never known a time at which the nation was not at war. This in itself is not so strange, as the United States has been at war for 93 percent of its history.[1] The conflicts in Afghanistan and Iraq stand out as what we might consider traditional, full-scale wars measured by the invasion and occupation of national territories by air and ground forces supported by nation-states. But these confrontations are the least of it, because the United States has also been embroiled in an ongoing "War on Terror" with the forces of Al-Qaeda and ISIS emanating from Afghanistan and Iraq, as well as Libya, Pakistan, Somalia, Syria, and Yemen. President Barack Obama looks set to become "the only president in American history to serve two complete terms with the nation at war."[2] The cost in lives and dollars has been enormous, and the outcomes are hard to reckon with, as the war on terror shows no signs of ending and the Middle East remains the most unstable and troubled region in the world. One might imagine that given such circumstances, the U.S. population would be in a continual state of mobilization, rather like during the great wars of the twentieth century, or at least there would be a pronounced and significant antiwar movement such as emerged during the Vietnam War in the 1960s. But neither has been the case.

Indeed, for most U.S. citizens, most of the time, there is no clear recognition that the country is involved in all-out warfare. Fought largely by a volunteer force or by privatized and professional armies, the national sacrifice has been minimal, ritualistically recognized at sporting events or on designated holidays, but hardly shared across the citizenry as one might expect in a national crisis. Attempting to gloss "the difference between being a war president and a president at war," Derek Chollet, a former U.S. assistant secretary of defense, notes that it comes down to not subordinating all of American power to fighting the war.[3] Perhaps it means something that the United States is not a "war nation" but only "at war," but the denial inherent in Chollet's prevarication should not be ignored. In the wake of 9/11, the first attack on American soil since Pearl Harbor, the U.S. Congress hastily passed the Patriot Act followed in 2002 by the Homeland Security Act. Both are indicative of the ways in which the War on Terror declared by President George W. Bush on September 20, 2001, emphasized the domestic threat to the United States. Although the United States did indeed launch the invasion of Afghanistan on October 7, 2001, unlike World War II the country seemed to be more concerned with security at home (e.g., the panic over the anthrax attacks) than the war overseas. National security and terrorism continue to be of concern, yet the threat of terrorist attacks is generally framed as a matter of homeland security (as with the Boston Marathon in 2013 bombing or the Orlando massacre in 2016) rather than as a war that entails sustained international military combat. The threat of such attacks emerges from time to time but dissipates as the news cycle proceeds along its relentless path, and on the whole life goes on, as if the nation's military excursions abroad were of little more than passing concern. Even when the terrorist threat is seen domestically, the war conducted by the United States elsewhere in the world goes largely unseen by publics in the homeland.

Yet something more complex than either seeing or not seeing, being visible or invisible, is going on. What we call the paradox of the in/visibility of war entails that war is simultaneously seen and unseen, both visible and invisible at once. One of the registers in which in/visibility occurs is displacement. Sights of the wars overseas are displaced on to the signs of the war on terror at home. Civilian patriots act by dutifully removing their shoes at airport security, but there is nothing that inclines them to picture the boots on the ground at war thousands of miles away. Awareness of and anxieties about such persistent and repeated military conflict have been not only displaced but also normalized in public discourse about mass shootings, immigration, police brutality, the carceral state, and the list goes on. For example, does the United States need a wall on the Mexican border to keep immigrants out or because terrorists might sneak in? The two possibilities become conflated in demands to secure the borders. Immigrants become potential terrorists, and domestic terrorists are perceived as immigrants who should have been screened out before admission. It becomes normal to perceive and respond to violence and threats at home in articulation with the war on terror, such that in an oblique, displaced way the wars being fought overseas are visible in militarized police facing (often African American) protestors at home, or when college campuses buy military equipment at a discount just in case of an active shooter incident. Oddly, then, "war" as a series of threats to domestic security is visible to and experienced by U.S. residents as normal life, and yet the deployment of lethal hardware abroad remains foreign. It is the disparity between the actuality of persistent and repeated military conflict—with all that such conflict entails—and the absence of a sustained and acknowledged, lived experience of war on the U.S. home front that directs attention to the paradoxical in/visibility of war in the twenty-first century: a public culture in which war is continuous and altogether present, but largely unseen and/or unacknowledged.

FIGURES OF THE IN/VISIBILITY OF WAR

To take the full measure of this paradox one need only recognize the degree to which U.S. society has become fully assimilated to a war culture that is no longer recognizable as such. No longer the exception—or even the presumed exception—war has become the norm in the same way that anything that becomes ordinary escapes regular notice. And ironically enough, it is this normalization that has rendered it simultaneously hyper-visual and unnoticed. Legitimated by a popular and commercial mass mediated culture, what has been dubbed the Military-Industrial-Media-Entertainment (MIME) Network, it is made visible as spectacle in the form of films and television shows, a billion-dollar video game industry, flyovers and other military ceremonies at sporting events at every level from high school football games to the Super Bowl, and so on.[4] By contrast, the reality of war is made visible through carefully managed journalistic access to arenas of conflict by a news industry that relies upon the banal representation of such warfare by downplaying the real cost—death and devastation of our military involvement around the world—in order to address the demands of ratings and profitability. And throughout, the militarization of American society proceeds apace, evident in the continued centrality of the military-industrial complex in public policy decision making and the consistent emphasis on international and homeland security. The paradox of in/visibility is thus manifest in the gap between the lived-experience of life in a war zone—or its aftermath, as manifest in all manner of traumatic effects both at home and abroad, including the toxic impact of military bases on the environment, an epidemic of suicides among soldiers suffering from posttraumatic stress disorder (PTSD), drug abuse and domestic violence among veterans, the destruction of civil society in occupied lands, and so on—and the visual, mediated experience of war in public, popular culture. Indeed, the latter mitigates the effect of the former, rendering it beyond ordinary sight. To be clear, by "in/visibility" here we do not mean a lack of visual content, but rather call attention to the active elisions and occlusions that produce a cultural optic in which some things are seen and others are either taken for granted or altogether ignored.

As a case in point, consider the photograph in figure I.1.

In the event that you do not follow American football, that is Peyton Manning at the Indianapolis Colts training camp in the summer of 2007 after having won the Super Bowl. Both authors lived in Indiana at the time, and it is not likely that we would have given the photograph a second thought if it had appeared on the front page of the *Indianapolis Star* or one of the local suburban newspapers. After all, Peyton Manning was a hometown hero, regularly celebrated by the local media. But the photograph did not show up in a local newspaper. Rather, it appeared in the *New York Times*'s "Pictures of the Day" slideshow for August 17, 2007, nestled in with photographs of the tragic (a Peruvian earthquake, a Utah mine disaster), the mundane (a longtime congressional leader announcing his retirement, political and religious celebrations), and the downright silly (the Dutch Office Chair Racing Championship).[5]

What makes the photograph notable is how truly ordinary it is: a revered sports figure attending to his doting fans. Even the irony of "real" warriors

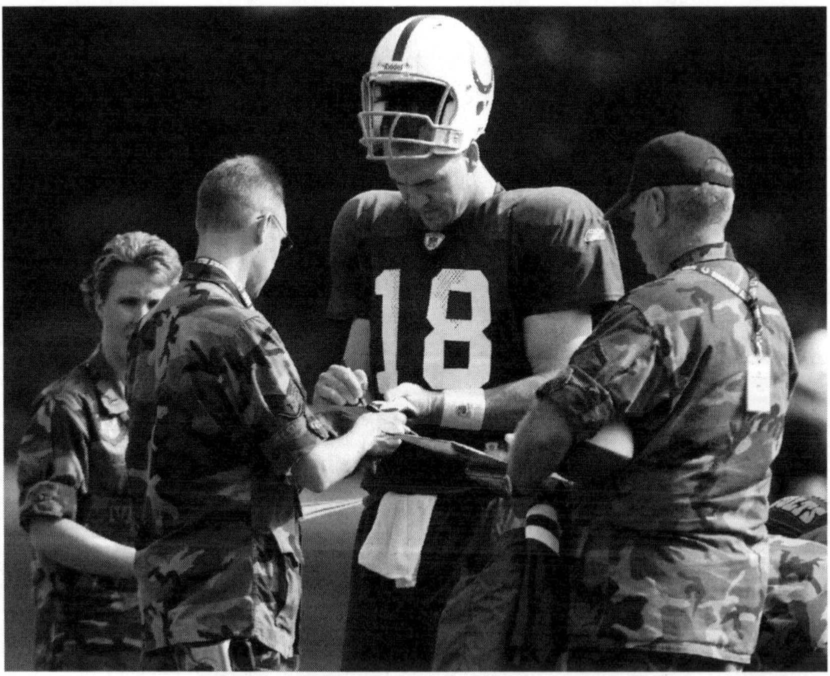

FIGURE I.1

seeking the attention of a professional "weekend" warrior seems to slip past notice with a wink and a nod, as just another day at the office. As the caption reads, "Taking a break from preseason workouts, Peyton Manning, quarterback for the Indianapolis Colts, signed autographs for the members of the 181st Tactical Fighter Wing visiting training camp in Terre Haute, Indiana." And therein lies the problem, for August 2007 was hardly what we might call normal times. The United States was fully entrenched in a foreign war that had been going on for four years and at that point had taken the lives of 3,700 U.S. troops and at least 50,000 Iraqis. And yet for all of that, we have a "picture of the day" in what is generally recognized as the paper of record that shows absolutely nothing out of the ordinary—for civilians and the military alike. Indeed, in an array of fourteen pictures of the day, this is the only one to portray the U.S. military in any fashion whatsoever. The presence of soldiers is a visible sign of war, to be sure, but one so removed and distant from the site of combat that one might assume that they are training in a time of peace.

The photograph of a sports hero signing autographs for members of the 181st Tactical Fighter Wing is telling *both* for what it shows *and* for what it occludes. The faces of the autograph seekers are turned from the camera or obscured from view, their identities reduced to the anonymity of the uniform they share and the souvenirs that they carry; the only identifiable visage belongs to the successful warrior girded for battle. Manning towers over his suitors like a Titan. They seem to stand before him tentatively, respectfully; they are thus subordinate not only in stature, but in attitude and gesture (as is due the "conquering hero"). Winning the Super Bowl is no small feat, to be sure, and the obeisance to sport celebrities is a regular feature of late-modern consumer culture, but when military figures are visualized as supplicants to a civilian athlete during a time of war, our eyebrows should raise just a bit. But of course, the photograph hardly received any notice. What might raise our eyebrows would be Peyton Manning asking these soldiers for their autographs, but of course that photograph does not exist—or if it was taken it was not distributed.

By focusing too much on how such photographs helped to normalize the war in Iraq, we risk looking past the larger implications for how they contribute to creating a culture in which war is paradoxically in/visible. Note, for example, how the image in figure I.1 also visualizes conventional beliefs and attitudes about the constitutive identity between the military and sport culture. One need think only of the contemporary vocabulary for talking about sport: a season is a "campaign"; coaches, quarterbacks, and point guards are "generals"; contests are won or lost "in the trenches"; the playing field is a "war zone," and the list goes on.[6] Lest the connection be missed, in 2011 the NCAA collaborated with the Department of Defense (DOD) to promote the "Carrier Classic," a basketball game between two college rivals played on Veterans Day on the deck of an aircraft carrier with the players wearing uniforms made to resemble camouflage.[7] And then too there is this: between 2012 and 2015, the DOD spent $53 million in sport-related marketing, most of it by the U.S. Army and U.S. Marines, dedicated to recruitment advertising aimed at the seventeen- to twenty-four-year-old demographic.[8] Unable to recruit by celebrating nonexistent victories in Iraq or Afghanistan, or by calling young men and women to join a heroic military struggle, the appeal to volunteer is displaced on to the heroics of sport. By seeing struggle and victory on the athletic "battlefield," publics are invited to *not* see what cannot be seen because it is not there: victory on the battlefield of war.

A different optic, a different way of figuring war, might enable us to see what remains unseen, and perhaps even to see war's simultaneous in/visibility. Vik Muniz's "Toy Soldier" (fig. I.2) helps to illustrate the complexities of the paradox of war's in/visibility.[9]

At first glance and from a distance, one sees the portrait of a young soldier dressed in uniform. Closer examination reveals, however, that the portrait is composed of thousands of small, toy soldier figures mixed and matched in all varieties of angles. The point is poignant as it invites the viewer to see what might otherwise escape ordinary vision, that is, the ways in which the grown soldier is formed by earlier experiences or other aspects of the culture that we can see only if we train ourselves to look more intently, to attend carefully to what is before our eyes. Interpreting the meaning of the picture for ourselves we might think, for example, that if only he had not played with toy soldiers as a boy, he would not now, still young, be dressed in his military finery, embodying the virtues of a citizen serving his country as it is embroiled in an imperialist war. But there is more to it than a simple critique of the socialization to war, for notice how looking closer only underscores the paradox of in/visibility and thus frustrates our capacity to "see war": that is, looking closer only takes us so far. It allows us to see what is represented in a different register in the detail by which it is composed. But it does not allow us to see all that we need to see in order to make timely and productive critical judgments such as the practices and effects of war. We need to know what war is made of, but when we look closely, we see a child's playful version of war, as if to say, yes you can experience war, but only as a game. Muniz thus encourages us to recognize that looking "closer" is important, but that it is never enough. We cannot be assured that by looking more closely at the heroic presence of military personnel in an ordinary, everyday setting (such as being invited to applaud the presence of a veteran on an airplane journey or at a high school commencement) we will see the big picture. We—critics and citizens alike—need to know what *we are not seeing* as well as *what we can see* even when we look closely.[10]

The question, then, is how are twenty-first-century wars operating within the rhetorics and logics of in/visibility? The problem is not that we cannot access what is and has been happening in Iraq, Afghanistan, Pakistan, Syria, Yemen,

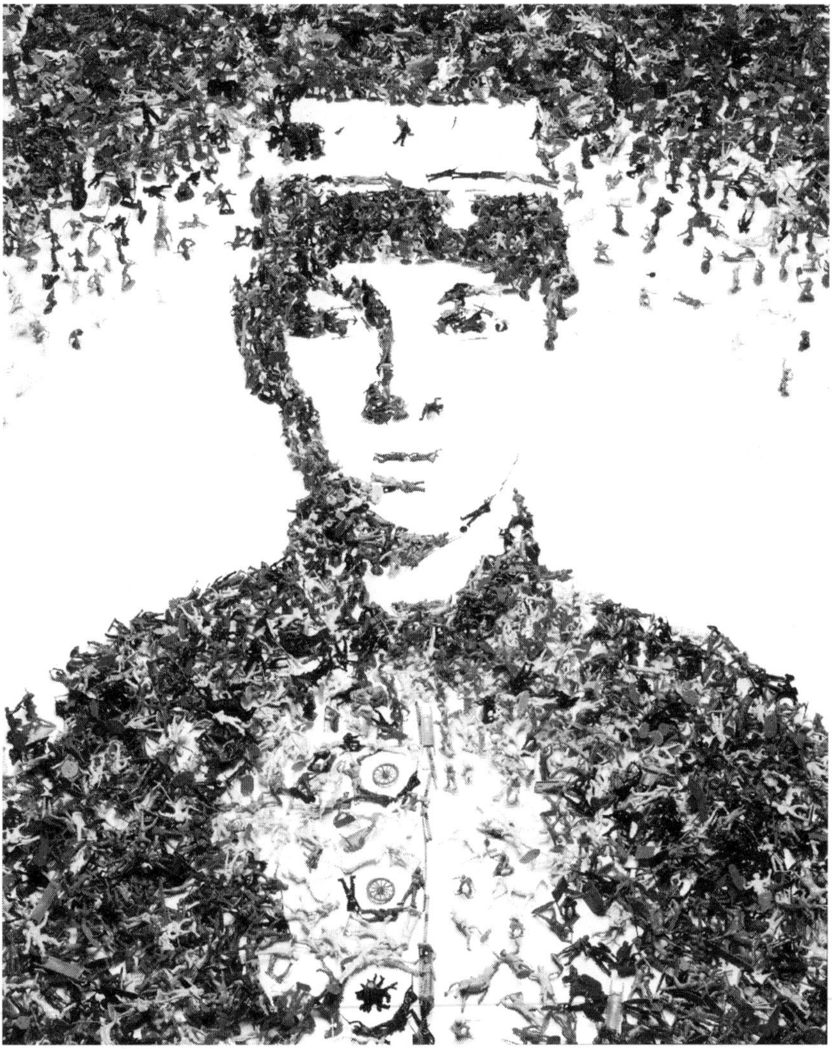

FIGURE 1.2

etc., even if we do not regularly encounter such information in television programming, popular films, social media newsfeeds, game consoles, and other popular cultural platforms. The facts are there for those who seek them out in less mainstream news sources and in academic journals. The problem is that they are generally unacknowledged and largely unknown. Consider, for example, that between 2001 and 2015, the United States dedicated $1.64 trillion to fighting the wars in Iraq and Afghanistan, as well as with Al-Qaeda and ISIS.[11] The cost in lives is a bit more difficult to get a handle on, but even the most conservative estimates make it overwhelming, with U.S. casualties numbering over 6,500 dead and 36,000 wounded, and over 240,000 deaths in Iraq alone.[12] Drone warfare in Pakistan, Yemen, and Somalia is another story. There are no ready estimates of the cost in dollars and cents, but since 2002 there have been between 3,000 and 5,000 deaths. More than 200 (and as many as 1,000) of these casualties were civilians, ten of whom were U.S. citizens and another twenty-eight were citizens of other western nations including Britain, Germany, Australia, and Canada.[13] These are of course raw numbers, abstractions that are difficult to process on their own, and they do not take into account the day-to-day stress and trauma that attends life in such war zones, as well as the epidemic of suicides among U.S. veterans suffering from PTSD. Nevertheless, they mark what is perhaps most significant about our twenty-first-century wars while underscoring the affordances and profound implications of the logic and rhetorics of in/visibility.

THE CRITIQUE OF WAR'S IN/VISIBILITY

The impulse to critique twenty-first-century U.S. wars is especially important insofar as they might be regarded as fundamentally distinct from the wars of the twentieth century. In the past century, the assumption was that wars were legitimized in liberal democratic terms by congressional approval and oversight, opponents were recognizable state actors, and the citizenry was mobilized in national campaigns for success—notwithstanding the eventual protest movement against the war in Vietnam. More recently, such wars have been recast as a "manageable security challenge," as "asymmetrical war" with "nonstate actors," and as a "war on terror." The post-9/11 invasions of Afghanistan and Iraq resembled post-Westphalian wars of nation-states against nation-states. Yet, and in spite of the urge to declare "mission accomplished," the United States remains embroiled in unending conflicts in which terrorists are replaced by insurgents and postconflict projects of nation-building. It is not new that these wars are "immeasurably more complex than the simple presence of military hostilities," but in contemporary times they are fought as much through covert operations and the use of sophisticated drone technologies as with troops on the ground. Indeed, these neoliberal wars entail "full-spectrum operations" that combine the civil and military functions of government and development, such that security in a given territory is made dependent on the governance of the population within it.[14]

How might such considerations bear on the in/visibility of war in the twenty-first century? In what follows, we consider some of the recent literature about the contemporary visual experience of war that helps in varying degrees to explicate the paradox of in/visibility. W.J.T. Mitchell suggests that the U.S. public has experienced its most recent wars as "war[s] of images," blinded by the rage animated by a series of particularly traumatic images. He notes that "2001–04 was an epoch marked and defined by unforgettable and traumatic pictures, from the destruction of the World Trade Center to the photographs of torture in Abu Ghraib prison."[15] From this perspective, the "war of images" turned against the United States in the spring of 2004 when the enemy's traumatizing photo ops prevailed over earlier, "forgettable" photo ops of the toppling of Saddam Hussein's statue and of the visual declaration of "Mission Accomplished." Mitchell observes how the "terrifying *immediacy* of viscerally intimate violence portrayed in real time [by the Iraqi resistance were] archaic forms of tribal violence designed to elicit the tribalistic reactions of the American public."[16] The difference here is telling, as from the latter perspective it is clear that the relay of atrocity images between 2001 and 2004 meant that the U.S. public experienced the war *as* images.

Mitchell's account of war images implies a version of the paradox of in/visibility that is close to the ideological critique of images as deceptive, distorting, and mystifying.[17] The public sees images but remains blind to what is needed for a critical understanding of war. So, for example, when he focuses attention on the now-infamous Abu Ghraib photographs, he urges his readers "to concentrate on the images as symptoms of a systemic problem," such as the racism and homophobia of U.S. culture.[18] Although the hooding of the most memorable figure from Abu Ghraib conceals the racialized enemy, it is also the case that U.S. viewers "have indeed hoodwinked themselves with a peculiar combination of ignorance and idealism, blindness and innocence."[19] And yet, Mitchell continues, with the prompting of Han's Hacke's *The Stargazer*, which shows a figure hooded in the U.S. flag, they are "capable of removing [the hood] and seeing things as they are."[20] This version of the paradox of in/visibility is as old as Plato's cave and follows a logic according to which civic sight is a form of trained blindness.[21] The systemic problems that lead to and sustain twenty-first-century wars against terror remain invisible unless civic vision is enlightened by art or by intellectual critics. The paradox of in/visibility from this angle is not much of a paradox at all, as it is resolved by looking past images to what lies beyond them.

An emphasis on the critique of visuality, of war as images, could then too easily follow the well-trodden path in cultural and political criticism that practices a hermeneutics of suspicion. In the mode of ideological critique, such an interpretive frame might simply aim to bring what has been hidden and invisible into the clear light of visibility. Such work can be found in more vernacular forms than Mitchell's scholarship such as the pressure put on the Pentagon to allow the press (and hence the public) to witness the coffins of fatal casualties arriving at Dover Air Force Base.[22] Or, alternately, it can be found in documentary films such as *Invisible War* (dir. Kirby Dick, 2012), which exposed the scandals of sexual assault in the U.S. military that were otherwise hidden from public view. Some have argued that if the public was shown the kinds of pictures that emerged during the Vietnam War (public executions, mass murders, the effect of napalm on children, etc.) that opposition to more recent wars would be more intense. Critiques of this sort are good as far as they go, but they fail to address the fundamental paradox of in/visibility when the complex task is to help us to acknowledge *what is already visible and yet remains unseen* because it is so ordinary as to go unnoticed . . . unremarkable threads in the fabric of a normalized culture of war.

To this end it becomes important to attend to how publics recognize and interpret what they see such that the visible becomes invisible (and vice versa). The issue here is one of framing and the ways in which various narratives "organize visual experience" so as to determine "what can be seen and what can be heard."[23] The words here are from Judith Butler, and from this perspective the material circumstances of war are rendered invisible by how they are situated within (or outside of) the visual frame. For Butler the primary concern is with how non-U.S. citizens—civilians and combatants alike—are rarely if ever recognized as "grievable" subjects. So, for example, we know that Iraqis and Afghanis have been injured and killed, but because they are not framed as grievable, we are inclined to disavow their wounds and trauma.

Disavowal is closely related to the critical practice of diagnosing symptoms, but in this case the cure is even less easily attainable than for bodily diseases. The nature of disavowal is to be aware of some problematic thing, to see it, but not to acknowledge its disturbing presence. It is worth expanding on disavowal in the Freudian sense as a structure of in/visibility. The subject is split between satisfying a driven desire and acknowledging the danger of fulfilling the desire, between rejecting reality and recognizing the dangers of reality.[24] Octave Manonni formulates it thus: "I know very well, but all the same. . . ."[25] U.S. citizens can know very well that there is war, that it entails very real dangers for the U.S. and inflicts a heavy cost on its military personnel, its national budget, and on the civilians in the countries in which wars are fought, and yet for all of that they do not experience war, do not acknowledge directly that the nation is at war, and thereby they sustain their desire to live normal lives. They can, as Mitchell points out, continue to regard themselves as idealistic pursuers of freedom and innocent victims of aggression and terror while U.S. forces wreak death and destruction on Iraqis and Afghanis. Yet, there are visible symptoms indicating that the reality of war is nonetheless acknowledged in normal life: playing computer war games for entertainment, focusing on canine-rescue narratives, watching alien invasion action movies, wearing military-style camouflage (simplified in the vernacular as "camo") as a fashion statement, and perhaps above all, fetishizing "our heroes," our service men and women, and our veterans without actually valuing them materially. Disavowal cannot be undone in a straightforward way by showing that there is war—by removing the hood—but instead entails bringing citizens to acknowledge what they already know, to look differently at what they already see.

To be clear, we do not wholly resist the trope of ideological unmasking, nor do we disagree that art and photographic appropriation are valuable in training citizens to look differently at both the images of war that populate the media and the circumstances and reasons for war. But again, such an approach oversimplifies the problem, and not only because it evades the sheer difficulty of working through disavowal. In addition to attending to the critical capacity of citizens, or the power of certain images to enliven those capacities—as important as both are—we also focus on the inherent structures of the regime of visuality according to which the key concern is to *look at* and *to think with* images that do not appear to be about war at all, however spectacular or banal they might be. Put differently, sometimes we need to look elsewhere than images of war to see the symptoms of war in the public culture.

Consideration of war's visibility are of course not new, but the shifting nature of war and global conflict has been accompanied by important changes in the technologies of visual representation and the ways in which we have come to encounter and engage war's visual presence.[26] Paul Virilio observed that at the same time as the camera seemed to bring war closer to home by showing us pictures of it, it also distanced the killer from the killed through visual techniques such as filmed aerial reconnaissance. He thus argues that as war has increasingly entailed technologically supported visual perception, particularly with moving pictures, it has disappeared or been "derealized."[27] As he notes, "The world disappears in war, and war as a phenomenon disappears from the eyes of the world."[28] Put differently, war produces spectacle rather than being turned into spectacle by visual and cinematic representation. From this perspective, there was a qualitative shift between the extreme visibility of the Vietnam War, the so-called television war, and the spectacle of the Gulf War.[29] As Laura Marks puts it, the rhetoric of clean war, as evidenced visually by the use of "smart bombs" in the Persian Gulf, kept the bloody reality of war out of sight even as TV screens were repeatedly filled by bomb's-eye views. And yet, in another play of in/visibility, the presence (and absence) of Osama bin Laden and terror in general is a challenge to "the global powers of visibility."[30] Even, then, if military power has enhanced itself with technologies of visibility, techniques of in/visibility are no less significant assets for the terror it counters.

More recent developments in media and society suggest another form of in/visibility which, following Jean Baudrillard's term "hyper-real," we might call "hyper-visuality." Along these lines, war is so visually present that it is not seen at all. From the start of the war on terror, the symbolic challenge of the attack on the Twin Towers on 9/11, we have seen too much, and our desire to see has not come as a critique of war but as an incitement of it.[31] Let us see the worst we can imagine, our own death, which we visualized in all manner of entertainment media before 9/11 and which we continue to enjoy in refracted forms such as the alien invasion genre. War is simulated, as Baudrillard puts it, not only as mass media, but also through the visualizing technologies and preplanning of war such that that the latter has already happened bloodlessly before its actual and bloody shadow is enacted on the ground.

Nicholas Mirzoeff offers a version of the paradox of in/visibility that echoes some of Baudrillard's claims, noting that the proliferation of media images of the war saturated the public sensibility to the point of "banality." Drawing on Walter Benjamin's notion that excessive information can overwhelm the capacity to establish meaning through the telling of stories, Mirzoeff maintains that "the immense surfeit of visual information during the [Iraq] war was conducive to the annihilation of effective narratives about what was happening."[32] From this perspective, the paradox of in/visibility calls attention to the fact that the war was not hidden from the U.S. public, displayed as it was under the caption of "shock and awe" in the case of the Iraq War. Rather, citizen-viewers, treated more as consumers, watched the war unfold on big screen TVs in the comfort of their own homes through a nonstop, twenty-four-hour news cycle. Such media saturation, cast in an altogether domesticated environment, thus produced a banal archive of images that mitigated any real experience of the war.

From this perspective, the problem was not a lack of images, but the "relentless persistence" of images that functioned as "weapons in the military-visual complex . . . designed to overwhelm response."[33] Mirzoeff perhaps focuses rather too much on images deployed by the U.S. government to foreclose public criticism of the war up to 2003 without attending to the images circulated by the government's adversaries or other alternative framings of war. Yet, the implication of his approach is still valid: namely, as critics we need to resist the urge to look behind the images as a way of demonstrating that they are unrepresentative of the realities of war. Consent to the Iraq War in 2003 was not sustained because of a lack of images of death and destruction, but because the measure of the war images of the time was not their accuracy but their performative character as events of national identification.

This brief review is not intended to be comprehensive in covering all aspects of the paradox of in/visibility (nor for that matter will the collection of essays in this volume satisfy such a need), but we hope it demonstrates the sense in which questions of visuality and visibility in war have been recognized and engaged in critical work. In/visibility is complex, not defined by a single feature but operates according to different, overlapping registers. We have touched on these registers in the discussion so far, namely normalization, displacement, disavowal, and simulation. "Normalization" perhaps can serve as an umbrella term for the various registers, and illustrates both the complexity of the in/visibility of war in recent times and the difficulty of figuring out how to unravel the logic and rhetorics of in/visibility, of rendering visible that which is already visible and yet unseen. Normalization of war is woven within the very fabric of everyday life. When visualizations of war are deeply embedded in cultural, political, and social norms—wearing camouflage, driving Jeeps and Humvees, hunting with a military-style AK47, celebrating sports heroes as warriors, playing video games or other simulated versions of war such as paintball, reading and watching comic book versions of *Captain America*, or nostalgic remembrances of World War II, and the list goes on—then war is no longer the state of exception but the rule. Visualizations and representations of war are embedded deeply in cultural, political, and social norms that are themselves a feature of the everyday injustices and oppression of everyday life. Such visualizing practices have their own norms, which render twenty-first-century wars as regular and ordinary as other wars. War then appears as the regularization of normal injustices in the militarization of society. War becomes the norm, or as we might put it while alluding to Giorgio Agamben, a "state of exception . . . in which fact and law coincide."[34] And when that happens war escapes active judgment on the part of the polity. It moves all too subtly and almost without notice from the world of "ought," where choice and judgment are always necessary, to the world of "is," where it becomes all too easy to be resigned to the way things are. The imperative to defend society translates into "America must be secured." Thus a key practice for rendering visible that which is simultaneously seen and unseen is to unravel the fabric of the normal in which in/visibility is produced. Similarly, non-normative practices of seeing and showing war, or alternative optics, are vital as a conduit for critical opposition to normalized war. The essays in the volume engage in these critical practices.

THE ESSAYS

The authors in this volume all seek to interrogate the paradox of the in/visibility of wars in the twenty-first century. Key questions include: How does in/visibility contribute to a militarization of society that operates almost imperceptibly in visual public culture? How do militaristic spectacles serve to hide war's costs while simultaneously putting war on display? How does the in/visibility of war articulate with other political and cultural structures, processes, and practices of social power, such as racism, sexism, and class inequality? Does dissent from militarism depend on other ways of seeing war and rendering it visible? *In/visible War* addresses these questions by considering the rhetorical, cultural, social, economic, and political processes and structures of power that craft and imbricate war's in/visibility. Explicitly or implicitly, the essays tackle in/visibility according to the different registers of normalization, displacement, disavowal, and simulation. As the same time, the various essays investigate the practices of seeing and showing war which simultaneously occlude it, even as they normalize and reinforce a belligerent militaristic culture. Finally, the volume explores alternative optics or ways of seeing our contemporary wars designed to invite critical insight and civic engagement.

The essays that follow examine a wide array of texts and practices that contribute to the public culture of war in the United States in the twenty-first century, including journalism, photojournalism, documentary photography, cinema, television, fiction, nonfiction, and war games. Though the volume is organized in three parts that emphasize one or another aspect of the condition of war's paradoxical in/visibility—"Seeing War," "Not Seeing War," and "Theorizing the In/visibility of War"—we want to underscore the ways in which each contribution both clarifies and complicates the problem of war's in/visibility. For some authors the key problem circulates around the challenges that the citizenry in a liberal-democratic polity face if they are to reverse (or at the very least acknowledge) the state of war's in/visibility. What do they need to be able to see in order to make the most important judgment citizens in a democratic polity have to make: whether or not to go to war. For others, the problem is that the normalcy of war is part and parcel of a system of normalized abnormalities that are endemic to a capitalist, neoliberal democracy, including class inequalities, sexism, and racism. For all, however, including Nina Berman's photo-essay, which connects all three sections, the difficulty is in seeing in/visibility itself and by so doing to invigorate the critical, political energies in opposition to war.

Part 1 focuses on "Seeing War," and each of the essays here emphasizes the ways in which contemporary wars are put on display in one or another form of documentation. The focus is on photography and videography because those are the two most prominent media that purport to accommodate the conventions of realism we typically affiliate with historical representation. This is not to say that such imagery is any more real than any other representation, but rather to call attention to how publics are typically shown war as it unfolds in so-called real time and in its immediate aftermath. This is when we are supposed to see war as it is. The focus of these essays is not on the most obvious issue of how wars are framed in televisual and other news journalism, and how such framing shapes perception of war along national or other lines that appeal to particular audiences. If American audiences had watched (and understood) the news on Al Jazeera in Arabic, they would have seen much more death and destruction than on U.S. news channels.[35] Rather, we focus on the medium of photography, which might seem to stand apart from the infotainment qualities of the more popular broadcast medium. As each of the essays demonstrates, the commitment to a realist aesthetic does not mitigate the paradox of in/visibility but, indeed, may well enable it to unfold in powerful and seamless ways.

Photojournalism is among the chief modes of representation through which war is put on display in something approximating real time. We begin with two essays that explore the conventions and implications of the aesthetic norms employed by photojournalists and the ways in which they have functioned in recent times to normalize our most contemporary wars and the culture of war that underwrites it. David Campbell analyzes the debate about acceptable technical and aesthetic norms of photojournalism that erupted after the publication of Damon Winter's award-winning Hipstamatic photographs taken on his iPhone in 2010 and featured in the *New York Times*'s "Year at War" project. That debate circulated around the question of what was a legitimate photojournalistic image and what was not, the key claim being that the Hipstamatic App processes images in a way that undermines the commitment to presenting an unfiltered reality that presumes to underwrite photojournalism. From Campbell's perspective the appeal to an "unfiltered reality" is unrealistic, gesturing to an aesthetic of objectivity that has never truly been practiced and is at best nostalgic, a point he demonstrates by returning to Robert Capa's photographs during the Spanish Civil War. The bigger point is not only that photojournalism operates within the logic of an outmoded aesthetic sensibility, but that debates surrounding such norms contribute to the depoliticization of war photography. In short, public attention to the horrors and other realities of war is reframed, literally displaced upon an aesthetic and technical debate that not only ignores the role of photojournalism as a mode of public art but, more to the point, helps to make important public questions about the legitimacy of war increasingly in/visible. The photographs are seen, but the issues of war per se are not the primary concerns debated by the community of photographers.

Christopher J. Gilbert and John Louis Lucaites turn attention to how one aspect of the aftermath of war is shown in their study of Craig F. Walker's photo-essay "Welcome Home, the Story of Scott Ostrom." Walker's Pulitzer Prize–winning photo-essay offers a view of the war veteran's struggle to return home, purporting to show what cannot be seen, that is, the psychic trauma that haunts Ostrom and the thousands like him. And it does a pretty good job of doing just that as it portrays the daily struggles that make it difficult for Ostrom to assimilate back into a home front where most of the people he encounters have no direct experience with the war he volunteered to fight. Trauma might be expected to be a subject that shocks viewers of the photographs to recognize the huge cost of war paid not only by U.S. troops but also by a multitude of traumatized combatants and civilians. The problem, as Gilbert and Lucaites demonstrate, is that Walker's view of the returning war veteran normalizes the struggles of returning home within the narrative of the ex-soldier's "war within." War cannot be seen as anything other than a metaphor that treats trauma as a personal and private disorder that is the responsibility of the traumatized individual to overcome rather than a public problem that needs to be shared by the society that supported and "benefited" from the war in the first place. Showing us the path from war's inevitable trauma to individual recovery, the photo-essay thus normalizes war as a persistent feature of the social landscape (rather like alcoholism or drug addiction). Under the cover of making the outcome of war visible as a privatized condition of abnormality (PTSD), the photos obscure the critical and active role that citizens should have with regard to their country going to war.

Jeremy G. Gordon also takes up the problem of war's trauma. From Gordon's perspective, a key problematic of the public understanding of the trauma experienced by war veterans is how it is made in/visible by being framed in a narrowly limited tragic narrative of the Homeric warriors Achilles and Odysseus. In Gordon's terms, war veterans are cast in a "cult of hardness . . . [which entails] an epic effort to repair and maintain performances of militarized masculinity." This mythic narrative is prominent in professional clinical discourses as well as in a broader public discourses, and the combination normalizes the war veteran's already limited agency to negotiate his or her trauma. The concern here is less with recognizing the normative practices for seeing—and by implication failing to see—the effects of war on its veterans, and more with teasing out the complexities of the mythic framework of war trauma through non-normative practices of showing and seeing. Drawing on Michel Foucault's appeal to refashion the lives of "infamous men," Gordon reads a series of portraits of veterans by photographer Susan Opton to demonstrate the sense in which the PTSD experienced by war veterans is inherently in/visible—both material and psychic, affecting both body and spirit—and argues for the importance of maintaining and living within the paradox as part of the reality of war, rather than assuming that it can be resolved (or cured) once and for all. The alternate mythic optic that Gordon offers is thus an effort to manage the paradox of in/visibility by (re)fashioning it rather than succumbing to its more conventional and banal normalizations.

Gordon's essay is thus illustrative of how normative practices of showing war inform the normalization of its traumatic consequences, such as bodily and psychic injury, and how different ways of seeing can challenge those norms. Whereas Mirzoeff critiques the banality of proliferated war images for "disappearing" war, Rebecca A. Adelman and Wendy Kozol treat the banality of war as the ground on which an alternative optic can be developed and war can be seen. Their essay studies "The Day Nobody Died," a 2008 video made by artists Adam

Broomberg and Oliver Chanarin, which immerses the audience in the logistical banality that connects a metropolitan center of war (London) with its imperial outpost (Afghanistan). The video follows the transport of a box of unexposed film from London to Afghanistan and back again, tracking the tedium and indeterminacy of life in a war zone, including not least the persistent fear of violence that sometimes occurs but is in any case always a threat. It is this banality that punctuates and interrupts ordinary life in a war zone and to the extent it can be represented it invites a non-spectacular vision of war that disrupts more conventionalized notions of war's affect. The encounter with the lack of affect that "The Day Nobody Died" represents encourages a critical engagement with the direction of our attention to visualizations of war that do not show us war at all. Rather than seeing nothing by seeing too much, in the optic of banality proposed by Adelman and Kozol we can see much more of war by seeing almost nothing.

The tension between seeing too much and seeing nothing is taken up in Jody Madeira's ethnographic study of the survivors, rescue workers, and relatives of the victims of 9/11. Though still concerned with realist, journalistic representation of the war on terror, Madeira's essay marks a transition between such representations and other, mostly fictional, visual media that show war by not showing it. According to Madeira, the media and the government offered competing frames for the pursuit of bin Laden as either a criminal manhunt or as a war enemy, thereby obliging family members and survivors to negotiate their emotional needs for consolation and/or revenge between these competing frames. In actively attending to the appearances and disappearances of bin Laden through visual media, including Osama bin Laden's own videos, they were witnesses to the displacement between a domestic threat and an external foe. And yet, although they were in a position to question the casting of the pursuit of criminal justice as an act of war, the critical questions about the post-9/11 wars do not come into sight in the fissure between the frames.

The transition between realist representations of war and visions of war as forms of entertainment is also evident in Nina Berman's photo-essay, "War Is Fun." Berman draws our attention directly to the banality of war, the banality of images, and the banality of the normalization of war in everyday life. When it becomes normal to see an armored vehicle exhibited in Times Square, the landing of a military helicopter in a park as a family attraction, a flyby of a stealth bomber as an addition to a day of family fun at the beach, then something weird has happened. It is not that these objects go unnoticed, but that their presence is domesticated, displaced almost entirely from the field of combat, and experienced very differently than they would be in the skies and ground where the war on terror is fought. As war becomes a feature of family entertainment, it is not seen as war per se. Berman's photos focus on the banal scenes of ordinary life in order to turn the normal into the uncanny. More to the point, these photos are not realist indices of war, its violence and horror, but oblique pictures of wars that happen elsewhere and that invite us to look again at the abnormal normality of a country that sees war as theme park attractions.

Part 2, "Not Seeing War," deals with fictional and literary media genres that entail a good deal of looking at images of war—video games, films, narratives—without seeing war. As above, the essays analyze the in/visibility of war through such mediated representations according to the registers of normalization, displacement, and disavowal, but the section begins with Roger Stahl's analysis of the video game *Call of Duty* in which he considers an additional register closely associated with simulation: immersion. Such video games have emerged from the Military-Industrial-Media-Entertainment complex, a concept that helps to understand how the technologies of waging war and communicating public entertainment are identical with one another. It is through the MIME complex that immersive, interactive technologies and aesthetics provide audio-visual simulations for the pursuit of pleasure and military prowess while simultaneously obscuring the actuality of war and the conceptual means to understand and critique it. Stahl notes that players immersed aesthetically and sensuously in video games are trained to treat their immersion in combat as given, as a situation into which they are thrown and must act. Consequently, they are trained not to question why they are fighting, and hence why the United States is even at war. Rather, players learn how to be compliant citizens who never question or criticize their government's actions. They learn only how to act. They are immersed in and looking at war simulations, but they do not see that their country is at war.

Another popular genre that might be seen as an immersive displacement of investment in war into the entertainment industry are the movies that combine the formulae of action heroes and alien invasion. As DeWitt Douglas Kilgore indicates, the industry of Marvel movies does not directly represent our nation's twenty-first-century wars, but they are symptoms of the war culture in which such wars have occurred—a culture smarting over the 9/11 terrorist attacks and all that has followed in its path. Accordingly, these movies tell a story of war and conflict in which the United States—cast as a metonym for humanity writ large—is threatened and wounded by an alien force only to survive and be saved. The formulaic repetition of this genre of movies thus serves as consoling relief for a war-stricken society, but not as cure. Accordingly, the United States is damned and destined to repeat the urge to defeat the alien, whose attacks on its symbols are witnessed in each reiteration of the genre. We have seen this movie before, and boy, we'll be back next time. And still, we won't see that we are at war.

Both Claudia Breger and Purnima Bose counter the normalization of war by unraveling it from the normalization of other social oppressions that are themselves both visible and invisible. The immersive aesthetics of the computer games that most obviously simulate war find a match in the aesthetics of war movies that are now far less common and lucrative than video games. As Breger's chapter illustrates, films ostensibly offer critiques of war, but more generally they serve as evidence of the disappearance of critique from public culture. *The Hurt Locker* is one of the few films that markedly addresses twenty-first-century wars directly and which won critical praise in liberal circles. Does it not then show us war, albeit in fictionalized form? Breger turns to narrative analysis in showing how the film's affect focuses our attention on the experience of trauma and away from what it normalizes. The hegemonic norms of white masculinity and (post)racial politics thus remain in/visible in visual representations of war. Similar to what happens to those immersed in video games, the critical sensibilities of viewers of *The Hurt Locker* are dulled as they are simultaneously immersed in domestic norms of masculinity and race. While war is shown visibly, the normal injustices of U.S. society are veiled in a fog of war trauma.

Purnima Bose analyzes the emergent genre of narratives about dogs being brought back from Iraq and Afghanistan. While these stories tell us little about the conduct of such wars, they are visible symptoms of the failures of such wars to bring about democracy in the occupied nations, a painful failure that is compensated by the difficult journeys of the dogs who are brought into the embrace of U.S. consumer citizenship. Arguing that citizenship has been rearticulated in the language of consumerism, Bose illustrates how pets in general have been recast as quasi-citizens. This anthropomorphization paves the way for the canine rescue narratives in which the failed efforts to democratize Iraq and Afghanistan are compensated by and displaced on to fables of saving dogs for democracy by returning them to the United States, the alleged "home of democracy."

Part 3 of the volume, "Theorizing the In/visibility of War," turns attention to more sustained theoretical consideration of the implications of war's in/visibility. Jon Simons focuses attention on the implications of war as a feature of normalized injustice and hegemonic power by considering the in/visibility of liberal conceptions of peace. Arguing that the everyday practice of liberalism is deeply implicated in the normalization of a war, Simons maintains that war is thus constituted against the abnormal both at home and abroad. Beginning with Immanuel Kant, he examines key texts in liberal political theory in order to make the case that peace is the in/visible liberal justification for war. Significantly, he maintains that the postconflict regimes of Iraq and Afghanistan combine military force and civil governance into a single spectrum of normalizing governmentality. Accordingly, twenty-first-century wars, like all wars justified by liberal theory, are normal. The central point here is that we see this justification all the time, yet we do not see it as an argument for war. The conduct of war against others as visualized in mainstream media is thus continuous with the practices and processes of governing the homeland, especially the defense of society from internal dangers and abnormalities. As a result, America is at war with itself: it disavows that it is at war, even as its many screens repeat the traumatic and yet banal scenes of war in the name of peace.

Is it possible to pass through such disavowal, and if so, how? In her chapter, Diane Rubenstein indicates that we cannot be sure. Discussing an encounter between French philosophers and public intellectuals Jean Baudrillard and Jacques Derrida with regard to the impact of television on public engagements with twenty-first-century wars, Rubenstein argues that the most we can do is to wager on the best theoretical strategy—critical or radical—in opposition to war. Derrida critically places his hopes on the way that a televisual image (of mass protestors or a vote within the United Nations, for example) offers a conditional affirmation of an international law or democracy "to come" that could contest post–Cold War U.S. hegemony. Yet such images also threaten to reveal these institutions or protests as forms of empty speech. Baudrillard radically focuses instead on the hypervisuality of the terror of 9/11 and the anticipated wars to follow. The former is the pinnacle of simulated events that are the mirror of the mediated images that precede them. So it is that Baudrillard maintains that the Gulf War did not take place. And the question is, how can the disappearance of such a reality be challenged? How do we counter the Iraq War that followed the image event of terror? It will take another event with the force of the challenge of 9/11 to shake us out of the disavowal in which we fetishize war images while not seeing the war that has become simulation. As the volume as a whole attests, the critical operation of seeing war as it is in order to subject it to the democratic jurisdiction to which Derrida appeals is a strategy we cannot forgo. But we cannot place all of our bets on it, because the confluence of war, image, and global order requires a radical challenge to all three together.

James Der Derian offers another explanation of how difficult it is to counter the in/visibility of war, arguing that such in/visibility is inherent to the character of what he dubs "War 2.0." Drawing explicitly on Virilio's articulation of warfare and visual perception, Der Derian outlines how war's indeterminacy currently evades our perceptions and hence also the methodologies and aesthetic genres that rely on the real. Neither the conceptual apparatus of International Relations as a realist academic discipline nor the linguistic tropes of linearity and causality can capture how a war of images prompted by the spectacle of 9/11 set off an "information bomb" that triggered a series of global events. It is not that ubiquitous cameras—whether held by civilians or mounted on armed vehicles as military hardware—fail to show us the events of war, but that war nonetheless escapes our visual and cognitive perception. Quantum war, rather like Schrödinger's cat, is necessarily in/visible even as we try to look at it.

LOOKING FORWARD

War 2.0 captures the complexity and difficulty, if not impossibility, of overcoming the in/visibility of war. For that reason, this volume has been able to rely only partially on the critical trope of unmasking, of making visible what is invisible in twenty-first-century wars. Rather, our effort has been to make invisibility itself visible, not in order to evaporate it, but to bring it to mind, the object of attention for scholars and citizens alike struggling to understand a perpetual war that has become the new normal. In/visibility is itself normalized, and if we cannot undo it by looking at it head on, we can at least see it as a phenomenon by looking obliquely, askance, by peering through the lenses of different optics that we find within, or grind for ourselves from, the visual representations of war that surround us. If we cannot simply displace the meta-frame of in/visibility in order to see what lies outside the frame, we can at least see the frame itself. If we cannot simply extract ourselves from the visual aesthetics of immersion within which we experience war, we can at least feel that which touches us like a second skin. If we cannot simply avow the visions of war, we can disavow them by looking at images of war without seeing the war itself.

As scholars—as with the vast majority of citizens—we see war only at a distance even as it touches us deeply.[36] We can train ourselves to see more closely, but we cannot rely only on more attentive vision to overcome our distraction. The immense, horrific impact of our distant vision cannot simply be brought closer to us in acts of human empathy by looking at the suffering we so seldom see. Most humbling of all, as scholars we cannot stop the wars that vex us, nor organize the popular, civil movements in the United States and abroad that will be necessary to confront the normalized structures of global power for which wars have become ordinary and necessary states of affairs. What we can do is to educate ourselves and each other to look differently and elsewhere, both at the disavowal of war, the displaced symptoms of war, and at each other. Perhaps if we want war to disappear, above all we must appear to each other by recreating the cultural and political spaces in which we can collectively turn our most contemporary, normalized, perpetual wars into the abnormality of a peaceful, nonviolent future. War, after all, is an inhuman(e) condition.[37]

NOTES

1. "List of Wars Involving the United States," *Wikipedia*, https://en.wikipedia.org/wiki/List_of_wars_involving_the_United_States.
2. Mark Landler, "For Obama, an Unexpected Legacy of Two Full Terms at War," *New York Times*, May 14, 2016, online edition, http://www.nytimes.com/2016/05/15/us/politics/obama-as-wartime-president-has-wrestled-with-protecting-nation-and-troops.html?_r=0.

3. Ibid.
4. See Nick Turse, *The Complex: How the Military Invades Our Everyday Lives* (New York: Metropolitan Books, 2008) and Roger Stahl, *Militainment, Inc.: War, Media, and Popular Culture* (New York: Routledge, 2010).
5. http://www.nytimes.com/slideshow/2007/08/17/nytfrontpage/081707POD_13.html. For fuller analysis of the photograph see John Louis Lucaites, "The Conquering Hero," http://www.nocaptionneeded.com/2007/08/the-conquering-hero/, originally posted on August 20, 2007.
6. See Stahl, *Militainment*, 49–68; Michael Butterworth, "American Football, Flags, and 'Fun': The Bell Helicopter Armed Forces Bowl and the Rhetorical Production of Militarism," *Communication, Culture & Critique* 2, no. 4 (2009): 411–433; and Tricia Jenkins, "The Militarization of American Professional Sports: How the Sports-War Intertext Influences Athletic Ritual and Sports Media," *Journal of Sport and Social Issues* 37, no. 3 (2013): 245–260.
7. The Carrier Classic was cancelled after 2013 because of a range of technical difficulties, but there is strong interest in bringing it back. In 2012 an "Armed Forces Classic" was begun in which a basketball game is played on an army base.
8. Laura Barron-Lopez and Travis Waldron, "Pentagon Paid up to $6.8 Million of Taxpayer Money to Pro Sports Teams for Military Tributes," *Huffington Post*, November 4, 2015, http://www.huffingtonpost.com/entry/defense-military-tributes-professional-sports_us_5639a04ce4b0411d306eda5e.
9. Vik Muniz, "Toy Soldier," from Monads, 2003, available at http://vikmuniz.net/gallery/monads.
10. On the normalization of war thesis in contemporary photojournalism, see "Watching War," in Robert Hariman and John Louis Lucaites, *The Public Image: Photography and Civic Spectatorship* (Chicago: University of Chicago Press, 2016), 171–226.
11. "Notes and Sources: Cost of National Security Counters," https://www.nationalpriorities.org/cost-of/resources/notes-and-sources/.
12. "America's Wars," Department of Veteran Affairs, http://www.va.gov/opa/publications/factsheets/fs_americas_wars.pdf; "Iraq Body Count," https://www.iraqbodycount.org.
13. Chris Woods and Jack Serle, "Hostage Deaths Mean 38 Westerners Killed by US Drone Strikes, Bureau Investigation Reveals," *Bureau of Investigative Journalism*, April 23, 2015, https://www.thebureauinvestigates.com/2015/04/23/hostage-deaths-mean-38-westerners-killed-us-drone-strikes/.
14. Brad Evans, "The Liberal War Thesis: Introducing the Ten Key Principles of Twenty-First-Century Biopolitical Warfare," *South Atlantic Quarterly* 110, no. 3 (2011): 748.
15. W.J.T. Mitchell, "Cloning Terror: The War of Images 2001–4," in *The Life and Death of Images*, edited by Diarmud Costello and Dominic Willsdon (Ithaca, NY: Cornell University Press, 2008), 185. For a fuller development of Mitchell's argument see W.J.T. Mitchell, *Cloning Terror: The War of Images, 9/11 to the Present* (Chicago: University of Chicago Press, 2011).
16. Mitchell, "Cloning Terror," 196.
17. See W.J.T. Mitchell, *Iconology: Image, Text, Ideology* (Chicago: University of Chicago Press, 1986).
18. Mitchell, "Cloning Terror," 197.
19. Ibid., 207.
20. Ibid. For Hans Hacke's *The Stargazer* see: http://williswillkillus.tumblr.com/post/26492214602.

21. For an argument that urges moving beyond Plato's Cave and to learn how to think with and through photographic images, see chapter 1 in Hariman and Lucaites, *The Public Image,* 2016, 1–28.

22. See Ray Rivera, "Images of the War Dead a Sensitive Matter," originally published in the *Seattle Times* on April 22, 2004, and reprinted along with an archive of articles on the topic at *Media Literacy Clearinghouse,* http://frankwbaker.com/mlc/images-of-war-dead. For a detailed analysis of the controversy, see William O. Saas and Rachel Hall, "Restive Peace: Body Bags, Casket Flags, and the Pathologization of Dissent," *Rhetoric and Public Affairs* 19, no. 2 (2016): 177–208.

23. Judith Butler, *Frames of War: When Life Is Grievable?* (London: Verso, 2009), 3. See also Dora Apel, *War Culture and the Contest of Images* (New Brunswick, NJ: Rutgers University Press, 2012), 151–182.

24. Sigmund Freud, "The Splitting of the Ego in the Defensive Process," in vol. 5, *Miscellaneous Papers, 1888–1938, Collected Papers,* 5 vols. (London: Hogarth and Institute of Psycho-Analysis, 1924–1950), 372–375.

25. Octave Mannoni, "I know well, but all the same," in *Perversion and the Social Relation: Sic IV,* edited by Molly Anne Rothenberg and Slavoj Žižek (Durham, NC: Duke University Press 2003), 68–92.

26. The study of the relationship between war and visual representation has generally focused attention on photography predating 9/11. A brief list of some of the most important work would include Susan Moeller, *Shooting War: Photography and the American Experience of Combat* (New York: Basic Books, 1989); Alex Trachtenberg, "Albums of War," in *Reading American Photographs: Images as History, Mathew Brady to Walker Evans* (New York: Hill and Wang, 1989), 71–118; John Taylor, *War Photography: Realism in the British Press* (New York: Routledge, 1991) and *Body Horror: Photojournalism, Catastrophe and War* (New York: NYU Press, 1998); George H. Roeder Jr., *Uncensored War: American Visual Experience during World War Two* (New Haven, CT: Yale University Press, 1993); and David A. Perlmutter, *Visions of War: Picturing Warfare from the Stone Age to the Cyber Age* (New York: St. Martin's Press, 1999). More recent work that bears relevance includes Barbie Zelizer's important *About to Die: How News Images Move the Public* (New York: Oxford University Press, 2010); Liam Kennedy, *Afterimages: Photography and U.S. Foreign Policy* (Chicago: University of Chicago Press, 2016); and *The Violence of the Image: Photography and International Conflict,* ed. Liam Kennedy and Caitlin Patrick (London: I. B. Taurus, 2014). An important recent book that looks beyond photography to the broader visual culture is Apel, *War Culture and the Contest of Images.*

27. Paul Virilio, *War and Cinema: The Logistics of Perception* (London: Verso, 1989), 1.

28. Ibid., 5, 83.

29. See this summary of Virilio's views in Laura Marks, "Invisible Media," in *The New Media and Technocultures Reader,* edited by Seth Giddings and Martin Lister (London and New York: Routledge, 2011), 249–250.

30. Ibid., 250.

31. A more expansive explication of Baudrillard's treatment of images of war and terrorism is given by Diane Rubenstein in her chapter in this volume.

32. Nicholas Mirzoeff, *Watching Babylon: The War in Iraq and Global Visual Culture* (New York: Routledge, 2005), 90.

33. Ibid., 13, 75.

34. Giorgio Agamben, *State of Exception,* trans. Kevin Attell (Chicago: University of Chicago Press, 2005), 26. Agamben argues that phenomena such as Guantanamo are indications of the suspension of law that becomes the rule by being a feature of a more or less permanent state of emergency. We do not necessarily adhere to the thrust of Agamben's argument in our consideration of in/visibility. Although images of Guantanamo have been visible on the public screen, the political conditions for this state of exception—war—remain in/visible. Normalized war does not entail "the suspension of the entire existing order" (12) but its continuity.

35. For one of numerous examples of framing analysis of war coverage, see Christian Kolmer, "Framing the Iraq War: Perspectives from American, U.K., Czech, German, South African, and Al-Jazeera News," *American Behavioral Scientist* 52, no. 5 (2009): 643–656.

36. Two important books that address the issue of negotiating war at a distance are worth paying attention to in this context. Mary Favret discusses the "absent presence" of distant wars with a focus on the role that Romanticism has played in how we understand modern warfare in *War at a Distance: Romanticism and the Making of Modern Wartime* (Princeton, NJ: Princeton University Press, 2010). By contrast, Wendy Kozol focuses on how visual representations of distant wars animate an "ambivalent witnessing" in *Distant Wars Visible: The Ambivalence of Witnessing* (Minneapolis: University of Minnesota Press, 2014).

37. We gesture here to the political philosopher whose work encapsulates the darkness of the twentieth century without a hint of unfounded optimism that the twenty-first century would be any better, Hannah Arendt, *The Human Condition* (Chicago: University of Chicago Press, 1958).

PART I SEEING WAR

1 • HOW PHOTOJOURNALISM HAS FRAMED THE WAR IN AFGHANISTAN

DAVID CAMPBELL

Images are central to contemporary geopolitics. We encounter other people and places in a "field of perceptible reality" that is enacted by visual representations, making some things visible while rendering others invisible.[1] Photographs, paintings, video, film, computer games—each and every pictorial artifact—helps establish what can be represented and how it can be shown. In turn, those images are made possible by a series of historical, cultural, and political frames or infrastructures.[2]

In this essay I consider how one set of pictorial artifacts—the contemporary war images of photojournalism—were produced in Afghanistan during U.S. military operations there. In particular, I explore how the discourse of photojournalism has become one of those frames that makes aspects of the war in Afghanistan in/visible. This means that, in addition to reading specific war photographs, I consider how the discourse of photojournalism—that is, the way photojournalists speak about and justify the practice of photojournalism—has been complicit in the production of the field of perceptible reality.

The modern discourse of photojournalism, which dates from the 1930s onward and is usually grounded in claims about how Robert Capa and his associates operated, is based on the premise that power is held accountable by making visible a different picture of war than that offered by the state. The claims of this discourse are grounded in terms of objectivity understood as immediacy, indexicality, and impartiality, and it reached its apogee in the Vietnam War, where an allegedly uncensored visual account supposedly hastened the end of the U.S. involvement.

However, as I argue in the later stages of this essay, these claims fail to appreciate both how Capa practiced his craft, and how visual media functioned in the Vietnam War. My thesis is that the modern discourse of photojournalism has never been able to grasp the problematic of in/visibility in terms of the state frame and its alternatives. Indeed, I propose that the modern discourse of photojournalism has become exhausted, bogged down by the reiteration of familiar concepts—especially aesthetics and a particular notion of objectivity—that no longer have critical purchase when it comes to understanding the late modern and digital production, circulation, and consumption of photographic images. I examine this through a point of contention in the practice of photojournalism during the war in Afghanistan, namely the status of pictures produced with applications (apps) on mobile devices. My claim is that the problems with the modern discourse of photojournalism mean we are unable to properly consider the function and effect of images and how they establish what is in/visible in the field of perceptible reality. These familiar concepts have produced the mystical foundations of authority, driven by certain desires to overcome particular anxieties.

We need to understand the intersection of anxiety and desire in order to fathom why photojournalism does not contribute to a critical rendering of our fields of perceptible reality as often as it could. A critical rendering would expose and contest the geographic imaginary enabled by photography's geopolitical function. If we understand geopolitics in the sense articulated within critical geopolitics—that is, as a writing of political space—then the affordance of photography as a technology of visualization involves a spacing and writing of the political, in which sight enacts site, thereby structuring our encounters with others. More often than not both the discourse and practice of modern photojournalism has helped sustain an "imagined geography" in which the dichotomies of West/East, civilized/barbaric, North/South, and developed/underdeveloped have been prominent.[3] The hope is that a critical reading of the kind offered here will open the way to a better consideration of how contemporary photographs of war function.

EMBEDDED IN AFGHANISTAN

The field of perceptible reality that is the war in Afghanistan has been enacted in large part through news imagery and photojournalism.[4] We have seen a steady stream of familiar pictures made up of allied forces, Afghan civilians, Taliban casualties, and American military families. Photojournalism on the front line has focused on the military struggles of international forces as they combat an "elusive" opponent, with soldiers and their weaponry front and center. There is also an inevitable regularity to the style of these images. As Associated Press photographer David Guttenfelder notes, the work of photojournalists in Afghanistan "sometimes looks very uniform."[5]

"Embedded journalism" has been a frame commonly focused upon to explain the nature and limits of what we do and do not see. That analysis sometimes proceeds on the assumption that there was once a time when photography's contribution to the field of perceptible reality was free from government controls. As Judith Butler claims in her assessment of the ethics of photography:

> Recent war photography departs significantly from the conventions of war photojournalism that were at work thirty or forty years ago, where the photographer or camera person would attempt to enter the action through angles and modes of access that sought to expose the war in ways that no government had planned. Now, the state works on the field of perception and, more generally, the field of representability, in order to control affect.[6]

But the frames through which the visualization of Afghanistan is enacted have a longer and deeper history than is suggested by this view. The conventions of war photojournalism have been frequently aligned with the state, thereby making the production of an alternative picture a more difficult task. The embedding of journalists during operations in Afghanistan—which grew out of the media's experience in the U.S.-led invasion of Iraq—is simply the latest in a long line of regulations governing relations between the military and the media.

Embedding involves journalists linking up with military units so they can report from the front lines, and it began formally with the invasion of Iraq. After agreeing to follow the U.S. Public Affairs Guidance or the Ministry of Defense's "Green Book," more than 700 journalists embedded with American forces and nearly 130 with British forces (although they were outnumbered by the more than 1,400 "unilateral" journalists who were in the war zone). Embedding involves a tradeoff between "generous access and narrow-aperture coverage." In Iraq, being able to witness war close-up and live was new, but being on a "slack leash" without the ability to set things in context constrained coverage. With only two dozen personnel "dis-embedded" by the U.S. military, the majority of journalists lived happily on the leash. Indeed, when U.S. officials reviewed the system, embedded reporters "were always spoken of as homogeneously supportive of the Pentagon effort."[7]

Coverage of the invasion of Iraq demonstrated in part the value to government of the embedding process. A survey of U.S. newsmagazine photographs showed "a highly restricted pattern of depiction limited largely to a discourse of military technological power and response."[8] The number of combat photographs from Iraq increased from those published in the 1991 Gulf War, but still only made up 10 percent of published pictures. This was less than expected from front-line reportage, and demonstrates that news pictures are less concerned with the firsthand recording of events and more with the repetition of familiar subjects and themes. Although individual photographers believed they operated with freedom within the system of embedding, and sometimes even broke the rules, the way their pictures were used in publications did not challenge the official war narrative.[9]

Embedding has played a role in the visualization of Afghanistan, though not from the beginning. When Operation Enduring Freedom began in October 2001, the Pentagon had not yet conceived the specific system of embedding. Moreover, given that the first military operations in Afghanistan were covert actions by Special Forces against a non-state actor, embedding was from the military's viewpoint untenable. As a result, the U.S.–led strikes in Afghanistan proceeded with minimal media access, but there were few if any serious protests about this lack.

The early photographic coverage of Afghanistan was, therefore, part of the overall coverage of the "War on Terror" arising from the September 11, 2001, attacks on the Pentagon and the World Trade Center in New York. That series of events was shaped through its immediate visual representation and saw an expanded realm of the visible. Photography is deployed to mark globally significant events, and some U.S. newspapers underwent a "sea change" in their use of news pictures, doubling the number prior to 9/11. Part of this proliferation of images was the use of pictures that, although showing something from the general area, did not depict the specific events being reported. This symbolic function, where the repetition of icons associated with 9/11 provided cues and prompts for viewers, meant photographs became a means of moving the public through its trauma, enabling support for the military action in Afghanistan.[10]

When combat began in Afghanistan, the media's absence from the front lines meant that the pictures came after the event, showing newly pacified landscapes, families in flight, and women enjoying new freedoms. As Barbie Zelizer argues, "Images were used in a way that showed less of the war itself and more of the assumptions about the war held by the forces responsible for its prosecution. U.S. journalism was thus complicit, if not consciously so, in using images in ways that upheld larger strategic aims."[11] This is the problematic of a particular in/visibility at work.

Embedding first came to Afghanistan in March 2002 when eight journalists accompanied units engaged in Operation Anaconda. The first combat operation involving conventional units as opposed to Special Forces, the Anaconda coverage produced pictures that would become a template for later reportage: combat troops hunkered down in wild terrain, helicopters kicking up dust as they ferried in men and material, and the bodies of Taliban fighters strewn among the rocks, all seen from an allied perspective.[12]

The narrow range of visual subjects in the coverage of Afghanistan is evident in two of the most prominent images of the conflict, one celebrated and the other controversial. In May 2009 Associated Press photographer David Guttenfelder was in the Korengal Valley and captured a moment of combat. It showed three soldiers peering into a remote valley, rifles at the ready, the enemy seemingly elusive (fig. 1.1). It evokes a war machine looking for a reason, certain a threat is out there, but unsure of its form. There's even a moment of pathos, with the man on the left in his red shirt, pink boxers, and exposed legs lining up with his comrades. Army Specialist Zachary Boyd was the casually dressed soldier, and after this photograph was widely reproduced in the American press, the secretary of defense declared his fondness for it: "Any soldier who goes into battle against the Taliban in pink boxers and flip-flops has a special kind of courage. . . . I can only wonder about the impact on the Taliban. Just imagine seeing that: a guy in pink boxers and flip-flops has you in his cross-hairs. What an incredible innovation in psychological warfare."[13]

Three months later, another Associated Press photographer, Julie Jacobsen, drew the secretary of defense's ire for her combat photograph. Jacobsen was on patrol with a Marine unit near Dahaneh in southern Afghanistan when the Taliban ambushed them. She photographed the scene, including images of a badly

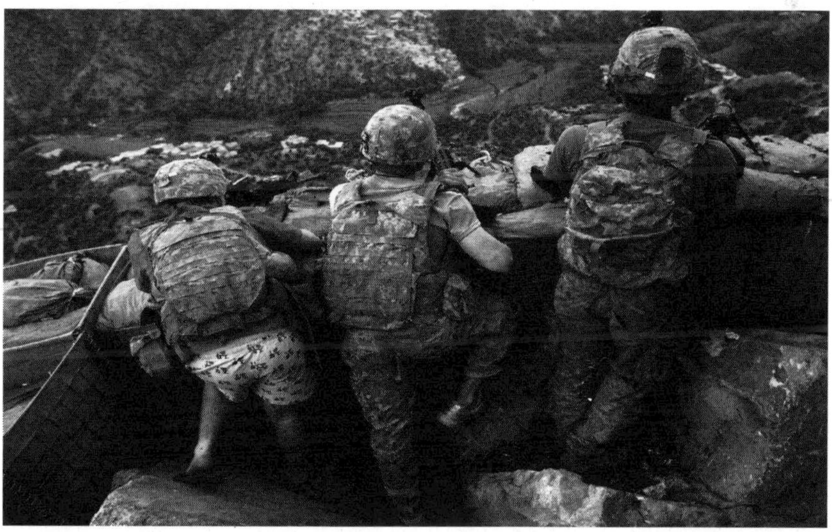

FIGURE 1.1

wounded Lance Corporal Joshua Bernard, who later died in the Camp Leatherneck medical unit. The blurred photograph of Bernard shows him slumped in a gully, a bloody leg wound visible, being hurriedly tended by two colleagues. Taken from a distance such that neither the faces nor the uniforms of Bernard and his helpers were identifiable, Jacobsen doubted the photograph would ever be used:

> I shot images that day well aware that those images could very possibly never see the light of day. In fact I was sure of it. But I still found myself recording them. To ignore a moment like that simply because of a phrase in section 8, paragraph 1 of some 10-page form would have been wrong. I was recording his impending death, just as I had recorded his life moments before walking the point in the bazaar. Death is a part of life and most certainly a part of war. Isn't that why we're here? To document for now and for history the events of this war? We'd shot everything else thus far and even after, from feature images of a Marine talking on a SAT phone to his girlfriend, all the way to happy meetings between Marines and civilians. So shooting the image was not a question.[14]

The embedding agreement in fact permitted Jacobsen to take the photo of Bernard. The Second Marine Expeditionary Brigade's regulations stated, "Casualties may be covered by embedded media as long as the service member's identity and unit identification is protected from disclosure until OASD-PA [Office of the Assistant Secretary of Defense, Public Affairs] has officially released the name. Photography from a respectful distance or from angles at which a casualty cannot be identified is permissible." Jacobsen had also shown the image to other members of Bernard's squad who raised no objection, and the photograph was withheld by the Associated Press until after the lance corporal's burial in the United States. Nonetheless, when Bernard's father objected to publication, he was supported by the secretary of defense, and many American newspapers refused to print the picture.[15]

The widespread publication of the Zachary Boyd photograph, in contrast to the limited circulation of the Joshua Bernard picture, demonstrates that embedding is just one of the frames that structures the in/visibility of Afghanistan. Whatever is produced within the confines of the embedding process has to be taken up by the mainstream press before a wider public can see. Photo agencies, picture editors, journalists, and news editors form a decision-making chain that, working with a set of assumptions about what their audience wants to view, winnows down the range of options to a few chosen images. The news photographs that the public ends up seeing are chosen less for their descriptive function or disruptive potential and more for their capacity to provide symbolic markers to familiar interpretations and conventional narratives.

iPHONE IN AFGHANISTAN

The global spread of mobile technology is changing the photographic landscape. There are currently 2 billon Android and iOS devices in the world, all of them possessing the capacity to capture images, and that number will soon rise to 3 billion. In the United States, smartphones equipped with high-quality cameras have outpaced almost every other technology in the speed of mainstream adoption.[16] Although these changes have led many professionals to fear replacement by an army of citizen photojournalists, other practitioners have embraced this technology and deployed it in their coverage of Afghanistan. Has this embrace resulted in a different visualization of the war?

Most notable among the iPhone series was Damon Winter's story, "A Grunt's Life," which was part of the *New York Times*'s extensive "Year at War" project.[17] Winter's photo-essay was a color piece following the First Battalion, 87th Infantry of the 10th Mountain Division in northern Afghanistan, and images from it ran on the paper's front page in November 2010.

Winter's photographs were produced with an iPhone using the Hipstamatic app, and he was far from the only established photojournalist employing this technology. For example, in March 2010 David Guttenfelder produced a portfolio of Polaroid-like pictures (using an app called ShakeIt Photo) detailing daily military life in Afghanistan. Balazs Gardi and Benjamin Lowy also used iPhones in some of their Afghan stories, while the Ukraine-Russia conflict over the Crimea has seen some novel mobile images on social media.[18]

The *New York Times*'s use of cell phone pictures on the front page was taken as a major endorsement of them as legitimate photojournalism. When Winter's Hipstamatic images won third place at the Pictures of the Year International contest in the newspaper feature category—and were also part of the portfolio with which Winter was named the 2011 news photographer of the year—there was a professional reaction one scholar has called the "War on Instagram."[19]

The lead protagonist in this industry "war" was photographer Chip Litherland, who wrote a scathing post entitled "There's an App for Photojournalism." According to Litherland:

> What we knew as photojournalism at it's [*sic*] purest form is over and POYi just killed it. Well, they didn't kill it so much as just dig another knife deeper into the back of its decaying corpse. . . .
>
> The fact that Damon Winter's "Grunt's Life" was just awarded a third place at POYi is a game changer. The fact it was shot on a phone isn't relevant at all and fair game, but what is relevant is the fact it was processed through an app that changes what was there when he shot them. It's now no longer photojournalism,

> but photography. That transition happens when images become more about the photographer and less about the subject of said photos.[20]

The debate about these images operated in terms of a discourse that tells us much about the nature of photojournalism and how it is conventionally understood. It is this discourse of photojournalism that is also a frame that contributes to the "field of perceptible reality" through which the war in Afghanistan has been in/visible. To be fair, a number of commenters on Litherland's blog praised Winter for exploring new techniques and extending the way stories could be told. Even those, like Litherland, who were critical of the awards, were careful to say they continued to respect Winter as a practitioner and that they liked the pictures in question. They just thought it wasn't photojournalism, and for that they directed their ire at the contest judges.

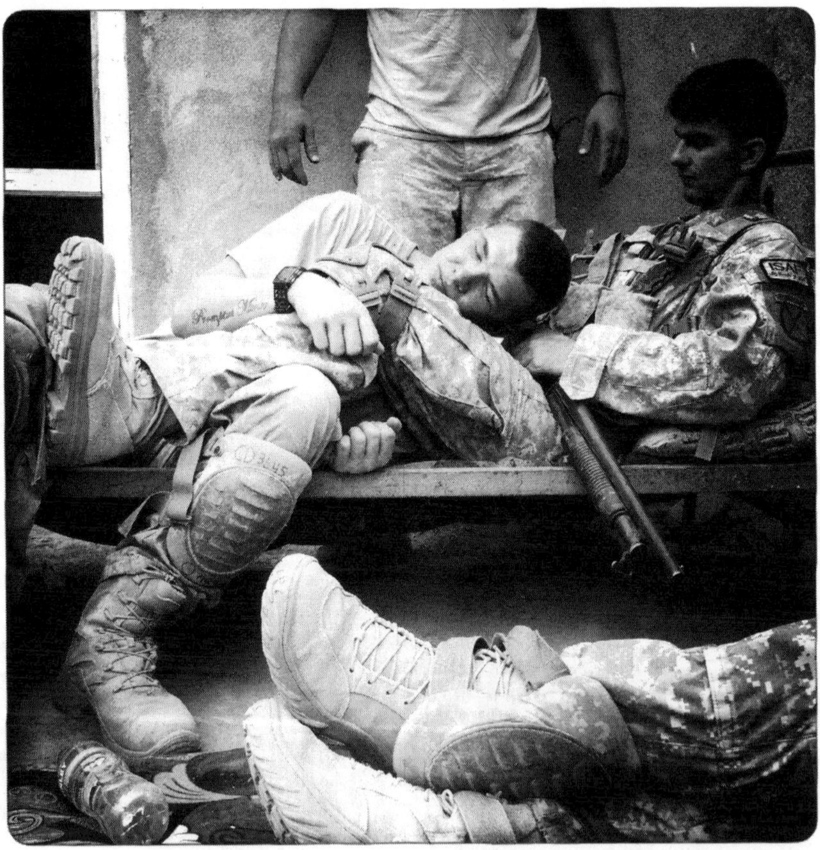

FIGURE 1.2

What concerned these professionals was that the award legitimized the Hipstamatic app. Their problem with this was that the images were, in Litherland's words, "processed through an app that changes what was there when he shot them." In the debate on Litherland's post one person endorsed his complaint, arguing, "The app has changed what was recorded. Photojournalism is about recording, unfiltered, what was in front of you." Another commenter argued that the images clearly violated the POYi rules that state that "no masks, borders, backgrounds or other artistic effects are allowed."[21] In a follow up, Litherland remarked, "I don't have an issue with it being shot on an iPhone. More power to him for doing so and making compelling photos with it. My only problem is Hipstawhatever photos being awarded in a photojournalism contest and processed through that app. *If the images were toned to reflect reality,* then the whole debate would be—well, not a debate" (emphasis added)." It is not difficult to see in these remarks traces of conceptual notions that shape the conventional discourse of photojournalism. Most obvious is the idea of objectivity, the belief that "photojournalism is about recording, unfiltered, what was in front of you." In this sense, because Winter's pictures were "processed through an app that changes what was there when he shot them," they cannot, by definition, be photojournalism.

This understanding of the objective production of images depends upon the untenable idea that "unfiltered recording" is possible. As some contributors to the debate noted, professional DSLR cameras process their images internally as soon as they are captured. Although the raw formats professionals use to enable later modification is conventionally considered to be as close to a film negative as is digitally possible, raw formats require in-camera processing in order for the sensor's information to appear to the photographer as a picture. Indeed, processing is the condition of possibility for the digital image, as digital cameras collect data rather than capture pictures.[22] Moreover, there is a range of proprietary RAW formats used by different camera manufacturers (i.e., CR2 for Canon and NEF for Nikon) that vary in their processing styles. When one takes or outputs a photograph in the JPEG or TIFF formats, even to the LCD screen on the back of the camera, the amount of in-camera processing is greater still. This means, as one commenter observed, "there is no such thing as a pure image" even at the moment of capture. Nor has there ever been a pure, original image, even in the pre-digital period. Even those nostalgic for analog film technology recognize that there was never a singular, standard black-and-white or color film. All films (for example, Kodachrome versus Ektachrome) differed in their chemical details and those details gave pictures different characteristics. A number of the contributors to the debate sparked by Litherland's post recognized that the Hipstamatic app offered digital options that replicated previous analog choices of camera, lens, and film. As Zach Wise argued:

> You should know that Hipstamatic is an app that automatically applies toning etc at the time of creation, NOT after the fact. The photographer makes a decision on lens and film in the app before making a photo. In theory this is no different than choosing to shoot with a lomo, holga or leica because of the unique aesthetic quality they produce. There are no "after the fact" effects applied. I hope this ends the argument.[23]

Of course this didn't end the argument. Wise drew the fault line of legitimacy in terms of effects at "the time of creation" versus those "after the fact." Litherland was not persuaded: "I understand that . . . my problem is what is added is completely fake and foreign. It masks a truthfully composed image with fake borders/ toning. My only rub lies with awarding it as photojournalism on POYi."[24]

This brings us to the second conceptual issue in the debate that revealed how the discourse of photojournalism acts as a frame, namely aesthetics. The app is illegitimate, Litherland says, because it adds something "completely fake and foreign" to what would otherwise have been a "truthfully composed image." We should though recall his earlier remark that suggested it was the particular type of toning, rather than toning per se, that was the problem: "If the images were toned to reflect reality," he said, "then the whole debate would be—well, not a debate." We have, then, a sense that something other than a simplistic objectivity, or faith in naïve mimesis, drives professional practice, even among those protesting the legitimation of Hipstamatic images.

As much as "unfiltered reality" is complicated by the technology of image capture on both film and digital sensors, photojournalism has long accepted "after the fact" alterations as legitimate. The most obvious is the credence given black-and-white pictures in the documentary tradition. In the predigital era that involved the choice of a particular film, which meant going into a three-dimensional world of color to produce two-dimensional black-and-white photos, something that surely replicates the concern about pictures being "processed through an app [here, film] that changes what was there when he shot them." Then there were differences in the chemistry of film developing, the choice of paper to print on, and dodging, burning, and other techniques at the time of printing. All these were and are legitimate professional practices that change the aesthetics of the photograph after the moment of capture.

Moreover, in the digital era, "after-the-fact" toning—often to consciously change or highlight something—is legitimate. The production of black-and-white photographs is the most obvious case in point, because it involves either altering camera settings to enable non-color capture, or color raw files are later desaturated in image editing software. While various photojournalism competitions have seen recent controversies over the perceived excessive saturation of color images, no one has ever been disqualified for submitting a desaturated photograph where the desaturation was achieved after the fact to produce a prize-winning black-and-white photograph.[25]

As an example, consider the Afghan war photographs of freelancer Victor Blue. According to *Photo District News,* "Blue is shooting the project primarily with a Canon 5D Mark II, and converting his images to black and white. 'I envisioned Afghanistan in gray tones. I saw color as a distraction,' he explains."[26] Blue's photographs, perfectly legitimate according to professional norms and excellent in many regards, invoke the traditional aesthetic of Vietnam-era photojournalism, but achieve it through after-the-fact toning that cannot be defended in terms of being "closer to reality."

There is also an accepted practice of toning in color digital images. The well-known Italian 10b Photography Lab wants to define digital manipulation only as the "moving of pixels," equivalent of Walker Evans's analog stipulation that photographs are documents if one does not stick something in or take something out. This is an argument that Damon Winter also makes about his Hipstamatic photos: "At the heart of all of these photos is a moment or a detail or an expression that tells the story of these soldiers' day-to-day lives while on a combat mission. Nothing can change that. No content has been added, taken away, obscured or altered. These are remarkably straightforward and simple images."[27] However, the 10b Photography Lab has been open about the changes it makes in the post-production of photographs for some well-known photojournalists. As 10b notes, these images "were intentionally shot underexposed in order to keep maximum detail in the highlights. The post-producer developed the pictures in a very flat style, with soft neutral [colors], then printed them on a file format that is intended to be an aesthetic interpretation of the scene."[28]

There are, then, many complicating factors in accepted professional practice that blur the lines for those who maintain somewhat simplistically that photojournalism is about the unfiltered capture of reality. It may be that people want to draw clear lines demarcating the legitimate from the illegitimate precisely because it is nearly impossible to draw such lines. If so, the debate is about a desire that is impossible to address, a nostalgic desire to recapture from photojournalism's history something that would make judgment easier.

One of the ironies of the "war on Instagram" (and other apps) is that the Hipstamatic app manifests a nostalgic desire. First, its design is "skeuomorphic": it is (as the *Oxford English Dictionary* defines it) "a derivative object that retains ornamental design cues to a structure that was necessary in the original." The app presents itself as a plastic Instamatic-style camera even though it is obviously digital, and one gets different processing effects by changing on an iPhone screen a lens that looks like a glass lens, and a film option presented as though it were a metal canister with rolled cellular film inside.

Second, the images produced by the Hipstamatic app are what Nathan Jurgenson has called "faux-vintage" photography, which manifests a "nostalgia for the present." Heightened by social media's power to view the present as always a potentially documented past, Jurgenson argues that images from Hipstamatic, Instagram, and other services work to make our prosaic and vernacular images "seem more important, substantial and real."[29] In the latest versions of the iPhone, the internal camera has come with some of these same toning filters allowing effects to be applied to images at the point of capture. Aesthetically, all this is achieved by reclaiming forms associated with the materiality of analogue photography. On this reading, Hipstamatic images are creating something with signifiers of authenticity from a predigital reality. As Jurgenson notes, "Perhaps this is a reason for the popularity of faux-vintage war photos: saturated, vignetted, faded, scratched and portrayed on simulated photo paper, Hipstamatic war photos frame contemporary conflict as like the wars our parents and grandparents fought."[30] This is profoundly ironic given the way much of the heated debate inside photography following the publication and recognition of Winter's photographs saw Hipstamatic pictures as by definition unreal. The major conclusion is that the controversy surrounding the Hipstamatic pictures demonstrates the limits and exhaustion of photographic critique based on naïve realism, claims about objectivity, and the attendant issue of aesthetics as something supposedly foreign to photojournalism. A particular failure is that the terms of this debate focus on the status of the image rather than the way photographs are themselves geopolitical.

RETURNING TO ROBERT CAPA

Although there is some distance between the iPhone and Robert Capa, and even though his legacy is not explicitly mentioned in the controversy surrounding Damon Winter's Hipstamatic photos, I argue that the contours of that debate demonstrate how an implicit set of assumptions about what constitutes legitimate war photography is based on traditional, but questionable, interpretations of Capa's work. If we want to consider how the discourse of photojournalism in relation to war acts as a frame for the contemporary representation of conflict, making particular things in/visible, then looking at aspects of the conventional history of war photography is unavoidable.

A full discussion of the history of war photography would recite many familiar names, beginning with the likes of Roger Fenton in the Crimea and Matthew Brady and his associates in the American Civil War, and a full consideration of their legacy is beyond the scope of this essay. However, it is important to note that even these "founding fathers" quite consciously staged some of their most iconic images. Another example worth noting is the Australian World War I photographer Frank Hurley, who believed that he could present the truth of the conflict only by the construction of an image that combined twelve different glass negatives.[31]

Although the history of war photography extends back 150 years, the consensus is that the Spanish Civil War, largely because it was conducted at the same time that picture magazines were rising to prominence in the media economy, was the first war to be extensively photographed for a mass audience. According to Caroline Brothers, it "marks the establishment of modern war photography as we know it." It "raised the visual expectations of the image-viewing public ever after. . . . It established the visual vocabulary of war photography as a genre."[32]

It was the dramatic Spanish coverage of Robert Capa—along with his colleagues Gerda Taro and David (Chim) Seymour—that is said to have created the style of modern war photography. Their black-and-white reportage is now familiar to us, but at the time it was a new form of visual journalism with a distinctive way of seeing.[33] As Susie Linfield has observed, "Capa's photographs from Spain plunged viewers into the heart of battle in ways that now seem iconic, even clichéd, but at the time were radically new: unsettling, nerve-wracking, scary. His photographs were closer, faster, *denser*, than any that had been seen before; Capa wasn't a witness to war so much as a visual participant in it."[34]

For those who see contemporary developments like the Hipstamatic photos from Afghanistan as a transgression of the traditional genre of photojournalism, the work of Capa and his colleagues is, implicitly at least, one of the foundation stones against which such transgressions can be judged. Yet within Capa's working biography during the twenty years between his Spanish Civil War photographs and his death in Vietnam in 1954, we can see many of the issues and themes that currently animate concerns about the contemporary state of photojournalism. These concerns—about the economy of photojournalism and its function in the contemporary media world—are often behind the anxieties that erupt in the wake of controversies like those surrounding Winter's Hipstamatic pictures. These anxieties produce the desire to draw clear lines between legitimate and illegitimate practice.

However, if the foundational tradition of war photography manifested in the work of Capa is more complex than that assumed by those who fear that the present is a perversion of the past, this resituates the contemporary complaints, demonstrating their dependence on mythical foundations of authority, the exhaustion of the concepts and terms through which they criticize new developments, and their resultant inability to develop a critical perspective on how photojournalism should be developing.

Given the significance of embedding to the visual representation of the war in Afghanistan, it is important to recognize that like many photojournalists in

Spain, and subsequently in World War II, Capa was in practice embedded. Moreover, Capa's practice required him to be embedded. His famous dictum that "if your pictures aren't good enough you aren't close enough" meant being an accredited member of military units.

At the same time, much of Capa's practice diverges from the traditional understanding of photojournalism and is more closely aligned with the contemporary age of professional anxiety. Capa and his associates were working in a period of change in the media economy. The illustrated magazines that had emerged in France and Germany in the 1930s were replicated in the United Kingdom and the United States, and though many now take the likes of *Life* to be the apogee of the golden age of photojournalism, Capa saw the limits of the print publishers and came to dislike *Life* with a passion. The magazine's disregard for copyright led to the resultant formation of Magnum as a collective to increase the photographers' control over the story. At the same time—again showing there was no golden age of abundance for social documentary—the dependence of Magnum on corporate work and a select few outlets to finance their work shows that the current crisis in the business models that support journalism have their historical antecedents. Notwithstanding those issues, Capa was creative in his approach, collaborating with writers like John Steinbeck and Irwin Shaw on photo stories. And Capa's belief that cinema and television would replace the still image as the predominant visual medium might be seen as presaging the recent advent of video capable DSLRs and the production of Web video stories.[35]

That said, perhaps the most significant thing that emerges from Capa's biography for thinking about the photojournalism of war in the present was his overt partisanship. On occasion, Capa expressed beliefs that could be considered consistent with the idea of objectivity, as when in a September 1937 interview with the *New York World-Telegram* he said, "No tricks are necessary to take pictures in Spain. You don't have to pose your camera. The pictures are there, and you just take them. The truth is the best picture, the best propaganda."[36] But as the mention of propaganda suggests, Capa was quite open about taking sides. He once told Martha Gelhorn, "In a war you must hate somebody or love somebody. . . . You must have a position or cannot stand what goes on."[37]

In assessing the reportage of Capa and his colleagues, Brian Wallis concluded photojournalism required three things, the last of which was "that the photographer had to be engaged, had to have judged the political stakes in that story, and had to have taken sides."[38] This engagement certainly had negative consequences. As one of his biographers, Andy Kershaw, remarks, "Capa was not an impartial reporter. He ignored atrocities committed by the Republicans, and would soon stage at least one documented [scene] as well as serve as an ideological cheerleader to the communist cause in Spain."[39]

Despite Capa's legendary status in the field, it would be hard to imagine a contemporary photojournalist embodying similar positions and being regarded, rightly or wrongly, as "professional." The interesting question here, then, is when the professional codes of objectivity came to infuse photojournalism in such a way that we would now regard one of the founding fathers of modern war photography as somehow illegitimate, and new imaging techniques like the Hipstamatic app as beyond the pale.[40]

To think about this we have to understand that the professional codes have depoliticized photojournalism. This depoliticization comes from the acceptance of what Simon Dell calls a "fantasy," the belief that in photographic practice the world makes in its own image. As Dell writes, "The fantasy represses that which precedes and conditions the making of the exposure; here the instant of the shutter release is made over into the immediacy of the image."[41] We saw this clearly in the debate about Winter's Hipstamatic pictures—a privileging of the immediacy of the image and an erasure of "that which precedes and conditions the making of the exposure" for all forms of photojournalism, leading to the attempted delegitimization of different techniques like the Hipstamatic app.

What the privileging of the immediacy of the image does is sustain a belief in photography's naïve realism by attempting to marginalize the question of aesthetics. But aesthetics cannot be marginalized when it comes to photography. As Damon Winter wrote about those who criticized his POYi award:

> We are being naïve if we think aesthetics do not play an important role in the way photojournalists tell a story. We are not walking photocopiers. We are storytellers. We observe, we chose moments, we frame little slices of our world with our viewfinders, we even decide how much or how little light will illuminate our subjects, and—yes—we choose what equipment to use. Through all of these decisions, we shape the way a story is told.[42]

Here we come to another irony in the critiques of the Hipstamatic images. Although those critiques were undertaken in terms of the real versus the aesthetic, all the responses from within photography dealt with the aesthetic at the expense of the substantive. While they protested the aestheticization of these particular images, the photographic critique was itself an instance of aestheticization—paying attention to the way Hipstamatic images look rather than what they show or the issue portrayed.[43] Indeed, it was striking that none of the criticisms aired in photojournalistic circles following Winter's award dealt with the perceptible reality such images enact for us.

The result of this is that the discourse of photojournalism itself has acted as a frame to secure a visual representation of Afghanistan that, although produced through new mobile technologies, continues to offer a rendering as partial as that achieved through embedded journalism. That is because the conventional discourse of photojournalism reverts to the exhausted ideas of naïve realism and objectivity thereby excluding or marginalizing questions of the function and effect of images.

The photographer Nina Berman has a succinct view of what Winter's pictures do: "The images are beautiful, sensual, and conjure feelings of romantic love. They have zero journalistic value and function more like a huge kiss to their subjects and the DOD."[44] Similarly, Michael Shaw of *BagNewsNotes* wrote that Winter's photos manifest "an intense emotional identification with U.S. soldiers divorced from their identity as the embodiment of the U.S. war machine," something achieved by "the transformation of the soldier and killing agents (the gun notwithstanding) into innocent man-child."[45] Although Alper makes "non-soldiers mimicking the imagined hand of the modern smartphone-equipped [U.S.] soldier" an overlooked ethical issue, the function and effect of all images, however they were shot, on what is both visible and invisible in the perceptible reality of Afghanistan has to be the primary concern.[46]

CONCLUSION

This persistent faith in photography's naïve realism and objectivity prevents us from moving onto the question of the political effect of these pictures because we cannot get beyond a clichéd "introduction to philosophy" in which opponents shout each other down by saying what is or is not real. Debate has ossified at this point because photojournalism tries to deny an essential part of itself: the unavoidable centrality of aesthetics in the production of any image. As David Levi Strauss writes, "To represent is to aestheticize, that is, to transform."[47]

For photojournalism to enhance its contribution to a critical rendering of our fields of perceptible reality, it must acknowledge that attempts to draw the line between legitimate and illegitimate modes of representation always turn in on themselves and displace the more important political questions of what images do. The major change in the photojournalism of war since Capa's formative work is not so much the evident technological developments that have increased the speed and scale of contemporary photographs. The major change has been the way the photojournalism of war has been depoliticized—that is, rendered uncritical—by a set of outmoded conceptual assumptions that deny photography's central characteristics to such an extent that Capa's images might themselves have fallen foul of these concerns.

We have to, as Mark Reinhardt has noted, "relax the aesthetic anxieties of critique."[48] It's not a matter of being for or against something like the Hipstamatic app. It is a question of how we think about such developments, invoke assumptions, and frame any concerns. When we realize the problems with how that controversy has unfolded, then, finally, perhaps we can focus on photojournalism's contribution to narrative and its political effects so that a different picture of Afghanistan might come into view.

It will take more than reworking the discourse of photojournalism, however, to ask these questions. Much of our media operate within the limits of official discourse, with journalists working on the field of perception through commitments to their national frames. Although we still harbor a belief that journalism is indebted to the ethos of the Pentagon Papers or Watergate, fearlessly investigating government failings, much contemporary war coverage directly or indirectly supports military strategies. For example, although British television broadcasters exhibit more faith in the idea of impartiality compared to the overt patriotism of their American counterparts, a review of their Iraq invasion coverage found that "when it came to contentious issues such as [weapons of mass destruction] WMDs or the mood of the Iraqi people . . . overall, all the main television broadcasters tended to favor the pro-war, government version over more skeptical accounts." The media's failure to continually exercise its watchdog role is one of the reasons for the emergence of Wikileaks, which has been described as a "stateless" news organization precisely because of its freedom from national limits.[49]

Hovering over and shaping the field of perceptible reality that is Afghanistan, especially as visualized through news photographs, is a mythic understanding of how the media and the military operated in Vietnam. The conventional wisdom is that Vietnam was a "living-room war," in which a highly critical media subjected its audience to a stream of graphic combat images showing both uniformed and civilian casualties, such that public opinion eventually turned against the war. It has been promulgated by both the military, who blame the media for a lack of patriotism and the eventual loss of the war, and the military's critics, keen to draw the lesson that if injustice can be shown it can be overcome. This mythic understanding has been behind both the array of post-Vietnam regulations governing the media's place on the battlefield that culminated in embedding, and the countervailing demand for an unsanitized view of war.

What happened in Vietnam is the opposite of this myth. The best analyses of American coverage demonstrate that newspapers, magazines, and television endorsed administration perspectives on the war even as the peace movement grew. Far from showing an incessant diet of gory visuals, the U.S. media shied away from graphic images. Although journalists and photographers on the ground in Vietnam operated with relative freedom compared to their World War II counterparts, their reports were woven into a narrative consistent with the national frame. The visual icons we now associate with the war—the pictures produced by the likes of Larry Burrows, Philip Jones Griffiths, and Don

McCullin—were rejected by the U.S. media, published after the event, or simply unrepresentative of most coverage.[50]

Vietnam has shaped both how we came to see Afghanistan, and how we respond to the visual enactment of such a war. There is also an historic connection between the two conflicts. Allied military involvement in Afghanistan between 2001 and 2014 surpassed both the length of the Soviet occupation and the formal duration of the Vietnam War. When NATO formally ended combat operations in December 2014, Afghanistan had become America's longest war. Looking at the role photojournalism has played in structuring the visual reality of Afghanistan we need to be free from the mythic understanding of the media's role in Vietnam.

Throughout the past decade, whatever the intentions of individual practitioners, news photography (whether shot on professional cameras or mobile devices) has represented Afghanistan in ways consistent with military strategy. Much photojournalism exists within and reproduces an "eternal present," obscuring the frames that narrow its perspective. Embedded journalism has contributed to this confined view, and this practice has also been constrained by the way the media generally offers a limited challenge to established positions. In addition, the way the professional discourse of photojournalism depoliticizes issues occludes questions of the images' effects and functions. In this context, calling for an unsanitized view of the war is bound to be insufficient as a strategy for challenging the official narratives of Afghanistan. What we require is the exposure of all the frames that produce in/visibility in the field of perceptible reality.

ACKNOWLEDGMENTS

This chapter is based on "From Robert Capa to the iPhone: How the Photojournalism of War Has (and Has Not) Changed," which I gave as the Branigan Lecture, Institute for Advanced Study, Indiana University, on February 2, 2012, and the Peter Gould Lecture, Colgate University, on April 25, 2012. I am grateful to both audiences for comments and questions, as well as to the reviewers of this essay for constructive suggestions.

NOTES

1. Judith Butler, *Frames of War* (London: Verso, 2009), 64ff.
2. David Campbell, "Geopolitics and Visuality," *Political Geography* 26, no. 4 (2007): 358–361.
3. Ibid.
4. Although the U.S. war in Afghanistan officially lasted from 2001 until the end of NATO combat operations in December 2014, some U.S. forces remain involved in combat. See "Taliban Gains Pull U.S. Units Back into Fight in Afghanistan," *New York Times*, April 29, 2015, http://www.nytimes.com/2015/04/30/world/asia/more-aggressive-role-by-us-military-is-seen-in-afghanistan.html. The imagery considered in this essay comes from the main phase of operations before 2014.

5. Coburn Dukeheart, "Shaking It Up: A New Look at Afghanistan," *The Picture Show*, National Public Radio, April 7, 2010, http://www.npr.org/blogs/pictureshow/2010/04/07/125664494/guttenfelder. For samples of the conventional imagery, see Boston.com's monthly Afghanistan galleries at http://www.boston.com/bigpicture/afghanistan/.
6. Butler, *Frames of War*, 72.
7. Bill Katovsky and Timothy Carlson, *Embedded: The Media at War in Iraq* (Guildford, CT: Lyons Press, 2003), xv, xvi; Christopher Paul and James J. Kim, *Reporters on the Battlefield: The Embedded Press System in Historical Context* (Santa Monica, CA: RAND Corporation, 2004), 54–55; Cardiff School of Journalism, Media and Cultural Studies, *Too Close for Comfort? The Role of Embedded Reporting during the 2003 Iraq War: Summary Report* (Cardiff, Wales: Cardiff University, 2004), 12.
8. Michael Griffin, "Picturing America's 'War on Terrorism' in Afghanistan and Iraq: Photographic Motifs as News Frames," *Journalism* 5, no. 4 (2004): 383.
9. Ibid., 397. For a photographer's reflections, see Cheryl Diaz Meyer, in *Reporting from the Front: The Media and the Military*, ed. Judith Sylvester and Suzanne Huffman (Lanham, MD: Rowman and Littlefield, 2005), 93.
10. Griffin, "Picturing America's 'War on Terrorism' in Afghanistan and Iraq"; Barbie Zelizer, "Photography, Journalism, and Trauma," in *Journalism after September 11*, edited by Barbie Zelizer and Stuart Allen (London and New York: Routledge, 2002); Zelizer, "When War Is Reduced to a Photograph," in *Reporting War: Journalism in Wartime*, edited by Stuart Allen and Barbie Zelizer (London and New York: Routledge, 2004).
11. Barbie Zelizer, "Death in Wartime: Photographs and the 'Other War' in Afghanistan," *Press/Politics* 10, no. 3 (2005): 34.
12. The view from the Taliban perspective is rare, with Gaith Abdul Ahad's November 2010 photographs an exception. See http://www.guardian.co.uk/world/gallery/2010/nov/23/taliban-bagland-afghanistan#/.
13. Michael Shaw, "Pink Skivvies: Whitewashing the Afghan Campaign," *BagNews Notes*, May 24, 2009, http://www.bagnewsnotes.com/2009/05/pink-skivvies-whitewashing-the-afghan-campaign/.
14. Julie Jacobsen, "Journal Entries of AP Photographer Embedded with U.S. Marines in Afghanistan," *Digital Journalist*, September 2009, http://digitaljournalist.org/issue0909/journal-entries-of-ap-photographer-embedded-with-us-marines-in-afghanistan.html; Michael Shaw, "Photo of a Dying Marine: The Larger View," *BagNews Notes*, September 5, 2009, http://www.bagnewsnotes.com/2009/09/photo-of-a-dying-marine-the-larger-view/.
15. David Dunlap, "Behind the Scenes: To Publish or Not?" *New York Times Lens Blog*, September 4, 2009, http://lens.blogs.nytimes.com/2009/09/04/behind-13/.
16. See David Campbell, "Media Disruption (1): The Primacy of the Screen and Mobile," May 19, 2015, https://www.david-campbell.org/2015/05/19/media-disruption-part-one-primacy-of-screen-and-mobile/; and Michael DeGusta, "Are Smart Phones Spreading Faster Than Any Technology in Human History?" *MIT Technology Review*, May 9, 2012, http://www.technologyreview.com/news/427787/are-smart-phones-spreading-faster-than-any-technology-in-human-history/.
17. "Year at War," *New York Times*, http://www.nytimes.com/interactive/world/battalion.html.
18. Balazs Gardi, Basetrack, "Afghanistan July 2011," http://www.foreignpolicy.com/articles/2011/07/25/the_war_in_hipstamatic, which is part of a five-part series, as clear here: http://www.iphoneography.com/journal/2011/7/28/hipstamatic-on-the-front-line-in-afghanistan.html. For Benjamin Lowy, see his "Afghanistan October 2011" work

(http://www.nytimes.com/2011/10/23/magazine/bad-guys-vs-worse-guys-in-afghanistan.html) and comments on it by picture editor Kathy Ryan at http://6thfloor.blogs.nytimes.com/2011/10/20/hipstamatic-in-kabul/. On Crimea, see Uri Freedman, "In Defense of Instagramming Conflict in Crimea," *The Atlantic*, March 7, 2014, http://www.theatlantic.com/international/archive/2014/03/in-defense-of-instagramming-conflict-in-crimea/284279/.

19. Pictures of the Year International, "Photographer of the Year—Newspaper," http://www.poyi.org/68/37/first_01.php; Meryl Alper, "War on Instagram: Framing Conflict Photojournalism with Mobile Phone Apps," *New Media Society*, September 18, 2013, http://nms.sagepub.com/content/early/2013/09/16/1461444813504265. The focus on the Hipstamatic app in photojournalism peaked in 2011–2013, and although it continues to be used, it has been overtaken by Instagram.

20. Chip Litherland, "There's an App for That," February 9, 2011, http://chiplitherland.com/blog/2011/02/09/theres-an-app-for-photojournalism/.

21. Pictures of the Year International, "Picture Rules," http://www.poyi.org/64CFE/rules.html.

22. David Campbell, *The Integrity of the Image*, World Press Photo Academy, November 2014, http://www.worldpressphoto.org/academy/integrity-of-the-image.

23. Comment on Litherland, "There's an App for That."

24. Ibid.

25. See David Campbell, "Photographic Truth and Photoshop," April 17, 2009, http://www.david-campbell.org/2009/04/17/photographic-truth-and-photoshop/ and Olivier Laurent, "World Press Photo Controversy: Objectivity, Manipulation, and the Search for Truth," *British Journal of Photography*, May 22, 2013, http://www.bjp-online.com/2013/05/world-press-photo-controversy-objectivity-manipulation-and-the-search-for-truth/.

26. Quoted in David Campbell, "The Aesthetics of the War in Afghanistan," December 17, 2010, http://www.david-campbell.org/2010/12/17/aesthetics-of-war-in-afghanistan/.

27. Damon Winter, "Through My Eye, Not Hipstamatic's," *New York Times Lens*, February 11, 2012, http://lens.blogs.nytimes.com/2011/02/11/through-my-eye-not-hipstamatics/.

28. 10b Photography, http://www.10bphotography.com/index.php?page=ethic&lang=eng.

29. Nathan Jurgenson, "The Faux-Vintage Photo: Full Essay (Parts I, II and III)," May 14, 2011, http://thesocietypages.org/cyborgology/2011/05/14/the-faux-vintage-photo-full-essay-parts-i-ii-and-iii/.

30. Nathan Jurgenson, "Faux-Vintage Afghanistan and the Nostalgia for War," August 2, 2011, http://thesocietypages.org/cyborgology/2011/08/02/faux-vintage-afghanistan-and-the-nostalgia-for-war/.

31. See Anne Wilkes Tucker and Will Michels, with Natalie Zelt, *War/Photography: Images of Armed Conflict and Its Aftermath* (New Haven, CT: Yale University Press, 2013).

32. Caroline Brothers, *War and Photography: A Cultural History* (London: Routledge, 1997), 2, 210.

33. Brian Wallis, "Rediscovering the Mexican Suitcase," in *The Mexican Suitcase: The Rediscovered Spanish Civil War Negatives of Capa, Chim, and Tar*, vol. 1: *The History*, edited by Cynthia Young (New York and Gottingen: International Center for Photography and Steidl, 2010), 13.

34. Susie Linfied, *Cruel Radiance: Photography and Political Violence* (Chicago: University of Chicago Press, 2010), 190.

35. See Alex Kershaw, *Blood and Champagne: The Life and Times of Robert Capa* (London: Pan Books, 2001).

36. Ibid., 38.

37. Ibid., 223–224.
38. Wallis, "Rediscovering the Mexican Suitcase," 13.
39. Kershaw, *Blood and Champagne*, 47.
40. See Dona Schwartz, "To Tell the Truth: Codes of Objectivity in Photojournalism," *Communication* 13, no. 2 (1992): 95–109.
41. Simon Dell, "Mediation and Immediacy: The Press, the Popular Front in France, and the Spanish Civil War," in *The Mexican Suitcase*, 37.
42. Winter, "Through My Eye, Not Hipstamatic's."
43. Mark Reinhardt, "Picturing Violence: Aesthetics and the Anxiety of Critique," in Reinhardt et al., *"Beautiful Suffering" Photography and the Traffic in Pain* (Chicago: University of Chicago Press, 2007), 13–36.
44. Nina Berman, comment on Michael Shaw, "War vs. Summer Camp: Hipstamatic Debate Just More Distraction Game?" *BagNewsNotes*, February 16, 2011, http://www.bagnewsnotes.com/2011/02/war-vs-summer-camp-hipstamatic-debate-just-more-distraction-game/.
45. Shaw, "War vs. Summer Camp."
46. Alper, "War on Instagram."
47. Quoted in Reinhardt, "Picturing Violence," 27.
48. Reinhardt, "Picturing Violence," 36.
49. Cardiff School of Journalism, Media and Cultural Studies, *Too Close for Comfort?* 14; Jay Rosen, "The Afghanistan War Logs Released by Wikileaks, the World's First Stateless News Organization," *PressThink*, July 26, 2010, http://pressthink.org/2010/07/the-afghanistan-war-logs-released-by-wikileaks-the-worlds-first-stateless-news-organization/; Rosen, "From Judith Miller to Julian Assange," *PressThink*, December 9, 2010, http://pressthink.org/2010/12/from-judith-miller-to-julian-assange/.
50. Michael Griffin, "Media Images of War," *Media, War and Conflict* 3, no. 1 (2010): 7–41. The seminal account of Vietnam is Daniel Hallin, *The "Uncensored War": The Media and Vietnam* (New York: Oxford University Press, 1986).

2 • RETURNING SOLDIERS AND THE IN/VISIBILITY OF COMBAT TRAUMA

CHRISTOPHER J. GILBERT AND JOHN LOUIS LUCAITES

I am lost in my world,
Invisible—unknown.
—Susie Clevenger, *Dirt Road Dreams*

The signs and symptoms of combat trauma are all around us: in images of troops under attack on the battlefield; in photographs of resuscitative and surgical procedures performed in the line of duty; in pictures of soldiers in combat fatigues affecting the thousand-yard stare; in videos of families grieving over a loved one, now a military casualty; in snapshots of wounded warriors, their damaged bodies, their severed limbs, their prostheses; and in statistics that report our wartime death toll in terms of veteran suicides. We encounter these tragic effects of war on an almost daily basis if for no other reason than that they are visible everywhere, part and parcel of a culture in which war and its aftermath have been normalized. Yet the question remains: What do we actually see? Or perhaps more to the point: What are we not seeing? And why?

The surface manifestations of our war culture are again and again reflected in the images and discourses that encircle it, mediated through countless journalistic and photojournalistic dispensaries of war's trauma. In each such documentary representation we are encouraged to see combat for what it is: sacrifice and sufferance. And one figure in particular carries much of the weight of such witnessing in U.S. public culture: the returning soldier.[1] Sometimes, of course, the returning soldier is made more or less invisible, entombed in a flag-draped coffin.[2] Our concern here, however, is with representations of the returning soldier who comes home alive and animates a form of witnessing that goads us to glimpse a less obvious trauma, or posttraumatic stress disorder (PTSD), which was called a "growing epidemic" by the National Institutes of Health (NIH) in 2009—the same year in which the U.S. Department of Defense lifted its ban on the publicity of images showing flag-draped coffins returning to U.S. soil.

But how do publics witness the publicity of sufferance in the perpetuation of what the NIH also dubs a "terrifying ordeal"? How do we make out the returning soldier's emotional numbness? How do we sense his or her deep-seated shame? How do we recognize the flashbacks, panic attacks, insomnia, or overweening hypervigilance? And more, how do we see the now-conventional commentaries about family troubles, relationship quandaries, frustrations with social institutions and bureaucracies, run-ins with the law and its multifarious machineries of criminal justice—all alongside a popular notion that experiences of war are as incommensurable with civic life as they are incommunicable? These are not simply questions of social knowledge; they are questions of civic responsibility to combat repercussions.

To tease out the complexities of these civic responsibilities, we turn to the photo-essay, a modern genre of photojournalism that situates the returning soldier as visibly embodied evidence of war's aftermath. Photo-essays are telling for what they reveal about the in/visibility of combat trauma. To begin, their depictions of returning soldiers portray the trauma in transitions to civic life. What we see in these portrayals is not the trauma of war, but rather the trauma of returning from war. This transition, idiomatically characterized as "the return," is wrought on the one hand with our cultural pathology toward public optics around violence, trauma, and sufferance, and on the other hand with the tension that comes from "public spectacle[s] of private exposure."[3] The photo-essay "Welcome Home, the Story of Scott Ostrom," published online by the *Denver Post* on December 30, 2011, is exemplary in this regard. With Pulitzer Prize–winning photographs by Craig F. Walker and copy by Michael Bryant, the essay documents (Bryan) Scott Ostrom's struggle to return home. More specifically, it provides a normalized view of combat trauma in the publicity of a soldier's pain. As we demonstrate in what follows, the photo-essay pegs Ostrom as an all-too-obvious threat to himself (and, by extension, to others), victimized by a violence that is neither immediately discernible nor visible to the naked eye. Ostrom is traumatized by "combat," which here vaguely signifies both the horrors of unseen warfare and the fight for homecoming. He is tormented by his own psychosis, and we are reminded that his first step to recovery is admitting that he has a problem. He is pitied for his alienation while, with expressions of guilt and self-reproach, he reinforces the shame so many returning soldiers bear upon themselves. Put simply, "Welcome Home" encapsulates the culture shock endemic to the return, and the pacification of our need to share in Ostrom's pain.

The photo-essay as a journalistic genre is significant because it perpetuates a standard narrative in serial form. As such, it carries cultural memory, expectations, predestinations, and the satisfaction of social cravings that come with news discourse more broadly. "Welcome Home" exemplifies the generic quality of PTSD in the notion that a soldier, physically maimed or not, will return with posttraumatic stress. Furthermore, the photo-essay collects and organizes a cultural narrative about the privatization of soldier sufferance even as it insinuates the in/visibility of pain in its photographic capture. In these ways, the form of the photo-essay serves a civic function as it purveys a recognizable subject matter. Nevertheless, it is revealing for what it exposes about the in/visibility of combat trauma and the unrecognizability of inner demons. "Welcome Home" shows the soldier as the object of sufferance. We see the victim. What we do not see is the "war/enemy within," or Ostrom's hidden wounds.

The photo-essay exposes us to the private world of PTSD along with its physical manifestations of distress. What it does not necessarily render is the particular psychology of the stressful malady. So, for example, in many images, Ostrom appears normal. But it is not until we apply the conventional combat labels that we see him as a ticking time bomb. Without the story, we do not witness the marks of trauma. Our burden is therefore to see in the photo-essay a parallax view, and glean different perspectives on the same image in order to derive different images in and from the same pictures. For our part, within the deep surfaces of the visible impacts of war are the very foundations of a war culture—a culture from which Ostrom and others cannot escape. These foundations tend to function as abstractions that, in many journalistic accounts, purge explicit evidence of war itself. Rarely do we see war. We witness its fallout in the personal struggles of soldiers who have themselves witnessed war and its atrocities. Yet, in identifying with them, we cleanse ourselves of war itself as a source of pain. This is the potentially damaging part of cathartic responses to soldier sufferance: something or someone is always cast out, making the publicity of "the return" both very selfish and very social.

Our aim is to understand the tension between visible and invisible combat trauma as a means for understanding the willful disregard of civic responsibility for returning soldiers in the ways in which we tend to regard them as a problem for our body politic. To do so, we hone in on three major themes that emerge out of "Welcome Home" and, coincidentally, shape our conventional conceptions of soldier sufferance, if not sufferance more generally. The first is shame, which is expressed in the conflict of Ostrom's thoughts, speech, and actions, and his express disgrace that is underwritten by social norms of honor and indignity, which tend to go unseen. The second is alienation. If shame mortifies and "performs culturally to mark out certain groups,"[4] alienation disaffects. In "Welcome Home," we see Ostrom turn away from the body politic at the same time as we are allowed to transfer to him any and all ownership of the responsibility, shame, and guilt that suffuses our war culture. As Norman Manea might attest, alienation is forced assimilation.[5] Last, the photo-essay reifies the role of self-reliance in the maintenance of our neoliberal state. Out of the shameful conditions of war we witness, in the end, a sense of community that relies upon the individual to take responsibility for his or her condition. We come, in turn, to how these shameful and alienating conditions might implicate representations of trauma in broader images of neoliberal subjectivity.[6] However, first and foremost we attend to how Ostrom reduplicates the human cost of war in the cultural purchase of "self-help." In this sense, it is no surprise that "Welcome Home" begins with an image of panic and ends with anxiety, all of which is not *ours* but *his*. Accordingly, "Welcome Home" is an ironic, even hostile title. To combat the ironies and hostilities in public portrayals of returning soldiers, it is vital, we argue, to consider the damage done by witnessing their return.

SHOWING AND TELLING TRAUMA

Trauma is complex. As numerous studies have shown, its implications are clinical, personal, social, phenomenological, existential, bureaucratic, institutional, political, cultural, and more. But as Lisa Lopez Levers demonstrates, the "core consequence . . . is human suffering."[7] Arguably, PTSD is from diagnosis to treatment to public perception far more a matter of rhetoric and politics than either science or medicine.[8] Since Freud began to systematize the study of trauma in psychiatric patients in order to understand its relation to psychoses, neuroses, war injuries, sexuality, hysteria, and catastrophe, many in the medical profession (and now in popular news outlets) have adopted "the traumatic" as a wide-angle lens for considering how and why we suffer. Academics have not been far behind. For example, Ruth Leys argues that such multifarious motivations have long led to inconsistencies and incoherencies in studies of trauma.[9] Claire Sisco King further establishes the contradictions and discrepancies as part and parcel to a "trauma culture" upheld by obsessions with the possibilities and problems of human sufferance.[10] As much is apparent in prevailing public discourses around veterans dealing with PTSD.

At its base, PTSD is an archetypal metaphor—"war/enemy within"—that signifies a foe within the body and mind of returning soldiers who, upon their return, are identified as "victims of an inner war."[11] This trope is part of a larger conversation about survivor's guilt, depression, isolation, drug abuse, crime, and panic, as well as the daunting problems veterans face acquiring benefits at home, attaining counseling, or receiving adequate medical treatment. And it is most salient when situated alongside "war's" definitive end for such veterans: suicide. In the past decade, numerous reports have documented shocking statistics about soldiers committing the ultimate (and arguably most shameful) crime against themselves.[12] Indeed, by June 2012, reports held that nearly one active duty member per day was committing suicide, rendering suicide itself a larger killer than the war in Afghanistan.[13]

The trope of "the return" and the psychosocial bane that it triggers is as old as the tales of Odysseus. Nonetheless, "thanks to modern armor and medicine, [soldiers] increasingly return home in one piece, but because of the unchanging viciousness of war, psychologically, they are often in pieces."[14] This is journalist David Phillips's response to the tales of Jose Barco and Kenneth Eastridge, two veterans who escaped combat only to later be imprisoned for attempted murder and murder, respectively. Much of the blame for severe outbursts, self-inflicted violence, and even more generalized repercussions of PTSD has fallen on the Department of Veterans Affairs, which has struggled to fulfill claims from troops returning from Iraq and Afghanistan.[15] All manifestations, however, are popularly attributed to the hidden wounds of combat, the cures for which are so often put on the soldiers themselves.[16] Photojournalism, too, has added to the poignancy of the discourse. All in all, there is an overwhelming prevalence of neoliberal frameworks operating in and through a privatized social economy of recovery, cataloguing the countless soldiers who, wrought by flashbacks, night terrors, insomnia, hypervigilance, and uncontrollable anxieties about social contact and emotional interactions, simply cannot cope with or live in the "civilized world." Instead, they survive and are survived by evaluations of their social status based on perceptions of shame and self-loathing.

CUT TO SHAME

Walker and Bryant's "Welcome Home" provides a penetrating look into what appears as a typical soldier's return home. Scott Ostrom, a veteran Marine who completed two tours of duty in Iraq, is pictured straining to find employment, laboring to maintain a rocky relationship with his girlfriend (then enduring a break-up), receiving rejections on applications for apartment residence, appearing in court on charges of aggravated assault, contemplating suicide, swallowing alcohol, self-medicating, weeping, screaming, and generally fighting back an invisible foe. He is also portrayed as having a closer relationship with his dog than with fellow humans (except, in some instances, for fellow veterans), which not only corroborates the proliferation of stories about military dog adoptions, dogs as curative agents, and even dogs with PTSD, but also suggests further the divide between soldiers and civilians as decade after decade we "cry havoc and let slip the dogs of war."[17] By and large, though, "Welcome Home" shows and tells just how much combat trauma pushes Ostrom to wreak havoc on himself.

This image in Figure 2.1 seems to tell it all.

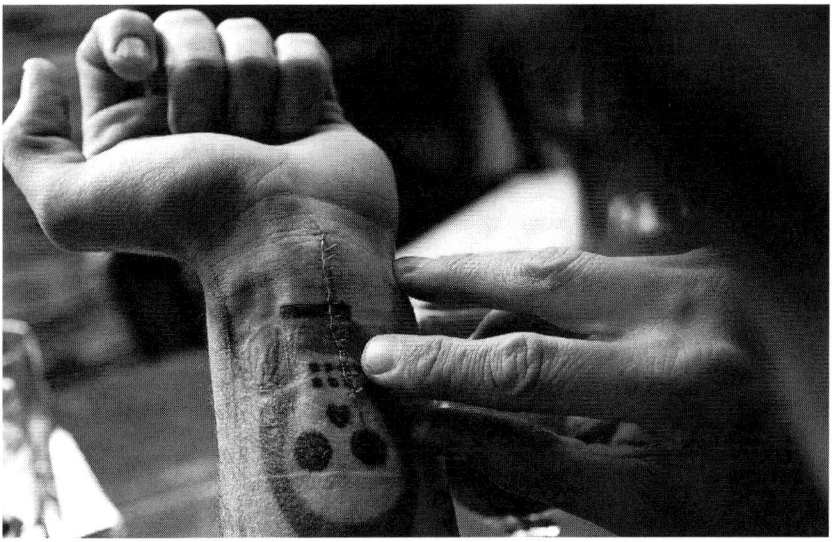

FIGURE 2.1

With his right hand, Ostrom fingers the edges of a stitched wound. He had recently attempted suicide following a verbal altercation with his now ex-girlfriend. In a fit of rage, Ostrom grabbed a pair of scissors. In his words, "I just tried jabbing them into my neck, but they were closed, so I just gave myself a nice laceration. So, I grabbed a nice kitchen knife and cut my wrists."[18] Ostrom's notion that both his laceration and the knife are somehow "nice" presents a sense of (incomplete) satisfaction that is as eerie as the evidence of his self-mutilation. The wound is disturbingly allegorical, cutting through the face of death, which is itself encased in what appears to be a grenade. What is more, the photo offers a symbolic representation of a returning soldier's desperate attempt to control the will to death that is integral to the will to survive. What we see is in fact a failed attempt at suicide, and in it a visible trace of internal trauma. From the narrative, though, we also get a glimpse into a strange paradox of success wherein Ostrom made it out of combat alive only to wish that he had died.

According to Ostrom, suicide is the "contingency plan" for the returning soldier, and it is predicated upon a socialized and militarized discourse of regret that goes beyond survivor's guilt. In one iteration, Ostrom articulates his sense of shame before a culture of scrutiny animated largely by survivors of World War II—the "good war"—that disallows any measure of pride in an unpopular war. One photo shows Ostrom walking in civilian clothes past a World War II veteran who sits in a wheelchair in front of a Veterans Affairs Medical

Center in Denver. The caption below the photo shares Ostrom's assumed position as a victim of shame, having not fought in a "real war." Here, the guilt he feels, not to mention the posttraumatic stress, is presumably unwarranted, the implication being that he should feel ashamed of his guilt. Then again, Ostrom is mortified by his recollection of the inhuman acts he carried out on the battlefield. "I'm just feeling guilty about the things I did," he laments. "I was bred to be a killer, and I did it. Now I'm trying to adapt and feel human again. But to feel human, I feel guilty." This is not survivor's guilt, but soldier's guilt. And it exposes a troublesome reality in Ostrom's appeal to the burden contingent to his return: either you die in combat or come home to suffer shame. As much is emblematized in both his failed attempt at suicide and his misfired self-sacrifice. The real honor, says Ostrom, would have been to die for his country. "I regret coming home safely," he admits. "I regret not getting seriously injured or killed." What should haunt us here is the idea that it was all along Ostrom's plan to die, and that his suicide attempt was in fact an effort to shame himself.

This points to the problem of traumatic representation and a central concern of this essay: the trouble with fostering a public identification between sufferers and witnesses, particularly as it recognizes combat trauma as socially shared in public memories, painful chronicles, social practices, and mediated experiences. Much of what we encounter relies upon what Leys calls a "transmission of the unrepresentable," whereby we are told of trauma and hailed into experiences of the traumatic and its enveloping events.[19] King suggests that traumatic narratives function as symbolic stand-ins, or "allegorical displacements," which often show and tell less about the soldier than they do about a society that transmits such stories.[20] We would be remiss if we did not admit that soldiers experience and remember war differently than civilians; that, in general, some know war definitely and directly while others know it through dissimulation and abstraction. In E. Ann Kaplan's terms, there is a difference between trauma and "vicarious trauma."[21] Accordingly, "trauma discourse works to construct trauma as a unifying experience that bonds survivors through shared suffering *at the same time* that the experiential authority assigned to the survivor gets used to distinguish and elevate that subject position as extraordinary and exemplary."[22] As such, trauma culture overlaps with what Jenny Edkins dubs a "testimonial culture," or a "culture of victimhood,"[23] indicating that a key dilemma has to do with how we share experiences of trauma as a social reality.

Shame entails the perception that one is uncovered, and more pointedly that one is exposed beyond one's control.[24] That shame is also both socialized and transmissible through public media should give us pause. Veteran suicides have been recently referred to as evidence of our nation's shame. But this claim to national ignominy leaves unexamined the particular ways in which we circulate a sense of shamefulness in the survival of returning soldiers: presence and absence, *fort-da*. In "Welcome Home," we witness the distinctly visual dimension of shame as it is implicated in public acts of bringing sufferance to the surface and covering it up. This visual dimension simultaneously exhibits shame as contained within and cast upon particular bodies. Still, as social as it is, shame is individualized, "relat[ing] to the self rather than to society."[25] When mapped onto the bodies of returning soldiers, shame isolates the trauma of war onto those who have been afflicted, and reinforces the shared experience of traumatized persons as somehow contaminated, defected, and unworthy of normalized civic life. To scroll through "Welcome Home" is therefore to look upon an individual who feels shame, who has nonetheless subjected himself to a photojournalistic exposé, and who still seems to want to hide his face. We are encouraged to experience pity. A returning soldier tried to commit suicide, and his scars might even be considered marks of cowardice. As we see Scott Ostrom in his diminished state,[26] we see our own righteousness in his failings, and we reaffirm our own position as supportive onlookers even as we avert our eyes. Additionally, as we discuss in what follows, we might see simultaneously a scapegoat for our own neoliberal failings.

The simple truth is that shame is underwritten by norms of public judgment that tend to go unseen.[27] Its psychosociality requires, at least in our war culture, that certain public experiences and their relational contents sustain a separation of the good from the bad, the civil from the savage. From a social standpoint, Ostrom's shame transcends his feelings of guilt, his enduring impulse to kill, and his symbolic efforts to cut from his life (and, indeed, from his body) the evil face of death. It traverses the confines of combat and folds into his civic campaign to recover a sense of himself, which has "died inside." But as the narrative suggests, those who escape death in war must face a second escape upon their return home—a paradoxical fight with and flight away from themselves.

RESIDENT ALIENS

Representations of returning soldiers bring us face to face with alienation. Alongside dominant narratives of soldiers who return home only to retreat from the normal strictures of civilized life is a powerful image of citizen-soldier relations built on the socialization of estrangement. This estrangement, in turn, is fostered by certain contradictions that demand the detachment of combat from civic existence. We separate ourselves from war even as war itself is carried out in the name of our society and its social institutions. To enlist is to withdraw from society. To return is to reconnect, but under severe scrutiny and with less care than concern.

Scott Ostrom's story rewrites alienation as a tale of belonging. Where Ostrom belongs, though, is elsewhere. To be alienated is to be out of place, quite possibly to have no place, to belong nowhere. A major theme that emerges from Ostrom's shame is the idea that while wars stop, for returning soldiers they never end. Just as traumas persist, so do the ordinary burdens of ordinary, everyday life fly in the face of unity in the trenches. We see these annoyances in the pathological interactions that Ostrom has with the society in which he now resides: he fights with his girlfriend, battles with bureaucracy when applying for an apartment, confronts the criminal justice system, spends his leisure time with his neighbor, playing video games (*Call of Duty*, no less) and lounging about his living room, and perhaps most tellingly, the only place he finds solace is in his relationship with his dog, Jibby.

"Welcome Home" is littered with images of Ostrom attempting to reenter civilization. The overarching impression is that, upon returning, a soldier is simply folded back into society as just another individual. Early on in the photo-essay, Ostrom likens his romantic relationship to a combat situation. Visual imagery displays its aftermath: bruised knuckles from punching walls, holes in wooden doors, vacant apartments. Soon he is on his own, trying to find a new place to live but being rejected once a background check reveals an assault charge. "Thank you for your service," Ostrom mocks, calling attention to the empty gesture that he reads into his rejection. "Thanks for your service . . . now go f____ yourself." Later, he is shown entering a vacant apartment with Jibby. In it, he is eventually seen "self-medicating" with marijuana; smoking alone, he fights off the depression that follows memories of when he "used to maka maka people."[28] He stands in his kitchen, clenching his fist with a look of terror on his face, fighting off a sudden onset of intense apprehension. And in a sentiment that seems to encompass the very condition of PTSD, he portrays his day-to-day life as "one long panic attack."

It is telling just how much these combative exchanges resonate with how even a non-soldier might interpret particularly confrontational interactions. In fact, it is not uncommon for civilians to experience administrative bodies and/or institutional bureaucracies through a similar combat optic, and thus a similarly aggressive—if not violently evasive—attitude. What makes Ostrom's negotiation of organizational conflict and interpersonal contact more jarring in this regard is his inability to tell the difference between military and putatively nonviolent civic contexts. Indeed, for Ostrom everything is embattled. Each social situation presents itself as a combat scenario. Any time he has to engage in what many would consider the most mundane aspects of living, he is moved to detach himself from society and its machinations. How appropriate, then, that just over halfway through we find this image (fig. 2.2).

It appears just after a photo of Ostrom gazing at a stormy sky from his apartment while regretfully remembering his actions in war, and just before a series of images of him with other soldiers or veterans. Shot from above at an angle

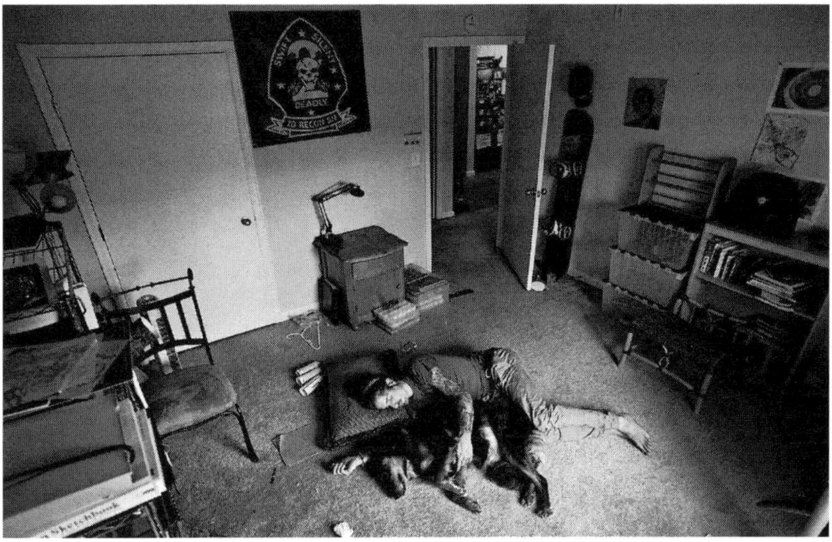

FIGURE 2.2

that casts the viewer as an omniscient spectator and apart from the immediate scene, we witness Ostrom lying on the floor with Jibby. They are in a spare room in the apartment, which is cluttered with a random array of items—a snowboard tucked behind the door, an empty CD rack, partially filled storage containers, a chair, a clothes hanger, and so on. A cold, blue light covers the scene and casts a sharp contrast with a warm, orange glow that emanates from the living room just beyond the open door. The utter disarray of material signifiers for modern living corresponds to the general disorganization and disorientation that characterizes Ostrom's life. More perturbing, though, is the position in which we find Ostrom and his dog.

The two are "spooning," or lying together back to front so they fit together like spoons. There is, prima facie, nothing particularly upsetting about this image. Many, as Donna Haraway would attest, find comfort in their companionship with pets. "Dogs are people, too," as the normative saying goes. They are "man's best friend." But "spooning" carries palpable connotations of romance. What is more, it suggests in this scene that Ostrom is attempting to mimic human relations with a social being that is not human. What stands out is the notion of overwhelming intimacy that Ostrom seems to attach to alienation. Throughout the photo-essay, Ostrom is seen in isolation, turning himself away from the civilian world and the social interactions that come with being a part of it. In this image, we see the resignation that comes with entering, in human relationships, a community of one. Even though Ostrom might not be committing himself to loneliness, he nevertheless resigns himself to being alone. In lockstep with this sentiment is the idea that, for a soldier to return to citizenship, he must involve himself in his own recovery or else suffer the alienation that follows a refusal to socialize. This does not suggest a wholesale loss of meaningful social interface; it does intimate a different type of relationality that suppresses (human) interpersonal relationships.

The caption corroborates this sense of self-alienation as a complement to socially prescribed disaffection:

> Scott said he was exhausted, and then went quiet and motionless. Eventually he broke the silence and said, "I'm tired of having bad f_______ dreams. I can't take a nap because I'll feel worse. I fall asleep, but it doesn't make it better. Everybody says, 'With time, with time it will all go away.' So I'm waiting." He got up, smoked a cigarette, made coffee and complained about the dirty dishes and his messy apartment. Just as he started cleaning, he said, "I don't have the motivation to do this s____. I don't have any motivation." Scott returned to the spare room, smoked some pot and pulled out his journal from Iraq. While he read, he laughed hard. Then shortly after his burst of laughter, he verged on tears. He put the journal aside and laid back down, Jibby joining him.

A turning point of "Welcome Home" therefore meditates on combat trauma as the soldier's burden to bear. At the same time, it recollects the combination of "visual shame" and "auditory guilt" that gets generally attached to returning soldiers in the photo-essay form.[29] Acknowledging this does not mitigate the fact that emotional turmoil is genuine, or that the impulse to recoil is real. However, with regard to the public responsibility for returning soldiers, complicity in the soldierly retreat within oneself is not the answer.

In Figure 2.2, we witness Ostrom's retreat. And we do so in a way that seems even more voyeuristic than many of the other photos—he seems to be asleep, and thus unaware of our presence. Or maybe he closes his eyes in shame, pretending that if he does not look at us we will not see him. As Erik Erikson notes, "He who is ashamed," after all, "would like to force the world not to look at him, not to notice his exposure. He would like to destroy the eyes of the world. Instead he must wish for his own invisibility."[30] But we see Ostrom, and by seeing him in this light we participate in his alienation as a transfer of ownership. Scott Ostrom must own his guilt. He must own his shame. And he must do so in a way that leads him to confront his problem. How troubling, in these terms, is the marine battalion flag that appears to bear down upon him as he rests. Back is the face of death, grinning over him. Like the PTSD that renders his existence a living nightmare, his former self is survived by the curse of combat, which is "swift," "silent," "deadly." We "welcome" him home. But we expect in return that Ostrom take responsibility for his demons, and kill that which is killing him.

THE STRESS AND STRAIN OF SOCIETY

The problem of combat trauma relates as much to processes of storytelling as to the labor of documentation.[31] Personal histories beget shared cultural fictions. For instance, a CNN story entitled "A War Hero Returns Home, 40 Years Later" offers a conventional narrative that draws distinctions between subjects of and to trauma, as well as to the traumatic object: a Vietnam veteran's life as a soldier, his experience of being decivilized for war, his petulant politics regarding warfare, his long road to personal recovery, and his admonition to veterans of the wars in Iraq and Afghanistan that their battles are "just starting."[32] A similar narrative emerges in a story that describes a private battle in the mind of Marine Corporal James Dahan, and one that, almost inevitably, ends in suicide.[33] The disturbing moral is that Dahan did what he was trained to do: he killed his enemy. For Cathy Caruth, these sorts of renderings engender "ignorance," or vast disconnections between soldier sufferance and public experiences of war.[34] We lose individual subjects in these accounts and instead find a metonymic returning soldier. For Leys, such examples foreground the problematic distinction between literal and figurative representations of trauma, on a presumed powerlessness of the victim, and on a view of trauma as a cycle of repression and expression. Tellingly, Leys likens the process of coping with war to culture shock. Soldiers suffering from PTSD, it seems, are shocked when they are forced to reimagine themselves as civilians.

"Welcome Home" crystallizes these narratives. In particular, it demonstrates the extent to which "the return" capitulates to the broader cultural burdens of neoliberal selfhood. The soldier self, like the civic self, is something to be managed. This is not difficult to imagine in military circumstances. Soldiers abide strict and regimented disciplinary guidelines in order to secure the safety and strength of a unit. Good conduct is comparable to staying in line. Socialization to civilization is not entirely dissimilar. However, while combat scenarios uphold the primacy of a unit, U.S. neoliberal society supports the primacy of the individual. Cultural and even constitutional frameworks provide for the privileged rights of singular subjects, which correspond to a public trust in the responsibility of individual agents as ethical beings and rational actors. The sustenance of civic selfhood, then, is in the public interest, rendering self-interest a civic good. Space precludes an in-depth analysis of neoliberal selfhood and the prospects of self-governance but the point to be emphasized is this: the discourse of self-reliance is carefully affixed to the returning soldier as he or she seeks to reintegrate with the civilian world.

It is a truism in U.S. public culture that the first step to confronting and solving problems—especially of the psyche—is admitting that a problem exists. It is central to the individuation of agency. It is also central to the proclaimed provision by society of resources for recovery, and by extension for "self" help. Ostrom typifies the returning soldier who is not at home in his own country. He cannot cope, he cannot interact and, more significant, he cannot discipline himself. Indeed, one of the most disturbing aspects of PTSD as a result of combat trauma is the subsequent inability of its victims to harness flight into fight modes, outbursts of aggression, night terrors, or environmental stimuli that might trigger flashbacks. Society, though, is often understood as the antithesis to war. It is controlled, governed, and ordered in ways that actual combat, with its (calculated) barbarism and its (proscribed) brutality, is not. Culture is also a controlled environment, closed off from the wildness and wiles of the natural world. These, at least, are the stories we tell ourselves. So when Ostrom says, "Society reminds me of war," we should consider what that says about society.

Ostrom appears alone in almost every image in "Welcome Home." He drinks alone. He shops alone. He separates himself from society. Then, in a striking series of four photos, he returns to nature. We first see him blowing on the embers of a small fire at his campsite on the Ceran St. Vrain Trail. He is center frame, and his surroundings are stunning. Large rocks cover the dirt floor around him along with a stack of logs for his fire. A river rushes by in the backdrop. And all takes on a cerulean hue, except for the red of the flames. Next we see a silhouette of Ostrom staring into a clear blue night sky. His body blends in with the tree line beyond him, which is also shaped in a shadowed contour against the firmament. By day, Ostrom is in a verdant field encased with evergreens. Jibby jumps expectantly before him as he readies to throw a stick for her to fetch. Then we find Ostrom lounging in a makeshift hammock. Tree trunks and pines fill out the background, along with a pile of his gear and a view of Jibby sprawled across the forest floor sleeping. Ostrom's face is blocked, covered over by a copy of *The Catcher in the Rye*, which he grasps with both hands.

The photographic account paints a picture of Emersonian serenity. But then we read the captions. Ostrom has escaped to the woods on Memorial Day weekend. He is not alone. He brought Jibby along with him. But he is very much by himself, without help, in his own head. This is initially apparent in the sense of necessary autonomy he feels away from social structures. "It feels good to be in a space this big and feel as safe as I do. . . . If anything bad were to happen, I would know exactly what to do. I can't say that about daily life." On the one hand, Ostrom points to the claustrophobia he experiences in civic interactions. In the woods he is safe because he does not have to deal with the bureaucracies, the administrative features, and the institutions needed to sustain neoliberal selfhood. On the other, he recognizes his responsibility over himself. In nature, "bad" things happening usually means that one must employ survival skills. In nature, staying alive is the thing, sustaining oneself. This realization is followed by a story that Ostrom recounts, relaying a day when an improvised explosive device (IED) blew up a guy he had met the very same morning—a guy whom he "knew right away" would be a friend. The story is tragic. Ostrom's chance at friendship, perhaps the most common and fundamental social bond, is put to an end before it can even begin. And so we see him socializing with Jibby, who he describes as at once a form of therapy and a source of unconditional kinship. It is no wonder that he later finds refuge in the antisocial world of Holden Caulfield, who, Ostrom notes, "lives in his own head. I can relate to that."

One could look upon Ostrom's weekend away and celebrate his retreat to nature: his decision, for instance, to put down the booze and "drink the wild air's salubrity."[35] Such self-reliance seems to bespeak a positive, albeit temporary, self-removal from society. Of course, it is only temporary, and eventually Ostrom must choose either to leave society (and commit social suicide) or return and face his fears. Here we witness his return (fig. 2.3).

The image is altogether banal. Ostrom stands on the side of a road, hunched over his camping equipment, indicating with the thumb on his right hand that he is in need of a ride. Both he and Jibby look beyond the frame with anticipation. Perhaps a driver is about to pull over. But there is an irony in this photographic allegory of neoliberal self-reliance. Hitchhiking is paradoxical. Unexcited about returning to society, he expresses his contentment in taking ownership over his own fate. Yet to get back to pick himself up as a participatory citizen, he must

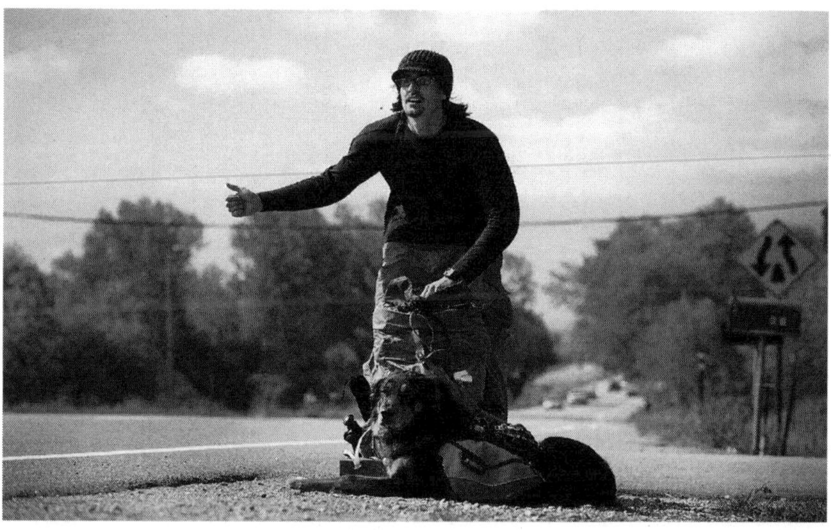

FIGURE 2.3

pick himself up. How ironic it is that he needs someone else to pick him up in order for him to do so. Ostrom cannot get himself back into society, though he can apparently get himself out (a problem made all the more poignant and transparent by the photographer who is with him and ready to capture the drama of Ostrom hitchhiking home). At war, Ostrom is burdened with the responsibility of protecting the private civil liberties so coveted in U.S. public culture. During his return, he cannot fully enjoy them, nor can he get past the social stigma that gets applied to demands on him to seek help. His return is hardly a free ride. Insofar as it amplifies the trauma of his transition from combat to civic life, Ostrom's retreat into nature betrays his avoidance of treatment and his will to escapism. Within the neoliberal framework, this adds up to an unwillingness to confront the problem. It appears as though he is not ready to admit his need for help. His escape is thus an extension of his self-alienation. His retreat, like his enlistment in treatment, requires his own initiative. Going back to civilization, Ostrom feels more alone than he does in the woods. This narrative is eerier than his reentry. No wonder society reminds him of war.

Ultimately, what we witness is a perversion of self-reliance. When the burden of re-socialization is brought to bear in images of retreat, "the call to action for soldiers to care for their mental health" comes off like "a campaign to screen AIDS or get a flu shot. Services are pitched as a potential solution, with the underlying assumption that the soldier or veteran is looking for a solution."[36] In other words, the options and services are there. The choice is theirs. Such an emphasis on self-sufficiency applies a market logic to civic responsibility, which means that as a society we do not need to feel responsible for the choices that soldiers do or do not make in seeking treatment.[37] What is more, discourses of heroism (that operate in "support our troops" campaigns despite appeals to the illegitimacy or inefficacy of contemporary wars) lionize soldiers and so further separate them from ordinary citizens. In this separation, traumatized combat veterans tend to disown their social responsibilities and seek solace in the comfort and understanding of their brothers and sisters in arms. As a public, we do them service by honoring and valuing their codes of silence, and so relinquish our responsibility.

It is fitting, then, that "Welcome Home" closes with images of Ostrom's spiral through depression to his enrollment in Denver's PTSD Residential Rehabilitation Program. In one of the last photos, Ostrom is packing recognizable accouterments for modern living: deodorant, toothpaste, shampoo, and so on. If not for the caption, we might think that he is packing for a camping trip. In the penultimate photo, he is in a parking garage walking away from his truck, a duffle bag slung over his shoulder. On display in the front window is his now familiar battalion flag, on which "DEADLY" is the only fully visible word. The final picture shows Ostrom from the waist up in a green marine hoodie. His head is cocked toward the sky. His eyes are closed. Large in the background looms the VA center, a cement structure utterly at odds with the earlier images of natural serenity, waiting to welcome him. Things are "looking up," he says.

We are left with a sense that it is unjust to look down on Ostrom or any other soldier unable to combat the traumas of war. However, we are also left without any "shame at witnessing a suffering."[38] Our concern is that trauma, in large part, is a social construction, and a particularly political construct insofar as it coincides with cultural beliefs and power relations that extend beyond the sites and subjects of trauma itself. As Jeffrey Alexander asserts, suffering is "social suffering," and trauma is "collective trauma," even if our cultural narratives tend to place its weight on some shoulders more than others. This is not to say that trauma or suffering is shared or felt in the same way. It is to say that both are a "result of . . . [an] acute discomfort entering into the core of the collectivity's [or individual's] sense of its own identity."[39] Representations of combat PTSD are therefore political actions in image construction, and "symbolic-cum-emotional . . . process[es] centering on [collective] meaning making."[40] Or, trauma is neither symptoms of anxiety nor a symptom per se of larger social unease about, say, war culture; it is rather "a rhetorical response aimed at assuaging such [anxieties]."[41] Herein lies a crucial move: we should not simply ask, "What trauma *does* to victims," but rather "What trauma *does for* the imagined U.S. community."[42] It is our sense that this move requires us to change the subject from soldiers (alone) to civic audiences of sufferance.

CONCLUSION

> They think that the war is over! Only the dead have seen the end of war.
>
> —George Santayana, Soliloquy 25

On October 9, 2013, satirical news source *The Onion* published an article entitled, "Military Unveils Bionic Super-Soldiers Capable of Withstanding Mental Toll of War." The article was accompanied by a mock image of the unveiling in which a military official stands behind a podium in a gymnasium and presents "the new guilt-free, psychologically advanced super-soldier[s]"—who appear in formation behind the official—to a public audience. The soldiers are touted for their capacity to "withstand limitless amounts of violence and bloodshed, which would then prevent them from experiencing future bouts of paranoia, anxiety, and crippling depression." Not a single one of the test soldiers committed suicide, we are told, and each one is engineered to remain emotionally stable in spite of traumatic events encountered in combat. Perhaps most important, the troops are trained for their return to "normal" life. "Now," says U.S. Secretary of Veterans Affairs Eric Shineski, "we can use these bionic troops on the battlefield to whatever extent we require, send them back to their hometowns, and never have to worry about providing them with costly medical treatment and counseling."

And that's just it. Though we are habituated to looking out for signature anxieties in returning soldiers, we are conditioned out of attending to our own civic anxieties about the embodied, emotional, and traumatic transitions our soldiers face in coming out of combat. As we have demonstrated, conventional forms of representing returning soldiers operate on and operationalize the privatization of pain. In channeling sentiments of shame, alienation, and self-reliance, photo-essays like "Welcome Home" in particular work to reify the social deaths of war veterans in our institutional machineries for cordoning, containing, and even decontaminating combat trauma. Such portrayals pretend to show and tell all, especially when they are disclaimed: "Warning: This photo-essay contains graphic images." A seemingly straightforward note of caution, this simple expression underwrites as it overdetermines a sense in which we as witnesses do not have to suffer through the pain and suffering of others. We do not have to subject ourselves to trauma. Soldiers, after all, are ultimately responsible for themselves, for their behavior, and/or their recovery of a civil independence in line with normative assumptions about what it means to live peaceably in a body politic. But even if we grant the visibility of "Welcome Home," even if we click on the links and bring Ostrom's combat trauma to light, we are still encouraged to turn a blind eye on our own collusion in a shameful politics of seeing, in our alienation of fellow citizens, and in our own reliance on social structures of blissful ignorance.

It cannot go unnoticed that there is a parallel between combat trauma and all of the other places where neoliberal ideology works to shame people for being poor, homeless, drugged, even disabled. To fall into poverty, for instance, is to fall into a state of wastefulness, which manifests in abstractions of individuals who are presented as unproductive and/or deficient members of society. In a neoliberal framework, this type of social collapse certainly fosters national shame for some. However, acknowledging such a parallel only gets us so far, especially if it ignores the fundamental uniqueness of a war culture that emphasizes the predicaments of citizen-soldiers as more righteous than routine. In war, the afflicted are first sent off to fight for the nation-state. The soldier's "fall" is thus a byproduct of war's fallout. Furthermore, returning soldiers are specific outcomes of combat trauma that are judged according to a rubric that recognizes sacrifice as greater than general social responsibility.[43] The post-9/11 context tends to prefigure embattlement as endemic to U.S. public culture (i.e., wars on poverty, wars on the poor, class warfare, etc.). Neoliberalism simply props up win/loss perspectives in an economy of trauma, which points less to questions of what to do after victories than what to do after losses. The citizen-soldier is part of a wider collectivity of individual losers, which reinforces the fact that there is today a broader conventional abandonment of public responsibility to the down-and-out. Alienation is therefore rife insofar as all are left to their own devices when it comes to grasping the proverbial bootstraps.

All too evident in this analysis is the irony that, even for a Romantic like Ralph Waldo Emerson, self-reliance depends upon aversion to custom rather than conformity. Norms blind. Conventions keep hidden the cultural codes of conduct that enable us to see and survive in certain ways. Yet even Emerson says that to thrive "alone" we must speak to and thus share with one another; we must strive "to live well," but to do so *together.* This implies that sociality in general, but something like civic friendship in particular, requires a delicate balance between similarities and differences. Drawing upon a conventional narrative of combat-induced trauma, the photo-essay reiterates a cycle of shame, alienation, and compromised self-reliance. As a rhetorical form of expression, it orients us towards a particular assessment of recurrent events and the "disorders" that they replicate.[44] However, the form also can reveal aporias that do not necessarily have to fold back into the recognizable narrative structure. As Kenneth Burke's psychology of form advises, such ruptures can be repaired as long as expectations are finally appeased.[45] Since such ruptures are caught up in a politics of witnessing, and since witnessing means to be intercessory as much as accessory to an event,[46] "Welcome Home" can serve as a remediation of combat trauma and its call for a civic gaze.

First, it might demand that we ask what images of war burden us to see. To witness is not just to see something happen; it is also to be victimized by something seen, to be subjected to an event against one's will, and to be overwhelmed by an occurrence. As Nancy Sherman pronounces, "As a public we, too, need to know how war feels, for war's residue should not just be a soldier's private burden."[47] We need to know how the organization of feeling is caught up in what we see. This suggests that, should we choose to look through the photo-essay of Ostrom, we should not then imagine ourselves free from the responsibility to intercede in it through forms of public testimony. It is willful disregard to presume that, in looking alone, we have done our civic duty. Instead, we call for a revision of ourselves as civic audiences within a sociality of pain. Calling attention to the potential damage done by the photo-essay form is a start inasmuch as form itself presumes the preeminence of an audience. We begin to do justice to Ostrom's sufferance when we move to strengthen the visual weight of trauma in the fragility of public appearances by expressing our discontent with the form of appeal.

Second, and by extension, in turning to the politics of witnessing we are burdened with the prospect of turning away from the almost unqualified agency of willing spectatorship. We are also shifting toward the unpredictability and the potential for upset expectations that come with being confronted by new ways of seeing. The plea here is to see in Scott Ostrom an image of ourselves. Politics of witnessing, after all, are implicated in the capacity to comprehend relationships. Seeing relationships means that looking at photos is an active enterprise, as is the willingness to see or not to see. There is no such thing as an innocent bystander in this notion because the concern is less about what is actualized than what is activated in what is seen. In attending to the in/visibility of combat trauma, we have implied an additive aspect of what it means to see the pain in a returning soldier's transition from war to civic life. An opening question asked what it means to witness a transition, which implored us to look for the hidden agendas and assumptions—both unseen and unspoken—within the deep surfaces of photojournalistic representations. Consequently, we hope to have modeled a critical practice of inserting a certain civic responsibility for soldier sufferance that is normally purged in the consumption of photo-essays like "Welcome Home." It is only when pain is directed outward that others can be affected. And to affect civic relations is to goad a public response, which makes a politics of wait and see irresponsible.

NOTES

1. Consider the following for just a small sample. Nina Berman and Verlyn Klinkenborg, "Returning from Iraq, the Damage Done," *Mother Jones,* March 2004, http://www.motherjones.com/photoessays/2004/03/returning-iraq-damage-done/01; Peter Van Agtmael, "A Farewell to a Fallen Service Member," *Time,* April 12, 2010, http://content.time.com/time/magazine/article/0,9171,1977142,00.html; Peter van Agtmael, "A Soldier's Final Journey Home," *Time,* April 12, 2010, http://content.time.com/time/photogallery/0,29307,1976918,00.html; James Estrin, "Home from Afghanistan to New Battles," *New York Times,* June 7, 2011, http://lens.blogs.nytimes.com/2011/06/07/home-from-afghanistan-to-new-battles/?_r=0; David Finkel, "The Return," *The New Yorker,* September 9, 2013, http://www.newyorker.com/reporting/2013/09/09/130909fa_fact_finkel; and others.

2. Tellingly, until 2009, there was a "coffin ban" on photographs that captured the caskets of soldiers killed in action. Defense Secretary Robert M. Gates announced a lifting of the ban, which would allow pictures to be taken of coffins arriving at Dover Air Force Base. Controversy over the ban persists and centers on whether or not a public should see the evidence of war's toll.

3. Mark Seltzer, "Wound Culture: Trauma in the Pathological Public Sphere," *October* 80 (1997): 26.

4. Sally R. Munt, *Queer Attachments: The Cultural Politics of Shame* (Burlington, VT: Ashgate, 2007), 2.

5. Norman Manea, "Exile," in *The Fifth Impossibility: Essays on Exile and Language* (New Haven, CT: Yale University Press, 2012), 3–12.

6. For discussions of neoliberal subjectivity within contexts of civic alienation, nationalistic selfhood, and "free market" governance of sociopolitical relations, see Bradford Vivian, "Neoliberal Epideictic: Rhetorical Form and Commemorative Politics on September 11, 2002," *Quarterly Journal of Speech* 92 (2006): 1–26; Trent H. Hamann, "Neoliberalism, Governmentality, and Ethics," *Foucault Studies* 6 (2009): 37–59; Lynne Layton, "Irrational Exuberance: Neoliberal Subjectivity and the Perversion of Truth," *Subjectivity* 3 (2010): 303–322; and

Jennifer Wingard, *Branded Bodies, Rhetoric, and the Neoliberal Nation-State* (Lanham, MD: Lexington Books, 2013).

7. Lisa Lopez Levers, "An Introduction to Counseling Survivors of Trauma: Beginning to Understand the Context of Trauma," in *Trauma Counseling: Theories and Interventions*, edited by Lisa Lopez Levers (New York: Springer, 2012), 11.

8. Mary Sykes Wylie, "The Politics of PTSD," *Psychotherapy Networker*, January 2, 2009, http://www.psychotherapynetworker.org/magazine/recentissues/2011-julyaug/item/486-the-politics-of-ptsd.

9. Ruth Leys, *Trauma: A Genealogy* (Chicago: University of Chicago Press, 2000), 6.

10. Claire Sisco King, *Washed in Blood: Male Sacrifice, Trauma, and the Cinema* (New Brunswick, NJ: Rutgers University Press, 2012), 7.

11. Erica Good, "After Combat, Victims of an Inner War," *New York Times*, August 1, 2009, http://www.nytimes.com/2009/08/02/us/02suicide.html?pagewanted=all.

12. Marilyn Elias, "Many Iraq Veterans Fighting an Enemy Within," *USA Today*, June 30, 2004, http://www.usatoday.com/news/health/2004-06-30-vets-mental_x.htm.

13. Alexander Abad-Santos, "Suicide Has Killed More Troops Than the War in Afghanistan This Year," *The Wire*, June 8, 2012, http://www.thewire.com/national/2012/06/suicide-has-killed-more-troops-war-afghanistan-year/53310/; see also "Survivors of War Struggle with Life at Home," *CNN*, May 5, 2012, http://johnkingusa.blogs.cnn.com/2012/05/25/survivors-of-war-struggle-with-life-at-home/?iref=allsearch; and Chris Miller and Patrick Bellon, "The U.S. Army Can't Stop Soldiers from Killing Themselves," *The Atlantic*, October 12, 2012, http://www.theatlantic.com/national/archive/2012/10/the-us-army-cant-stop-soldiers-from-killing-themselves/263540/.

14. David Philipps, "Veterans' Lingering Wounds," *Washington Post*, November 11, 2010, http://voices.washingtonpost.com/political-bookworm/2010/11/veterans_lingering_wounds.html.

15. See "From War Injuries to PTSD to Backlogged Claims, New Veterans Battle New Foes after Coming Home," *Washington Post*, May 27, 2012, http://www.washingtonpost.com/national/health-science/from-war-injuries-to-ptsd-to-backlogged-claims-new-veterans-battle-new-foes-after-coming-home/2012/05/27/gJQAuygWuU_story.html; Mike Scotti, "The V.A.'s Shameful Betrayal," *New York Times*, May 28, 2012, http://www.nytimes.com/2012/05/28/opinion/the-vas-shameful-betrayal.html; and Nicholas D. Kristof, "A Veteran's Death, the Nation's Shame," *New York Times*, April 15, 2012, http://www.nytimes.com/2012/04/15/opinion/sunday/kristof-a-veterans-death-the-nations-shame.html.

16. "The Hidden Wounds of Combat," CNN, May 27, 2012, http://www.cnn.com/video/#/video/bestoftv/2012/05/27/exp-ptsd-suicide-kravis-and-lyles.cnn.

17. For a more in-depth discussion of the relationship between dogs and war, see Purnima Bose's chapter in this collection.

18. All quotes and captions are gleaned from the photo-essay "Welcome Home," unless otherwise noted.

19. Leys, *Trauma*.

20. King, *Washed*, 14–15.

21. See E. Ann Kaplan, *Trauma Culture: The Politics of Terror and Loss in Media and Literature* (New Brunswick, NJ: Rutgers University Press, 2005).

22. King, *Washed*, 39–40.

23. Jenny Edkins, *Trauma and the Memory of Politics* (New York: Cambridge University Press, 2003), 18.

24. Stephen Pattison, *Shame: Theory, Therapy, Theology* (New York: Cambridge University Press, 2000), 71.

25. Ibid., 70.

26. Alex Tyree, "Shame: A Hospice Workers' Reflections," in *The Shame of Death, Grief, and Trauma*, edited by Jeffrey Kauffman (New York: Routledge, 2010), 88.
27. Martha C. Nussbaum, *Hiding from Humanity: Disgust, Shame, and the Law* (Princeton, NJ: Princeton University Press, 2004), 174.
28. *Maka maka* is military jargon for killing.
29. These phrases are borrowed from Erik H. Erikson, *Childhood and Society* (New York: W. W. Norton, 1963).
30. Ibid., 256.
31. Dominick LaCapra, *Writing History, Writing Trauma* (Baltimore: Johns Hopkins University Press, 2001).
32. John Blake, "A War Hero Returns Home, 40 Years Later," CNN, April 9, 2012, http://www.cnn.com/2012/03/24/living/karl-marlantes-war-books/index.html.
33. Dahleen Glanton, "Iraq War Is Over, but Effects Linger for Veterans," *Chicago Tribune*, December 20, 2011, http://articles.chicagotribune.com/2011-12-20/news/ct-met-iraqwar-ptsd-20111220_1_steve-nardizzi-ptsd-iraq-and-afghanistan.
34. Cathy Caruth, "Trauma and Experience," in *Trauma: Explorations in Memory* (Baltimore: Johns Hopkins University Press, 1995), 8.
35. Ralph Waldo Emerson, "Considerations by the Way," in *The Collected Works of Ralph Waldo Emerson: The Conduct of Life*, edited by Douglas Emory Wilson (Cambridge, MA: Harvard University Press, 2003), 129.
36. Rajiv Srinivasan, "Soldier Suicide: The Stigma to Seeking Help," *Time*, July 12, 2012, http://ideas.time.com/2012/07/12/soldier-suicide-the-stigma-to-seeking-help/.
37. David J. Morris, "How Much Does Culture Matter for P.T.S.D.?" *The New Yorker*, July 16, 2013, http://www.newyorker.com/online/blogs/elements/2013/07/ptsd-and-its-critics.html.
38. Michel Haar, *Nietzsche and Metaphysics*, trans. Michael Gendre (Albany: State University of New York Press, 1996), 136.
39. Jeffrey C. Alexander, *Trauma: A Social Theory* (Malden, MA: Polity Press, 2012), 15.
40. Ibid., 2.
41. King, *Washed*, 13.
42. Ibid., 11.
43. Of course, this is even more pronounced when one considers that something like structural impoverishment pushes many of the already unfortunate and/or disadvantaged into the military in the first place. Hence the enduring significance of Jean-Paul Sartre's quip in *The Devil and the Good Lord* (1951): *Quand les riches se font la guerre, ce sont les pauvres qui meurent* ("When the rich wage war, it's the poor who die"). Jean-Paul Sartre, *Le diable et le bon dieu* (Paris: Flammarion, 1951).
44. See Kenneth Burke, *Counter-Statement* (1931; rpt. Berkeley and Los Angeles: University of California Press, 1953), 31; See also Carolyn Miller, "Genre as Social Action," *Quarterly Journal of Speech* 70, no. 2 (1984): 151–167.
45. Burke, "Psychology and Form," 29–44.
46. John Durham Peters, *Courting the Abyss: Free Speech and the Liberal Tradition* (Chicago: University of Chicago Press, 2005), 250.
47. Nancy Sherman, *The Untold War: Inside the Hearts, Minds, and Souls of Our Soldiers* (New York: W.W. Norton, 2010), 8.

3 • (RE)FASHIONING PTSD'S WARRIOR PROJECT

JEREMY G. GORDON

On the surface, veteran trauma is layered with mythic references that make it in/visible to those not materially, literally experiencing it, rendering it legible, but in ways that naturalize and invoke unreflective ways of seeing. Put differently, the struggle with combat trauma is envisioned as a warrior project in which only those who embody a heroic, if not Homeric, ethos are able to take on and defeat the shock, pain, and distress of posttraumatic stress disorder (PTSD). Indeed, one does not have to look hard to see how images of Achilles and Odysseus saturate cultural attempts to redress the phenomenon, assembling a coherent and cohesive mythic formation that guides the attitudes, investments, and affective attachments that make PTSD matter (both in terms of material manifestation and felt as a matter of concern).[1]

Kevin Sites, for example, fashions combat trauma as a Trojan horse, a metaphorical structure ready to let loose hidden destruction on a nation presumed to be at peace.[2] In his telling, Corporal William Wold becomes Achilles, a warrior with a mortal flaw, while Lance Corporal James Sperry is an "allegorical Odysseus, who . . . finally makes it home."[3] Sites's journalistic accounts parallel Jonathan Shay's seminal work that enmeshes Achilles's flaws and Odysseus's journey with veteran experiences of coming home.[4] The Wounded Warrior Project (WWP) animates one of the most prominent public spaces in which mythic touches are relied upon to see and attend to PTSD in epic proportions.[5] Part of the organization's mission is "Project Odyssey,"[6] a noble endeavor, the name of which derives from Odysseus's epic quest to find his way home from war. Of course, if trauma is an epic quest, armor is needed, preferably something with a degree of sheen. Therapist Major Thomas Jarrett describes it as a need to "polish many ideals . . . soldiers already know, and remind them of their

Greco-Roman tradition of excellence and emotional control," with Spartan finish: "We have the same blood and ideals as those who defended [to the death] Thermopylae."[7] The use of armor is not lost on Odyssean projects. The WWP is sponsored by Under Armour, a company that has "muscled" its way into favor by manufacturing form-fitting athletic wear that is most popular for fighting men.[8] The relationship between Under Armour and military personnel is a deliberate market choice. Founder Kevin Plank is proud to supply the textures for war and its aftermath. For a minimal price, one can share in the battle against trauma. At $24.99, Armour seems like a good deal.

Fashioned for allegories of homecomings, set as models for reintegration programs, and drawn upon for clinical attempts to "communalize trauma," Achilles and Odysseus help craft combat trauma in epic terms.[9] More to the point, the contemporary presence of these mythic forms situate combat trauma as a "virtuous war."[10] Envisioned as such, negotiating trauma becomes an either/or proposition of heroically masculine proportions: to overcome and live or fail and die.[11] Homer's warriors make PTSD matter in the public eye, yet their well-worn presence leaves little for expanding the ways in which combat trauma's complexity might be seen.[12] Relying on Achilles and Odysseus to make veteran trauma visible turns the "fabric of character," to use Nancy Sherman's phrase, into a stiff and seamless layer of stoic armor.[13] At first glance, such surfaces provide protection during battles with trauma, seemingly most fitting for efforts to overcome it and claim ultimate victory. Yet mythic armor also hinders the development of other legendary layers that might expand the kinds of visions and encounters we have with veterans, not to mention the ways in which veterans might rely on mythic cover for cultural legibility and recognition.

This essay emphasizes trauma as a fundamentally mythic phenomenon. Associations with the Homeric tradition continue to shape visions of PTSD as a "war after war," a "battle," and ultimately a warrior project.[14] Figured as such, combat trauma becomes a "cult of hardness."[15] Favoring a warrior project helps establish veteran trauma as a hard Homeric contest of virtue, a mythic effort to repair and maintain performances of militarized masculinity in hopes of reaffirming empire and a culture of ongoing war.[16] In the process, clear demarcations are made between those who are most able to resolve trauma's effects and those who fail in the war after war.[17] Myths of overcoming mark masculine adherence to individualism, reaffirming simplistic sights of "male armor," militarized bodies worthy of valorization, and the further privatization of PTSD.[18] The "battle to regain dignity in the face of . . . trauma is arduous enough without . . . having to battle the image, internal and external, that a real warrior is self-reliant" and can prove virtuosity in the quest for overcoming illness.[19] Ultimately, with a condensed range of mythic layers, we lose sight of those who live with trauma without the armor of mastery.

One response to mythically hardened visions of PTSD is to strip away the armor, to lay bare the "merely" mythic surfaces that impede exact views of trauma. We might align with medical anthropologist Allan Young, who deems PTSD a "harmony of illusions."[20] An assemblage of "practices, technologies, and narratives with which it is diagnosed, studied, and represented," veteran trauma is an illusion, a false cover akin to bad ideology.[21] Situated as such, trauma becomes what Cathy Caruth calls a "crisis of truth," a phenomenon that shifts and moves, evading epistemological categories and vision.[22] Accordingly, trauma is made invisible as a contingently structured logic, even as such logics are naturalized. Young and Caruth reveal any illusions we might have about seeing and knowing trauma. I am sympathetic to their efforts, but I am also concerned about how ongoing critique strips away necessary illusions and layers that make combat trauma matter. Shredding mythic surfaces risks leaving veterans bare, our encounters without texture, and limits the cultural resources we might rely on to render trauma visible as a social phenomenon.

Leaving us in a crisis of truth risks reliance on expertise to see sickness hidden deep within the subject, further privatizing PTSD. However, veterans rely on myth as much as truth for negotiating everyday life.[23] Mythic forms, like medical diagnoses, paradoxically provide legibility with categories that can render life unlivable.[24] Even as Homeric shades shape PTSD as a matter of mastery hinged to military masculinity, they are attempts to constitute trauma "culturally rather than clinically," as a "collective experience that generates collective responses."[25] Mythic forms do have the potential to expand trauma "beyond the confines of the narrowly medicalized or privatized encounter," particularly if we consider encounters with trauma as moments of invention rather than discovery.[26] Myth has potential to "forge creative responses to it that far outstrip even the most utopian of therapeutic and political solutions."[27] We just need more than Homer.

This project, then, is to work with myth so as to reanimate its layers in ways that expand visions of combat trauma and loosen hardened cultural formations that inform encounters with veterans. Reanimating mythic layers helps to maintain surfaces that make trauma culturally legible while leaving open the possibility for looser forms that expand visions of it. In the context of this essay, it is more fitting to say that myth helps to (re)fashion combat trauma's surfaces and render it more than a warrior project. Suzanne Opton's *Many Wars* inspires just such a mythic (re)fashioning of veteran trauma.[28] As a photographic collection of veterans diagnosed with PTSD, *Many Wars* provides the textural surfaces for expanding trauma's rigid mythic look and feel. Filled with veterans draped in loose, breathable fabrics, Opton's work enlivens an archive of legendary forms that allow for movement and flexibility in how PTSD is made legible, making for more capacious visions of how to live with trauma. The fabric veterans use for cover gestures toward softer, more malleable mythic layers. Seen as remnants of legend, pieces of cloth become robes, cloaks, and shrouds, all of which expand combat trauma's mythic forms and amplify the potential of less polished figurations. This becomes especially apparent when approaching Opton's photographs with Michel Foucault's textural orientation.[29] With Foucault, we become attuned to seeing how "bits of cloth" and "make-shift scraps of old finery" provide for embellished appeals beyond "dreary" technical reports and expert diagnostics.[30] Favoring embellishment over austerity, Opton and Foucault urge us to see PTSD as a matter of refashioning surfaces that reorient our eyes toward thicker visions of trauma.

LEGENDARY DRAPERY AND SOFTER VISIONS OF PTSD

There are not many contextual clues in *Many Wars.* Against nondescript backdrops, veterans compose cover with swaths of drapery and arrange their bodies into gestural poses. Opton's photos lack "the action-packed 'kinetic' combat photos we have become accustomed to. Her stripped-down images omit the context we seem to need as viewers."[31] According to photojournalist Ann Jones, the lack of context animates internal inspection. Opton's photos are a "kind of Rorschach test to reveal to ourselves what we think about war."[32] The "nondescript fabric" worn by veterans in *Many Wars* magnifies how envisioning trauma is dependent on culturally informed, habitual ways of seeing. Nondescript fabrics paradoxically hide and show. Drapery prevents penetrating sight, leaving us at a loss for meaning, yet displays the ways in which PTSD is negotiated culturally. By extension, *Many Wars*'s drapery magnifies how tight our prominent modes of vision might be and impresses the need for cultivating others. Lacking hints of a war after war, narrative understanding is limited. The photos are fragments, remnants that evade linearity, closure, or clear knowledge. What we do see are tactile surfaces and a variety of cloth material that evoke engagement with how particular textures make trauma tangible in the social imaginary. What is more, Homer is absent. There are hints of archetypal presences, but muted tones and frays make warrior projects difficult and mythic forms imperfect. And though Jones considers Opton's photographs as still and revealing, the abundance of fabric situates them as dynamic and layered with movement. Jones's rhetoric of revelation reaffirms seeing PTSD as getting beneath the surface for a stark truth of trauma. Opton's drapery worries a hermeneutics of uncovering and requires "textural analysis," attention to discerning surfaces and the kinds of contact, cultural associations, attachments, and meanings that might be available.[33]

A textural approach is certainly speculative, even uncomfortable, given expectations of how trauma should look and how we should look at trauma. Yet it is precisely this fraught, fragmentary speculation that leaves open the possibility for ongoing alteration of the mythic forms that dictate the look and feel of

PTSD. The textural approach I take here is guided by Foucault, whose "Lives of Infamous Men" offers a lively visual grammar for considerations of how legendary fabrics dress up unheralded appeals for political recognition. Brief statements "dressed up in grand rhetoric" by ordinary people lead Foucault to arrange such "rudiments" into a legend of the obscure. "A 'legend' because, as in all legends, there is a certain ambiguity between the fictional and the real," an ambiguity that makes a multiplicity of lives possible.[34] For Foucault, shabby statements have more "thickness," more legitimate presence when figured as legend. Legend "covers them with so many wonders, embellishing them with so many impossibilities, it is as almost as if they had never lived."[35] The paradoxical status garners attention without requiring revelation of a definitive identity. With a Foucauldian inflection, Opton's photos become embellished remnants arranged into a legend of obscure veterans. As such, they provide a recognition that is neither quite real nor quite fictional:

> They bring tramps, poor wretches, or simply mediocre individuals onto a strange stage where they strike poses, speechify, and declaim, where they drape themselves in bits of cloth they need if they wish to draw attention in the theater of power. At times they remind one of a poor troupe . . . who deck themselves out in make-shift scraps of old finery to play before and audience . . . they are staking their whole life on the performance.[36]

We might see veterans in *Many Wars* similarly decked out in bits of old finery striking poses to declaim, and staking lives on being.

To see *Many Wars* with a Foucauldian eye is to envision Opton's photos as "singular lives, transformed into strange poems" embellished by unsung persons petitioning for visibility.[37] To such ends, I assemble a few of Opton's photographs into strange poems of singular lives, an initial, suggestive, invitation to loosen armor by spinning out less harmonic legends. There is no assumed narrative that links what follows. It is episodic, tentative, frayed, neither rigorous nor rigid. And that is the point. The arrangement is not authoritative. It might be better to see what follows as incomplete glances and makeshift, imperfect legends of drapery, fitting for expanding the archetypal fabrics of combat trauma's character. Consider, for example, the shroud worn by veteran Steven Hensel (fig. 3.1).

Right arm extending to clasp the edge of his swath of fabric, Hensel seems to be drawing the ends closer together. It may be that there is hope of becoming even more enveloped, especially when we see his left arm reaching for the other edge and take note of how far up the neck the piece of fabric reaches. Looking over his right shoulder with eyes down, there is the sense that Hensel is careful in not being noticed. There is a slight hunch in his posture, marking a desire to become smaller. Drawing the edges together, shrinking beneath fabric, Hensel

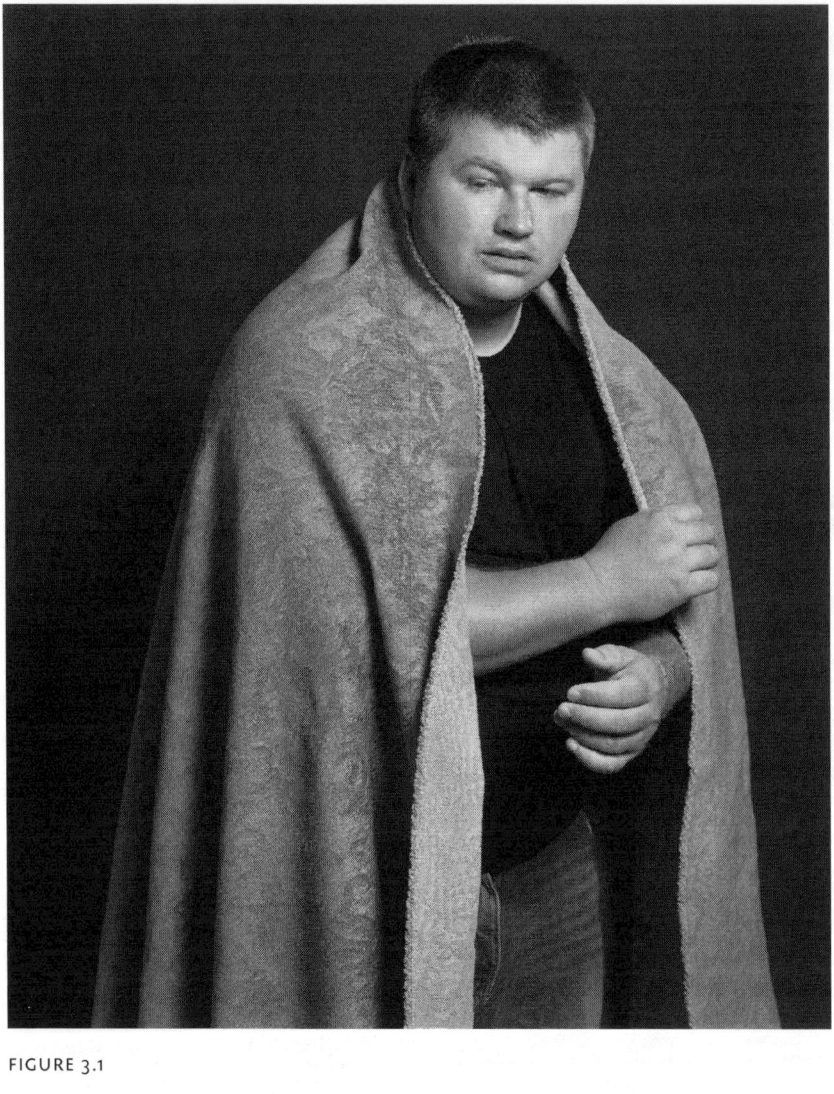

FIGURE 3.1

seeks cover from whatever might be over that shoulder. In contrast to becoming visible and revealing trauma by baring himself, Hensel marks himself as cloaked from sight, hidden away from, as he tells it, a ghost that haunts him.

We might see Hensel as posing to be seen as something other than a warrior, a confrontational stance his posture renounces. Haunted and feeling for cover, he relies on fabric turned talisman, a magical item of protection against spirits of dread. In this case, the fabric gives off a slight shimmer, an effect that accents a mystical feel. This is amplified by the embossed design that winds around the cloak, even as its composition is an unclear, cryptic shape. To say that Hensel relies on a cloak to ward off shades is not to treat the scene lightly. Nor is it a critique or statement of preference for a more rational, less superstitious rendering of trauma. Rather, it is to accept Hensel's surface attempt to render living with trauma legible in ways other than a warrior look and feel. Hensel's cloaking of trauma suggests something other than armor as cover can provide for softer kinds of eye contact with veterans. It is not welcoming by any means, as getting close does not seem to be offered with cloaks. Nor does the cloak offer material for simple identification. The cloak, magical or not, affords a "legendary" status without a perfect fit, archetypal material enabling distinct encounters with veterans like Hensel.

The look and feel of cloaks and the kind of mystical valence they take on for Hensel also suggests vulnerability. This is especially the case if we see the cloak as a talisman for protection. Once more, haunted gestures and more permeable material do not provide the confidence in victorious quests that armor might. The look backward does not evoke progression to healing, only regression with hauntings. With cloaks and glances back, we have to live with ghosts. Though Hensel's look over his shoulder might elicit unease at what is in the shadows, what has followed him home, it may provoke a more entangled consideration and confrontation with what refuses to stay in the past or to be overcome: the ghost that Hensel sees, the ghost that might provide some sense of forgiveness. Forgiveness from ghosts cannot be reached with diagnoses, a harder look, or stripping away mythic cover. It is the very mythic cover—the talismanic cloak—that provides the style for living with the unforgiving shades of traumatic experience.

ORATORICAL ROBES OF OBLIVION

> Some of the other milder symptoms are short-term memory; long-term memory, word retrieval—things like that.
>
> —John Kipp

John Kipp tells of being in a space of oblivion.[38]

The gestures and pose seem to match (fig. 3.2). Looking intently into empty space, there is the sense that Kipp is focused on recalling memories that might be revealed for confession. The raised arms and active hands gesture toward trying to catch something ephemeral that refuses to be located. Note especially the left hand that is ready to grab at the thing coming before Kipp's eyes. If he can grasp it, perhaps he can make it known to an audience, to show us trauma. Seen as a lack of memory and a seeming failure to recall, the scene evokes loss of the past, a loss of truth, and an ongoing struggle to retrieve accurate information.

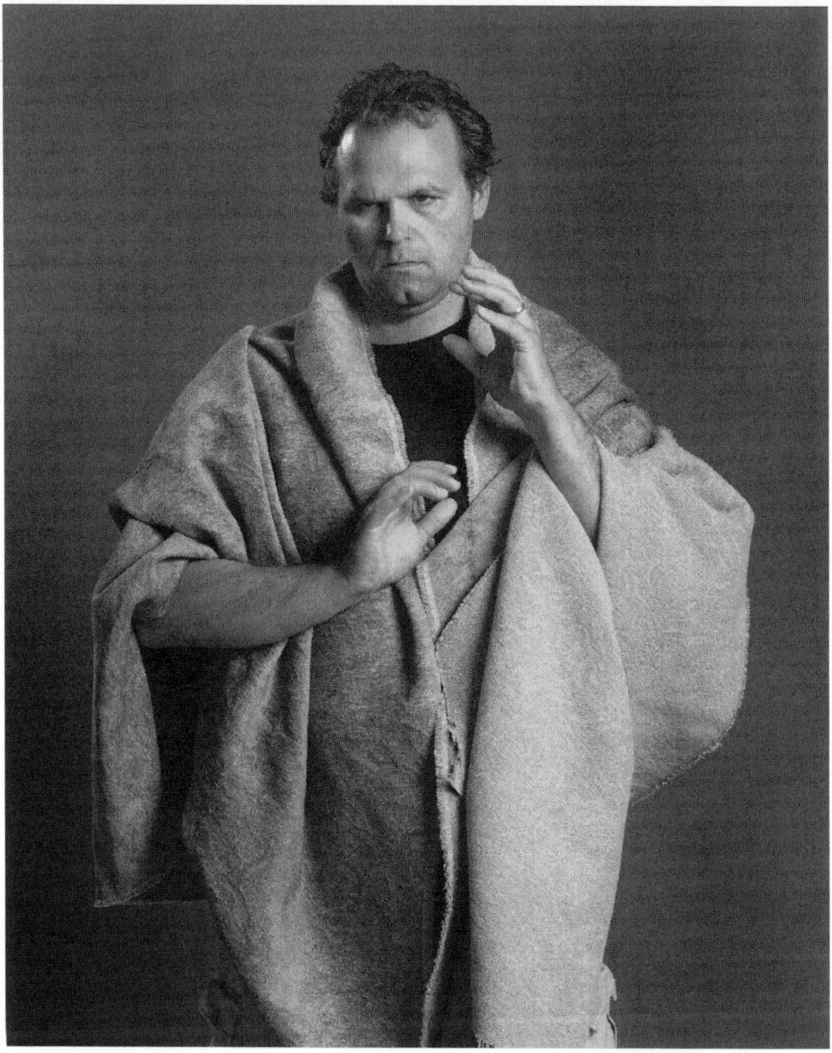

FIGURE 3.2

The assumption here is that the revelation of traumatic experience will put us on the path to healing. But with ongoing loss of memory, that vision fails us. And Kipp. It leaves us lost in oblivion. The term is derived from the French *oublier*, "to forget," and is intimately tied to *oblivion*, from the Latin *oblivisci*. According to Harald Weinrich, sinking into emptiness of a formless oblivion has been a dominant metaphor for forgetting. Forgetting "occupies primarily the desert wastes, the sandy areas in which what is to be forgotten is gone with the wind."[39] In such a landscape, armor loses it sheen. Dust settles and sand sinks under the weight of it. This landscape requires a looser and lighter drapery—more relaxed expectations of revelation—that enables other ways to envision and encounter Kipp.

If one is not versed in *ars memoriae,* the brighter arts of memory, there is a failure in the virtuous search for truth. Here, Kipp fails in *ars memoriae,* necessitating his efforts in *ars oblivionis,* the arts of forgetting. To envision Kipp as performing the arts of forgetting is to feature a softer sense of memory bound to imagination rather than truth. Memory is associating contents into images by use of the imagination. This conception of memory might be more fitting and have more potential for envisioning how it is to encounter Kipp without relying on total recall. Put another way, memory seen as an inventive art rather than an act of recall of accurate truths provides us with a way to see Kipp as not failing in confession and revelation. Rather, we might see him as amidst invention, which alludes to legendary styles less related to revelation and Stoic, heroic armor. We might see Kipp as in the process of fashioning a stature more associated with legendary robes of oratory.

The folds form as the fabric becomes twisted over Kipp's shoulders and around his raised arms. As a whole, the swath is bunched around the elbows, adding to the number of folds and thickness of the material. The bunched material also allows for the rest of the robe to drape from Kipp's arm, inviting the sense that there is a great deal of fabric collected here, an excess that is yet to be fashioned. Even with excess, the robes do not look as if they were haphazardly fitted. The folds might even be purposefully arranged, their flow artfully worn to feature a certain stature. It appears that these robes have been stylized for excess embellishment. Adding to the stylized folds is the patterned ornament. Woven into the fabric is a fluid design that speaks of flourish. Parts of the design seem to be flowery and organic, accenting movement and ornament. The stylized folds, the bunched material hanging from kinetic limbs, the touches of embellishment and flourishing all foreground another way to see Kipp—as a figure attentive to style and ornament over revelation and bare words. Wearing oratorical robes suggest a legendary cast that is more covered, perhaps even more stylistic, and a monument to flourish. Purposefully or not, Kipp's gestures and robes take us to legends of oratory in which form and style matter more than recall, pressuring us to reconsider what and how we pay attention to when we look at veterans practicing *ars oblivionis.*

The legendary cast we might reference belongs to famed Roman orator Cicero. Cicero stands as a legendary figure, as a reference point for Renaissance humanism, a model of political adeptness, a political theorist, professor of moral duty and Stoicism, defender of republics, and teacher of eloquence.[40] "Cicero's ghost" still haunts and informs the way current laws are formed and used to deny "enemy combatants" legal protection.[41] Accounts of Cicero's death have made him "into poetry" that politicians, poets, theorists, and orators draw on for defending political speech.[42] There is also Robert Hariman's argument that Cicero's "Republican Style" serves as a model for comportment and action in civic performance.[43] Ciceronian style guides aesthetic performances of civility and eloquence, as well as an appreciation for the art and performative nature of public work. Cicero is a legend that informs how one is recognized as practicing civic involvement. The robes are not insignificant in this regard. Cicero's folded robes help mark the legendary texture of civic recognition. They are a part of the legendary form of political style and civic legibility. John Kipp's adoption of folded robes and oratorical gestures might be seen as a vision of a non-heroic attempt at a political style that provides for civic legibility and recognizability guided by Cicero's legendary appearance.

Cicero is also part of Nancy Sherman's "cast of characters" for rethinking Stoicism as the predominant aesthetics of military character.[44] To loosen the Stoic armor that still informs contemporary military decorum, Sherman highlights Cicero's less rigid ideas about seemliness and comportment. As Sherman argues, Cicero recognizes that decorum is stylistic and that seemliness "does not have to demand absolute conformism."[45] If a Ciceronian style of Stoicism provides a more generous fit without battling the warrior image, it appears as if Kipp is trying on that more generous fit. It is not a perfect fit to be sure, nor should it be. The edges of the fabric are frayed and there is a slight tear where the sides of the robe come together. The jagged tear amplifies the shabbier texture of legendary covering, the infirmity of the mythic layers that allow for reshaping and refitting the drapery. The robe might be a Stoic cover that allows for living between self-mastery and vulnerability. In addition, seeing a robed Kipp stylized into a shabby Ciceronian legend allows us to extend Sherman's observations and theories of softer Stoicism. In addition to Cicero's philosophies about moral duty, we can foreground Cicero's concern for oration in claiming civic recognition.[46]

Centering Cicero's rhetorical treatises allows us to see Kipp's reach for memory as a complex inventive gesture. Seen as a Ciceronian effort to live with trauma, embellishment becomes more vital and important than clear expression of remembered content. His rhetorical robes, embellished with touches of Cicero, provide for legendary layers that adjust for oblivion. Foucault explains that those who drape themselves in bits of cloth for political and social recognition and attention "speechify" and "declaim" rhetorical acts and postures that accent practicing arts of embellishment and invention over and above a systematic process of recall and revelation. As such, Kipp's embellished folds and heightened gestures mark inventive postures and activity. The robed nature calls attention to the inherent slipperiness of memory, giving us pause before situating Kipp as opposite those of us who might assume to have privileged access to memory.

Accenting the folds of robes—both Kipp's and Cicero's—registers the inherent slippage of memory and its expression. Memory involves unfinished folding that leaves crevices and cracks, requiring embellishment, wonder, and imagination, all of which Cicero promotes. According to William Covino, Cicero's *De Oratore* is a treatise on the art of wondering, "irresolution and ambiguity."[47] Ciceronian style is an art of bewilderment, wondering, and physical delivery. This is especially important to how we might see Kipp as draped in remnants of Ciceronian legend. Seeing ornamental, oratorical robes as suggestive of wondering and bewilderment seems more fitting for an encounter with Kipp and his loss of memory. We might then see the ready hands and focused gaze as something other than trying to catch an ephemeral thing that is lost. Instead, it is possible to see such gestures as in the process of shaping memory and wisdom, with a look or wonder at what it might be and become. Memory for Cicero is not a "repository for all things," but a "faculty for invention of narrative and knowledge, not for the storing and retrieval of 'facts.'"[48] Wrapped in the folds of the robe, then, is it possible to see Kipp as engaging in a dynamic practice of invention, of making trauma matter without revelation?

The alternative, of course, is still visible. It would be understandable, given more rigid notions of memory and consistent expectations of recalling hard evidence, to see Kipp as entangled in a jumble of heavy fabric that prevents the ability to bare all and see what might be bared. However, this risks seeing failure to recall as a symptom of sickness and a sign of lack against a presumed normal capacity to remember—the ability to easily recall deposited, ordered narratives that have been hidden and protected. But amid folds of Ciceronian legend, the scene accents how we all negotiate oblivion and work to weave remnants of experience together for shaping memory. At the very least, Kipp's oratorical drapery might highlight the contingent nature of confession and revelation. As such, Kipp's fashioning of his robes with rhetorical flare might help reorient our attention towards more varied expressions, looks, and feels of PTSD. If we are attuned to the surface textures of the robe, with its ample layers and decorative look, we may become more aware of the kinds of formal expectations we have when envisioning veteran trauma and how we might expand our visions for richer encounters. There is potential for seeing PTSD as a robed activity that expands the ways trauma is and might be made manifest, felt, imagined, and delivered.

To see veteran trauma here is to envision Kipp as decked "out in make-shift scraps of old finery to play before an audience" in a visual theatre of PTSD.[49] I stress, this is not to valorize or make light of Kipp's trauma. The emphasis on oratorical robes is part of an ongoing attempt to develop a variety of responses to trauma, taking part in refashioning the mythic and legendary layers relied on to live with and envision PTSD. Envisioning Kipp as one of Foucault's shabby "poem lives" allows for the addition of layers when seeing him and his negotiation of living with and without memory.[50] Doing so expands and slackens our forms of contact for encountering Kipp as more than a hardened warrior in battle after battle. Kipp's oratorical stance invites seeing veterans as in the midst of civic life, robed not armored, adding to PTSD's mythic imaginary and the legendary influences that shape the way we expect PTSD to look.

MAGICAL CLOAKS AND HAUNTOLOGICAL CONJURING

> It's like, I should do something but what am I gonna do? I mean you can't bring somebody back from the dead.
>
> —Steven Lopinto

We began with how Steven Hensel's (fig. 3.1) cloak urges us to consider how the drapery in *Many Wars* helps (re)fashion PTSD's warrior project. The impulse here is to create more expansive and inclusive legends of combat trauma, and, with a Foucauldian orientation, take up bits of fabric to animate alternative forms of recognition. Reanimating mythic cover is a knack for seeing how remnants might reconfigure our attention. It is nothing short of spinning out the mythic fabrics we use to texture trauma. As such, it may be fitting to take another look at cloaks as part of the archetypal collection we have scrapped together.

Cloaks are garments often affixed to conceal in the shadows, worn by the likes of highwaymen, spies, bandits, mysterious riders, and sorcerers. Seeing Steven Hensel's swath of fabric as a cloak suggests that it might be a magical talisman shaped for protection from the figures that seem to be following him from war. Again, the cloak takes us into the realms of seeing PTSD as something mystical or paranormal. For those held to a modernist separation between the medical and the mystical, "cloaking" Hensel's trauma is problematic. Once more, I stress that rendering Hensel's very real suffering as cloaked is not to take it lightly or to deny his physical and psychological suffering. It is to stress that medical and modern ways of seeing trauma are inadequate to address Hensel's own admission that "shades" have followed him. To dismiss his cloaking with technical expertise, without giving due to its mystical or mythical dimensions, is to be dismissive of Hensel's efforts to live with trauma. To seriously see his cloaked comportment as protection from ghosts is to become entangled with how trauma is made to matter as a social, political, and cultural phenomenon—where the forms of living with trauma are made possible, fashioned, and (re)fashioned. Thus, to see and speak of magical cloaks in *Many Wars* is to accent the always/already mythical, and mystical, dimensions of visuality. Entangled with multiple forms of knowledge, whether we see it or not, situates us as nonmodern, or cognizant that the categories between science and myth are not so clearly marked.[51]

This entanglement is where we also see subtle differences between the scraps of legend and remnants of old finery. As noted, Hensel's cloaked comportment suggests a move to invisibility and protection against shades that continue to haunt him. The cloak is a talisman, a magical fabric shaped for warding off spirits that refuse to go away, that won't let him escape. His left hand reaches outward, perhaps readying to complete the cloaking. Or perhaps the gesture is the beginning of an abrupt turn around, an attempt to confront whatever and whoever might be drawing his indirect glance over the shoulder. Either way, the cloak is a marker of a failed warrior project. The shades of war are not so easily forgotten, nor dismissed. However, the cloak does mark an attempt to negotiate living with trauma's ghosts. Clinging to the cloak may offer some protection, even though fabric does not offer armor. Critically, cloaks do not guarantee victory over shades, leaving us to consider what happens when a warrior quest fails, when armor is untenable, when all there might be to live with ghosts are talismanic cloaks. With cloaks as cover, we as onlookers have to live with trauma's haunting presence.

This might especially be the case as we attend to Steven Lopinto's cloaked posture (fig. 3.3).

We could first note the pattern on his drapery. The repetitive squares, alternating in their pattern, create optical confusion. As solid squares blend into a pattern filled with wavy lines, the cloak seems to move or change. It is almost animated. Focusing on the cloak is difficult because its kinetics seem to blur vision. It is difficult to look at the cloak for long, perhaps because the shimmering evokes a challenge to vision. We might also say that the cloak, with its confusing and yet alluring pattern, invites visibility and attempts to see something that is not there. It is hypnotic and appealing, drawing our eyes to it yet showing little. All of this is only amplified when taking note of how the cloak falls from Lopinto's frame. It hangs loosely off of the left shoulder as his left arm seems to move outward from beneath the fabric. He doesn't seem to be trying to draw further into a cloak. In contrast to the first cloak we saw (fig. 3.1), this version is more slacked, leaving room for more outwardly animating gestures. Drawing the focus to Lopinto's gestures, there is what appears to be an outward attempt to animate, hold, and shape. Note how the hands are curved and the fingers stretched in his reach. Lopinto's hands also seem to move together, working around something that our eyes cannot reach. But it does look as though Lopinto can see it, just not directly in front him. Eyes closed, he focuses on something from beyond what is immediately visible. We might picture him as searching another realm for the images and figures, or rather, conjuring something immaterial.

The hypnotic swathe of fabric, the animating gestures, and otherworldly focus all come together to form a vision of combat trauma as a practice of conjuring. To conjure involves making something appear, seemingly from nowhere.

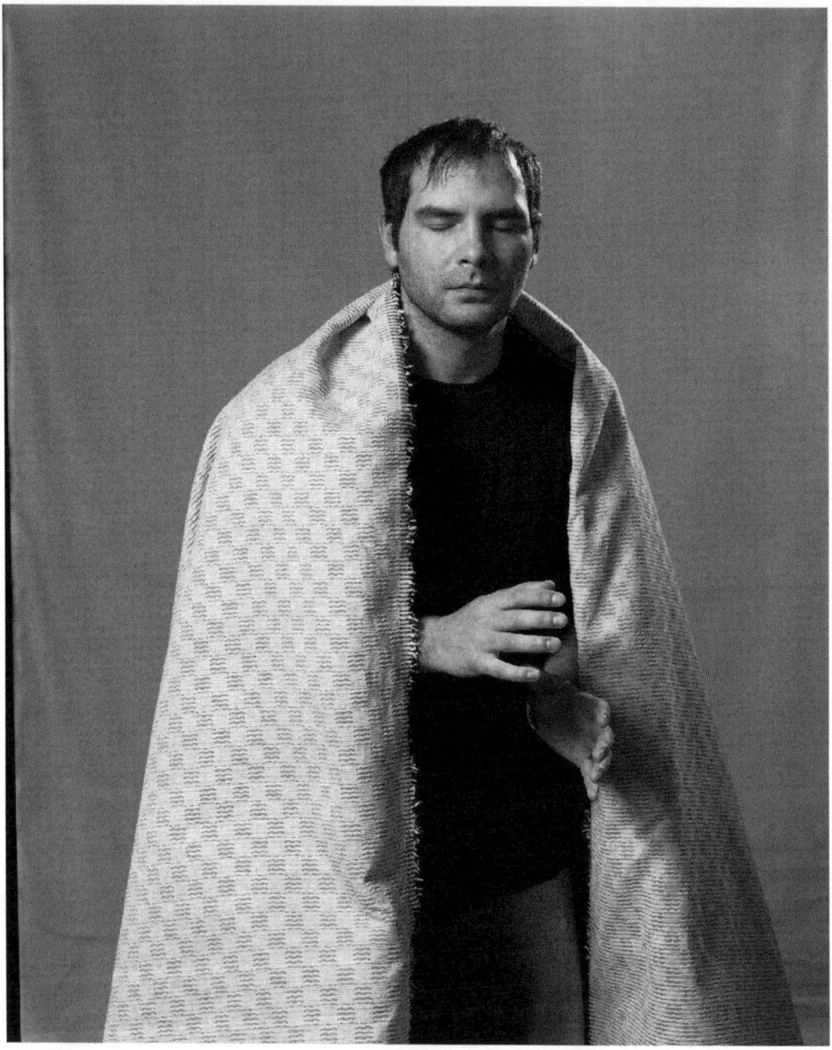

FIGURE 3.3

It also involves calling on something to appear. Seen as in the midst of a cloaked conjuring, Lopinto is attempting to bring before our eyes, to captivate and make manifest a vision. The cloak here is less a talisman for protection than it is a remnant that helps to conjure for spectators the shades that haunt Lopinto. It should be noted that Lopinto was a medic who "never had the opportunity to care for the wounded because everybody died."[52] According to him, there are times he slips into other realms while sleeping, where visions haunt. With his eyes closed, he sees his failure as a medic: "That image [of death], it's like an ongoing thing.

The scenario, the whole situation is never gone. The reason . . . it stuck with me so much is because I was a medic. . . . It's like I should do something but what am I gonna do? I mean you can't bring somebody back from the dead."[53]

It appears that Lopinto is trying to do just that. His efforts at conjuring may only be in spirit, but they might also be seen as efforts to bring before spectators' eyes the shades of combat that might otherwise go unnoticed. In a magical attempt to make manifest what and how he could not medically save, Lopinto is not simply attempting to reveal otherworldly trauma. He is, in performing this cloaked posture, enticing us to see. The visions Lopinto might be attempting to animate are not exact. His hands are still in the active process of shaping what we might be seeing. As such, Lopinto is not simply showing what is. Rather, he is participating in an invocation of something yet to be seen, something we have to imagine. At one level, his attempt to conjure coaxes us to confront the beguiling and paradoxical nature of seeing trauma, especially attempting to see trauma with instruments of precision. What his cloaked conjuring emphasizes is that even though we cannot see trauma, it is there. Whatever it is that Lopinto is animating, shaping, and trying to show can be neither evaded nor evacuated. The alluring cloak that he wears accents the magical nature of seeing, the invocative activity that vision involves. In sight, we invoke visions as much as we see what is simply there. An attempt to see trauma in a photograph is an invocation, a mythic recitation with gestures and reaches that might seem antithetical to seeing clearly.[54] Lopinto's attempt to conjure trauma before our eyes might be seen as a failure of vision, especially given the mystical qualities of the scene. Inflected by more modernist and advanced modes of sight, his invocation and invitation to "look" could be considered a regressive failure, a lack of vision. Maybe he is stuck seeing visions from the past.

Yet, Lopinto's cloaking of trauma might easily be seen as attempting to give presence to unwanted ghosts, a cloaked, gestural hauntology—an ongoing negotiation with ghosts that refuses strict categories of the living and dead.[55] Hauntology, as outlined by Jacques Derrida, is an act of attending to whispers that continue to haunt and defy categorical ways of knowing. Seen as conjuring ghosts, Lopinto's stance refuses to let restless spirits lie. Remains must be buried in order to construct life and progress. Pronouncing the dead entombs the unfamiliar and renders us safe at home. His cloaked conjuring interacts with the restlessness of what refuses to stay buried. As an invisible materialization of what might be laid to rest, Lopinto does not protect himself or us from the uncanny enterprise of encountering the undead. The invisible is in the process of becoming visible. The nature of the scene is not unlike Odysseus's hailing of shades to help him find the way home. But his cloak stresses that this is not merely the use of the dead for homecoming. The patterned cover confuses the scene, leaving the encounter uneasy. By extension, Lopinto's conjuring leaves us without enjoying good or clean conscience.

This need not be seen as tragic failure to bury the dead in the past. Following Jacques Derrida, hauntology is an ethical orientation that attempts to "conjure a plurality of histories" while forestalling any satisfaction that complete inclusion and rematerialization is possible.[56] Seeing cloaked conjuring is to see Lopinto's otherworldly focus as an ethical orientation towards uneasy and uncertain rematerialization ghosts of trauma that haunt us.

Those presences, especially if unseen, are surely less appealing to warrior project logics. Enchanting visions of trauma being cast out are unsettled, even denied. Perhaps what is most threatening in Lopinto's focused invocation is the sense that harder, more rational, technical, and verifiable logics hold little sway when it comes to provoking the unseen. The shaping gestures, closed yet seeing eyes, and an illusionary cloak all make for seeing PTSD as a magical matter of conjuring ghosts for spectators to see, which involves, in accordance with Lopinto's experience, reviving rather than leaving the dead behind. Thus, we might see Steven Lopinto's cloak marking him as more prophet than warrior, adding to our expansion of PTSD's legends.

TYING UP A FEW LOOSE ENDS

Veteran David Morris argues that envisioning combat trauma depends on seeing strangely.[57] Living with trauma is something that happens in the liminal space where visions warp. *Apophenia,* the habit of finding patterns where there are none, is what Morris promotes. Looking to clouds, shooting stars, and other mystic phenomena provide for speculative looking that makes more sense for encountering what trauma is: paradoxical, pieced together, and surreal. Without such speculative interpretive work, visions of trauma become flat and repetitive. This essay is an attempt to practice the speculative looking that Morris cites. With Suzanne Opton and Michel Foucault, I have tried to find patterns of PTSD that might otherwise be smoothed out by predominant visions of warrior projects. The essay offers an assemblage of legendary patterns from which to begin expanding the mythic dimensions of PTSD. To find ways we might see unexpected associations and relations is to gather a range of cultural resources to engage in inventive forms of spectatorship. In doing so, envisioning PTSD becomes a collaborative, collective, poetic, even mythic endeavor. The mythic formations made become cultural spaces of contestation and deliberation, where meanings of PTSD are publicly visible and made to matter. Veteran trauma, so often invisible, becomes present as part of a public culture, intimately entangled with the everyday contingent figures and forms that inform our social imaginaries. It becomes visible as a starting point for constituting relations.

The inventive inflection of seeing trauma assumes that the in/visibility of PTSD is a lively paradox full of potential. The ways in which veterans in *Many*

Wars drape PTSD emphasize that envisioning PTSD always involves hiding and showing, a frustrating oscillation that keeps us between surface and depth, where rich and dynamic engagement happens. There is also a sense of imprecision or incompleteness in Opton's photographs and my arrangement of them. There is no single mythic figure or form present. This is one of the most productive dimensions for thicker engagements and more substantial visions of how it is to live with the rougher edges of PTSD. Without specific warrior markers, gestures layered with drapery keep us in the paradox of in/visibility, emphasizing a tension with desires for tales of do or die victory or defeat. Celebrations of epic victories and valorization of warrior projects reaffirm seemingly inevitable and ongoing war. If warriors can defeat the shadows of combat, then why worry about war's after-effects? We might surmise that warrior projects offer another way to celebrate myopic versions of heroism. And with Achilles and Odysseus leading our eyes, visions of heroism are easy to discern—particularly when they are inflected with a hardened brand of male armor. The battle with PTSD ends in either victory or sacrifice, both of which provide for clean, clear ends worthy of epic visions.

(Re)fashioning the legendary status of PTSD is about maintaining rather than resolving the in/visibility of PTSD, about living in the paradox where beginnings and ends cannot be seen. This is the paradox in which veterans live—at once required to show trauma, even as it evades visibility. And if they can show it, there are parts that remain covered. Veterans are always/already between fiction and reality, the ambiguity Foucault features as the space where potential for political recognition exists. It is fitting then, that as spectators we also find ways to remain in the paradox and live with what we see, and what we do not. But it is important that the paradox remain alive and lively. Attention to the textural dimensions of PTSD's regimes of perception allows for movement that provokes a range of ways we might take part in shaping more creative, even irreverent responses to veteran trauma. And by extension, taking an active role in animating attitudes about treatment and attachments to how we redress trauma. With a textural orientation, pieces of fabric and frayed remnants—even in the most mundane images of PTSD—might signal alternative, even unlikely patterns that leave room for animating seams and layers that enliven trauma's varied look and feel.

NOTES

1. Mythic forms guide how we might see, but it also provides felt texture to everyday life. See William Doty, "Myth," in *Encyclopedia of Rhetoric and Composition: Communication from Ancient Times to the Information Age*, edited by Theresa Enos (New York: Garland, 1996), 449–452; Stephen Daniel, *Myth and Modern Philosophy* (Philadelphia: Temple University

Press, 1990). "Affect is what gives 'color,' 'tone,' or 'texture' to the lived." It "identifies the strength of investment which anchors people in particular experiences, practices, identities, meanings and pleasures, but also determines how invigorated people feel at any moment in their lives, their level of energy or passion." Lawrence Grossberg, *We Gotta Get Out of This Place: Popular Conservatism and Postmodern Culture* (New York: Routledge, 1992), 80–82.

2. Kevin Sites, "The Unforgiven," *aeon*, April 9, 2014, http://aeon.co/magazine/psychology/how-do-soldiers-live-with-their-guilt/.

3. Ibid.

4. Jonathan Shay, *Odysseus in America: Combat Trauma and the Trials of Coming Home* (New York: Scribner, 2002); Shay, *Achilles in Vietnam: Combat Trauma and the Undoing of Character* (New York: Scribner, 1994).

5. For more on the Wounded Warrior Project, see *The Wounded Warrior Project*, "Project Odyssey," https://www.woundedwarriorproject.org/programs/combat-stress-recovery-program/project-odyssey.aspx.

6. Tim Mak, "'Wounded Warrior' Charity Unleashes Hell on Other Veteran Groups," *Daily Beast*, May 4, 2105, http://www.thedailybeast.com/articles/2015/05/04/wounded-warrior-charity-unleashes-hell-on-other-veteran-groups.html.

7. Cited in Nancy Sherman, *The Untold War: Inside the Hearts, Minds, and Souls of Our Soldiers* (New York: W. W. Norton, 2010), 188.

8. David Colman, "Muscling Into the Mainstream," *New York Times*, August 7, 2008, http://www.nytimes.com/2008/08/07/fashion/07ARMOUR.html?pagewanted=all&_r=0.

9. See, for example, Charlotte Higgins, "The Odyssey: A Soldier's Road Home," *The Guardian*, November 30, 2013, http://www.theguardian.com/books/2013/nov/30/odyssey-soldier-afghanistan-military-homer; Robert E. Meagher, *Herakles Gone Mad: Rethinking Heroism in and Age of Endless War* (Northampton, MA: Olive Branch Press, 2006); Peter Meineck and David Konstan, eds., *Combat Trauma and the Ancient Greeks* (New York: Palgrave Macmillan, 2014).

10. James Der Derian, *Virtuous War: Mapping the Military-Industrial-Media-Entertainment Network* (New York: Routledge, 2009).

11. Dhruv Khullar, "The Trouble with Medicine's Metaphors," *The Atlantic*, August 7, 2014, http://www.theatlantic.com/health/archive/2014/08/the-trouble-with-medicines-metaphors/374982/.

12. Christopher Coker, *The Warrior Ethos: Military Culture and the War on Terror* (New York: Routledge, 2007).

13. Nancy Sherman, *Stoic Warriors: The Ancient Philosophy Behind the Military Mind* (New York: Oxford University Press, 2005); Sherman, "The Look and Feel of Virtue," in *Virtue, Norms, and Objectivity: Issues in Ancient and Modern Ethics*, edited by Christopher Gill (New York: Oxford University Press, 2005), 59–82.

14. Sherman, *The Untold War. Battle* seems to be a prominent term used to describe how veterans approach trauma. For example, see Craig Walker, "Photos: Welcome Home, the Story of Scott Ostrom," *Denver Post*, January 5, 2012, http://blogs.denverpost.com/captured/2012/01/05/captured-welcome-home-the-story-of-scott-ostrom/5172/#photo43; David J. Morris, "After PTSD, More Trauma," *New York Times*, January 18, 2015, http://opinionator.blogs.nytimes.com/2015/01/17/after-ptsd-more-trauma/?_r=0.

15. Susan Bordo, *The Male Body: A New Look at Men in Public and in Private* (New York: Farrar, Straus, & Giroux, 1999), 55.

16. Jerry Lembcke, *PTSD: Diagnosis and Identity in Post-empire America* (Lanham, MD: Lexington Books, 2013); Susan Jeffords, *The Remasculinization of America: Gender and the Vietnam War* (Bloomington: Indiana University Press, 1989).

17. Claire Sisco King, *Washed in Blood: Male Sacrifice, Trauma, and the Cinema* (New Brunswick, NJ: Rutgers University Press, 2011).
18. Jon Robert Adams, *Male Armor: The Soldier-Hero in Contemporary Military Culture* (Charlottesville: University of Virginia Press, 2008).
19. Sherman, *Stoic Warriors*, 192.
20. Allan Young, *The Harmony of Illusions: Inventing Post-Traumatic Disorder* (Princeton, NJ: Princeton University Press, 1995).
21. Young, *The Harmony of Illusions*, 5.
22. Cathy Caruth, "Trauma and Experience," in *Unclaimed Experience: Trauma, Narrative, and History*, edited by Cathy Caruth (Baltimore: Johns Hopkins University Press, 1996), 6.
23. Coker, *The Warrior Ethos.*
24. Judith Butler, *Gender Trouble* (New York: Routledge, 1990).
25. Anne Cvetkovich, *An Archive of Feelings: Trauma, Sexuality, and Lesbian Public Cultures* (Durham, NC: Duke University Press, 2003), 18–19.
26. Ibid., 5.
27. Ibid., 3.
28. Suzanne Opton, *Soldier/Many Wars* (Seattle: Decode, 2011).
29. Michel Foucault, "Lives of Infamous Men," in *Power*, edited by James D. Faubion (New York: New Press, 1994), 157–175.
30. Ibid., 162.
31. Ann Jones, "Soldiers, Who Are They," in *Many Wars*, Suzanne Opton (Seattle: Decode Books, 2011).
32. Ibid.
33. Jennifer M. Barker, *The Tactile Eye: Touch and the Cinematic Experience* (Berkeley: University of California Press, 2009).
34. Foucault, "Lives of Infamous Men," 170, 162.
35. Ibid., 162.
36. Ibid., 171.
37. Ibid., 162.
38. Cited in Opton, *Many Wars.*
39. Harald Weinrich, *Lethe: The Art and Critique of Forgetting*, trans. Steven Rendall (Ithaca, NY: Cornell University Press, 1997), 4.
40. Cicero has made a mark in popular culture as well. See *Rome*, DVD, directed by William J. MacDonald (Burbank, CA: Warner Home Video, 2007).
41. Ian Baucom, "Cicero's Ghost: The Atlantic, the Enemy, and the Laws of War," in *States of Emergency: The Object of American Studies*, edited by Russ Castonovo and Susan Gillman (Chapel Hill: University of North Carolina Press, 2009), 124–142.
42. Amy Richlin, "Cicero's Head," in *Constructions of the Classical Body*, edited by James Porter (Ann Arbor: University of Michigan Press, 1999), 190–211. Richlin's study speculates on how Cicero's decapitation and loss of tongue made Cicero into poetry, in which parts became animated embodiments of losing capacities to speech and voice.
43. Robert Hariman, *Political Style: The Artistry of Power* (Chicago: University of Chicago Press, 1995).
44. Sherman, *Stoic Warriors.*
45. Ibid., 53.
46. George Kennedy, *The Art of Rhetoric in the Roman World* (Princeton, NJ: Princeton University Press, 1972). It is also worth noting, I think, that Kipp is a teacher, a relevant observation given how Cicero is positioned as a teacher of citizens who rhetorically participate in affairs of the republic.

47. William A. Covino, *The Art of Wondering: A Revisionist Return to the History of Rhetoric* (Portsmouth, NH: Boynton/Cook Publishers, 1988), 34.
48. Ibid., 40.
49. Foucault, "Lives of Infamous Men," 181.
50. Ibid.
51. Bruno Latour, *We Have Never Been Modern,* trans. Catherine Porter (Cambridge, MA: Harvard University Press, 1993).
52. Opton, *Soldier/Many Wars,* 41.
53. Ibid.
54. Photography is a "form of hallucination." Roland Barthes, *Camera Lucida: Reflections on Photography,* trans. Richard Howard (New York: Hill and Wang, 1980), 115.
55. Jacques Derrida, *Specters of Marx,* trans. Peggy Kamuf (New York: Routledge, 2006).
56. Michelle Ballif, "Historiography as Hauntology: Paranormal Investigations into the History of Rhetoric," in *Theorizing Histories of Rhetoric,* edited by Michelle Ballif (Carbondale: University of Southern Illinois Press, 2013), 150.
57. David J. Morris, *The Evil Hours: A Biography of Post-Traumatic Stress Disorder* (New York: Houghton Mifflin Harcourt, 2015).

4 · UNREMARKABLE SUFFERING

Banality, Spectatorship, and War's In/visibilities

REBECCA A. ADELMAN AND WENDY KOZOL

Critics of the U.S. War on Terror have long called for an alternative optic to the relentlessly myopic perspective of American news media. The presumption behind this call to look elsewhere is that doing so will reveal images that are authentic or compelling enough to disabuse American spectators of their ambivalence about the casualties of militarized violence. This logic imagines the grisly "truth" of war to happen somewhere beyond or outside the frame of mainstream representations of combat. What happens, however, when conflict photographers who seek visually graphic and affectively searing images of war find evidence of its banality instead? In this essay, we focus not on how suffering becomes banal in and through representation, but on the spectatorial possibilities opened up by visual objects that endeavor to capture the nonspectacular conditions that war engenders.

FINDING BANALITY ON A DAY NOBODY DIED

In 2008, photographers Adam Broomberg and Oliver Chanarin arranged to be embedded with the British Army in Afghanistan for their video and photography project, "The Day Nobody Died." Rather than documenting staged public relations events, military actions, or civilian conditions, they instead tracked a large box of light-sensitive photographic paper as it traveled from London to Helmand Province in Afghanistan and back. Broomberg and Chanarin opened the box to expose segments of the paper at significant moments when photojournalists might otherwise have taken pictures. This process generated images that precisely mark a particular space, time, and happening, but do not create a visual index of the event. "The Day Nobody Died" disrupts our expectations about what conflict photography will show us, and in so doing, it highlights the limitations of photojournalism. As the artists explain, "The main protagonist of this performance, The Box, became a sort of proxy, a mute witness, at times it even seemed to represent a coffin on its repatriation journey."[1] Despite the enticing title and its promise of witnessing, the project's refusal of indexicality directly confronts a major conceit of conflict photojournalism (that war can be visually documented) and spectators' expectations for it (that seeing images of war leads to knowing it). "The Day Nobody Died" undertakes this disruptive work in two forms: one, an exhibition of large-scale, single-frame, abstract photographs created through the chemical process of exposing film to sunlight; the second, a twenty-three-minute videographic depiction of the box's journey to, around, and from this war zone, in which tedium and repetition visualize the banal processes endemic to military operations.

At odds with conventional efforts to make visible the violent impacts of war, Broomberg and Chanarin's work provides a visual record of commonplace and seemingly unremarkable affective elements of soldiering that is both exceedingly accurate and minimally precise. As the title of the project suggests, "The Day Nobody Died" engages the viewer without ever capturing the graphic suffering presumed necessary for meaningful spectatorial engagement with war. Broomberg and Chanarin's project thus calls attention to the ways in which banality infuses and, in many cases, defines contemporary conflict and its attendant violence(s). Of all the things to be concerned about when considering the constitutive elements of the Global War on Terror, banality seems underwhelming, unimportant, and incapable of exposing the strategies of in/visibility that have dominated the visual culture of this war. Yet, we argue, the banality that pervades scenes of war in "The Day Nobody Died" conveys something of how ordinariness couples with (rather than contrasts to) extreme vulnerability in the everyday struggles that proliferate in conflict zones. We use the term *banality* to reference the tedious and quotidian aspects of war, phenomena that generate images containing no overt evidence of blood, combat, or suffering, in which violence permeates the landscape but remains largely invisible. The banal, in other words, is fundamental to militarized experiences, but its affective significance is often underestimated.

Unlike spectacles of violence, elliptical and destabilizing elements in these images create only ambiguity and uncertainty. Indeed, the most visually interesting pieces of "The Day Nobody Died," the lavishly colored photographs, pointedly refuse spectacular tropes of conflict photography, inviting the gaze with lurid captions that the images vividly fail to illustrate. Visual culture studies scholars have long been concerned that the endless proliferation of images of suffering risks making such harm so familiar as to appear boring or ineffectual. Confronting the seeming inability of images to effect social change, scholars employ concepts like compassion fatigue and denial to critique the routinization of war photography that apparently results in viewer disengagement.[2] Although spectacularized depictions of combat seem to run the risk of desensitizing viewers, critics might worry that decidedly unremarkable images would leave them unmoved or underwhelmed.[3] Our inquiry, however, begins from precisely this site of ostensible failure in order to explore the ways in which images of unremarkable suffering pose an alternative visuality to historic conventions of war representation.

Focusing on discordant affects resulting from the quotidian redirects theoretical attention beyond the endlessly iterable questions that images of violence, conflict, and suffering might tempt us to pose.[4] Robert Hariman and John Louis Lucaites identify an emergent aesthetic vocabulary in conflict photography intent on mapping the everyday routines that accommodate or normalize social violence in twenty-first-century conflict zones. They argue:

> Banality carries the dual recognition that ordinary people adjust to violence and deprivation and of necessity can become accustomed to anything, and that this capacity for survival can be used against them. By documenting small gestures instead of dramatic events, photographs that draw upon banality as an aesthetic resource reveal what otherwise risks going unseen: how violence is being normalized.[5]

Hariman and Lucaites's description of banality as an aesthetic resource poses a methodological challenge for prevailing visual practices intent on "uncovering" the spectacular harms of war.

Taking up that challenge, in this essay, we propose an asymptotic analytical method to investigate how banal images produce a different aesthetic resource for engaging the visual culture of the Global War on Terror. We adopt the notion of the asymptote from analytical geometry, where it describes a line that a curve approaches, but will never cross, as it moves toward infinity. The asymptote functions here to model the relationship between the truths of war and images that purport to document them. The figure of the asymptote serves as a reminder that images can get really close to the essence of war or violence, maybe even increasingly close, but never actually meet or cross it. In short, the asymptote dramatizes the intellectual and affective unknowability that structures these unsettling representations of war.

Banality in war representation, as we theorize it, is not a politically or ideologically 'pure' alternative either to gruesome images of death, injury and suffering or to the sanitized depictions of war deployed by the state to serve its jingoistic purposes. Instead, images of banality can direct spectatorial gazes to the quotidian forces that drive militarized geopolitics. We are not suggesting that the richly colored abstract photographs or the monotonous video that comprise the two parts of "The Day Nobody Died" are somehow better or more truthful than other representations of war. Rather, we aim to disrupt those critical and intellectual hierarchies by courting visual representations that deliberately fail to make war visible in familiar terms.

Conflict photography, photojournalism, and documentary film have trained generations of viewers to expect graphic renditions of military violence, and images seemingly designed to shock viewers into recognition of the other's suffering. "The Day Nobody Died" intentionally challenges these spectatorial expectations by drawing attention to the affective and political investments that often adhere to the act of looking at war "over there." Like many other critics, we are concerned with how a Western gaze envisions violence in ways that put the anguished other on display.[6] Recent theorizations of affect provide a framework for thinking through this phenomenon, which affixes to the underside of the narratives valorizing the West. For example, Lauren Berlant argues that contemporary experiences of labor and citizenship in the United States and other Western nations require enactment of a "cruel optimism."[7] Optimism, as a way of clinging to a fantasy of the "good life," functions cruelly because the good life can only be achieved by pursuing goals antithetical to flourishing in the present. Alternatively, the Western gaze at conflict zones hinges on something like its inverse, what we call benevolent pessimism, in which the superiority of the West is secured by a vision that anticipates suffering, chaos, instability, and violence everywhere else.[8] We endeavor to write against the spectatorial desire for displays of suffering that promise the affective frisson of enacting grief over a distant other.

Spectatorial emotions typically align with ideological and affective systems predicated on and perpetuated by the suffering of others. Sara Ahmed describes the processes by which happiness becomes coercive, a norm that must be upheld despite the material or political circumstances in which the subject finds herself, a burden that often falls upon the marginalized: women, colonized subjects, immigrants, queers. The gaze that seeks the misery of others, which looks expectantly for their suffering, is a corollary to the coerciveness of happiness.[9] Ostensibly, concerned spectators look to images of abject suffering in the hopes of uncovering some knowledge or emotion that might result in an amelioration of the other person's precarious circumstances. However, this pessimistic gaze, with its long and problematic history, too often remains complicit with the systems that generate that suffering in the first place. Banal images, alternatively, have the potential to deflect that gaze and defuse its performative capacity to conjure a vision of suffering that gratifies the spectator. Therefore, we ask: what new ethical and political possibilities emerge when the spectator gazes at scenes that reference, but do not visibly represent, suffering (or much of anything at all)? Using the analytic of the asymptote, we explore what occurs in the variable space between the asymptote and the line in "The Day Nobody Died," a space in which ostensibly "nothing happens."

FINDING BANALITY ELSEWHERE

The box first appears in "The Day Nobody Died" video propped inert on its end on a sunlit wood floor. For almost a minute, nothing happens until a pair of disembodied hands picks it up and loads it into a hatchback. Lying amid other cargo, the box sits in the corner of the frame, which otherwise displays a passing London streetscape: other cars, double-decker buses, buildings, bicyclists, pedestrians, trees, traffic lights. The box jiggles slightly with the motion of the car, and the only sounds are muffled road noise and the quiet creaking of the car's interior. This is wartime in London, where the video begin and ends. Bookending the film in the heart of the imperium refuses the growing invisibility of the war in Afghanistan for many Western viewers, while also subverting the function served by embedded reporting as the primary channel by which citizens of the United States and Britain receive news of the war.[10] The apparent disinterest with which everyone handles the box evinces the widespread lack of interest in seeing this war, even among the people who fight it. The circular nature of the film further underscores the lack of temporal limits in the Global War on Terror, in which the passage of time does not guarantee any kind of progress.[11]

"The Day Nobody Died" stages a visual encounter in which discordant affects may arise in response to images of banality intent on unsettling the viewer not by shocking her with carnage, but by perplexing her with the absence of gore. Affective unsettlement here is different from both spectacular and sentimental modes of representing suffering. Of course, we do not presume to know how other spectators respond to "The Day Nobody Died"; the affective unsettledness of the work, with its lack of familiar markers about what to think or feel, opens up a multiplicity of viewing positions and forms of spectatorship. As a project, "The Day Nobody Died" is essentially itinerant, resulting in artifacts that refuse fixed affective or epistemological positions. Because the video depicts the box being moved but never opened, even spectators who watch the full twenty-three minutes are left no more informed than at the outset. Viewers can only imagine what the box looks like inside, and what might have transpired off-camera when it was opened, which leaves them with nothing more than speculation about what kinds of affects might have arisen if they could have seen more.

We situate the politics of discomfiting affects in dialogue with recent critiques of the role of spectacle in international human rights discourse. Wendy Hesford, for instance, examines the ways in which a visual economy of victimization privileges Western viewers as world citizens of a "global morality market." "Spectacular rhetorics" of suffering, she argues, consolidate identities and "configure material relations of power and difference to produce and ultimately govern human rights subjects."[12] While documentary representations of warfare tend to create spectacular rhetorics by isolating violence to locally specific temporal and geospatial registers, unsettlement in "The Day Nobody Died" functions as a critical mode of accounting for the boundlessness of violence across spaces and times.[13] A very different spatial and temporal sensibility evoked by the trope of "boots on the ground" conjures embodied experiences of conflict and risk, what Kevin McSorley describes in his study of soldiers' helmetcam videos of firefights as "often radically indistinct and chaotic, a ragged fusion of rapid panning, shuddering reverberations, and clamorous noise."[14] Images of banality can provide a similarly proximate, albeit differently angled, view of the confusions of war. Banal images can disrupt spectatorial expectations about linear progress that scaffold conventional stories of conflict with definitive beginning and ending points. Instead, as the asymptotic model demonstrates, the visual and material conditions of war proceed through time along axes that never quite meet. In Broomberg and Chanarin's video, for instance, the box traverses geopolitical spaces without providing any temporal guidance for the viewer. Beyond the "June 2008" intertitle at the beginning of the video (and only brief references in the documents surrounding the project), "The Day Nobody Died" could be almost any day at all.[15]

Unknowability in this video challenges spectatorial expectations embedded in war reportage that hail viewers to witness the suffering of others. Broomberg and Chanarin describe the box itself as "utterly banal yet somehow mysterious."[16] The inscrutability of this central character compounds the affective dissonances produced by the video's refusal to provide locational or temporal information. Impenetrability at the heart of the project (the box remains securely closed throughout the video) combines with aesthetic and narrative strategies to unsettle conventional representations of space and time. Most notably, given the box's journey across the historical terrain of British and U.S. imperialism, temporal disorientation and spatial unknowability aim to disrupt hegemonic narratives of neocolonial militarism.

The one thing spectators can know with any certainty is that the box is continually elsewhere. Even in those moments when landscapes become visible, place is only identifiable in generic terms: London streets, an Afghan airport, a British military installation. The box is usually in motion, so that place is often only a transitory space in-between locations. And so viewers see the box inching around a baggage carousel, flying in a helicopter, driving through a military base. Though there appears to be intention to this journey, no clear logic defines this peripatetic travel as soldiers move the box and load it on to vehicles whose drivers deliver it . . . somewhere. In one scene, a soldier carries the box on his shoulder while walking down a dirt road in a desert terrain with no locational markers. He then stops and puts the box on the ground. Next, a female soldier appears in front of the camera, stops walking, and they both look around. After a few moments, the male soldier picks up the box and they move on. Broomberg and Chanarin refuse to satisfy expectations that a video about war will provide a narrative anchored by cues about time and place even as temporality, spatiality, and mobility figure prominently in "The Day Nobody Died.".

In addition to temporal and spatial fragmentations, aural features in the video are equally cryptic. The exclusive use of ambient noise and a hand-held microphone result in muffled sounds with few distinguishable words. Moreover, the video relies almost entirely on natural or atmospheric light, creating a visual unevenness and occasional inscrutability. Interior shots, especially in vehicles, are often shadowy. At other times, the film literally contradicts the promise of enlightenment as blinding infusions of natural light obscure the very thing it was supposed to illuminate, such as when someone opens the door of a building or vehicle onto the bright desert sun. Spectators acculturated to the conventions of commercial narrative film have been trained to expect film to orient them within the diegetic world created by the story; these expectations are especially pronounced for documentaries. Yet, visual, aural, and narrative strategies in this video fail to provide such information, instead producing disorienting affects that reverberate back onto the viewer's expectations of what a documentary should do.

Unsettledness here, though, does not produce anxiety as it might in horror movies, thrillers, or even in traditional wartime documentary, where unknowability signifies imminent threat. In "The Day Nobody Died," there are no strong affects, no clear directions, and nothing obvious happens beyond the process of traveling to and fro. With no story to tell, the procedures of moving and carrying the box become the purpose and telos of action; the video camera merely tracks the box of light-sensitive paper as it travels through airports and luggage conveyors; onto transports including Chinook helicopters, tanks, and Jeeps; hangs around with soldiers; and then travels back to London. The video captures movement for the sake of being on the move or for reasons unknown to those who are compelled to move. This visualizes the ordinary, routine, and often repetitive conditions that British soldiers face, except, of course, in moments of hostile interactions and combat.[17] Comporting themselves in a casual way that evokes none of the intense affects that mark iconic images of conflict, soldiers stand around, move gear, take pictures of each other, ride in trucks, and doze on a helicopter. Movement that has little apparent energy or desire affectively registers the quotidian banality of military duty.

Perhaps because they fail to visualize scenes with more familiar affective intensities, banal images typically do not garner much critical attention. A prominent approach in visual studies aims to identify good examples as a constructive effort to showcase images that somehow avoid the visual problem under critique. Scholars often turn to art or independent journalism for representations of conflict that promise to provide a better, fuller, somehow more human truth.[18] In many ways, this strategy is a laudable alternative to a hermeneutics of suspicion that laments what is wrong but gives no indication of how anything might ever be different.[19] But it can also be an overly optimistic strategy, one that can too quickly assume that there is a better (more progressive) outside to dominant visualities, appealing to spectators who are only too eager to flee to this optical elsewhere. In her study of "ugly feelings" like envy and irritation, Sianne Ngai considers the political potential in emotions that are "explicitly *a*moral and *non*cathartic, offering no satisfactions of virtue, however oblique, nor any therapeutic or purifying release."[20] Images of banality leave spectators similarly and productively mired in uncertainty; as the asymptote demonstrates, going elsewhere is difficult because banal images do not always provide a clear place from which to depart, nor a clear path forward to some kind of better, purer, or truer image.

Banality operates in a different register from those good images, neither providing grand visions of a better society nor the tools to radically undermine the status quo. It is more of a shrug or, at best, a noncommittal nod of the head. In this regard, the politics of unsettledness in "The Day Nobody Died" emerge through the indecipherability at the heart of this video. Writing about "bad" feelings in contrast to the promise of happiness, Ahmed comments, "We might need to attend to bad feelings not in order to overcome them but *to learn by how we are affected by what comes near,* which means achieving a different relationship to all our wanted and unwanted feelings as an ethical resource."[21] In other words, the potential to envision war beyond a framing of negativity or suspicion may require just sitting with, or dwelling in bad feelings, or non-feelings, especially those discomfiting *meta*-feelings that come from acknowledging one's lack of bad feelings.[22] Yet, banality, unlike negativity (whether of an affective or critical sort), is not judgmental, for there are neither good nor bad actors to identify with or against. To reiterate, we are not talking about how suffering becomes banal through repetitious representation but about how representations of banality might convey lived experiences of non-spectacular suffering. The visual aesthetics of banality in the video—slow pacing, repetitive actions, and awkward framings that offer no narrative insights into the war in Afghanistan—generate dissonant affects that produce a space of looking within which to abide. That dwelling place, the permanently encrypted heart of this video, positions the viewer within the frame of the more insidious aspects of militarization in which things happen for reasons unknown to those most affected.

AN ASYMPTOTIC APPROACH TO THE SCENE OF VIOLENCE

War images can get exceedingly, even ever-increasingly, close to the truth of violence, but never actually arrive at, cross, or capture it. Mimetic oscillations between violences that can never be fully known and representational efforts to record, document, and remember asymptotically produce a perpetual approach and an arrival endlessly deferred. The curve moves toward infinity, and so does the line, but even with a radically unlimited horizon, they will never intersect. In the asymptotic model of violence and visibility that we propose, the violence itself takes the shape of the curve (with its connotations of change, diversion, and perturbation), while the visual artifact of violence, the image, is the unchanging, unwavering line as it moves through time and space. Banal images, even as they apparently "fail" to capture the visceral truth of combat, have a unique potential to force spectatorial reckoning with this asymptotic truth of representation. Spectators occupy the space between the curve and the line, and might find themselves closer to one or the other at various moments. One crucially important feature of the asymptote as a theoretical model is that it does not presume a fixed position or singular kind of spectator; banal images, with their ties to the in-between space where nothing apparently happens, remind spectators of their distance from both the line and the curve; that terrain produces a multiplicity of perspectives but none of them provide a fully revelatory view of militarized violence.

Images that operate asymptotically frustrate expectations that visual documents of violence have a unique political potential to illuminate spectatorial desires and investments. In her analysis of the political importance of less dramatic affects, Susan McManus proposes an "ambivalence-project": "simply eliciting and attending to the multiplicity of possibilities that take shape in affective series, in sites of proximity and in-betweenness, torsion and inflection of object/subject, affect/agency, affect/emotion."[23] Banality is precisely one of those sites of proximity and in-betweenness that result in torsions among ideologies of war, unsettled affects, and the limits of visibility. Banality exemplifies the potential of the space between the line and the curve, between the image and the truth of violence, to engage with that which is visible but cannot be represented, despite this impossibility.

Broomberg and Chanarin's embrace of visual and narrative inadequacy as a productive political and creative expression of unrepresentability enacts a fundamental principle of the asymptote—the failure of the line and the curve to meet. Consequently, this unceasing divergence may not be precisely a failure as opposed to a success (after all, we are not suggesting that there could be some perfectly complete or faithful visual representation of war), but rather the fulfillment of an ingenuous promise to fail. Scholars have recently begun to conceptualize failure as a potent strategy of resistance, intent on disrupting the normative, progressive drives of the neoliberal political economy. In *The Queer Art of Failure,* Judith Halberstam argues that failure can be understood not as an inability to be successful, but as a refusal to participate in the political economy, a way of lodging oneself in the present rather than a fanciful orientation toward a utopian future. Failure, in other words, can be an expressive participation in the world and in relation to others that refuses inscription into the position of the disciplined liberal consuming subject. "Under certain circumstances," Halberstam writes, "failing, losing, forgetting, unmaking, undoing, unbecoming, not knowing may in fact offer more creative, more cooperative, more surprising ways of being in the world."[24] In contrast to Halberstam's emphasis on the kinds of failure embodied in "the embrace of the absurd, the silly, and the hopelessly goofy," we want to consider the deathly serious but deeply productive failure of banal images of warfare.[25]

Scholars and artists have long grappled with the ethical implications of visual media's limited ability to motivate political actors to intervene in conflict or disrupt brutality.[26] Avoiding the entrenched debate between efficacy and voyeurism, Sharon Sliwinski persuasively argues that failure, rather than a mark of shame, can be both politically and ethically meaningful. As she notes, the magnitude of atrocities and catastrophes cannot be represented or imagined in their totality. Sliwinski writes, "Aesthetic encounters with these successive breakdowns of society oblige us to enter the political and historical scene with no false innocence, bearing no redemptive offering for human subjects who have suffered, but instead to recognize the difficult relation we have to the shared landscape in which we must participate, negotiate, and ultimately reside."[27] For Sliwinski, an ethic of failure acknowledges the "difficult" relations that spectators have with experiences of suffering accessible only through representation while rejecting idealist assumptions about imagery's capacity for redemption.

What kinds of affective and ideological "failures" can facilitate such a potentially transformative encounter? Visual artifacts like "The Day Nobody Died," which deliberately and meticulously stage failure, provide an opportunity to take up the challenge posed by Sliwinski, Susie Linfield, and other critics questioning the ethics of representing contemporary violence and suffering. The asymptotic territory of failure can, we suggest, become a space that generates questions about the process of spectatorship itself, including the intricacies and complicities of viewers' own gazes. Consequently, we want to distinguish the affective or visual blandness of banal images from failure conceptualized as something unproductive, irremediable, or paralyzing. Nominally, "The Day Nobody Died" is a condemnation of global media's failure (perhaps even its essential incapacity) to see the quotidian, living, breathing structural movements of imperial militarism at work. Beyond that, we argue, affective dissonances that swirl around the banality in this project have the potential to provoke viewers to confront unanticipated and even unwelcome affective responses to its failures. By displacing attention from scenes of conflict onto the mechanisms that produce and circulate these scenes, "The Day Nobody Died" exposes the limits of those mechanisms as both beautiful and absolute. The photographs created when someone opens the box are tethered to the conventional contexts of war reportage, but make visible nothing of its typical content, flooding the space between them with color.

Rather than documenting a failure to achieve an intended objective, Broomberg and Chanarin catalogue disappointment as an affective residue of failure. For example, a cryptic twenty-eight-second scene appears twenty-one minutes into the video, after a troop movement that is never explained or contextualized. In this scene, a group of soldiers sits on gymnasium-style bleachers in the bright white interior of a makeshift building, watching a television show and ignoring a ringing phone. The men are a study in ambivalence and disinterest. Some talk and laugh quietly, not acknowledging the screen at all. Others fidget. Among those who stare straight ahead, one appears to lean forward in his seat, as if compelled by the television program, but even his attention seems habitual and dull rather than actively engaged. This short sequence dramatizes a disconnected form of spectatorship, shows what it looks like when an image appears but does not matter. Even less consequential, apparently, than the television is the box of photo paper that sits on the floor with a few other pieces of luggage. The box's record of war, it seems, is even more insignificant than the generic programming flashing uselessly on the screen. If this is war, it is war at its most inactive, unemotional, and uninspiring—a disappointment if one is expecting to see intensely fearful or aggressive affects conventionally associated with military action.

Although failure has an obvious opposite in success, disappointment does not have a direct or precise antonym; what Broomberg and Chanarin capture, therefore, is a visual field in which there is no obviously better visual alternative. In his analysis of snapshot photographs of and by Nazi officers, Paul Lowe discusses pictures that do not show acts of violence but are only linked circumstantially to the Holocaust.[28] These snapshots do not gratify the spectators' desire for graphic depictions of violence or provide an intense affective encounter. Instead, Lowe argues that banality finds its political usefulness elsewhere, prompting imagination while also deflecting the gaze and (potentially) provoking a confrontation with the underpinnings of the desire to look in the first place.

In "The Day Nobody Died," banal scenes like that of the soldiers watching television illuminate a common wartime spectatorial position between the line and the curve, a location in the gap between physical spaces of the Global War on Terror and their visual traces in the military armament, transportation vehicles, buildings, and soldiers that inexplicability move in and out of view. Critics define affects as intensities registering physiological reactions or shifts that occur as people interact with other beings, objects, and environmental factors.[29] The dislocation caused by banal images can be slight, perhaps just a waver or a wobble, but potentially enough to reorient spectators to each, ultimately incommensurate side, at once. If one were to graph the dislocations caused by viewers' reactions to banality in "The Day Nobody Died," this might take the shape of the curve that does not cross the line, the asymptote, the unbridgeable distance between encountering violence at a mediated remove and inhabiting it in all its intensity. Tracing this asymptotic curve, we propose, can be a way around the intractable debates about whether or not violence can ever be truly represented.

This question about the unrepresentability of violence—a foundational debate in trauma studies, with roots in questions about whether the Holocaust can ever be represented—may be misguided. Jacques Rancière argues that the question of whether a thing or event is (un)representable ought not be framed as a yes or no inquiry. Instead, he refocuses attention to the epistemic circumstances that create representability by asking "Under what conditions might it be said that certain things cannot be represented? Under what conditions can an unrepresentable phenomenon . . . be given a specific conceptual shape?"[30] Following Rancière's critical admonition, to move along this curve is to move beyond a polarity of representable/unrepresentable. The resultant shift reveals not merely the need for documentation of suffering but also, and crucially, the inability of suffering ever to be documented fully. At the same time, the asymptote demonstrates that there is value in getting visually close to that experience, even if it can never be fully visualized.

The figure of the asymptote suggests a need to redefine "success" and "failure" in representation, to reconsider strategies for making war visible. Banal images of conflict zones complicate categories of representable and unrepresentable experiences and trouble the seemingly stable opposition between them. Linfield argues that the more "searing" an image is, the "more misleading it can be," and the asymptote reminds us that visual intensity is no guarantee of accuracy, that there is no necessary connection between them.[31] Rethinking the characteristics of a "successful" representation entails disaggregating unrepresentability and invisibility. Unrepresentability is not inherently a mark of failure; an image that fails to represent the graphic truth of a conflict, ostensibly leaving it invisible, may be succeeding somewhere else, or highlighting instead the impossibility of capturing such a thing.

One of the most curious aspects of the video for "The Day Nobody Died" is its focus on the box containing the light-sensitive paper, which commands the camera's continual attention. The camera does not seem to care much about the soldiers or civilians in the scene, filming them only incidentally. Whatever action or narrative exists in the video is always in relation to the continually visible box. Sometimes, the box is "one of the guys." For instance, in one of the scenes in the helicopter, the box leans against the wall between two bored soldiers. Alternatively, the box functions as an inert subject, appearing several times over the course of the video as part of the luggage, the quotidian but necessary accoutrements of the people fighting a long war and the journalists trailing them as they do.[32] Occasionally one of the soldiers will lean against or steady the box when they are in transit. But mostly the box just takes up space.

There is something absurd about this box traveling through a conflict zone, often being carried by soldiers in combat gear unwittingly caught up in this performance. Absurdity, Broomberg and Chanarin argue, here takes on a subversive quality, for "this is a war zone after all, soldiers are engaging in life and death battles, which we were disrupting by having them carry a cardboard box from place to place, with no intention of documenting anything but the performance itself."[33] The cardboard subject can move only where people put it, traversing the circular routes of an empire that melds an earlier British colonization with the current U.S. imperial adventure on a path whose logic is unknowable to the viewers. Importantly, the box is not an empty signifier or merely a conveyance for the rudimentary film that it houses. Instead, it directly references the disjunctures between the in/visibility of quotidian machineries of war and the history of conflict photography. Declining to spectacularize militarized violence by reshaping it into a clear visual sign, with all the attendant affective intensities, the box is a different kind of subject, a subject situated in "sites of proximity and in-betweenness" in which oscillations among objects, subjects, and visuality produce often destabilizing affective responses.[34]

The box contains the paper that will make the visual record, but that consequently also will index the impossibility of a comprehensively or faithfully "truthful" one. In many ways, the box embodies the impasse captured in images of militarized banality. Berlant uses the concept of the "impasse" to designate a time of dithering, stasis, a wheel spinning that prevents forward movement; it "is a stretch of time in which one moves around with a sense that the world is at once intensely present and enigmatic."[35] And so it is with the box. Just as the asymptote and line can only ever approach but never reach one another, the box as subject in the video can only ever approximate experiential truths about conflict zones that documentary genres, especially embedded journalism, promise to capture.[36] Nevertheless, this approximation documents an essential visual characteristic of conflict; it does not simply (or even) fail to show violence clearly. Instead, in a very technical but not insignificant sense, it represents violence at least as faithfully as the sharpest, most graphic photographs. For the box dramatizes the dilemma of witnessing, in which witnesses record the best available imprint of the scene. This imprint, though, is necessarily inadequate to the event; witnesses can never do more than provide an approximate memory, and hence an approximate validation of the suffering of others.

The large, single-frame photographic records that make up the exhibition of the same name, "The Day Nobody Died," vividly address the dilemma of witnessing, for they log the observational work that the box did. Among these pictures, "The Day of One Hundred Dead, June 8" would perhaps be the climax of "The Day Nobody Died" as a whole, if such a thing could be said to exist. This image marks the day, in the middle of the photographers' week in Afghanistan, when three British soldiers died, increasing the number of British casualties to one hundred. The work of record keeping or documentation that the box does is not "mechanical reproduction," but is instead a low-tech, mostly manual process in which the content of the images it generates are dictated almost entirely by external variables such as light and temperature, rather than the human actions of the operator.

Like all the still photographs created for the project, "The Day of One Hundred Dead, June 8" is seven meters long; the project website features a detail from the chromatic abstraction that documents this grim milestone. Most of the frame is bright white, with colors around the edges that grow paler as they reach toward the puzzlingly colorless middle of the shot: reds soften into pinks, blues bleed into plums, until they give way to nothing. There are striations in the color, vague shapes that invite speculation but resist interpretation; really, they are nothing at all, just a trick of the light. Juxtaposing this abstraction with knowledge of death and suffering provided by the caption confronts multiple limits: of the photographic medium, of imaging technologies, of an authoritative spectatorial position, and indeed of visibility itself. In this way, "The Day of One Hundred Dead, June 8" enacts a double default on the avowals of photojournalism.

Distinct from graphic scenes of violence that war reportage offers to distant spectators, this image takes excess to its outer limit of abstraction. And rather than the indexicality promised by the mechanically produced photograph, the light-sensitive paper here is a non-mimetic and happenstance form of representation. It operates according to a different logic that raises a crucial question: What happens to an indexical medium like photography when its actual referent cannot exactly appear? Broomberg and Chanarin describe the images that resulted from their openings of the box as the "inverse of traditional reportage" and, relatedly, "useless as evidence."[37] The bloody-looking but meaningless palette of "The Day of One Hundred Dead" results from nonfigurative action shots that present only the traces of violence. A mark of its overload, violence exceeds the capacity of this rudimentary device to visualize it, even as violence saturates the medium itself. *This is what unrepresentability looks like.* It is unreadable, but not invisible. "The Day of One Hundred Dead" illustrates the visuality of the asymptote, providing a record of the distinct series of seconds during which Broomberg and Chanarin left their box open to the air and the Afghan sun.

The box, and the images that ultimately emerge from it, nudge us toward a spectatorship dependent not on an affective encounter with the sight of violence but on a critical reflection on the conditions of visibility itself. Broomberg and Chanarin's photographs and video urge a readjustment of expectations, an acknowledgment of the epistemological limits of the visual. By foregrounding the impossible promise of representation, these cryptic images necessitate relinquishing the demand that pictures of war show us everything, or anything, about it. They have the potential, therefore, to refract the spectatorial gaze inward, onto the problematic desire to look itself. The appreciation, or perhaps even the embrace, of this ostensible failure is a crucial step in the formation of a different visuality that resists the fantasy of militarism.

AGAINST THE FANTASY OF MILITARISM

The aesthetic power of the video "The Day Nobody Died" lies in the affective pull of scenes that promise but limit vision, the monotonous and often indistinguishable ambient sounds, and a repetition of movement made tedious because it never yields insight into where we are or why. Overtly challenging U.S. and British triumphalist claims about the Global War on Terror, banality as a strategy of visibility refuses the promises of security, heroism, national sovereignty, and imperial power central to the fantasy of militarism. How, though, to activate the political potential of banality and other emotions that do not seem to get us anywhere? In other words, what do we gain in a consideration of the in/visibilities of the War on Terror by foregrounding affective phenomena that do not really seem to be worth thinking about?

As critics have long pointed out, spectacles of suffering, even those intended to denounce violence, can just as easily reinforce as undermine militaristic agendas. Such projects of exposure assume militarized violence to be an exceptional crisis, an abrupt and radical change that shatters ordinary life. Without discounting the impact of moments of radical disruption, Berlant insists that in order to understand conditions of ongoing precariousness within the current global political economy, we also need to recognize traumas of the everyday, what she calls systemic crisis or "crisis ordinariness" where trauma is structurally embedded.[38] In looking beyond the spectacular, "The Day Nobody Died" produces a visual aesthetic about the Global War on Terror not as a punctuation or interruption of life, but as the everyday grammar of the historical present. The box as subject functions as the silent witness to the machinations of that militarism, including anxious encounters with potential and actual violence that never happens, but always threaten to; the location of the box in an active war zone cues spectators to the hovering possibility of a violent happening. The fact that the camera captures no such thing indicates not an absence of violence, but only that we as spectators have been protected from it by the happenstances of distance and good fortune.

If the fantasy of militarism produces what Berlant might characterize as an optimistic attachment to the state, in Broomberg and Chanarin's project aesthetic strategies relentlessly refuse the spectator's desire to be a part of the narrative. The video, for instance, primarily captures incomplete human bodies—typically legs, feet, hands, torsos, or whole bodies but only from behind—anonymous and indistinguishable parts of the machinery of war. Repetition and fragmentation thus create an affective space of tedium and indeterminacy in contradistinction to the state's militaristic fantasy.

These non-spectacular visual artifacts of conflict reject the premise and aesthetics of photographic exposure, and thus their asymptotic approaches to the visual have a unique potential to re-angle political and affective perspectives on conflict. Broomberg and Chanarin's photographic abstractions, like the video's repetitive and aimless banality, powerfully critique journalistic complicity with the fantasy of militarism and its attendant promise that war progresses toward peace. Yet, as we cautioned at the outset, we are under no illusions that the turn to banality or other noncathartic emotions can do a "better" job than news reportage or conflict photography. A tautology in this project constrains its politics, for the box as silent witness can only see what the soldiers see, thus reproducing even as it critiques the machineries of war.

The "crisis ordinary" of military life that is visualized here, the constrained but continually suspenseful way of living without knowing, living in fear but also in boredom, inevitably (and perhaps predictably) excludes Afghan civilians and combatants. Even as Broomberg and Chanarin critique U.S. and British policies of embedding journalists, the box as witness does little to call attention to militarism's ordinary but always potentially catastrophic impact on Afghan communities. Thus, as much as "The Day Nobody Died" explores the political potential of noncathartic emotions, these representations risk understating the significance of their abstracted referent, particularly because Western spectators are conditioned to use their own emotions as a gauge for the import of what they see. Though "The Day Nobody Died" aims to deflect the probing, voyeuristic gaze of the spectator looking for carnage, that spectator can become differently mired in the images, entranced by their nonsensical beauty or distracted by the work of trying to decode them. Thus, even as this project refutes the epistemologies of photojournalism, the affective and visual legacies of photojournalism pattern the coordinates through which the asymptote runs, endlessly.

NOTES

1. Adam Broomberg and Oliver Chanarin, "'The Day Nobody Died' Presented at the Barbican Art Gallery, 4th December 2008a," http://www.broombergchanarin.com/barbican-gallery-presentation.

2. See, e.g., Susan D. Moeller, *Compassion Fatigue: How the Media Sell Famine, War, and Death* (New York: Routledge, 1999) and Stanley Cohen, *States of Denial: Knowing about Atrocities and Suffering* (Cambridge: Blackwell, 2001). For another consideration of the concept of banality, see Carrie A. Rentschler, "Witnessing: US Citizenship and the Vicarious Experience of Suffering," *Media, Culture & Society* 26, no. 2 (2004): 296–304. Rentschler suggests that mediated witnessing is integral to the experience of American citizenship, but also that representations of suffering are so ubiquitous as to become banal, and that most spectators consume them accordingly.

3. Much of the scholarship that engages questions of ethics and spectatorship focuses on graphic images of suffering, perhaps on the often-tacit assumption that these provoke the most urgent ethical questions. See, for example, Susie Linfield, *The Cruel Radiance: Photography and Political Violence* (Chicago: University of Chicago Press, 2012). We urge an expansion of the critical view beyond these rather more spectacular depictions.

4. For a more sustained reflection on the discordant affects prompted by banal images and their implications for ethical spectatorship, see Rebecca A. Adelman and Wendy Kozol, "Discordant Affects: Ambivalence, Banality, and the Ethics of Spectatorship," *Theory & Event* 17, no. 3 (2014).

5. Robert Hariman and John Louis Lucaites, "The Banality of Violence," *Flow* 15, no. 5 (2012), http://flowtv.org/2012/01/banality-of-violence/.

6. Asma Abbas, "Voice Lessons: Suffering and the Liberal Sensorium," *Theory & Event* 13, no. 2 (2010).

7. Lauren Berlant, *Cruel Optimism* (Durham, NC: Duke University Press, 2011).

8. Wendy Brown writes eloquently of the limitations of a politicized "attachment to injury" as a motivation and framework for activism by marginalized groups; this benevolently pessimistic gaze is perhaps a related orientation, turned outward. See Brown, *States of Injury: Power and Freedom in Late Modernity* (Princeton, NJ: Princeton University Press, 1995).

9. This gaze is akin to what Sara Ahmed characterizes as the "perverse performative," the "speech act that brings into existence what it cannot admit that it wants, or even the very thing that it says it does not want" (201). See Ahmed, *The Promise of Happiness* (Durham, NC: Duke University Press, 2010).

10. Broomberg and Chanarin, "The Day Nobody Died" (2008a)

11. For a critical history of the idea of wartime as discrete from peace, see Mary L. Dudziak, who asks, "How Can We End a Wartime When War Doesn't Come to An End?" (Dudziak, *War Time: An Idea, Its History, Its Consequences* [New York: Oxford University Press, 2012]), 4. Broomberg and Chanarin pose a filmic counterpart to that question.

12. Wendy Hesford, *Spectacular Rhetorics: Human Rights Visions, Recognitions, Feminisms* (Durham, NC: Duke University Press, 2011), 9.

13. Dudziak writes, "As a wartime without boundaries, the war on terror broke the problem of war's temporality into the open, revealing anxiety over the impact of perpetual war on American democracy itself. Americans disagreed deeply about this war, but coalesced around the idea that the times were not normal times. As war goes on, Americans have lapsed into a new kind of peacetime. It is not a time without war, but instead a time in which war does not bother everyday Americans" (*War Time*, 135).

14. Kevin McSorley, "Helmetcams, Militarized Sensation and Somatic War," *Journal of War and Culture Studies* 5, no. 1 (2012): 47–58.
15. As American citizens, we take up this analysis as a rejoinder to the United States' renewed commitment to the Global War on Terror without temporal or geographical limits, evident most recently in the intensification of drone warfare in the Middle East and now in northern Africa (Charlie Savage, "Debating the Legal Basis for the War on Terror," *New York Times*, May 16, 2013; Eric Schmitt and Scott Sayare, "New Drone Base in Niger Builds US Presence in Africa," *New York Times*, February 22, 2013; and Mark Mazzetti. "A Secret Deal on Drones, Sealed in Blood," *New York Times*, April 6, 2013).
16. Broomberg and Chanarin, "The Day Nobody Died" (2008a).
17. This is, we argue, akin to Ahmed's discussion of the figure of the killjoy who refuses to smile if there is reason to smile; see *The Promise of Happiness*.
18. See for instance Kyo Maclear's comment about "art's potential to convey the unsignifiable, its capacity to provoke questions that can take us beyond what is already understood. . . . Through art, we encounter the prefigurative movement of memories which test our shrunken imaginings of history, community and responsibility" (Kyo Maclear, *Beclouded Visions: Hiroshima-Nagasaki and the Art of Witness* [Albany: State University of New York Press, 1999], 15). Lisa Parks, though, cautions against privileging art as a radical space for this diminishes the possibilities of "critical engagement with and accountability for the images of war that circulate *within television culture*" and other dominant media (Parks, *Cultures in Orbit: Satellites and the Televisual* [Durham, NC: Duke University Press, 2005], 99, emphasis in the original).
19. Coined by Paul Ricoeur in *Freud and Philosophy: An Essay on Interpretation*, trans. Denis Savage (New Haven: Yale University Press, 1970), a hermeneutics of suspicion references a critical framework, as Eve Kosofsky Sedgwick explains, that seeks "an unmystified view of systematic oppression" (Sedgwick, *Touching Feeling* [Durham, NC: Duke University Press, 2003], 127). Feminist and postcolonial critics have powerfully refined a "hermeneutics of suspicion" about the Western mediated gaze at Third World violence (e.g., Inderpal Grewal, *Transnational America: Feminisms, Diasporas, Neoliberalisms* [Durham, NC: Duke University Press, 2005]; Lilie Chouliaraki, *The Spectatorship of Suffering* [Thousand Oaks, CA: Sage, 2006]; Jasbir Puar, *Terrorist Assemblages: Homonationalism in Queer Times* [Durham, NC: Duke University Press, 2007]; and Julietta Hua, *Trafficking Women's Human Rights* [Minneapolis: University of Minnesota Press, 2011]). Without rejecting the contributions of this theoretical frame, Sedgwick suggests that its dominance in critical theory may have led to a "stultifying side effect: they may have made it less rather than more possible to unpack the local, contingent relations between any given piece of knowledge and its narrative/epistemological entailments for the seeker, knower or teller" (*Touching Feeling*, 124). We are curious here about the potentials of making war visible when visual practices, such as Broomberg and Chanarin's, move away from a hermeneutics of suspicion and toward a reparative epistemological approach.
20. Sianne Ngai, *Ugly Feelings* (Cambridge, MA: Harvard University Press, 2007), 6, emphasis in the original.
21. Ahmed, *The Promise of Happiness*, 216, emphasis in the original.
22. Writing against the common desire to avoid, accelerate through, or medicate away unpleasant feelings like depression, Ann Cvetkovich proposes that a person experiencing depression might instead "let depression linger, to explore the feeling of remaining or resting in sadness without insisting that it be transformed or reconceived" (Cvetkovich, *Depression: A Public Feeling* [Durham, NC: Duke University Press, 2012], 14). We are talking about a slightly

different set of feelings (or non-feelings) here, but—insofar as we believe there is political and ethical potential resident in this unpleasantness—share Cvetkovich's critical investment.

23. Susan McManus, "Hope, Fear, and the Politics of Affective Agency," *Theory & Event* 14, no. 4 (2011).

24. Judith Halberstam, *The Queer Art of Failure* (Durham, NC: Duke University Press, 2011), 2–3. Halberstam's critical project is to "use these negative affects to poke holes in the toxic positivity of contemporary life" (3).

25. Ibid., 186–187.

26. Human rights and media scholars have long debated whether television, photojournalism and other visual media have the potential to mobilize empathy and action or if they simply produce spectacles that lack the critical insights necessary to foster political engagement. For two discussions on this debate, see David Campbell, "Horrific Blindness: Images of Death in Contemporary Media," *Journal for Cultural Research* 8, no. 1 (2004): 55–74; and Rosalind C. Morris, "Images of Untranslatability in the US War on Terror," *interventions* 6, no. 3 (2004): 401–423. Susan Sontag's final work also addresses this debate; see *Regarding the Pain of Others* (New York: Farrar, Straus and Giroux, 2003).

27. Sharon Sliwinski, *Human Rights in Camera* (Chicago: University of Chicago Press, 2011), 137.

28. Paul Lowe argues that "such images of the *absence* of visible violence can lead the viewer into an imaginative engagement with the nature of atrocity, and the nature of those who perpetrate it" (Lowe, "Picturing the Perpetrator," in *Picturing Atrocity: Photography in Crisis*, ed. Geoffrey Batchen, Mick Gidley, Nancy K. Miller, and Jay Prosser [London: Reaktion Books, 2012], 189).

29. Teresa Brennan, *The Transmission of Affect* (Ithaca, NY: Cornell University Press, 2004), 5.

30. Jacques Rancière, *The Future of the Image*, trans. Gregory Elliott (London: Verso, 2007), 109. "Nothing," he emphasizes, "is unrepresentable as a property of the event. There are simply choices" (129). He concludes, "In order to assert an unrepresentability in art that is commensurate with an unthinkability of the event, the latter must itself have been rendered entirely thinkable, entirely necessary according to thought. The logic of the unrepresentable can only be sustained by a hyperbole that ends up destroying it" (138).

31. Linfield, *The Cruel Radiance*, 50.

32. Broomberg and Chanarin observe, "The box becomes an absurd, subversive object, its non-functionality sitting in quietly amused contrast to the functionality of the system that for a time served as its host" (Broomberg and Chanarin, "The Day Nobody Died," 2008b, accessed October 17, 2012, http://www.choppedliver.info/the-day-nobody-died/).

33. Broomberg and Chanarin, "The Day Nobody Died," (2008a).

34. McManus, "Hope, Fear, and the Politics of Affective Agency."

35. Berlant, *Cruel Optimism*, 4.

36. Broomberg and Chanarin (2008a) are directly critical of the enterprise of embedded reporting, describing it as more "collusion" than journalism. It may be that the limited visual repertoire of the box dramatizes the narrow perspective afforded to embedded reporters.

37. Broomberg and Chanarin, "The Day Nobody Died" (2008a).

38. Berlant, *Cruel Optimism*, 10.

TRANSITION

WAR IS FUN

A Photo-Essay

NINA BERMAN

Fans cheer as billion-dollar weapons systems fly over baseball stadiums. Attack helicopters touch down on state parks while families run to greet armed Marines. On beaches and boardwalks, military recruiters teach children to aim assault rifles. An armored vehicle arrives in Times Square. Crowds dance to "Locked and Loaded," a song by the Air Force rock band. This year's Navy campaign is #selfiewithasailor.

The U.S. military sells its image to the public by sponsoring hundreds of family-friendly events that bring civilians face to face with the nation's fighting forces. Central to the audience experience is the invitation to participate in military power while remaining in the comfortable role of consumer and spectator. These events—there are hundreds a year—allow the public to experience a version of warfare absent of carnage, defeat, destruction, and loss. In other words, war is fun.

Local lawmakers enlist corporate partners for sponsorship and branding. Atlantic City's Air Show, Thunder Over the Boardwalk, launched in 2003, is now the signature summer event seen by hundreds of thousands of people. Sponsored by Geico, the show features the military's most expensive bombers from the B-2 *Stealth* to the F-22 *Raptor*. Along the boardwalk, recruiters set up booths promoting the Army, Navy, Air Force, and Marines with model weapons, blow-up mascots, toy giveaways, videos, and posters.

These events, which so smoothly conflate war and play, exist in parallel with the growth of military training and terrorism preparedness exercises that rely on civilian participants to authenticate their narratives. Vast lands of the American landscape are used by the military as staging areas for War on Terror performances with increasingly elaborate scripts, stages, casts, and crew.

In southern Indiana, on the site of a former residential center for the mentally disabled, an elaborate game of nuclear war is played out as thousands of civilian extras, covered in fake blood, lie on piles waiting to be rescued. The $12 million NORTHCOM exercise, which imagined Islamic terrorists detonating a dirty bomb, was such a popular draw that many locals took vacations from work in order to participate. At $15 an hour and a promise of overtime, playing a victim in the War on Terror was a chance not to be missed.

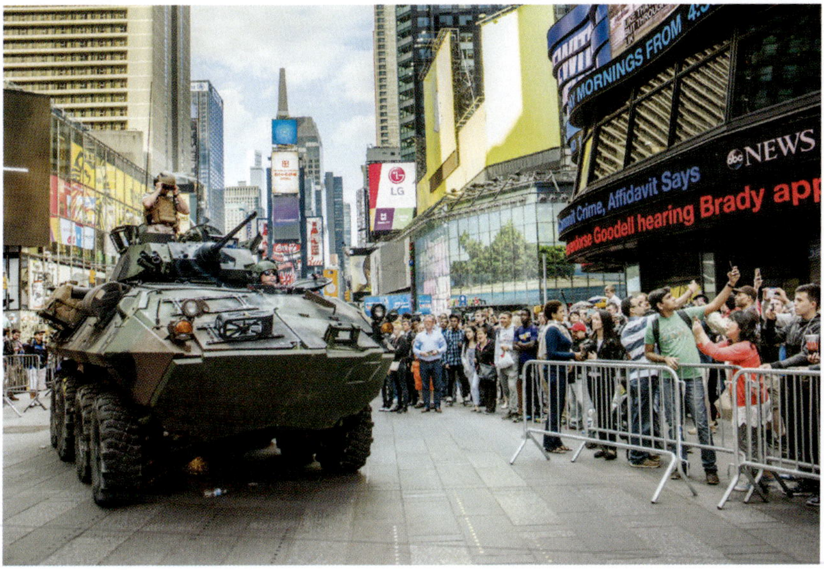

Armored vehicle, Times Square, New York, NY, 2015

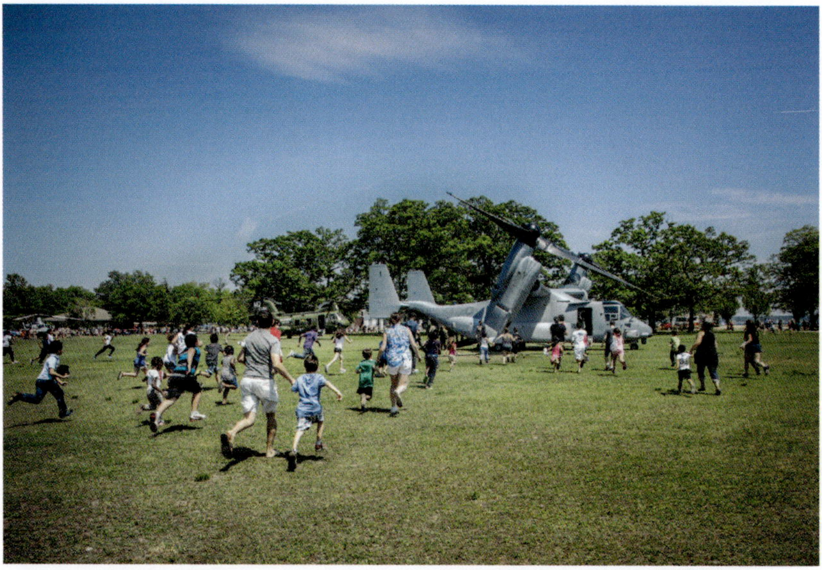

Running to the Osprey, New Rochelle, NY, 2015

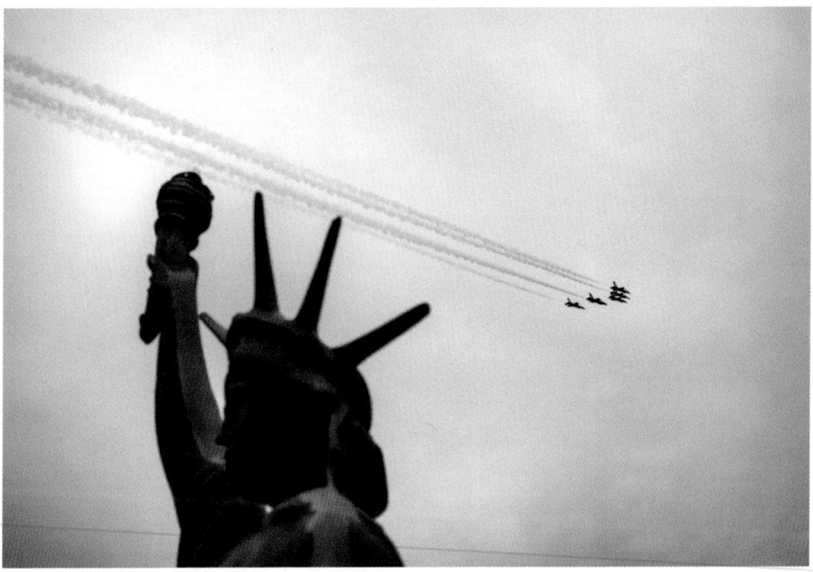

Souvenir liberty, real bombers, New York, NY, 2012

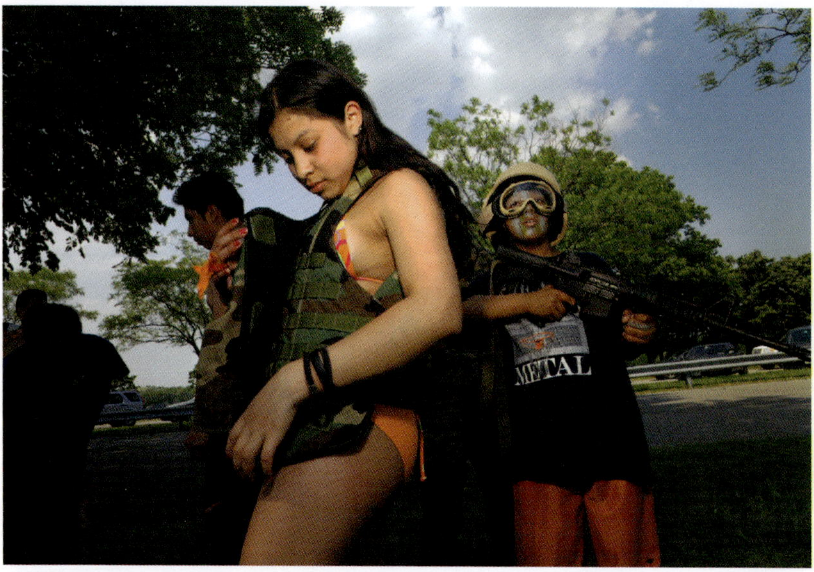

Girl and boy play Marines, The Bronx, NY, 2007

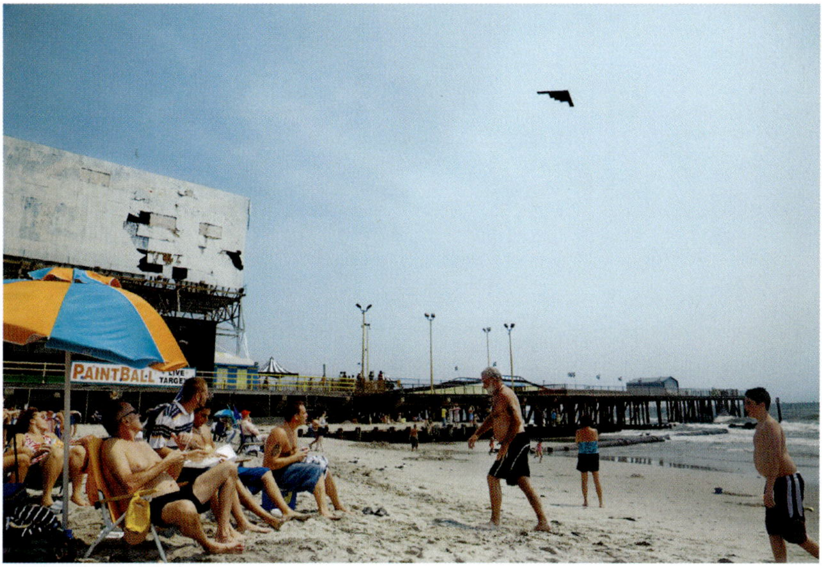

B-2 Stealth bomber, Atlantic City, NJ, 2007

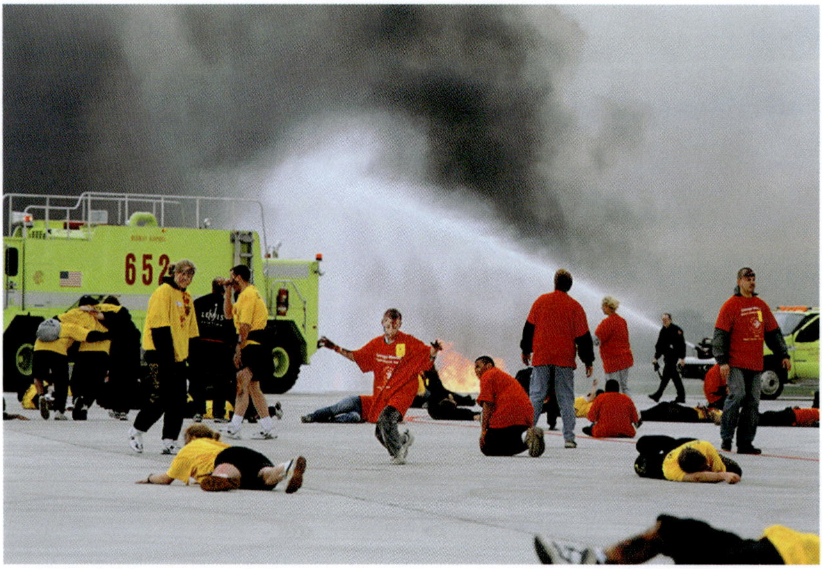

Terrorists attack Midway Airport, preparedness drill, Chicago, IL, 2003

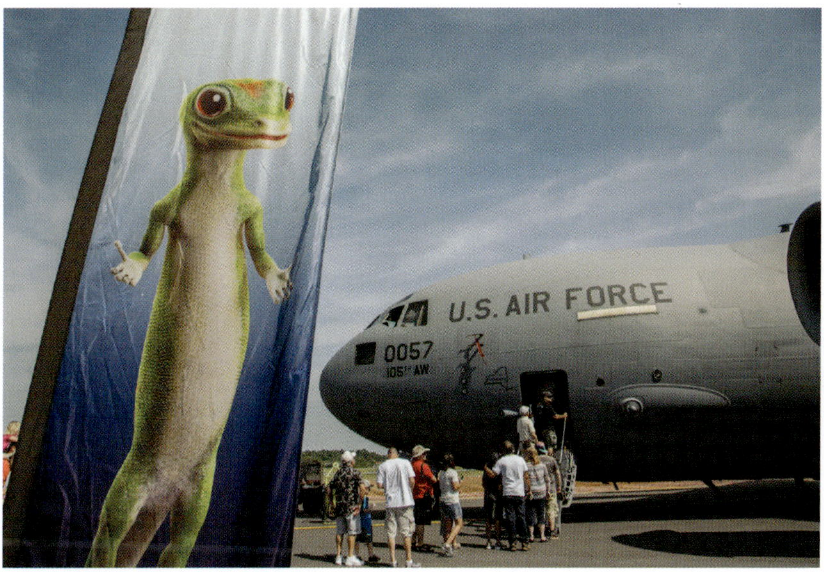

Geico display, New York Air Show, Fort Stewart, NY, 2015

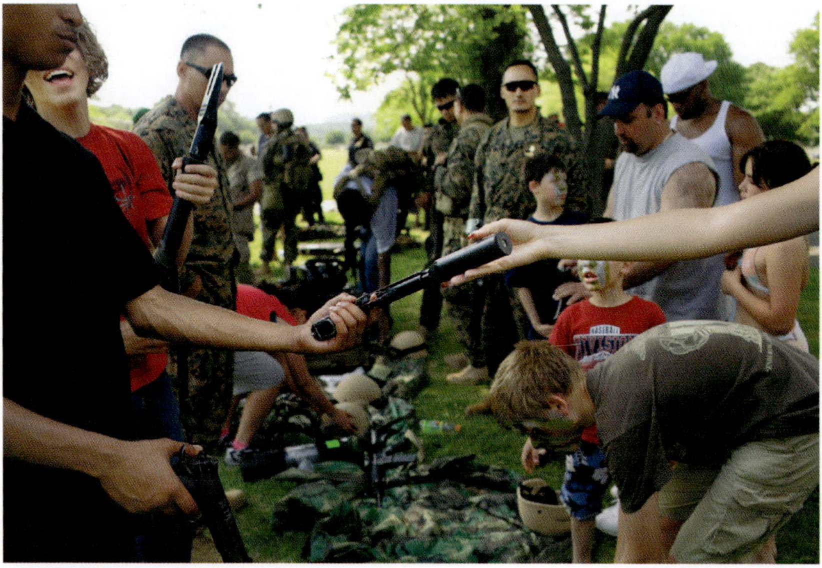

U.S. Marines weapons display, The Bronx, NY, 2007

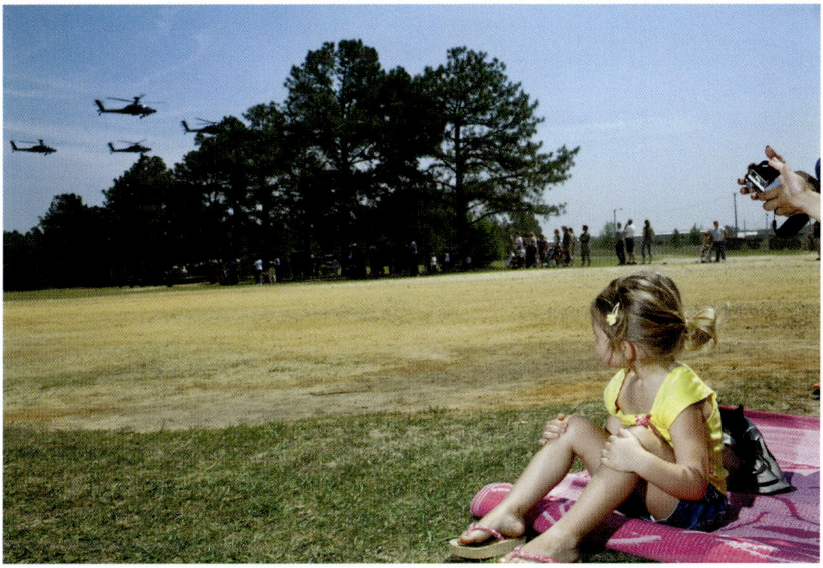

Helicopter fly-by, All America Day, Fort Bragg, NC, 2006

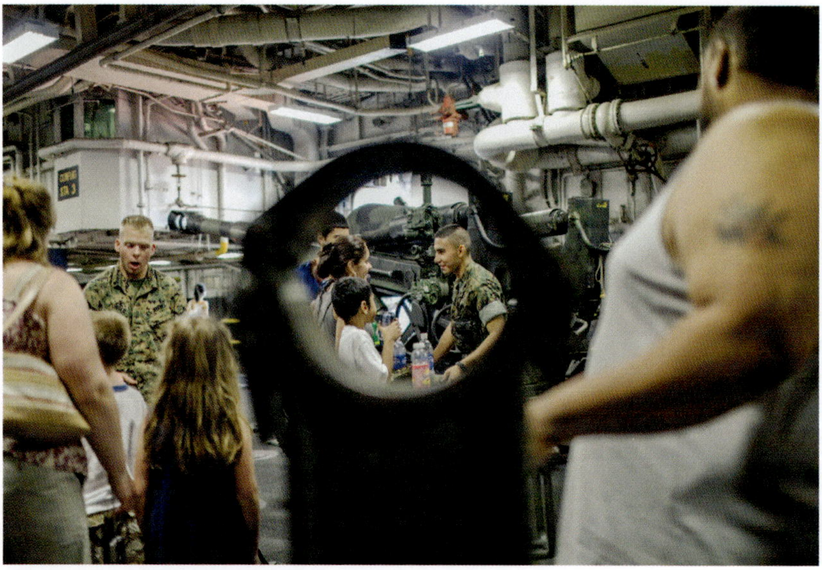

The *Intrepid,* New York, NY, 2007

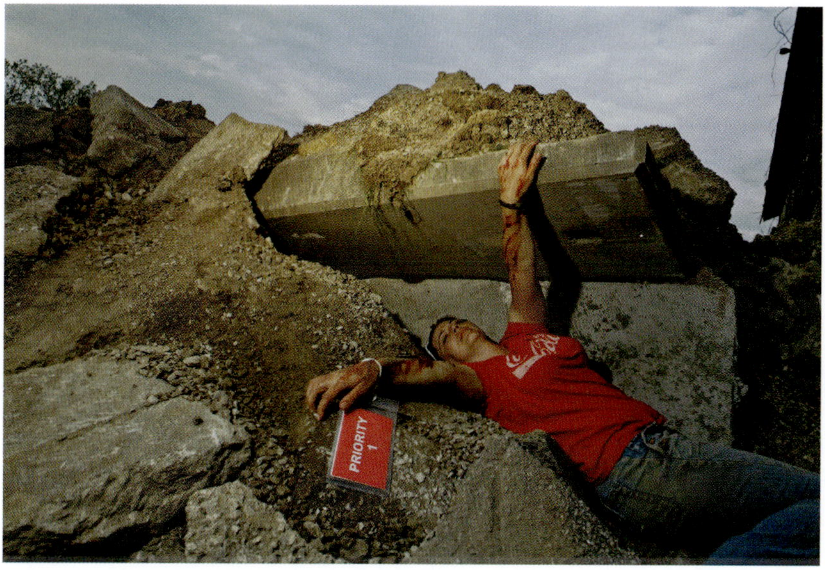

Priority 1, nuclear war drill, Butlerville, IN, 2007

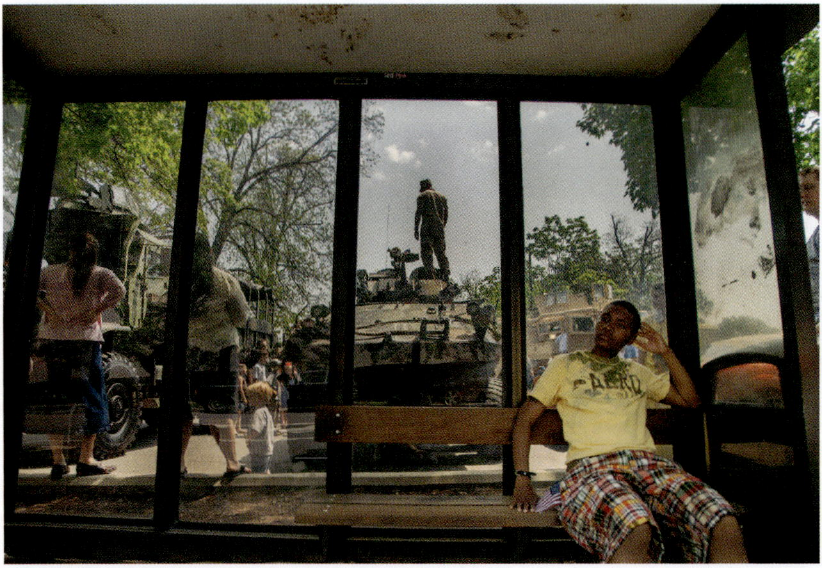

Salute Our Troops, Raleigh, NC, 2008

5 · LAYING BIN LADEN TO REST

A Case Study of Terrorism and the Politics of Visibility

JODY LYNEÉ MADEIRA

Early on the morning of September 11, 2001, nineteen terrorists hijacked four planes and crashed them into the World Trade Center towers, the Pentagon, and a farm field near Shanksville, Pennsylvania. The attacks killed 2,996 people and spawned a global "War on Terror" in Iraq and Afghanistan. Al-Qaeda claimed responsibility for the 9/11 attacks; U.S. forces pursued its leader, Osama bin Laden, for more than nine years and ultimately killed him in a raid on his Abbottabad, Pakistan, compound on May 2, 2011. Following his death, soldiers removed bin Laden's body and transferred it to the U.S.S. *Carl Vinson*, where it was cleaned, photographed, and shrouded. Following a short ceremony, bin Laden's remains were buried somewhere in the North Arabian Sea. His death was witnessed only by Special Forces soldiers and key Obama administration personnel in real time; the administration debated whether to release photos but decided against it, though members of congressional intelligence committees were permitted to view certain images.

This essay explores the role of in/visibility—the paradox of being simultaneously seen and not seen—in the manhunt and subsequent assassination of bin Laden, prioritizing the reactions of 9/11 family members, survivors, and rescue workers. Although President Barack Obama and other officials invoked family members' needs for closure and justice to justify bin Laden's killing, the debate over publicizing photos of his corpse focused instead upon the American public's needs for credibility and safety, and whether these images could incite further violence. There was underlying uncertainty over how to regard, or frame, 9/11—as a crime, an act of war, both, or neither—as well as confusion over the appropriate role and prominence of 9/11 victims, especially in relation to other categories of victims, such as soldiers and their families and a deeply traumatized city and nation.[1] It was unclear which sorts of in/visibility pertained to the death of bin Laden, and how the relationships among media technologies, the government, and publics played out. In/visibility varies according to the media in which it occurs, to and for whom, and why.

How are the politics of in/visibility negotiated by the people who are most directly affected by it and in whose names bin Laden's body was procured—9/11 family members, survivors, and rescue workers? In the first section of this essay, I discuss bin Laden's manhunt and death in terms of in/visibility. In the second section, I explain how 9/11 family members, survivors, and rescue workers—those with a direct investment in bin Laden's identification and accountability—negotiated nearly a decade of bin Laden's in/visibility, his manhunt, and death.

THE POLITICS OF IN/VISIBILITY: THE MANHUNT FOR BIN LADEN

The Politics of bin Laden's Manhunt and the War on Terror

Bin Laden's death was a key event in the American "War on Terror"—a war not based on "territorial conquest, or on an easily locatable or identifiable enemy."[2] Moreover, bin Laden was killed in a Special Forces raid, engendering a confused mish-mash of criminal justice and martial rhetoric. Although both criminal justice and warfare attempt to render enemies identifiable and subject to capture, prioritize visuality, and are waged from the highest vantage point, they utilize different technologies and engender different politics of visibility. Criminal justice and warfare are also different frames through which the death of bin Laden was in/visible. According to David A. Snow and Robert D. Benford, media framing makes it possible to "assign meaning to and interpret . . . relevant events and conditions in ways that are intended to mobilize potential adherents and constituents, to garner bystander support."[3] Framing can accomplish numerous tasks, including "identification of a problem and the attribution of blame or causality," "identify[ing] strategies, tactics, and targets," and enunciating a "call to arms or rationale for action."[4] Bin Laden's death was framed in certain ways by the media, the government, and others, which 9/11 families, survivors, and rescue workers then negotiated.

War offers its participants greater freedom of action than criminal justice; in war, one can impose accountability at a distance with little procedure, unlike the prolonged doctrinal and procedural requirements demanded of law enforcement and criminal courts. War is always shaped by (and has in turn shaped) visual fields, each of which affects "the limits of leaders' sights and determine[s] what strategy and victory would look like."[5] According to James Der Derian, the medieval ideal necessitated waging war "from the highest vantage point," and we continue to privilege sight from drones and satellites.[6] The field of battle is also a field of perception,[7] so foreign cities such as Cairo and Baghdad must be mapped into "the cognitive space of European reason" so "everything seems ordered and organized, calculated and rendered unambiguous" and, crucially, visible.[8] In contrast, criminal justice prioritizes the collection and presentation of forensic evidence, constrained opportunities for using force, and specialized legal doctrines and forums, including trials and defendants' constitutional protections. Crime victims are inherently part of the criminal justice frame in ways they could never be in war; legal doctrines have cemented access to a perpetrator at trial and execution.

Bin Laden's death was the culmination of a "manhunt." Swati Pandey observes, "Manhunts promise a sort of tidiness. They begin and end with images—a charcoal sketch or youthful mugshot—and end with grizzled defeat or something gorier, confirmation that the good guys won."[9] But War on Terror manhunts were anything but tidy, and were not conducted solely to capture, but also to shame and kill. In/visibility is key to the manhunt; Pandey observes, "When [Khalid Sheikh] Mohammed was finally imagined, named, sought, and captured . . . a CIA agent mussed his hair, put him in an ugly t-shirt with a loose neck, and caught him making a haggard grimace."[10] Bin Laden was visible through photographs and videos as the terrorist mastermind; paradoxically, he remained invisible, prompting curiosity over how this aging man could continue to evade American forces and still manage to release videos.

The War on Terror and bin Laden manhunt have altered terrorism policies; prior American manhunts were led by law enforcement and facilitated criminal prosecutions. Manhunts that focused on "evidence, verdicts, and inmates" were in tension with war and its "intelligence, victory, and bodies"; older procedures were considered "ineffective and even dangerous: evidence exposes intelligence, verdicts threaten victory, inmates demand habeas corpus." Terrorists' trials have demonstrated criminal justice's limitations; it "confound[s] the American legal system" when suspected terrorists "soapboxed on an end to American involvement in the Arab world" during criminal proceedings. In the War on Terror, manhunt targets are often located and dispatched at a distance by drones, eliminating any need "for the complex lawyerly maneuvering that [some] rightly fear undermine the notion of American justice."[11]

States use in/visibility as a framing strategy to accomplish projects of control, accountability, and punishment. Perpetrators or foes are subjugated before being visibly "released" to the public gaze. After accountability proceedings (a trial or battle), they are made invisible, most often secreted away in prisons. This is one of in/visibility's paradoxes. Visibility—producing the criminal body—is essential to accountability; it alone can produce an efficacious invisibility; the perpetrator must be seen to be not seen. Yet the State cannot control in/visibility's parameters. Offenders who remain invisible because they are uncaptured produce credibility crises; the perpetrator and the media can become inadvertent collaborators in making states seem inept. A perpetrator's visibility may also violate norms when perpetrators gain access to media beyond criminal justice venues (for example, courtrooms) or martial forums. Because perpetrators who are captured and incarcerated must be accorded resources and legal rights, sometimes literal invisibility through death seems more appealing.

Bin Laden's Politics of In/visibility

Prior to his capture, bin Laden's appearances were orchestrated through videos and terrorist attacks for which he claimed credit. One might characterize this as "guerilla visibility": an unpredictable and strategic visibility intended to harass, undermine, and surprise the United States. He evaded capture by taking refuge in terrains of invisibility, such as underground caverns like Tora Bora. In the United States, it was crucial either to set parameters around the wily bin Laden's visibility or render him as invisible as possible. Bin Laden's visibility was linked in a triangular relationship to power (denying him opportunities for visibility and/or mayhem) and danger.

For nearly a decade, bin Laden was an evanescent phantom, whereabouts unknown. These were years marked by government silence, the invisibility of capture efforts, and a questionable government commitment to its capture promise. Many seemed to believe that bin Laden would eventually be located and subjected to the actuarial gaze, but not through normal criminal proceedings such as capture and imprisonment. Making bin Laden visible risked hypervisibility, a media circus in which he could haunt the United States much more thoroughly than ever before.

Nor was bin Laden's invisibility resolved when President Obama announced that he had been killed during a Special Forces raid and buried at sea. Denied visual confirmation, Americans had to be content with a description of the visible. Ironically, his death rendered bin Laden simultaneously visible and invisible; the cycle of visibility into invisibility was already complete when Americans learned that Seal Team 6 had located, shot, identified, and buried the body. These developments refine and redefine what means of visibility best hold terrorists accountable—whether the visible should be images or news copy, whether justice demands producing bodies of text or bodies of terrorists. Visibility—to see or not to see, to show or not to show—becomes a tragic choice for institutions, officials, and individuals. Accepting bin Laden's death meant reposing trust in the very same government that had taken so long to apprehend him.

Keith Feldman locates the final battlefield in the bin Laden manhunt in the White House Situation Room, captured in the infamous Peter Souza photograph where President Obama and senior advisors watched the raid on live video feed from the Abbottabad compound on May 1, 2011. We watch as they watch; Feldman remarks, "The target of imperial retribution remains just outside the visual field, even as its presence haunts our reading. We are drawn to witness the witnessing of Bin Laden's assassination, with its spectral performance."[12] Bin Laden seems to be just on the other side of the photograph, in sight if we could only turn our heads to peek around the image's corner. The intimacy of bin Laden's killing was in stark contrast to prior intelligence gathering to locate him, which was ambiguous imaging data gathered by a drone.[13]

This intimacy was deliberate; the Obama administration ruled out a *Hellfire* missile strike that would have destroyed the compound and intelligence within and rendered bin Laden's body unrecognizable. Instead, Special Forces were used to gain close contact with the target and to "capture the image of bin Laden on camera," which required a "different kind of 'human' encounter . . . a strategy of unmediated proximity whose 'rush to the intimate' could adequately respond to 9/11's wound of punctured domesticity." The Peter Souza Situation Room photo is the closest we come to seeing bin Laden. As Feldman explains, "We come to know the death of bin Laden through its absent presence," and the Situation Room photograph stands in for a "scalp on display." Here, we see the actuarial gaze in action, a penetration from "ideal safe space" into "duplicitous, dystopic, and risk-laden space."[14] Situation Room inhabitants became proxies who witness what the government believes the general public must not. This photo shows the fact of bin Laden's death but not its circumstances—unlike the kill photos, which officials subsequently refused to make available. Yet, the photo could not conceal as much as the government may have hoped. Initial reactions noting that Hillary Clinton covered her mouth with her hand prompted her to release a statement that her pose expressed neither anxiety nor horror but was a banal cough suppression.

NEGOTIATING THE POLITICS OF VISIBILITY: PERCEPTIONS OF FAMILY MEMBERS, SURVIVORS, AND RESCUE WORKERS

How did those whose family members bin Laden had helped murder, who narrowly escaped the death he intended, and rescue workers who labored within the rubble of lives and buildings negotiate the politics of bin Laden's in/visibility for nearly a decade? They had perhaps the greatest motivation and the largest disinclination to follow bin Laden's fate, the greatest personal stake in whether he was ever identified, captured, or killed. How did they see bin Laden's in/visible presence, and then his death?

Participants' remarks about bin Laden's visibility, negative reputation, and demise animate the following account. They highlight the mass media's key framing roles—of which 9/11 victims knew, and distrusted. They demonstrate visibility and its forms affect how victims work through traumatic events, and illustrate how a perpetrator's various visibilities—physical, audiovisual, postmortem, textual—can serve as proxies for and constructive influences upon a perpetrator's perceived importance and dangerousness. Participants were able to draw conclusions about bin Laden, his importance, and his deserved fate, and they gauged these factors in relation to his visibility. In the following section, survivors and family members are abbreviated as "S" and "FM," respectively, followed by an identifying number.

"Evil Personified": Bin Laden as an Unwelcome Presence in Participants' Lives

The concept of a perpetrator's "unwelcome presence"—being felt despite being unseen—illustrates the in/visibility paradox; it was usually triggered by bin Laden's visibility and his inaccessibility and invisibility. Moreover, it is connected to the U.S. government's strategic use of bin Laden's selective visibility to make citizens aware of his threat, although the fact that it could not procure bin Laden alive or dead highlighted its inability to quash that danger. Participants' remarks further demonstrate the interdependence of and profound impacts from bin Laden's negative reputation and visibility, and illustrate visibility's role in reinforcing, strengthening, and legitimizing certain conceptions of threat and the Other. Ironically, these strategies may ultimately backfire upon their framers; when officials construct a threat as serious yet diffuse, one man may symbolize the threat, yet his death will not quash the broader danger. Logically, then, most participants did not feel bin Laden was a strong, unwelcome presence. As S4 emphasized, "Just because it's a symbol, like I'm not stupid enough to think everything is better now; nothing is going to be better now."

The majority of participants (thirteen) believed that bin Laden had been an unwelcome presence in their lives, linked to their perceptions of danger and frustration over the lengthy manhunt, to bin Laden's effect on their personal lives or to America, and his media visibility. For S6, bin Laden's presence stemmed from him "being such an incredible strategist." For S9, the dominant source of the unwelcome presence was "fundamentalist, extremist terrorists," of which bin Laden was emblematic.

The pervasiveness of bin Laden's presence was also correlated with the drastic changes he wrought in family members' and survivors' lives and nations. S11 observed, "Yes, yes [he was an unwelcome presence]. I mean, well, obviously he's the one that changed my life, and interrupted my life, and destroyed my life.

I was very happy the day I found out that they killed him, yes." S3 observed it felt odd that bin Laden was a personal unwelcome presence: "I perceived him as evil personified? And so that evil infected our whole country." The United States' failure to capture bin Laden aggravated his presence for some participants. As S5 related, "He was the one that was . . . out there in the wind and that was the person we were supposedly focused on finding and then it was more annoying that as time goes by, why the hell can't we find him." Some characterized this unwelcome presence as a background awareness, a lingering of thought; others as "annoying" (S5) or "nagging" (S13). Only one survivor characterized this presence as life changing, terrifying, and visceral: "If I would be alone in a room and he'd come on the TV, I would have like a little mini panic attack. . . . There were times when my fear level would rise so high, like I said I dropped off different forms of transportation when I thought something was going to happen. . . . I just thought that if it was going to be a high alert day, something was going to happen to me" (S4).

For those afflicted by bin Laden's toxicity, media coverage often triggered this unwelcome presence. As FM1 remarked, "For him I would say yes, yeah, [he was an unwelcome presence] because he did get quite a lot of coverage." For FM4, it was the unexpectedness of 9/11 images: "I would see a picture and read the article. So it kind of drew me there, and that was fine for me, but once again, if my [child] was in, whatever, Shoprite, or getting a cup of coffee in Dunkin' Donuts with [a] friend, and he's on the front cover, I would have to hold my breath for that." Often, media coverage of bin Laden coincided with other events to form a perfect storm: "The . . . invasion of Afghanistan put a lot of focus on this issue. Even President Bush's speech to Congress on the 19th of September, all these things together reached a crescendo which was essentially a manhunt for one person" (S13). Sometimes the best response was just tuning out: "You get to a point where you are saturated with it and you don't want to look at it anymore. . . . So I'll turn it off if there are stories about him. . . . I don't care what garbage he is spewing tonight around the anniversary or whenever it was. Just turn it off" (S8).

Bin Laden's most memorable appearances in grainy videos rebroadcast on American news media were both threatening and mocking. Participants reacted both to bin Laden's *actual* visibility and threatening rhetoric, and to his untraceability, invisibility, and threat potential. Lacking control over whether and when such videos aired, participants had to develop strategies to mitigate this visibility. The videos' timing undermined some participants' conception of threat and increased their suspicion of officials' willingness to use in/visibility politics. Participants seemed unsure whether the applicable frame was criminal justice or war; either way, they expected that a manhunt's outcome—death—should be the same: the side with superior forces should win, and quickly.

Participants had varied reactions to these videos. Four participants each characterized them as upsetting, as strategic, or as images to avoid. Two participants each stated that the videos rendered bin Laden pathetic, were confusing or incredible, scary, and emphasized the frustrating lack of capture.

Participants who characterized the bin Laden videos as very upsetting had both physical and psychological reactions. Bin Laden was still very much a terrorist, only now through the medium of video footage. FM4 found it "very upsetting," and FM5 recalled, "It would make me sick to my stomach, I couldn't look at him. To see that he was alive, and living his life, and walking through the mountains over there. . . ." S4 described the terror as a type of "brain washing": "When he was going to talk, it was because something bad was in the planning. . . . So every time [he] spoke, I would think I was about to die the next day, that somehow I would be in the wrong place at the wrong time. . . . It's a brainwash thing for people who want to follow him, but it's a brainwash thing for people who are terrified." Most survivors did not find bin Laden's in/visibility threatening. His video appearances prompted S13 to take him less seriously: "Sometimes it was just kind of like, ok, there he goes again? Kind of lame actually. . . . I thought he was kind of a tool. I thought he was really pathetic, I mean almost laughable, just like . . . okay, you'll send nineteen men to do a job . . . but you're unwilling to come out of your cell." Others felt that the videos heightened concern and wonderment that bin Laden was still free, particularly when other American domestic manhunts had proven so successful. As S14 noted, "I couldn't understand how a New York City detective, with basic education, and no strategic machinery, could work in a city of 13 million and find a suspect within days or weeks. But yet the United States with all their machinery, and all their troops, thousands and thousands and thousands of troops, couldn't find this guy. . . . I don't get it. Maybe we should hire that cop."

Many participants felt that bin Laden meant these videos to be strategic, "sending out signals, telling people to do something" (S10). Again, this is part of the in/visibility paradox; bin Laden is seen on a video as a talking head, not as a dynamic terrorist leader. In this light, participants sensed these videos fulfilled egotistic, strategic, and propaganda functions but were unsure which purpose was paramount: "There's a portion of those tapes and things that he really said were as much for him to put himself in the media as it was to let others know that Al-Qaeda was still there. That's the perception I have . . . Did he try to embody Al-Qaeda? Like was he acting as a representative of Al-Qaeda, or was he acting just for himself, or both?" (S2). S2 opined that the videos' purpose was to distract America's attention from other terrorist activities that were going on elsewhere: "And if we stay focused on him, too, maybe we wouldn't notice the other pieces of the moving puzzle. . . . You'll miss what the people in Somalia are plotting. Or Yemen." Much of bin Laden's evil presence, then, stemmed from his involvement in 9/11, with media coverage serving only as a nagging reminder of the United States' ongoing inability to capture him. This invites the question of how participants as media audiences negotiated his media visibility and used it to glean information.

Negotiating bin Laden's Visibility

The mass media was undoubtedly the medium by which most participants "got to know" bin Laden. However, this information created more questions than it answered. How could this man ostensibly be both Al-Qaeda leader yet refugee, frail yet an escape artist, wealthy yet cave dwelling? To participants, bin Laden looked much as he had in the past—a robust, wealthy man, angrily speaking out against the United States—but was invisible as he actually was: an aged and ill man on the run, dying his hair to appear youthful.

Most disliked bin Laden's heightened visibility. S4 recalled that "Osama's picture all over the place was kind of daunting, in those first months." Participants attributed this increase in information to bin Laden's status as both an Al-Qaeda leader and Islamic fundamentalist symbol who was still very much alive:

> I think that the FBI, and the other government agencies, the CIA . . . were trying to feed the American people information as fast as they possibly could. I think bin Laden, being that he was always escaping being in our grasp, we followed him a lot more. And I also think it gave more . . . of an opportunity to accurately depict him versus, you're gonna sit there and talk about Atta, who is dead? (S6)

"Getting to know" bin Laden usually meant that participants believed they knew "a lot" about him (S11). The vast majority of participants (thirteen out of fifteen) learned about bin Laden through the mass media, in particular news coverage of which he was the focus. This knowledge was deeper than that acquired about most other terrorists; of fifteen participants, fourteen felt that bin Laden was the most familiar 9/11 figure. As S2 explained, "In some ways you got a more humanistic picture of him. Even before they went in and attacked his compound. Because you did get some more background on his history—where he started, who his family was, things he had published or said—which you didn't get from the other hijackers."

When asked to describe the most memorable media facts about bin Laden, participants most frequently recalled his past involvement in the Soviet-Afghan conflict: "One thing I kind of felt was odd that the United States helped him when the Russians were in Afghanistan. . . . And then he turns around and attacks us" (S10). The second most pervasively identified media theme was bin Laden's wealthy Saudi family; this characteristic seemed at odds with the third most memorable image of bin Laden, as a man dwelling in mountain caves. As S8 observed, "I remember him living in a cave. . . . This big guy with all this money and you're living in Pakistan or wherever in a cave. Just like when they caught Saddam, in a fox hole."

The idea of bin Laden living in caves was very evocative for participants. One was very critical of media coverage of bin Laden as a "cave-dwelling animal" (S6). But caves have messianic as well as primitive connotations. Thus, bin Laden's cave residence seemed to bolster his alleged claims to spiritual leadership, rendering him, in the words of S4, a "perverted version of, like, a Jesus."

Many participants also recalled bin Laden's kidney failure, at odds with cave dwelling and successfully evading international manhunts. Such facts undercut the government and media credibility; as S6 explained, "Bin Laden happens to be . . . one of the world's best strategists. He has the patience of a saint. . . . The news media always put him down, they sort of made him that cave animal. . . . If you really believe that, don't you resent the American government for letting a cave-dwelling, simple little animal put together such an incredible feat against the American people?"

Participants learned to negotiate this paradoxical in/visibility, including selectively paying attention to media coverage. Over the years, as the terrorists' message stayed the same and attacks were continually thwarted, participants found it easier to tune out: "All the tapes that they kept putting up . . . like right after, when he was saying, 'Yeah, we got you.' And you know, 'We're going to rain death down.' . . . Then after a while, I just stopped paying attention to be honest" (S9).

Another implication of bin Laden's in/visibility was what his death meant in terms of accountability proceedings. Some participants were thankful that the United States never had to imprison and thus support him: "Thank God they killed him. . . . They'd be putting him in a satin-lined cell and feeding him everything that he wanted, and giving him all of his rights. No, I am so grateful that they put a bullet in his head" (S5). This implies that bin Laden's visibility at capture and trial would have been damaging to private sensibilities or public security, and that his postsentencing invisibility would have come at too high and shameful a cost. But others thought these ends were best accomplished through life imprisonment: "If he gets the death penalty, he gets so much more credence, and like publicity, and authority in a sense" (S10).

These remarks illustrate how participants negotiated complex politics of in/visibility over which they had little practical control. Though participants thought they knew bin Laden as the best of the perpetrators, he seemed a figure caught in a series of paradoxes. Thus, bin Laden's visibility exacerbated the many questions participants asked in the years before he was captured and killed. How, then, did participants negotiate the moment when bin Laden would most logically be visible: his capture and death?

"At a Loss": Perceptions of bin Laden's Death

Bin Laden's death was the moment when he was simultaneously rendered visible and invisible; his whereabouts were known yet his death hidden. The Special Forces raid that killed bin Laden was both intimate and distanced. American soldiers were in the compound, yet body cameras ensured that military commanders and government officials thousands of miles away saw what was in their line of vision. After his death, bin Laden first was presented as a body of text, shrouded by official assurances that he was dead and buried. Bin Laden's death surprised many participants, along with the flat emotion they felt upon hearing the news; nonetheless, most were largely content with how events unfolded, and seemed content to live with the contradictions of bin Laden's in/visibility—a visible textual body and invisible flesh.

Most participants wanted to see bin Laden killed rather than captured because any other punishment would have been too lenient or expensive, his capture would have increased the risk of danger, he could not have been a valuable information source, and because his trial would create a media circus. Some were concerned that he would waste fiscal resources: "If he was captured alive, he would probably . . . get life in prison without parole, which again would be another waste of the taxpayer's dollar" (S14). For S4, bin Laden had little to no inclination to share intelligence: "The only people I would want alive are people who are going to say why, what else is out there, but he never would do that either." S8 found it "better" that bin Laden was ultimately confronted by the immediacy and inevitability of his own death: "The end result is the U.S. military shot him. To me that is a thousand percent better than capturing him or dropping a bomb on his head because he knew what was coming." Only death was practical; bin Laden's capture would increase the risk of terrorist attacks and produce a "media circus" (S10).

But other participants noted that bin Laden had to be made entirely visible for full accountability. FMs 1 and 6 believed that bin Laden's death diminished our ability to demand accountability: "It doesn't feel like really justice. I mean justice is something you do in a courtroom." S6 was concerned that bin Laden's death would create a new politics of in/visibility, in which bin Laden would gain cachet as a martyr and become more visible after his life was extinguished: "I think that it would have had a lot more impact on his people if their wonderful man spent the rest of his life behind bars."

Feelings About bin Laden's Death

Participants described complex reactions to bin Laden's death as well as to how it took place. By a slim majority, most reactions were positive; seven described themselves as "glad," four stated that they were very happy, three felt relief, and two participants each described feeling satisfied and supported by the American government. Six participants, however, felt little to no emotion, and others experienced negative emotions such as irritation, wariness, and a feeling that this event had come too late to be of much use.

Participants were often pleased that the situation was resolved in a way that kept bin Laden's visibility to a comparatively unthreatening and invisible minimum—without protracted litigation, media attention, or opportunities for revenge attacks. FM5 recalled that "it was very emotional for me, and I just [said] thank God." S4 felt that an ailing parent had waited until bin Laden's death to pass away: "My [parent] knew that I needed him dead.... [S/He] didn't leave before [s/he] knew he was gone, because he was the symbol of everything ugly and evil that ruined my life."

For these participants, bin Laden's death apparently resolved many of the paradoxes of his in/visibility. As the years passed without news of bin Laden's capture or killing, S11 had felt almost betrayed: "I thought the government let us down, and I thought, why are they not catching him? Are they even looking to get him at this point? Is it over?" Bin Laden's death provided reassurance that the American government had not forgotten either 9/11 or its victims; FM2 recalled, "It definitely makes a difference to have him gone . . . to feel like my government was doing something after all to protect us, like they had our back, that definitely felt better." Even participants who would have wanted a trial were partially relieved to have the affair over and done with, especially in light of the uncertainties and delays that plagued other terrorism trials; FM2 observed, "I would have wanted a trial, but there's part of me that's so glad it's just done." S1 described this event as a "turning point" that provided a sort of finality: "There was definitely a turning point in that there was a part of me that was glad the guy was dead, in that, I guess a certain closure... I think the closure was we knew what happened to him."

But for many participants, the unresolved contradictions in bin Laden's in/visibility dulled its emotional effects. One relevant contradiction was the disparity between bin Laden's continual visibility as an American threat and the comparative invisibility of both his person and manhunt developments during the nearly decade-long search. The second contradiction was between the United States' efforts to construct bin Laden as the sole visible agent of 9/11 on one hand, and its attempt to justify Homeland Security measures and wars in Afghanistan and Iraq by pointing to Al-Qaeda's continued threat on the other. Bin Laden was both seen—as the agent responsible for 9/11—and not seen, buried in the multitudes of Al-Qaeda adherents.

Upon learning of bin Laden's death, most survivors felt little to no emotion. FM1 recalled, "I didn't have a very strong reaction at all. For me, I was flat, to be honest." Similarly, FM2 observed, "What you realize is that you don't really feel that different. And you know why he's gone, but it's not a sense of relief."

Participants were often surprised by this subdued reaction: "I was just sort of stunned. I guess I hadn't thought about him in a while. Then it's like, 'Oh my gosh.' I guess it was something I thought maybe would never happen. It made me feel weird . . . and it surprised me that I was sort of at a loss for how I felt because I really expected to be like jumping up and down. It made me sad. Not for him" (S5). As if aware of these contradictions, participants struggled to identify reasons for this reaction. S3 attributed it to the distance between bin Laden and 9/11: "I kind of never really felt I had anyone to like really be able to pinpoint, even with bin Laden . . . I didn't get anything from that, and I don't know why that is." Others blamed the nearly decade-long gap between 9/11 and bin Laden's death: "I didn't have any huge sense of satisfaction, because in a way for me it was ten years too late" (FM1). Participants were also very conscious of danger still lingering from Al-Qaeda: "Now that he's gone, it's not done. Don't rest easy. They didn't kill terrorism" (FM4). Bin Laden's killing deprived Al-Qaeda of leadership, but might simultaneously have created different dangers: "I think he held things together as a ruler, as a leader. . . . Now, it's a lot less structured and you have . . . a lot of cells that don't have the power, the strength. . . . It's lost some of its oomph. But now it's more dangerous because it's not as organized" (S12). Even participants who expressed happiness at bin Laden's death often qualified their reactions by acknowledging it would not resurrect victims. S1 cautioned, "I'm glad they killed him, don't get me wrong, but it doesn't bring all those people back. It doesn't bring the Towers back, and it doesn't get these memories out of my head."

Finally, numerous participants hoped that bin Laden's death would not make it easier to forget 9/11. As bin Laden persisted, so did a continued focus on 9/11. "A neighbor, the kindest man across the street from me the next day, was like, 'Yay, we got him!'" FM4 related, "He was happy, but did that close the door for him on, on 9/11? I hope not." To keep 9/11 from being forgotten, one had to talk about it.

Finally, some found bin Laden's death annoying or its timing too politically convenient. FM4 was irritated that President Obama's announcement coincided with the final moments of the last episode of Donald Trump's reality show, *The Apprentice*: "He's screwing it up for Donald Trump." S14 was bothered that the event occurred during a presidential election year: "You found Saddam Hussein with no problem. . . . How come you couldn't find the other guy? . . . So that was the first thing that came to my mind, you need to get reelected now, so now you want to find the guy?"

Ultimately, then, participants felt bin Laden's visibility at the moment of capture and death would have been more burden than boon, feared it would heighten threat, spur additional terrorist activity, martyr bin Laden, and so on. They weighed these politics of visibility more in light of the prevailing cultural and political climate than in the context of their own personal desires. And it was this larger political and cultural context, ironically, that rendered bin Laden's death something of a non-event for many. Did this subdued reaction to bin Laden's death affect whether participants wanted to view death images?

"That Strange Mystery": Viewing Death Images

Bin Laden's death was the beginning, not the end, of opportunities for visibility. The question of whether to release postmortem images was a tragic choice, no matter the outcome. S2 recognized these tensions: "It also had that strange mystery to it, did we really get him, where's the body. It was good that we didn't give him a place to go to, but we also don't have our proof, and if we show proof we're animals."

Following bin Laden's death, there was no victim demand to "produce the body," nor did the government proffer visual evidence to the public. The United States had released postmortem photographs in similar contexts at least twice before. Postmortem photos of Saddam Hussein's sons Uday and Qusay, killed in an extended firefight with U.S. soldiers on July 22, 2003, were later released to provide "closure" to Iraqis, as were images of Abu Musab al-Zarqawi, the Iraqi Al-Qaeda leader who was killed in a U.S. airstrike on June 7, 2006. Participants readily accepted the Obama administration's justifications for not releasing the postmortem photographs, many of which bolstered the idea of a War on Terror regime and the need to police the jihadist threat.

If possible, bin Laden became even more phantasmal in death, a toxic presence whose release could be a source of contagion and incite violence. Choosing not to release the photos, or affirming a lack of desire to see them, was a way to mount the moral high ground; presumably, those who would have viewed the photos would distrust government assurances, and perhaps be unpatriotic. President Obama refused to release postmortem photographs of his body on the grounds that "we don't trot this stuff out as trophies."[15]

Most participants would not have wanted to view images of bin Laden's corpse, and often linked viewing to trust in government. S5 remarked, "I know people don't trust the government, but I trust them when they say they got him. That was good enough for me." FM7 similarly noted, "I took the word of the [United States] there, that he was gone. . . . I don't see him walking down the streets no more, do you?" FM4 described this trust as temporary, susceptible to future change: "I don't think I would have needed to see that. I mean I trust that he was killed, but you know what, I can say to you right now, ten years from now there might be an article that I read that doubts that that really went on."

Some participants felt that viewing these images would be outright harmful. "I saw those photos that they had of Saddam Hussein, I just feel like I saw bodies there," S5 reflected. "I just try to not have any other disturbing images in my brain as much as possible." S12 asserted, "It wasn't necessary to show pictures of him, his death. It really wasn't. I see enough death." S4 identified bin Laden's corpse as a potential trigger of additional violence: "Seeing something that might have looked horrifying, and you know what, it would cause even more problems, more people hating us."

A handful of participants would have wanted to see bin Laden's death images, just to provide confirmation that it was indeed him. FM3 recalled that her or his deceased loved one, a 9/11 site worker, had developed profound distrust of the government based on its unwillingness to acknowledge or compensate worker injuries and would have wanted to see such images just to know it was him. Participants were careful to disentangle the evidentiary benefits of viewing from voyeuristic or ghoulish impulses. S6 observed, "Not for the glory of seeing it . . . obviously after the assassination of bin Laden, there was a lot of, 'Oh yeah, they buried him at sea right away,' so that—it goes back to that whole Kennedy assassination thing. So, would I have liked to have seen documented proof? Yes." S10 did not want to view the images but remarked they could provide a different authenticity: "Who knows if our government is covering something up anyway. . . . I remember seeing pictures of JFK . . . and not that I'm gory or anything like that, but it was like, wow. He's, like, really dead."

Even though they would not have wanted to view these images, most participants felt that they should be made available to family members, survivors, and rescue workers who did desire to see them. FM2 remarked, "I think that should be an option, again, some people can take or reject." FM2 observed that viewing opportunities might cultivate trust: "I'm in a weird, different position since I have a lot of friends who have seen the photos, and I trust them, but I can imagine if you don't know people personally it would be hard to trust." S10 connected viewing to closure: "They probably should have only because I think for them more so it would be closure. . . . For family members . . . I think that would've been a little better."

CONCLUSION

Participants' remarks not only illustrate the mass media's and government's roles in constructing and framing bin Laden and his in/visibility, but also how aware most participants were of these processes and negotiated these representations. Their comments reflect sojourns through visibility's uncertain future—journeys and expected outcomes heavily influenced by the nature of the offense and the offender. It was hard, even impossible to imagine a captured bin Laden brought within U.S. borders to stand trial; moreover, American precedents as well as past experiences with government officials did not lead participants to believe that they would be accorded access to accountability processes.

The U.S. government was extraordinarily successful in constructing and framing an extensive terrorist threat that merited a "War on Terror." Ultimately, the demise of Public Enemy No. 1 affected the safety status quo but little. Americans had been focusing too hard for too long upon terrorist Others; the death of a terrorist Other nearly a decade later was not a glorious victory but rather emphasized that no single battle would win the War on Terror—and that indeed this war might be endless. These factors help to explain why bin Laden's death seemed to have little permanent positive affect; most participants not only were uncomfortable with any celebratory atmosphere but felt curiously "flat." When a threat is so diffuse that no individual's death can end it, reactive emotions can fall flat, and our technologies for observing instead become media of obscuring.

NOTES

1. See generally Jody Lyneé Madeira, "Clear and Ever-Present Dangers? Redefining 'Closure' in a Post-9/11 World," in *Capital Punishment: Part of a Sustainable Criminal Justice System?*, ed. Lil Scherdin (London: Ashgate, 2014).
2. Allen Feldman, "Securocratic Wars of Public Safety," *Interventions: International Journal of Postcolonial Studies* 6, no. 3 (2004): 300–350, 331.
3. David A. Snow and Robert D. Benford, "Ideology, Frame Resonance, and Participant Mobilization," *International Social Movement Research* 1, no. 1 (1988): 197–217, 198.
4. Ibid., 199–203.
5. Nick Cullather, "Bombing at the Speed of Thought: Intelligence in the Coming Age of Cyberwar," *Intelligence and National Security* 18, no. 4 (2003): 141–154, 141.
6. James Der Derian, Interview with Paul Virilio. http://nideffer.net/proj/_SPEED_/1.4/articles/derderian.html (1997).
7. Ibid.
8. Derek Gregory, "Dis/Ordering the Orient: Scopic Regimes and Modern War," in *Orientalims and War*, ed. Tarak Barkawi and Kieth Stanski (Ithaca, NY: Cornell University Press, 2013), 155.
9. Swati Pandey, "War by Manhut: Osama Bin Laden and Khalid Sheikh Mohammed," *Los Angeles Review of Books*, July 8, 2012, http://lareviewofbooks.org/review/war-by-manhunt-osama-bin-laden-and-khalid-sheikh-mohammed.
10. Ibid.
11. Ibid.
12. Keith Feldman, "Empire's Verticality: The Af/Pak Frontier, Visual Culture, and Racialization From Above," *Comparative American Studies* 9, no. 4 (2011): 325–341, 326.
13. Ibid., 336.
14. Allen Feldman, "On the Actuarial Gaze: From 9/11 to Abu Ghraib," *Cultural Studies* 19, no. 2 (2005): 203–226, 209.
15. Michael A. Memoli and Peter Nicholas, "No Release of Death Photos, Obama Cites Security in Keeping bin Laden Pictures from Public," *St. Louis Dispatch*, May 5, 2011.

PART II NOT SEEING WAR

6 · DIGITAL WAR AND THE PUBLIC MIND

Call of Duty Reloaded, Decoded

ROGER STAHL

In the dozen years since 9/11, the U.S. War on Terror has kept pace, complementing troop draw-downs in Afghanistan and Iraq with drone strikes that have expanded to at least six countries, sweeping surveillance of the global digital grid, and traditional air strikes in Libya and Syria. At the same time, however, the war has faded to invisibility as these conflicts precipitously dropped from the news screen. Beginning in 2005, the occupations of Iraq and Afghanistan migrated from lead story to background noise. By this time, reporters had disembedded en masse, handing over their significantly attenuated role as the "fourth estate" to the military's new in-house press corps, the Defense Video and Imagery Distribution System (DVIDS). With very little presence in occupied areas, press accounts dwindled, occasionally relaying what "U.S. officials say" while running footage U.S. officials had released. Despite exceptional events—such as the killings of both Osama bin Laden and Muammar Gaddafi in 2011—the war had effectively disappeared.

Hollywood's experiments with war film tapered off alongside the news. After a series of attempts—from the morose *Jarhead* (2005) to more critical fare like *The Green Zone* (2010) and even Katherine Bigelow's Best Picture–winning *The Hurt Locker* (2008)—the genre had proved to be a "toxic" commercial failure.[1] Some exceptions persisted. Due perhaps to the vacuum of journalism left by television news, the war documentary picked up steam with both investigative pieces like *Taxi to the Dark Side* (2007) and *Standard Operating Procedure* (2008), as well as embedded-experiential pieces like *The War Tapes* (2006) and *Restrepo*

(2010). Another exception was the surge of "Washington movies" in 2012 that followed on the tail-end of the ill-fated "surge" of troops in Afghanistan.[2] The White House worked closely with Katherine Bigelow and Mark Boal to produce *Zero Dark Thirty* (2012), which rewrote the killing of Osama bin Laden as a story about the efficacy and necessity of torture.[3] *Act of Valor* (2012) began as a Navy recruitment advertisement in 2006 and eventually grew into a feature film starring actual Navy Seals.[4] Despite this later infusion of activity, however, the film industry preserved only a tenuous, episodic relationship to military occupation and the War on Terror.

Unlike the big screen, the video game industry squarely embraced the thematic of contemporary warfare. Chris Suellentrop of the *New York Times* put it bluntly: games "have become the most popular fictional depictions of America's current wars."[5] Of the top ten highest grossing games in 2012, three had come from the popular *Call of Duty series.*[6] Franchises like *Battlefield,* the *Tom Clancy* series, and *Medal of Honor* rounded out the second tier. The enormously popular *America's Army,* a free recruitment game produced by the U.S. Army, also made the top ten list of most played games.[7] This popularity is even more significant given the growth of the video game industry as a whole: By 2010 the game industry was worth $56 billion, twice the size of the music industry and about three-fifths the size of the global film industry after counting both box office and DVD sales. Moreover, the video game sector has increasingly courted a mainstream audience. Nearly three quarters of households now play games, with players averaging thirty-seven years of age.[8] These numbers suggest that games hold a primary place in the media landscape, and that within this new landscape, the thematic of the War on Terror is front and center.

This essay tracks the rhetoric of the War on Terror through the storytelling power of the two primary series in Activision Blizzard's *Call of Duty* franchise since 2007, when it began to engage the contemporary period directly. The first series, *Call of Duty: Modern Warfare,* produced by Infinity Ward, released three titles: *Modern Warfare* (2007), *Modern Warfare 2* (2009), and *Modern Warfare 3* (2011). The second series, produced by Treyarch, includes *Call of Duty: Black Ops* (2010) and *Black Ops 2* (2012). Each of these titles have set their own sales records. The release of *Black Ops 2,* for example, set a record for biggest launch in the history of entertainment, reaching $1 billion in sales faster than its closest rival, the blockbuster film *Avatar* (2009). By that point, the *Call of Duty* franchise had netted more than the box office receipts for *Harry Potter* or *Star Wars,* the two largest movie franchises to date.[9] If war is rendered visible to civilian experience in the West largely as a mediated phenomenon, strange as it may seem, the *Call of Duty* franchise has been one of its primary manifestations on the screen. This essay proceeds first by sketching the major features of war and game studies, especially the way that game aesthetics have shifted from a spectacular mode that invites the player to observe from a distance to an interactive mode characterized by the player's immersion. The next section tracks the discourse of authenticity offered by war-themed game makers and what these claims about verisimilitude mean. Following that, I identify the dominant narrative features that animate the series, which include stories about the causes of conflict, the role of the War on Terror motif in understanding both the past and the future, the legitimacy of international law, and the security state's increasing control of the communications grid. I then offer some concluding thoughts about these games as markers of global privilege. Ultimately, I argue that the *Call of Duty* series, even as it poses as a subversive text that promises to reveal what is hidden by those in power, works to legitimate the War on Terror narrative and many of its most questionable premises.

WAR AND VIDEO GAME STUDIES

The literature on war and game studies is still relatively new, although there have been significant attempts to understand the video game's place at the military-entertainment nexus. Early studies took note of the developing political economy between the military-industrial complex and the commercial gaming industry after the Persian Gulf War in 1991, which, because of its push-button prosecution, earned the nickname of the "video game war."[10] Tracking these relations of political economy has occupied much of the scholarship since. James Der Derian's touchstone *Virtuous War* (2001) examined techniques of military training from the inside, describing the increasing reliance on gamelike simulations, many of which later spilled out onto the commercial market. Der Derian describes this as the Military-Industrial-Media-Entertainment Network (MIME-NET), a simulacral doubling of the war machine that substitutes virtuality, virtuosity, and thus virtue for the ugly realities of state violence.[11] Others, focusing more on the commercial sphere, describe similar institutional synergies from the dissemination of official recruiting games like *America's Army,* to military-commercial partnerships that attempt to brand branches of the military, to collaborations through which military technical expertise is offered in exchange for artistic influence over the game narrative.[12] Following these studies, Matthew Thomas Payne calls game companies "techno-cultural brokers" insofar as they are in the business of fusing one institutional apparatus to another through both command-and-control hardware and rhetorical software.[13]

When scholars attend to the close textual study of games beyond their political economy, they generally employ two broad analytical approaches, narratological and ludological.[14] A narratological analysis sees the game as an unfolding story with some representational relationship with the world outside the game. A number of studies have revealed powerful narrative patterns, especially as they shape collective memory.[15] Aaron Hess, for example, sees *Medal of Honor: Rising Sun* (2003) as part of a raft of World War II nostalgia in the vein of *Saving Private Ryan* (1998) that urged citizens to view the war as a blood sacrifice and a debt to be paid in an uncertain post–Cold War period through privatized patriotism and submission to official policy.[16] With regard to contemporary conflict, scholars have examined how war games enable conflict through vilification. In this vein, Vit Sisler and Johan Höglund survey the field of war-themed games and find all of the classic orientalist modes of constructing the Arab lifeworld.[17] (Sisler and others observe an entirely different set of narratives in games produced by Middle Eastern firms, some of which reside in occupied zones.[18]) Others, like Peter Mantello, have noted that the global neoliberalist forces that have produced the predominant Special Forces-type game have imprinted it with a signature narrative that challenges international law, privatizes conflict, and imbues military action with an overt market logic.[19] In contrast to narratology, the ludological perspective (from the Latin *ludere*, to play) contends that games cannot simply be read as one might read a film. This perspective pays attention to the algorithmic structure of the game in its parameters, possibilities, and procedures. In their respective landmark studies, both Ian Bogost and Alexander Galloway suggest that the aesthetics of subjectivity lie at the heart of the gamic universe, a media platform more significant in its interactive doing than in its static witnessing.[20] Patrick Crogan further suggests that commercial war-themed games, what he collectively regards as the cultural "shadow" of the high-tech military, are a way of inhabiting the world and not simply representing it.[21] Geographers Ian Graham and Ronald Shaw, using psychoanalytic theory, express something similar in the notion that the identity of the war gamer operates in "transitional space" between civilian and military realms, a character that I have called the "virtual citizen-soldier."[22]

Although the present reading of *Call of Duty* leans decidedly in the narratological direction, it acknowledges that the meaning of the narrative—the ability to navigate its crisis and resolution—depends on the formalities of the medium. Certain stories, after all, survive well in the genre of the war-themed first-person shooter, especially those that activate the pleasures of gaining entry into an exclusive world. Moreover, attention to the medium alerts us to the fact that the war-themed game ultimately works to craft the player-subject. With permission from Marshall McLuhan, we might say that the "medium is the metaphor" insofar its significance also resides not only in the way it delivers a "message," but also in the way it metaphorizes the self in the screen avatar.[23] Finally, acknowledging the ludological power of the medium allows us to understand how the war game aesthetic has come to condition the entire media environment as it drifts from spectacular to interactive modes.[24] To take an example from television, when news broke of the 2010 raid on bin Laden's residence in Abbottabad, Pakistan, by the celebrated Seal Team 6, outlets from CNN to CBS rushed to recreate the events using video game-like 3D graphics using first-person perspectives.[25] Even beyond rendering of computer-generated polygon environments, however, the interactive mode can be represented by the flavor and perspective of a practice like embedded reporting, which purported to put the citizen into the soldier's boots. Considering these dynamic shifts, I ask what narrative the game presents and, relatedly, what kind of subject-player the narrative invites. Before visiting what Walter Fisher calls the inner dynamics of "narrative coherence," however, it is necessary to describe how game companies produce authenticity, what Fisher calls "narrative fidelity," to the world the game seeks to represent.[26] In other words, just how seriously do these war games take themselves?

PRODUCING AUTHENTICITY

One of the fundamental appeals used in the marketing of war-themed games is verisimilitude to the real world, including a professed fidelity to the realities of weapons, ballistics, institutions, geography, and history. Alexander Galloway argues that unlike television and film, the interactive character of games exerts a particular "congruence requirement" to tie the "social reality depicted in the game and the social reality known and lived by the player."[27] War-themed games appear to exert this impulse more than most, presenting themselves as a route for taking part in violent struggles depicted via other conduits such as television news. Galloway differentiates, however, between "realism" (social reality) and "realistic-ness" (object reality).[28] As we will see, commercial war games are often high on object reality and low on social reality. The player-soldier has the opportunity to see war "as it is" with meticulously reproduced weapons, while the social and political causes of conflict, and even the distinguishing characteristics of the enemy, fade into obscurity. Borrowing from Jacques Derrida, Ian Bogost calls the intense drive for verisimilitude "simulation fever," which is often coupled with an equally intense disavowal of congruence ("It's just a game") that imbues the text with a profound instability.[29]

Simulation fever is indeed strong in war-themed games, particularly in the drive to recreate playable experiences based on real conflicts. In 2011, for example, Zombie Studies released *Blackwater* for the Xbox Kinect, a game that allows players to fantasize about conducting missions on behalf of the private military contractor, a firm that changed its name first to "Xe" and then "Academi" to flee its reputation for trampling human rights. An advertisement for the game features an immersion scenario that plays on the desires and paradoxes of selling "realism." The gamer dodges bullets whizzing through his living room before gleefully diving behind the couch to escape a grenade that falls at his feet.[30] Another game, *Kuma\War*, attempts to make good on promises of representational fidelity. For nearly a decade, the game, whose staff includes a stable of retired military personnel, has produced playable versions of news events, including the killings of Osama bin Laden and Muammar Gadaffi. The official military recruiting game, *America's Army*, operating since 1999, has staked much of its appeal on the premise that no one can produce a more realistic game than the Army itself. This kind of marketing represents a sharp departure from conventional practice in film and television. These media have traditionally avoided publicizing collaborations with the Pentagon, often burying these acknowledgments at the end of the credits lest they open the producers up to the charge of "propaganda."[31] Gamemakers, in stark contrast, appear to be in a kind of arms race to prove who has closer ties to the military. Big players like *Medal of Honor*, which aimed to reproduce the ongoing conflict in Afghanistan, ran television spots in 2010 that began with these words on the screen: "The following individuals are not actors. They are actual U.S. Special Operations soldiers that [*sic*] consulted on *Medal of Honor*."[32] The interviewees, with blurred faces and disguised voices, testify to the game's authenticity in the kind of dimly lit industrial settings that suggest an "undisclosed location." Gamemakers broadcasted the fact that, with the Pentagon's blessing, they had used more than one hundred microphones to record the sounds of helicopters, gunfire, and explosions at the mock-Iraqi village training facility in Fort Irwin, California.[33]

Beginning in 2007, the marketing of *Call of Duty 4: Modern Warfare* took this strategy a step further by elevating its military advisors to pseudo-celebrity status. In particular, the gamemakers forward-deployed a former Army officer and military historian named Hank Keirsey into a variety of promotional interviews and photo opportunities. Keirsey, whose persona resembled a cross between a jaunty Teddy Roosevelt and the archetypal barking drill sergeant from *Full Metal Jacket* (1987), served mainly as a signifier of authenticity, a liaison who celebrated the meticulously simulated weapons and explained how the game could be used as a tactical trainer.[34] His presence also served to smooth over the inevitable objection voiced, for example, when the Iraq Veterans Against the War lined up famously at an *America's Army* booth in 2007 and sounded off in unison, "War is not a game!"[35] Keirsey functioned as a synecdoche for every soldier's endorsement, neatly melding dissonant selling points: the game as both a hell of a lot of fun and a solemn tribute to the hell of war.[36] In a gesture that sutured the virtual world of the game to real-world conflict, gamemakers briefly flashed Keirsey's actual service dossier in *Call of Duty: Black Ops* (2012). The easy migration of his persona from actual Army officer to supporting role in the virtual world of the game worked to tighten the sense of congruence. With the 2012 release of *Call of Duty: Black Ops 2*, the franchise extended the figure of the celebrity military advisor further. Part of its promotional package was an "investigative documentary" featuring Peter Singer, the author of *Wired for War*, a best-selling exploration of the future of drone and robotic weaponry. Singer set up the game's dramatic arc as he opined about the wonders of a robotic Army. Oliver North also made a showing, advancing the plot by worrying about what happens when the enemy "gets the keys."[37] In the actual game North appears as himself representing the White House National Security Council as he attempts to convince an operative, in the style of the *Rambo* films, that he should get back out in the field. Other figures, voiced by actors, made cameos in the name of narrative fidelity as well, including Manuel Noriega, John F. Kennedy, Fidel Castro, and David Petreaus as future secretary of defense.

The will to represent conflict "realistically" naturally provoked conflicts over representation. In 2013 the International Red Cross launched an initiative to persuade developers to include representations of international humanitarian law.[38] As their website put it, "Game players [should] face the same dilemmas as soldiers."[39] The mere fact that the Red Cross recognized games as an emerging player in shaping public attitudes about real conflict speaks volumes about the centrality of authenticity discourse in games. The organization faces an uphill battle, however, in convincing gamemakers that representing humanitarian law should not make the games any less enjoyable or commercially successful. As we examine the narrative logic of *Call of Duty*, we discover among other things that the pleasures of its ilk fundamentally rely on the exclusion of international law from the frame and the normalization of exceptionalism.

FOUR NARRATIVE STRANDS

The narratives advanced in *Call of Duty*'s contemporary war series are surprisingly consistent in structure. At heart, they rely on the promise that the game will reveal the hidden truth of history, a feature that comports with the imperative to sell verisimilitude. Even as the game interpellates the player-soldier into this privileged world, the real causes of conflict become increasingly shrouded in mystery. The game reveals a multitude of secrets, but rather than complete an alternative picture of how the world works, these secrets only accumulate and feed a sense that conflict arises from an unfathomable evil. This narrative structure ultimately disavows the usefulness of searching for the political causes of conflict and instead automatically promotes the notion that the only reasonable response to a problem is military action. Thus the series has discovered a narrative formula that serves the needs of the gamemakers well, one that entices the player with exclusive entry into authentic conflict, propels gameplay by justifying military action as first resort, and extracts any political consideration that might inhibit the flow of gameplay or jeopardize the gamemakers' relationship with its Pentagon collaborators.[40] What remains is a very simple problem-solution design, where a threat arises practically *ex nihilo* and Special Forces must neutralize the threat by whatever means necessary. As the series repeatedly traverses this design, four narrative threads emerge that (1) suggest the origins of conflict are largely apolitical, (2) rewrite the history of modern conflict in accordance with the official frame of the War on Terror, (3) normalize violations of international law, and (4) advocate for the militarization of communications. The remainder of this section untangles each of these narrative threads in turn.

With respect to the origins of conflict, the prime mover in the *Call of Duty* universe is an aggressor who generally takes the form of a small-time extremist. The antagonist's backstory suggests that he harbors a personal grudge against the West, often for the death of a close family member. This character ultimately plans to exact revenge either by detonating weapons of mass destruction or sparking a global conflagration. Consider the backstory of Raul Menendez, the antagonist in *Black Ops 2*. Menendez was born into a drug cartel in Nicaragua and spends much of his life running drugs and weapons in support of various Marxist uprisings around the world. He is driven mainly by revenge against the "capitalist 1%" for an incident in his youth when an American burned down his own warehouse for the insurance money, a fire that left Menendez's sister badly burned. Later, he achieves worldwide fame and adoration as the leader of a billion-strong movement called Cordis Die. Intent on crippling the economy, Menendez orchestrates a number of attacks on Western interests. Occasionally, Menendez delivers a rationale for these wanton acts of destruction: the "economic anarchy of capitalism," "absurd materialism," and the "sin of opulence."

All of these explanations for violence are bound by their apolitical nature. Despite the veneer of ideological commitment, Menendez's pronouncements come off as weak excuses for violence that is driven purely by a sense of personal vengeance or whose cause is ultimately inscrutable. Such a narrative thus leans heavily on the "argument from evil" that became part of the official War on Terror narrative after 9/11, one that James Aune suggests is "inherently corrosive of democratic politics" and a preface to authoritarianism.[41] The story depicts terrorist motivations as deeply personal and singular, operating as the exact opposite of those that are historically and materially situated. Grievances cannot be addressed, for example, by examining the history of imperialism and revisiting the wisdom of foreign policy. The game methodically applies this depoliticized frame. In the *Modern Warfare* series, for example, what might otherwise be events driven by real political interests (a coup in a Middle Eastern capital and a Russian invasion of the United States) are only surface manifestations of a hidden global terrorist plot to drum up conflict for its own sake. Struggles for territory or resources appear as the product of a global and largely apolitical vendetta that has no discernible cause and thus no solution that can be addressed through policy, deliberation, diplomacy, or reconciliation. In other words, war appears as a purely technical problem amenable only to a military response.

The second dominant narrative reframes the history of conflict from the Cold War onward, suggesting that the logics of the War on Terror, as they have been officially articulated, have been the way the world has always worked. In the first *Black Ops*, for example, the main antagonist, Ivan Dragovich, fights alongside Fidel Castro at the Bay of Pigs invasion and is described by Robert McNamara as "Terrorist #1." One of Dragovich's partners, a man named Krevchenko, allies with the Viet Cong, which leads the player to engage in that conflict. (In a rather bold confusion of imagery, we are told that Krevchenko was "spraying nerve gas all over Vietnam" while photos of the My Lai massacre flash on the screen.) The narrative implies that Dragovich may have even brainwashed the main character to assassinate John F. Kennedy. *Black Ops II* performs a similar historical restitching. The villain this time, Raul Menendez, embittered by the slaying of civilians by the Contras in his native Nicaragua (a fact that the main storyteller in the game explains as "an accident"), builds a large drug cartel and "runs guns" for various "Marxist" groups all over the world. The player chases him to Afghanistan and ends up fighting alongside the Mujahideen against the Soviets, fights forces in Angola supported by both Menendez and Cuba, and travels to Panama as part of Operation Just Cause to squeeze Manuel Noriega for information as to Menendez's whereabouts. The *Black Ops* series in particular reframes conventional Cold War history as a facade behind which the player discovers the real story, which happens to be the War on Terror. In the first game, the story is told through an avatar character who goes through an extensive discovery that he has been brainwashed. A trailer for *Black Ops* conveys the dramatic kernel: "A lie is a lie. Just because they write it down and call it history doesn't make it the truth. We live in a world where seeing is not believing, where only a few know what really happened. We live in a world where everything you know is wrong."[42] The game thus participates in the economy of secrets and conspiracy theory that some scholars suggest is endemic to a contemporary techno-culture marked by distrust in civic institutions, surveillance, and information overload.[43] The revelation in the end is not that truth is ultimately unknowable, however, but rather that the War on Terror is the one true story that explains all that has transpired behind the curtain of received history.

This message also works to naturalize covert military operations while displaying open contempt for international law. The persistent aesthetic is one of redacted documents, hushed tones, talk of who gets to write history, and if-the-public-only-knew inside jokes. In *Modern Warfare 3*, one of the good guys waxes philosophical and paternalistic, lauding secret military operations as the true agents of history: "The duty of every soldier is to protect the innocent, and sometimes that means preserving the lie of good and evil—that war isn't just natural selection played out on a grand scale." The declaration congratulates the player for being in an inner circle where one understands the allegedly esoteric dictum that "might makes right" and thus persistently justifies the prerogative to conduct secret wars and break the rules. As the trailer for *Black Ops* puts it: "You will move without boundaries. You will act above the law. You will use every means necessary to stop the wars that are hidden from the world. And if you succeed, you will do so without recognition. Because you do not exist."[44] Although the game boasts about "preserving the lie of good and evil," it simply introduces a new moral frame to replace the old. Here the player's position is ostensibly defensive, to "stop the wars" begun by the equivalent of Satan in the Manichean tale, a figure cast out of heaven and forever taking revenge. Accomplishing this goal involves breaking the old moral or legal codes, such as the fundamental principles that prohibit state aggression. The action rhythmically hops from one end of the globe to the other in search of the terrorist mastermind, thwart imminent WMD threats, and rescue prisoners. The games' cinematic transitions visually reinforce this attitude toward the sovereignty of other states, typically describing the next mission using a 3-D line-art aesthetic that zooms in on a square in a planetary grid. In addition to maximizing consumer variety (invoking something akin to the Navy's old enticement to "see the world"), the use of disparate locales—from Siberia to Saudi Arabia—visually normalize a globe without state boundaries, a seamless target for clandestine Western military intervention.

The *Call of Duty* series goes out of its way to emphasize that this vigilante player inhabits a secret world where tactics like assassination and torture are not just tolerated but de rigueur. Although the goal of all the games is to hunt and kill the primary antagonist, the games give the nod to many other acts of extrajudicial killing. In *Modern Warfare,* for example, we learn that the U.S. government authorized the assassination of a man in possession of nuclear rods (a mission, incidentally, that the game suggests was not public knowledge by showing mainstream news clips) as well as another person responsible for staging a governmental coup in a Middle Eastern country. In *Black Ops,* one mission leads the player on an attempt to assassinate Fidel Castro just prior to the Bay of Pigs invasion, and in *Black Ops 2,* a briefing informs us that Menendez's father, a drug cartel boss, was "taken out by a sanctioned US assassination." Additionally, torture is a primary means for gaining information. One mission briefing in *Modern Warfare 3* shows before and after photos of a bomb maker who has been tortured (beaten black and blue) for information about the whereabouts of Makarov. "Did he talk?" one asks. "They always talk," comes the unequivocal endorsement of torture's efficacy and righteousness. In *Black Ops,* the player even undergoes torture in first person (in the form of electrical shocks) as U.S. operatives pry for information about nuclear launch codes. While in Afghanistan fighting alongside the Mujahideen in *Black Ops 2,* the player tortures (by beating, stabbing through the hand) and eventually kills a Soviet operative to extract the whereabouts of Menendez. Later, while walking through an abandoned compound in the year 2025, one of the characters motions to an empty room with more nostalgia than condemnation. "At one time the CIA had interrogation rooms like this all over the world," insinuating that perhaps the current terror could have been avoided had publicity not forced the black sites to close.

As the *Call of Duty* series has progressed, its narratives also have kept pace with real-world trends toward the militarization of domestic communications. *Black Ops 2* offers a storyline that legitimates these controls in the name of the War on Terror. Here the narrative recodes legitimate protest as an extension of terrorist violence and the communications grid as primary weapon of terror. The instigator of this violence, Raul Menendez, runs his operation, Cordis Die, specifically through social media. As we learn from news clips, Menendez "crowdsources" riots in various parts of the world by activating this network. To stop him, the U.S. government rather uncontroversially shuts down Cordis Die's Twitter account, which results in a reprisal the next day in which the FBI director is "burned alive." Combined with its rhetoric of the "capitalist 1%," it is not difficult to understand Cordis Die as an analogue for the Occupy movement (perhaps with a pinch of the Arab Spring), although its members are mainly portrayed as dupes of Menendez's anticapitalist demagoguery rather than agents of change: "A billion people think Menendez is their savior," says one of the Special Ops team. In addition to harvesting a legion of followers, Menendez uses the communications network as a weapon of mass destruction. In particular, he conducts a cyberattack on the Chinese stock market, setting Sino-American relations on edge. Here, Cordis Die appears as an overblown and leader-centric version of the hacking group Anonymous, which has conducted a number of comparatively small-time denial-of-service attacks against various corporate webpages. In the style of an Anonymous missive, Menendez communicates to the world via YouTube with his face blurred and under the name "Odysseus." (The "documentary" companion to *Black Ops 2* discussed earlier even directly references Anonymous, noting that this is a world where there is "no longer a defined battlespace," where "the enemy could be anywhere, could be anyone" while flashing a picture of the famous Guy Fawkes mask.[45]) In the ultimate merger of hacker and terrorist, Menendez uses a special code called "Celera" to take control of the U.S. drone fleet and use it to attack Los Angeles during a G20 summit. The narrative thus posits a chain of association linked through Menendez that spans from the crowdsourced riots of Cordis Die to the cyberattacks on global infrastructure to hijacking the American drone fleet. On the way, the narrative folds disparate nonviolent resistance movements into the threat matrix of the War on Terror. Beyond demonizing these movements and expanding the definition of "war," the narrative suggests that the heart of the terror problem is a vulnerable communications infrastructure, one in desperate need of surveillance, securitization, and control.

Each of these of these narrative threads functions on its own to make a particular argument, but together they paint a global conflict marked by invisibility. Here, battle is fought on the terrain of communications with worms and viruses that crawl along the dark hallways of the Web. Shadowy characters, whose motives are truly known only to themselves, instigate the violence. More often than not, the villain under pursuit turns out to be a puppet of an even more cloistered and shadowy villain, suggesting an infinite regression, or, as the Oliver Stone film *JFK* (1991) described the assassination conspiracy, "an enigma wrapped in a mystery." The game continually reminds us that *everything* we know is a lie, and knowledge necessary to make informed decisions as a democracy is simply unavailable. In doing so, the narrative transforms what might otherwise be a healthy critical impulse into a ritual of civic abdication. Moreover, the game normalizes invisible military action, which is carried out through means specifically designed to evade public scrutiny. From beginning to end, the game presents war as an object made real only insofar as it continually vanishes before our eyes. This logic ensures that this version of war extends infinitely into the future, forever evading public comprehension, and forever necessitating the blackest of ops.

CONCLUSION

This essay endeavored to track the narratives embedded in the *Call of Duty* contemporary war series and their relationship to larger political realities. After assessing the ways that the series establishes itself as an authentic representation of war, global political relations, and the military, I described four dominant narrative threads. The first reframes conflict as a largely post-political and post-ideological phenomenon. This premise obscures the complex history of imperial aggression, displacing it with a tale of defensive action. Second, the game rewrites history in the image of the War on Terror. Although feigning a critical posture toward official history, the game hegemonically reinforces the premises of the War on Terror narrative as how the world has always worked. Third, the game narrative normalizes the most controversial practices of the contemporary security state, including torture and clandestine operations. Fourth, the narrative, especially as it culminates in *Black Ops 2*, positions the communications grid as the ultimate battleground. Such a storyline, which collapses weapons of mass destruction into cybersecurity, hacking, and, importantly, the use of social media for protest activities, ultimately advocates folding civic expression into the terrorist threat matrix.[46] Together these narratives present a version of war that exempts itself from public oversight.

What subject does this interactive narrative sculpt? What character does the game invite to step into the *Call of Duty* universe, a world that claims to represent history, honor the troops, faithfully reproduce weapon specs with the military's assistance, and tell the esoteric story of the true extent of the terrorist threat? A clue may lie in the ad campaign for *Black Ops,* whose slogan is "There's a Soldier in All of Us."[47] This campaign's most circulated ad features regular folks and a few celebrities (Kobe Bryant and Jimmy Kimmel) in their civilian attire (business suits, hospital scrubs, construction outfits, flannel shirts, burger chef aprons) running around a desert-themed war zone with guns, grenades, and rocket launchers. The Rolling Stones' "Gimme Shelter" plays in the background, which, along with the "wall of napalm" shot that closes the ad, invokes the cinematic history of the Vietnam War. Halfway through the ad, a phone rings in the pocket of a hotel worker crouched behind a barricade. Although enveloped in explosions, he cheerfully and instinctively answers, "Concierge!," a response signaling that despite the realism and immersion of the game, the shelter of the comfort zone is "just a shout away." Here, the *Call of Duty* experience functions as yet another consumable antidote to the humdrum workaday world. Here state violence is a foregone conclusion, and any opportunity to consider one's civic role in its authorization has been thoroughly expunged. Indeed, the main storyteller in *Black Ops 2* describes the player's role in no uncertain terms: "I'm a soldier. I take orders and get shit done!" This character, even as it promises to empower the player with access to a secret world, casts participation in the game narrative as an exercise in taking orders. Assuming the shape of the soldier-avatar, the player glides through a cascade of "missions" that plot the game narrative, itself ultimately nested within the official narrative that has informed American life since 9/11. As such, one way of thinking about the player-subject of the game is as the final stop in a long chain of command.

The game also invites a particular relationship to danger and human suffering. To be sure, the game erases war's lasting horrors and substitutes a kind of "unreal" violence. Increasingly, however, the function of war-themed games like *Call of Duty* is not the erasure of violence but instead the erasure of a citizen subjectivity responsible for authorizing violence. In the past, the theme of the remote war governed this relation. Distance separated the conflict zone "out there" from the politically detached subject playing real-world violence from the couch. More recently, war games have challenged the aesthetics of remoteness with a more proximate and domestic version of conflict. *Modern Warfare 2*, for example, features combat episodes set in suburban America with tanks rolling down curved streets and bullet-riddled strip malls. *Modern Warfare 3* is set in Washington, D.C., New York, and Paris, and *Black Ops 2* takes place on home turf in a besieged Los Angeles. Such scenes intensify rather than compromise the basic dynamic of privilege. Here the space of social division is across the street rather than across the ocean. Here privilege resides not in the illusion of distance but in the illusion of aligning oneself with the directionality of military power and its payoffs, one of which is access to an expensive, high-tech gaming experience. In this way, entry into *Call of Duty*'s version of geopolitics is a ritual entry into a gated and fortified community, a secure green zone even if the sacrificial red zone is next door. It is no secret that entire game franchises have been built by offering the pleasures of identifying with the security apparatus. Less obvious, however, are the ways these orientations work to normalize civic powerlessness. The drama of the vanishing war, in other words, accompanies a vanishing critical consciousness regarding the ways the security state may be pitched against one's own interests.

NOTES

1. Martin Barker, *A "Toxic Genre": The Iraq War Films* (London: Pluto Press, 2011).
2. William Marsden, "Hollywood, Washington Getting Cosier; Unease Growing as *Zero Dark Thirty* Shows Extent of Co-operation," *The Gazette*, January 12, 2013, A17.
3. David S. Cloud, "Politics and 'Zero Dark'; A Draft Pentagon Report Includes Emails between Screenwriter and Defense Official," *Los Angeles Times*, June 6, 2013, D4.
4. John Andersen, "On Active Duty for the Movies (Real Ammo)," *New York Times*, February 12, 2012, AR16.
5. Chris Suellentrop, "War Games," *New York Times*, September 12, 2010, 62; see also Nina Hunteman, 'Playing with Fear: Catharsis and Resistance in Military-Themed Video Games,' in *Joystick Soldiers: The Politics of Play in Military Video Games* (New York: Routledge, 2010), 223–336.
6. Ana Douglas, "Here Are the 10 Highest Grossing Video Games Ever," *Business Insider*, June 13, 2012, http://www.businessinsider.com/here-are-the-top-10-highest-grossing-video-games-of-all-time-2012-6.
7. Corey Mead, "Military Recruiters Have Gone Too Far," *Time*, September 17, 2013, http://ideas.time.com/2013/09/17/military-recruiters-have-gone-too-far/.
8. Tim Cross, "All the World's a Game," *The Economist*, December 10, 2011, http://www.economist.com/node/21541164.
9. Nick Turner, "Call of Duty Tops $1 B in 15 Days," *The Gazette*, December 6, 2012, A28.
10. J. C. Herz, *Joystick Nation* (New York: Little, Brown, 1997); Busah Ebo, "War as Popular Culture: The Gulf Conflict and the Technology of Illusionary Entertainment," *Journal of American Culture* 18, no. 3 (1995): 19–25.
11. James Der Derian, *Virtuous War: Mapping the Military-Industrial-Media-Entertainment-Network*, 2nd ed. (London and New York: Routledge, 2009).
12. Marcus Power, "Digitized Virtuosity: Video War Games and Post-9/11 Cyber-deterrence," *Security Dialogue* 38, no. 2 (2007): 271–288; Roger Stahl, "Have You Played the War on Terror?," *Critical Studies in Media Communication* 23, no. 2 (2006), 112–130; Tanner Mirrlees, "Digital Militainment by Design: Producing and Playing SOCOM: U.S. Navy SEALs," *International Journal of Media and Cultural Politics* 5, no. 3 (2009): 161–181; Toby Miller, "The Shameful Trinity: Game Studies, Empire, and the Cognitariat," in *Guns, Grenades, and Grunts: First-Person Shooter Games*, ed. Gerald A. Voorhees, Joshua Call, and Katie Whitlock (London: Continuum, 2012), 113–130; Nick Dyer-Witheford, *Games of Empire: Global Capitalism and Video Games* (Minneapolis: University of Minnesota Press, 2009); Ed Halter, *From Sun Tzu to XBox: War and Video Games* (New York: Thunder's Mouth Press, 2006); Matthew Thomas Payne, "Manufacturing Militainment: Videogame Producers and

Military Brand Names," in *War Isn't Hell, It's Entertainment: Essays on Visual Media and the Representation of Conflict*, ed. Rikke Schubart et al. (Jefferson, NC: McFarland, 2009), 238–55; Robin Andersen and Marin Kurti, "From America's Army to Call of Duty: Doing Battle with the Military Entertainment Complex," *Democratic Communiqué* 23, no. 1 (2009): 45–65.

13. Matthew Thomas Payne, "Marketing Military Realism in Call of Duty 4 Modern Warfare," *Games and Culture* 7, no. 4 (2012): 305–327.

14. Jesper Juul, "Games Telling Stories?" *Game Studies* 1, no. 1 (2001), http://www.gamestudies.org/0101/juul-gts/; Markku Eskelinen, "The Gaming Situation," *Game Studies* 1, no. 1 (2001), http://www.gamestudies.org/0101/eskelinen/.

15. Patrick Crogan, "Gametime: History, Narrative, and Temporality in Combat Flight Simulator II," in *The Video Game Theory Reader*, ed. Mark J. P. Wolf and Bernard Perron (New York: Routledge, 2003), 275–302; James Campbell, "Just Less Than Total War: Simulating World War II as Ludic Nostalgia," in *Playing the Past: History and Nostalgia in Video Games*, ed. Zach Whalen and Laurie N. Taylor (Nashville, TN: Vanderbilt University Press, 2008), 183–200; Tracy Fullerton, "Documentary Games: Putting the Player in the Path of History," in *Playing the Past: History and Nostalgia in Video Games*, ed. Zach Whalen and Laurie N. Taylor (Nashville, TN: Vanderbilt University Press, 2008), 215–238.

16. Aaron Hess, "You Don't Play, You Volunteer: Narrative Public Memory Construction in *Medal of Honor: Rising Sun*," *Critical Studies in Media Communication* 24, no. 4 (2007): 339–356.

17. Vít Šisler, "Digital Arabs Representation in Video Games," *European Journal of Cultural Studies* 11, no. 2 (2008): 203–220; Johan Höglund, "Electronic Empire: Orientalism Revisited in the Military Shooter," *Game Studies* 8, no. 1 (2008), http://gamestudies.org/0801/articles/hoeglund.

18. David Machin and Usama Suleiman, "Arab and American Computer War Games: The Influence of a Global Technology on Discourse," *Critical Discourse Studies* 3, no. 1 (2006): 1–22.

19. Peter Mantello, "Playing Discreet War in the US: Negotiating Subjecthood and Sovereignty through Special Forces Video Games," *Media, War & Conflict* 5, no. 3 (2012): 269–283.

20. Alexander R. Galloway, *Gaming: Essays on Algorithmic Culture* (Minneapolis: University of Minnesota Press, 2006); Ian Bogost, *Unit Operations: An Approach to Videogame Criticism* (Cambridge, MA: MIT Press, 2006).

21. Patrick Crogan, *Gameplay Mode: War, Simulation, and Technoculture* (Minneapolis: University of Minnesota Press, 2011); Crogan, "Gametime."

22. Ian Graham and Ronald Shaw, "Playing War," *Social & Cultural Geography* 11, no. 8 (2010): 789–803.

23. Marshall McLuhan, *Understanding Media: The Extensions of Man*, paper ed. (Cambridge, MA: MIT Press, 1994).

24. Roger Stahl, *Militainment, Inc.: War, Media, and Popular Culture* (New York: Routledge, 2010).

25. "Who Really Killed Bin Laden? (2013)," http://www.youtube.com/watch?v=ZASyzwpZIfY&feature=youtube_gdata_player; "Minutes Felt Like Hours in Bin Laden Raid (2011)," http://www.youtube.com/watch?v=WzNzVQSmIac&feature=youtube_gdata_player; "CNN: Inside the Raid That Killed Osama Bin Laden (2011)," http://www.youtube.com/watch?v=THLcqxgkaok&feature=youtube_gdata_player.

26. Walter Fisher, "Narrative as Human Communication Paradigm: The Case of Public Moral Argument," *Communication Monographs* 51, no. 1 (1984): 1–22.

27. *Galloway, Gaming*, 83.

28. Alexander R. Galloway, "Social Realism in Gaming," *Game Studies*, 4, no. 1 (2004), http://www.gamestudies.org/0401/galloway/.
29. Bogost, *Unit Operations*, 108.
30. "Blackwater—Official Debut Trailer for Kinect (2011)," http://www.youtube.com/watch?v=c_VobftQAqc&feature=youtube_gdata_player.
31. David L. Robb, *Operation Hollywood: How the Pentagon Shapes and Censors the Movies* (Amherst, NY: Prometheus Books, 2004).
32. "Medal of Honor—PC | PS3 | Xbox 360—Monday Night Football TV Advert Video Game Trailer HD (2010)," https://www.youtube.com/watch?v=LRcxbB2jtFE.
33. Suellentrop, "War Games."
34. "Call of Duty: Modern Warfare 3—Interview W/ Military Advisor Hank Keirsey (2011)," 2013, http://www.youtube.com/watch?v=JbgkCZ1ekq8&feature=youtube_gdata_player.
35. "IVAW Confronts Military Recruiters in St Louis (2007)," http://www.youtube.com/watch?v=fHz4a_sgqCg&feature=youtube_gdata_player.
36. See an appraisal of Keirsey's role in Payne, "Marketing Military Realism in Call of Duty 4 Modern Warfare."
37. "Documentary—Official Call of Duty Black Ops 2 (2012)," http://www.youtube.com/watch?v=Gm5PZGb30yQ&feature=youtube_gdata_player.
38. "Red Cross Wants Video Games to Get Real on War Crimes," *NPR: All Tech Considered*, October 12, 2013, www.npr.org/blogs/alltechconsidered/2013/10/12/232480753/red-cross-wants-video-games-to-get-real-on-war-crimes.
39. *International Committee of the Red Cross*, "Video Games and Law of War—ICRC," http://www.icrc.org/eng/resources/documents/film/2013/09-28-ihl-video-games.htm.
40. These narratives are not necessarily restricted to games; they can also be found, almost point for point, in contemporary releases from franchises such as the Jason Bourne series, James Bond, and *Mission Impossible*.
41. James Arnt Aune, "The Argument from Evil in the Rhetoric of Reaction," *Rhetoric & Public Affairs* 6, no. 3 (2003): 518–522.
42. "Call of Duty: Black Ops—World Premiere Uncut Trailer (2010)," http://www.youtube.com/watch?v=OtRnpC7ddv8&feature=youtube_gdata_player.
43. Jodi Dean, *Publicity's Secret: How Technoculture Capitalizes on Democracy* (Ithaca, NY: Cornell University Press, 2002); Mark Andrejevic, *Infoglut: How Too Much Information Is Changing the Way We Think and Know* (New York: Routledge, 2013).
44. "Call of Duty: Black Ops—Single Player Trailer (2010)," http://www.youtube.com/watch?v=lJerWQhM16k&feature=youtube_gdata_player.
45. *Documentary—Official Call of Duty Black Ops 2*.
46. Michael S. Schmidt and Colin Moynihan, "F.B.I. Counterterrorism Agents Monitored Occupy Movement, Records Show," *New York Times*, December 25, 2012, A18.
47. "Call of Duty: Black Ops TV Commercial: 'There's a Soldier in All of Us' (2010)," http://www.youtube.com/watch?v=Pblj3JHF-Jo&feature=youtube_gdata_player.

7 · A CINEMA OF CONSOLATION

Post-9/11 Super-Invasion Fantasy

DE WITT DOUGLAS KILGORE

The striking thing about September 11, 2001, and the War on Terror that followed is the way in which a spectacular event was momentarily rendered invisible, placed beyond the seeable either by reason of its traumatic visibility or by responses to the political history of images inherited from previous conflicts—especially the Vietnam War. In the month following 9/11, the American film industry became embroiled in a moral panic about what to do with the iconic, cinematic visibility of the New York City skyline. One initial solution was to digitally excise the World Trade Center Towers (WTC).[1] This brief banishment of the Towers from sight, a hysterical attempt to exorcise an iconic vulnerability, is of a piece with the decision of the administration of President George W. Bush to censor images of the damage caused by a new War on Terror. By managing media access to battlefields, prisons, and returning coffins, the government hoped to hide the nature and cost of the war.[2] If one of the functions of mainstream cinema is to create moving pictures of the way we live, it can also conceal uncomfortable truths. But once seen, certain public events cannot be unseen. They also may be disturbingly insistent, either as artifacts of human memory or because they are things that we have seen before and expect to see again. The Twin Towers became an absent presence, lingering in memory but also almost instantly reappearing in U.S. visual culture.[3] Under these circumstances, the willful blindness of immediate post-9/11 censorship could not be sustained. Hollywood's panicked erasure of New York City's iconic towers created a hole that had to be filled.

In popular adventure films, invisibility became a challenge. It has been met by a cinema of consolation that filters the historic trauma through the well-established generic conventions of fictional alien invasions, renewing the cathartic potential of specular scenes of urban destruction for popular amusement. I argue that in the decade following 9/11, mainstream cinema found ways of addressing the trauma of that real-world invasion by taking the anxious tradition of alien invasion and linking it to the more optimistic romance of salvation by superheroes. Through the super-invasion genre, popular filmmakers solved the challenge of mounting spectacles that bore a resemblance to the 9/11 disaster while avoiding direct reference to its painful reality. I propose that the rise of the superhero genre in mainstream action and science fiction films and its imbrication with the alien invasion trope is a direct response to the disappearance of the WTC. The result is a hybrid that uses genre to make 9/11-style devastation newly visible (as entertainment) while accepting the physical disappearance of the old World Trade Center towers. The general effect is to offer an ending in which invasion is only a prelude for survival and renewal.

This conversion of two familiar genres into a new, vigorous cinematic hybrid allows several things: (1) Action adventure films can continue staging fantastic spectacles in which famous monuments and entire cities may be turned to rubble without regret; (2) diegetic worlds may be created in which heroic, super-powered American icons will save the nation from any outside threat; and (3) these films invite their audiences into a hyperreality (a nice description for multi-picture franchises such as *Star Trek, Star Wars, Harry Potter,* and the Marvel Cinematic Universe) that stands for but replaces the real world. Multiplex audiences—particularly for films that offer science fiction and fantasy realities—are asked to invest in coherently designed worlds that often operate according to an ahistorical narrative logic. If the invasion narrative often focuses attention on national vulnerability, the superhero genre gives us champions with the power to deny any invader ultimate victory. In this fantastic diegetic, the ramshackle historical circumstances of 9/11 and the War on Terror disappear. The world witnesses an invasion of a peaceful New York City but sees it saved by its heroic defenders. In the hyperreal visions offered by post-9/11 science fiction and fantasy films, invasions are turned back and invaders are defeated. This cinematic resolution helps conceal the upheaval caused by 9/11 and seeks to heal the cultural wounds it inflicted.

The immediate reaction to the World Trade Center tragedy was conditioned by how similar it was to a Hollywood movie. The disaster seemed too much like an outsized special effect to be real. This observation has been made so often that is has become banal. However, Jean Baudrillard produces an intriguing variant by making the link between "the countless disaster movies" and the destruction of the towers as not only something that the terrorists desired but that *we* wished for: "We have dreamt of this event. . . . Everyone without exception has dreamt of it—because no one can avoid dreaming of the destruction of any power that has become hegemonic to this degree."[4] This is why, Baudrillard argues, the destruction of iconic buildings/monuments like the World Trade Center has such hallucinatory, symbolic power: why we feel it as something that has happened before. Perhaps, we might add, this is also why the fictional devastation of American real estate remains politically viable, commercially profitable, and aesthetically satisfying. Images like the destruction of the World Trade Center towers persist because they conform to a tradition of cinematic invasion spectacles in science fiction from *Things to Come* (1936) to *The War of the Worlds* (1953) to *Independence Day* (1996).[5] These films are part of the archive that both prepared us for 9/11 and also made the event surreal. That archive constitutes a Baudrillardian simulation overlaying the actuality we inhabit.

Several decades of urban action-adventures such as *The Towering Inferno* (1974) and *Die Hard* (1988) and the science fiction films mentioned have accustomed American audiences to expensively crafted set pieces in which iconic buildings—representing democracy or capitalism—have been destroyed for fun and profit.[6] These artfully crafted sequences of devastation are an essential part of popular filmmaking, a significant commodity of U.S.-based cinema as a global business. They function not only as catharsis but also represent the cherished values that a foreign or alien power might threaten. Geoff King and Tanya Krzywinska, writing in 2000, note that in these films,

> we are able to experience the spectacle of New York and the White House being blown to smithereens in a convincing way, while knowing quite clearly that this is a sophisticated piece of artifice. We can enjoy the spectacular destruction of such hallowed landmarks, taking pleasure in what appears to be a highly detailed realism of images that we are unlikely ever to see in the real world. At the same time, we can enjoy the knowledge that this is not real, and that we are not so naïve as to be fooled; and, in case it matters to us, that such icons of Western democracy and power remain safely intact.[7]

These pleasurable cinematic shocks also work as narrative triggers that catalyze heroic action, the courageous response to the physical peril raised by external threats. Even as actual political and social forces sought to make the burgeoning violence of the War on Terror invisible, Hollywood's generic conventions, and the economic imperatives that secure them, could only seek ways to make it visible. This point can certainly be made with reference to documentaries and realist narrative films that have sought to capture the sights, sounds, events, and emotions of 9/11 and its aftermath. My interest, however, is in the popular cinema that both informed the initial perception of 9/11 as an unbelievable spectacle and has continued to produce visual narratives that both aestheticize and occlude violence.

In science fiction and fantasy film, visuality is strongly marked by nonrealist modes of storytelling. Genre, in other words, provides the vocabulary of particular plots and the iconography that makes them viable as effective cinematic experiences. Thus genre is the filter through which an audience's experience of and response to traumatic, politically charged events might be imaginatively rehearsed and remembered.[8] The western, for example, was not only a significant entertainment in the early to mid-twentieth century, it also served as the lens through which events such as the Battle of Little Big Horn (1876) [*Little Big Man,* 1976] and the Johnson County War (1889–1893) [*The Virginian,* 1929] were viewed.[9] Similarly, alien invasion films metaphorize internal and external threats to national security. This particular genre has a long history in American cinema, beginning with classic statements from the 1950s such as *The War of the Worlds* (1953), *Invasion of the Body Snatchers* (1956), and the cult B-movie *The Blob* (1958).[10] These Cold War–era thrillers are the direct models for the fantasy-oriented post-9/11 motion pictures through which the trauma of 9/11 and the War on Terror have been processed and resolved in American popular culture.

The continuous process of adaptation, even cannibalization, that is a signal feature of Hollywood image-making means that the narrative conventions of times past are exploited to explain immediate events: old bottles are used for new wine. In effect, current super-invasion films gain credibility from the familiar iconography and plots unique to their generic affiliations. The result is a fantastic estrangement in which real-world trauma is suspended and abstracted by a stable set of heroic images and a simple moral framework that invokes a terrible prospect only to console the viewer. The shock of an unprecedented invasion of American soil is transformed into a series of pleasurable spectacular effects under the filmmaker's control. From this emerges a cinema of consolation that softens the cultural shock produced by 9/11, allowing its audiences to accept the reality of the actual incursion and the War on Terror within the narrative frame of heroic science fantasy. What I am calling a cinema of consolation is a generic strategy that allows new events, fresh catastrophes, and recent trauma to be absorbed into well-worn modes of seeing. It is a way of defending us against new shocks; it forces rising problems into old solutions. The very visible destruction of the 9/11 attack is hidden, exchanged for invasion as an artful construct that is finely controlled and satisfyingly resolved.

The alien invasion genre, the popular form that helped found modern science fiction, was renewed through the emergence of the superhero genre in motion pictures after 9/11. In this regard, the superhero films of the Marvel Cinematic Universe (MCU), particularly *Captain America: The First Avenger* (2011) and *The Avengers* (2012) are striking in the ways they make the images produced by 9/11 disappear as a traumatic reality and reappear as adventure.[11] These films are high-technology visual contrivances offering a fantastic revision of actual historic events and political threats. As dramatic narratives, they are also heroic fantasies that conform to the narrative effects identified for fairy stories by J.R.R. Tolkien: recovery, escape, and consolation.[12] Critical to this structure are unambiguous heroes and villains, virtues and vices. The MCU provides its audiences with a fantastic transposition from a contemporary world characterized by terror and perpetual war to one in which the invading alien Other is placed beyond any sympathy, a fractured humanity finds a common salvation, and the besieged United States recovers its martial standing.

Heroic fantasy is a useful frame for this analysis because it clarifies what is at stake in the post-9/11 confluence of alien invasion with iconic superheroes. If historical reality seems uniquely troubled by conflicts over the response to Islamic extremism and concern about an increasingly powerful surveillance state in support of perpetual war, then super-invasion cinema offers narratives in which fantastic invaders are defeated in roughly two and a half hours. As high-tech fairy tales, the goal of these films is the thrill and relief experienced when the threatening Other is defeated, destroyed, or exiled. Such emotion is secured by images depicting the successful defense and restoration of an embattled New York City.

During the past eight decades superhero comics have ebbed and flowed in response to their engagement with domestic and international problems. They initially emerged as an inventive response to the stress of the Great Depression and reached tremendous heights of popularity during World War II. In some ways, the current cycle of superhero films recapitulates that foundational moment, creating a popular space in which its creators might make sense of a dangerous world and bring it under narrative control. The films of the Marvel Cinematic Universe have been the principal beneficiary of the political atmosphere produced by 9/11 and its aftermath. In this film franchise, the superheroes of Marvel Comics are deployed to face foreign or alien threats to American life. *Captain America: The First Avenger (CAFA)* best illustrates the cultural provenance of the popular invasion narrative and its recycling for current use.

CAFA reminds us that modern American invasion films often have World War II and that conflict's iconic adversary, the Nazis, as influential sources.[13] Indeed, comic books, the medium that created Captain America, popularized the superhero genre by pitting characters like him against Hitler and other cartoon avatars of fascism.[14] Captain America, created by Joe Simon and Jack Kirby in 1941, arrived just in time to gain immense popularity during the war. Bradford Wright notes that the first issue of *Captain America Comics* "depicted the ultra-American hero slugging Adolf Hitler in the face almost a full year before the United States declared War on the Axis."[15] The character is a deliberately patriotic symbol, a super-soldier whose mission was to be the incarnation of the

Allied nations' fighting spirit. *CAFA* places us within that history while producing a fantastic transposition that replaces German militarism with the world-conquering villainy of the cartoonish Red Skull, a Nazi super-villain. Though equally hyperbolic, the flag-draped Captain America was intended by his Jewish American creators to be a superman who embodied an idealized national character. In a medium that emerged from the pulp fictions of urban vigilantes, he was an explicitly political hero who fought fascism at the moment of that ideology's highest prestige in American life and thought.[16]

As nebbishy Steve Rogers, Captain America was initially too small and fragile for active military service. But, desperate to fight the Nazi menace, he volunteered to test a super-soldier serum. Crucially, he was not corrupted by his empowerment and maintained his ability to empathize with the weak and their aspirations; indeed, he is their champion.[17] It is these values that *Captain America: First Avenger* resuscitates in 2011 as a visible sign of a United States worthy of defense against the alien and illiberal forces his original creators despised.

This appeal to the motivations of a heroic soldier elevates the virtues presumed necessary to national security in invasion narratives. In *CAFA,* resistance is not premised on appeals to constitutional principles or democratic governance. Rather the film offers a soldier's ethos that valorizes the safety of fellow combatants. Indeed, this heroic ideal even allows for defiance of authority in defense of the soldier's battlefield-oriented morality. However, this perhaps admirable motivation deflects judgment about the reasons for war and diverts attention from the institutions that are invested in making war. By reminding us of a historically sanctified "good war," *CAFA* implies that the patriotic heroism of the past can save today's world.

September 11 produced a crisis in American values. It exposed their vulnerability, challenging culture-creators to rearticulate what those values are and why they are worth defending. The MCU uses Captain America to reinforce popular conceptions about what an American hero is and the values that spur him or her to act. That he represents an old-fashioned ideal is the point of the character's vivid cinematic incarnation in post-9/11 cinema. In this way, old images are used to secure the future. If we accept this premise, however, it looks like an exercise in simple nostalgia. The international conflicts of World War II were very different from the independent terrorism executed by Al-Qaeda. The key is in the way that superhero conflicts are personalized. The hero's personal virtue is levied against a wrong represented by a villain. In the super-invasion film, conflict with adversarial states disappear behind the cartoon adversary, who is an inhuman racial other. The human complexity that may be found in merely human insurgents, such as Al-Qaeda or the Taliban, is exchanged for a simple evil that must be defeated.

In the superhero invasion narrative adversaries are rarely pictured as conventional human beings. In *CAFA,* Captain America's nemesis, the Red Skull, sets the standard. Initially he appears to be an ordinary Caucasian man. Indeed, he could pass as the masculine embodiment of the Third Reich. When that human façade is stripped away to reveal a red-skinned, skull-like face, its death-like design signals that he is the Nazi superman as an inhuman demon. This fantastic creature literalizes the "satanization of the enemy" that Robert L. Ivie notes is part of dramas seeking the "utter extermination of the evil Others."[18] It is a difference that confirms the character's faith in the ideology of racial superiority he articulates. This Nazi superman is, therefore, the inhuman invader who may be destroyed without regret. In *CAFA*'s diegesis, this supervillain is a placeholder for national enemies such as Osama bin Laden and Saddam Hussein. But this fantastic creation also offers a momentary escape from the conflict represented by those figures, substituting well-established images of mid-century political villainy for the unsettled, often racialized iconography of Islamic extremism. Popular culture's permanent war against Nazi Germany implies that the values and symbols of World War II may be used to define what is at stake in the War on Terror.

Cinematic monsters are almost always avatars of racial difference, particularly in science fiction and superhero narratives.[19] Their existence constitutes a disruption of natural order that cannot be integrated into common experience. Their appearance implies that the good, familiar world could be transformed into something else; a terrible new order that would replace customary relationships and values. The monster always also invokes fear that others of its kind may appear. Like Frankenstein's creature, any particular monster may be only the first of a "race of devils" who will come to prey on and then, perhaps, replace humanity.[20]

The monstrous Other illustrates what is always at stake in invasion narratives. The figure's embodiment of a fantastic racialized physiognomy makes clear the difference between hero and villain. This type of villain is a sublime but comforting creature whose principal function is to gift the hero with moral clarity. Hero and monstrous alien occupy an ethical battlefield where the difference between right and wrong is clear and nonnegotiable. The often-metaphorical racial difference between antagonists is also an easily digestible way of marking the outlander as an implacable enemy who must be destroyed. Thus, although superhero invasion films seek to eclipse memory of the 9/11 attack, they also reinforce public sentiment in favor of a strong national defense.

The importance of a carefully designed alien Other to the moral impact of an invasion narrative is demonstrated in Joss Whedon's *The Avengers* (2012), the sixth film of the MCU franchise and, perhaps, a paradigmatic expression of the post-9/11 invasion fantasy that consoles its audiences. Here the supernormal enemies of the Earth-as-America are more than mere criminals within reach of the law. They are demons outside of it. They invade the world to remake it in their own image. Their motive is always absurdly simple and unsympathetic, lacking the complexities of real-world conflicts. Their invasion would eliminate any semblance of human heterogeneity, replacing it with totalitarian simplicity. Loki, the Asgardian god who is the principle antagonist of *The Avengers,* asks only one thing of the human race: kneel.

This demand is made not with the goal of extracting any particular material good but with the aim of securing a racial subjugation that would erase all notions of human rights, liberty, or independence. That Loki is a Norse god and makes his demand in Germany, and that an old man visually coded as Jewish stands up in defiance, underscores the cultural and historical resonance that Whedon builds into his screenplay. We are asked to understand this weird adventure picture in light of the great racial conflicts of the past century. Perhaps we do not need Captain America's red, white, and blue shield to make the case for defiance of this racist logic. He arrives in any case and declares the thematic link to Nazi Germany, the racist regime he helped defeat when it launched an attack on the United States of America. Thus the film's message is clarified, justifying the fight between good and evil that follows. If the images produced by 9/11 and the War on Terror are largely invisible, the superhero invasion film replaces them with a Manichean iconography. This makes it possible to see any threat from outside the nation as one between good and evil, freedom and slavery. If the free world is to endure, the alien must be fought. In *The Avengers* this point is amplified by the appearance of the Chitauri, reptilian extraterrestrials that use Loki as a scout for their attack.

The fear of invasion by a powerful alien culture, represented as a teeming, animalistic horde, links *The Avengers* to current worries about Al-Qaeda and its affiliated organizations.[21] However, as avatars of pulp villainy, the Chitauri represent no articulate political program or history in common with their terrestrial (Western) adversaries. Thus they are an empty image of difference onto which current fears may be projected. A principal effect of *The Avengers* is, therefore, to offer alien invaders as an image so open that topical reference to 9/11, Al-Qaeda or its leaders, and the overall War on Terror may disappear behind the spectacle. In this way, the superhero invasion genre manages audience perceptions by diverting attention from the real-world referents that inspire them.

Marvel's Chitauri fits the pattern that H. G. Wells established for evil alien conquerors more than a century ago in *The War of the Worlds* (1898).[22] Unlike his Martians, the Chitauri are humanoids and can communicate in a suitably distorted English. Like the Martians, they are rendered in a palette of dark metallic hues, signaling their racial difference from humankind. When their troops appear in earthly light they are shown as a peculiar amalgam of human and reptile. As the Chitauri army swarms from a dark hole in the clear sky above midtown Manhattan, they provide more than enough targets for our heroes to shoot, wrestle, and punch. It is the well-choreographed action that follows their arrival that makes the alien invasion, as a cinematic form, a visual and technological marvel that entertains us. The excitement generated by this battle sequence places an aesthetic polish on the film's overall theme of racial conflict. It provides the emotional release promised by character conflict and produces moments of kinetic beauty. As an aesthetic echo of 9/11, *The Avengers* provides the formal order possible only in cinema. Its iconic superheroes furnish a quick and visually satisfying victory. The actual event is thereby repositioned as a momentary nightmare that is banished by light from the silver screen.

The power of cinematic action to stand in for an actual event is highlighted by the professionalism of *The Avengers* set-piece invasion sequence. The film's attack on New York City is carefully controlled in a way that both excites and comforts the viewer. Whedon and his editors, Jeffrey Ford and Lisa Lassek, set up a sequence of tableaux and movements designed to awe but not frighten or confuse. The camera personalizes the action and makes it sharply legible. The invaders project overwhelming force into the city, demolishing a large part of midtown Manhattan. This is offset by the defensive actions of the Avengers as they take orders and deploy through rapidly shifting interior and exterior spaces. They rescue civilians and dispatch alien humanoids with a variety of fantastic weapons. The action is choreographed to avoid any depiction of human death or suffering on screen.

This hyperactive sequence is structured around a series of visual rests that create a distinct rhythmic pattern: a moment when Captain America picks himself up after saving a room full of citizens, a slow-motion tableau vivant in which Thor's hammer and Cap's shield return to their hands before being thrown again, and a comedic beat when the Hulk contemptuously punches Thor after they defeat a room full of enemies. By giving theatrical definition to the action, these moments humanize what would otherwise be a visual jumble. The filmmakers' fine control over their images takes an event that would be perceptually unintelligible in real time and creates thrilling amusement. Thus both filmmakers and audiences regain visual mastery over the devastation of a great American city. If the Al-Qaeda operatives who executed 9/11 can be said to have taken Hollywood spectacle into the real world, then *The Avengers* takes back the initiative.

The final battle of this superhero film indicates how current popular cinema aestheticizes invasion, making it safe to bring spectacular and lucrative destruction back to New York City.[23] Much of the battle takes place around Grand Central Station, the familiar entrance to the metropolis. The New York City skyline is imperiled by the Chitauri invasion, as well as by a nuclear missile fired by desperate politicians. Signature as well as fictional skyscrapers (the Stark Tower, which replaces the actual MetLife Building behind and above Grand Central Station) are heavily damaged or destroyed. Crowds of people are shown reacting to and fleeing from the chaos. Although the action is focused on midtown Manhattan, the audience cannot help but be reminded of the scenes that survive from 2001. We are invited to imaginatively rehearse 9/11 with the crucial difference that the spectacle is completely under the filmmaker's control. The heroic response is immediate, thrilling, and successful, with no lingering traumatic aftermath. The shock occasioned by the fall of the Towers finally fades before the return of a traditional "innocent" pleasure.

The post-invasion denouement of *The Avengers* is as important to the consolation offered by the film as its well-designed battle. The ruined city quickly rebuilds. A handcuffed Loki is taken to an Asgardian judgment, an ordinary woman recognizes the heroism of Captain America, politicians gesticulate before wrecked buildings in search of political advantage, Iron Man plans the renovation of Stark Tower with his lover, and the rest of the team leave for well-earned freedom. These vignettes signal the cozy restoration of ordinary life; salvation is a return to normalcy. If the post-9/11 film of alien invasion seeks to supplant the traumatic images produced by the fall of the World Trade Center towers, it does so by assuring its audiences that if war comes home, America's heroes and the way of life they represent will prevail.

As stated earlier, *The Avengers* follows the overall epistemological logic identified by Tolkien in "On Fairy Stories." The viewer is invited into a world on the brink of a technoscientific transformation that would reshape New York City (if not the world) into an energy-rich, ecological utopia. Loki's invasion forces a group of heroes together who must recover the communal, old-fashioned truths that make it possible to stand against extra-planetary invaders. The inhuman racial threat represented by the Other is defeated. The suffering, confusion, and destruction occasioned by the invasion turns to relief and then joy. As Tolkien would have it, the invasion might be interpreted as a eucatastrophe, the sudden joyous turn that leads to a happy ending.[24] The post 9/11 superhero invasion film follows a fairy-tale logic that underwrites the narrative consolation it offers.

Consolation, however, presumes the story has come to a satisfactory conclusion. Tolkien's high-fantasy model is premised on consolation that heralds a new age. Relief leads to a glimpse of the harmonious world to come.[25] However, Whedon's screenplay breaks this pattern by presenting a post-credit anticlimax in which joy is undercut by a tired melancholy. The exhausted Avengers visit a battle-damaged ethnic restaurant and eat *shawarma,* Arabic for the fast-food sandwich commonly known as a gyro in the United States. By signaling the existence of thriving Middle Eastern businesses in America's great cities, Whedon gestures toward the human diversity his superheroes defend. It is a subtle cue that the filmmaker's iteration of post-9/11 invasion fantasy seeks to offset the kind of xenophobia that would transform *shawarma* into "Liberty" or "Freedom" wraps. The world (as multiracial/multicultural New York City) is worth saving because it has such things in it; a representation of the human diversity that the alien Other would destroy. However, the scene strikes a pensive note, comically overturning the expectation of a trumpet-blaring victory march. This is a momentary return to ordinary life, the exhausted, distracted reprieve before the dawn of another battle. Perhaps the characters sense what we already know, that their hard-won peace is a preamble for the next bellicose episode in the MCU franchise. Victory is only the prelude to perpetual war.

The Avengers, however, works hard to avoid the notion that this anticipation endorses what Robert L. Ivie identifies as the "republic of fear" that characterized the Bush administration's rhetorical conduct of the War on Terror.[26] Joss Whedon flirts with this possibility only to diminish it as the true meaning of the film's post-invasion order. In another closing credit sequence when the Other reports failure to the architect of Loki's invasion, the audience is given an inspiring portrait of a free people: "They are not the cowering wretches we were promised. They stand. They are unruly and, therefore, cannot be ruled. To challenge them is to court death."

This chastened speech casts a flattering light upon the United States and its (super) heroes. The consolation offered by *The Avengers* is reinforced by a newly revived martial capacity that is shown as dangerous and wonderful. It is all too obvious that the film's domestic and international audiences are invited to accept the Other's judgment as both a call to arms and a warning (as well as an exciting teaser for future films in the franchise). This example of superhero invasion cinema shows its iconic heroes waging a successful fight for truth, justice, and the American way. The images broadcast by 9/11 are eclipsed by a powerful projection of cinematic art.

Although the consolation provided by *Captain America: First Avenger* and *The Avengers* offer an alternative to the republic of fear, it does not overturn the pattern of extreme othering that Ivie sees as authorizing an endless cycle of terror and counter-terror.[27] Though these films do represent a pluralist humanity worth defending against racist aggression, they do so using the old device of projecting otherness onto some fictive, inhuman, warlike species. This gesture leaves in place the rationale for permanent war that was normalized in American political culture following 9/11. The superhero invasion film encourages U.S. citizens to stand together against national threats rendered as racially outside any semblance of human comity or civilization. If, as Glenn Greenwald has argued, the cost of the United States' endless War on Terror has been rendered "largely invisible" to its citizens, these films help fill the discursive space left by the absence of images from the front.[28] They provide a way of seeing that helps us accept as normal a forever war. The United States of America is not only a target of demonic evil but also Theodore Roosevelt's "helmeted queen among nations."[29] It is through this popular cinema that our "invisible" war has found a visible analogue.

NOTES

1. Lynn Spigel notes that for a brief moment (about a month), culture industry producers "eager to censor trauma-inducing images of any kind" removed the Towers from movie posters and trailers. But they quickly returned to the "mass-destruction ethos" that is fundamental to their creative and commercial businesses. Lynn Spigel, "Entertainment Wars: Television Culture after 9/11," *American Quarterly* 51, no. 2 (2004): 235–270.
2. Robert Trager, Joseph Russumanno, Susan Dante Ross, and Amy Reynolds, *The Law of Journalism and Mass Communication* (Washington, DC: CQ Press, 2010), 30–31.
3. For example, Art Spiegelman's 2002–2004 comic strip, "In the Shadow of No Towers," offers a striking counter to the hysterical in/visibility caused by the their destruction. Art Spiegelman, *In the Shadow of No Towers* (New York: Pantheon Books, 2004).
4. Jean Baudrillard, *The Spirit of Terrorism and Requiem for the Twin Towers* (London: Verso, 2002), 5, 7.
5. *Things to Come,* directed by William Cameron Menzies (1936; New York: Criterion Collection, 2013), DVD; *The War of the Worlds,* directed by Byron Haskin (1953; Hollywood, CA: Paramount Pictures, 2005), DVD; *Independence Day,* directed by Roland Emmerich (1996; Los Angeles, CA: 20th Century Fox, 2013), DVD.
6. *The Towering Inferno,* directed by John Guillermin (1971; Los Angeles, CA: 20th Century Fox, 2003), DVD; *Die Hard,* directed by John McTiernan (1988, Los Angeles, CA: 20th Century Fox, 2013), DVD.
7. King and Krzywinska's formulation was written before the spectacular real-world destruction of the World Trade Center. Geoff King and Tanya Krzywinska, *Science Fiction Cinema: From Outerspace to Cyberspace* (London: Wallflower, 2000), 66–67.
8. As Tom Ryall notes, "For whatever else it is, Hollywood is surely a cinema of genres, a cinema of westerns, gangster films, musicals, melodramas, and thrillers." Tom Ryall, "Genre and Hollywood," in *American Cinema and Hollywood: Critical Approaches,* edited by John Hill and Pamela Church Gibson (Oxford: Oxford University Press, 2000), 101.
9. *Little Big Man,* directed by Arthur Penn (1976; Hollywood, CA: Paramount Pictures, 2003), DVD; *The Virginian,* directed by Victor Fleming (1929: KVC Home Video, 1989), VHS.
10. *Invasion of the Body Snatchers,* directed by Don Siegel (1956; Hollywood, CA: Paramount Pictures, 2012), DVD; *The Blob,* directed by Irvin Yeaworth (1958; New York: Criterion Collection, 2000), DVD.
11. *Captain America: The First Avenger,* directed by Joe Johnston (2011; Hollywood, CA: Paramount Pictures, 2011), DVD; *Marvel's The Avengers,* directed by Joss Whedon (2012; Burbank, CA: Buena Vista Home Entertainment, 2012), DVD.
12. J.R.R. Tolkien, *The Tolkien Reader* (New York: Ballantine Books, 1966), 77–85.
13. An important realist precursor is Orson Welles's efficient Nazi-hunting film noir, *The Stranger* (1946). *The Stranger,* directed by Orson Welles (1946; Narberth, PA: Alpha Video, 2002), DVD.
14. Paul Buhle, ed., *Jews and American Comics: An Illustrated History of an American Art Form* (New York: New Press, 2008), 57.
15. Ibid., 30.

16. Danny Fingeroth, *Disguised as Clark Kent: Jews, Comics, and the Creation of the Superhero* (New York: Continuum, 2007), 57–60.

17. Championing the oppressed is a key characteristic of the superhero. Superman, the character that launched the superhero genre in the late 1930s, was initially a socialist outlaw who fought political and social corruption. It is only in the 1950s that he became a "patriotic stooge" (Grant Morrison, *Supergods* [New York: Spiegel & Grau, 2011], 6, 16; Bradford W. Wright, *Comic Book Nation: The Transformation of Youth Culture in America* [Baltimore: Johns Hopkins University Press, 2001], 9–11).

18. Robert L. Ivie, *Democracy and America's War on Terror* (Tuscaloosa: University of Alabama Press, 2005), 137.

19. For an excellent investigation of how race functions in science fiction cinema, see Adilifu Nama's *Black Space: Imagining Race in Science Fiction Film* (Austin: University of Texas Press, 2008).

20. Mary Shelley, *Frankenstein* (1818; Oxford: Oxford University Press, 1998), 165. In her review of the relationship between *Frankenstein* and the early nineteenth-century Anglo-French science of teratology (the study of monsters), Melinda Cooper recalls that the racial implications of monstrous creation were important political components of the debates inspired by science. Melinda Cooper, "Monstrous Progeny: The Teratological Tradition in Science and Literature," in *Frankenstein's Science: Experimentation and Discovery in Romantic Culture, 1780–1830,* edited by Crista Knellwolf and Jane Goodall (Burlington, VT: Ashgate, 2008), 95–96.

21. Excellent visual references for the idea of the enemy as a racialized swarm may be found in such post-9/11 entertainments as *The Lord of the Rings: The Fellowship of the Ring,* directed by Peter Jackson (2001; Los Angeles: New Line Home Entertainment, 2002), DVD and *I, Robot,* directed by Alex Proyas (2004; Beverly Hills, CA: Twentieth Century Fox Home Entertainment, 2005), DVD.

22. H.G. Wells, *The War of the Worlds* (1898; New York: Penguin, 2005).

23. The superhero invasion film is a robust genre. Its practitioners are tasked with developing ever more inventive ways of imperiling great cities and rescuing them: Superman's Metropolis, *Man of Steel,* directed by Zach Snyder (2013; Burbank, CA: Warner Home Video, 2013), DVD; and Batman's Gotham City, *The Dark Knight Rises,* directed by Christopher Nolan (2012; Burbank, CA: Warner Brothers Pictures, 2012), DVD are models of the practice.

24. Tolkien, *The Tolkien Reader,* 85–86.

25. Tolkien identifies this moment as *evangelium*. It is for him the raison d'etre of cognitively effective fantasy. Ibid.

26. Ivie, *Democracy and America's War on Terror,* 5.

27. Ibid., 8.

28. Glenn Greenwald, "Washington Gets Explicit: Its 'War on Terror' Is Permanent," *The Guardian* (London, UK), May 17, 2013.

29. Mario R. DiNunzio, ed., *Theodore Roosevelt: An American Mind: A Selection from His Writings* (New York: St. Martin's Press, 1994), 185.

8 · DIFFERENTIAL CONFIGURATIONS

In/visibility Through the Lens of Kathryn Bigelow's *The Hurt Locker* (2008)

CLAUDIA BREGER

The critical reception of Kathryn Bigelow's *The Hurt Locker* (2008) presents a puzzle. Although Bigelow's more recent *Zero Dark Thirty* (2011) stirred significant controversy for its representation of torture during the "Wars on Terror," *The Hurt Locker*, which focuses on a three-man bomb defusal team in Iraq, was almost exclusively greeted with praise.[1] Not only did the film earn six Academy Awards, including those for Best Director and Best Picture, along with many other accolades, it also was an overwhelming critical success—although most commentators agreed that the film's visceral images of a series of dangerous bomb deactivation operations do not develop a critical stance on the Iraq War.[2] Some critics even asserted that, in failing to develop that stance through the portrayal of its lead character, Sergeant Will James (Jeremy Renner), the film effectively sends a pro-war message, or functions as "one of the most effective recruiting vehicles for the U.S. Army that I have seen."[3] If this diagnosis should present little trouble for conservative critics,[4] it seems surprising that the film-critical establishment, with its liberal reputation, was nonetheless so enthusiastic about *The Hurt Locker*. I do not believe that this enthusiasm is sufficiently explained by Bigelow's longstanding reputation as a bold, auteurist investigator of the gendered and racialized configurations of contemporary culture. And the lack of a critical response was not limited to the United States: at the film's premiere at the 2008 Venice festival, *The Hurt Locker* received a ten-minute standing ovation, along with five awards, including the Human Rights Film Network

Award, which would seem designed to honor precisely those political or ethical implications of a film that *The Hurt Locker,* according to many of its enthusiastic critics, failed to develop.

As I argue here, this absence of a critical response points to larger configurations of in/visibility in contemporary culture. In *The Right to Look: A Counterhistory of Visuality,* Nicholas Mirzoeff starts from the "apparent conundrum" that the shocking images of the Iraq War captured by photojournalists had "so little public effect": the gruesome visibility of violence and torture did not translate into political outrage.[5] With Jacques Rancière, Mirzoeff explains this configuration through the modern regime of visuality as that "division of the sensible whereby domination imposes the sensible evidence of its legitimacy," presenting "authority as self-evident."[6] His brief comments on *The Hurt Locker* offer a rare critical take on the film: as Mirzoeff suggests, it gives an "'aesthetic' form" to the contemporary, "post-panoptic" extension of this regime, which legitimates the "Wars on Terror in the name of the seemingly self-evident 'sacrifice and duty' of 'counterinsurgency.'"[7] My own reading in part confirms this claim. However, Mirzoeff does not discuss *The Hurt Locker* in much detail and does not give a fuller account of how the diagnosed process of legitimation operates in contemporary culture more generally. Instead, his argument about the twenty-first-century reconfiguration of the modern regime of visuality remains caught in a rhetoric of contradiction and paradox: On the one hand, Mirzoeff suggests, this regime has become "visible" as such; on the other hand, contemporary war "paradoxically" depends increasingly on invisibility, thus provoking a "'crisis of visuality' itself."[8]

Aiming to dissolve these paradoxes, my close reading of *The Hurt Locker* approaches the puzzle of its uncritical reception, and the in/visibility of contemporary wars more generally, through a focus on the film's aesthetics. The overwhelming praise for *The Hurt Locker* has been centered on the "spellbinding" force (Roger Ebert) and "viscerally exciting" (A. O. Scott), "totally immersive, off-the-charts high-anxiety experience" created by Barry Ackroyd's "brilliant" cinematography and quick, multiple point-of-view editing, which make "you feel as if you, like the characters, are under threat from all sides" (Amy Taubin).[9] In line with Ackroyd's earlier *United 93* (dir. Paul Greengrass, 2006), *The Hurt Locker* thus resonates with the paradigms of immersion through which Roger Stahl has characterized the trajectory of contemporary war mediations across media. Displacing the "third-person" experience of the "deactivated citizen-spectator" with "interactive war" to be played by the "virtual citizen-soldier,"[10] Stahl suggests the aesthetics of immersion has increased tolerance "of the presence of death in dealing with foreign populations" and undone the earlier hegemonic pretense to a clean war with a "more sadistic posture."[11]

As reviewers have underlined, *The Hurt Locker* is massively bloody, as well as dirty—the violence and destruction of war are highly visible in that (literal) sense. At stake in the puzzle of the in/visibility of contemporary wars, however, are relations between what is thus technically visible, what is perceptible as well as conceptually intelligible, and (in the metaphorical sense of visibility dear to generations of humanities scholars) available for a translation into critique. In untangling these relations, I discuss how *The Hurt Locker*'s aesthetics speaks to twenty-first-century aesthetic trends more generally, as well as corresponding habits of perception and scholarly fascinations and conceptualizations.[12] Specifically describing the film's first-person mode of narration as its phenomenological aesthetics, I suggest, in other words, that *The Hurt Locker* does not just exemplify contemporary modes of war representation, but more generally speaks to newly hegemonic ways of envisioning the world, in the cinema and beyond. In scholarship and cultural theory, phenomenological approaches have had a comeback in the twenty-first century as well. Both these new phenomenologies and the equally influential (in some respects quite different) paradigms of Deleuzian affect studies have contributed to an increasing questioning of scholarly methodologies of critique as such. In the place of "distanced" critique, their proponents have recommended more affirmative takes on affective experience and advocated for replacing third-person analysis with first-person modes of reading.[13] This methodological shift in current scholarship programmatically disrupts the continuum between "seeing" and "seeing critically" that most twentieth-century trained cultural studies scholars perhaps took for granted for too long.

SUN, SAND, AND SIGNIFICATION: PHENOMENOLOGICAL AESTHETICS AND NARRATIVE WORLDMAKING

For the professional reviewers of Bigelow's *The Hurt Locker,* not only its bloodiness, but also the film's reliance on cultural scripts of heroic masculinity are quite visible. Thus, reviewers have praised Renner's lead performance of the (safety rules–defying, all-too) fearless bomb defusal expert James as "a visceral projection of who this man is" (Ebert) and the film as one that "confronts the fact that men often take great pleasure in war" (Guy Westwell).[14] Although Westwell does caution that "this unapologetic celebration of a testosterone-fuelled lust for war may gall," he attributes "something original and distinctive" to "the film's willingness to admit that for some men (and many moviegoers) war carries an intrinsic dramatic charge." A more sophisticated, but also more categorical defense of the film's affirmation of such war lust is presented by Steven Shaviro, a major contributor to the "affective turn" in cinema and media studies. Shaviro underlines the role of "sensory immersion" for Bigelow's aesthetics in general and praises *The Hurt Locker* as "a film . . . in which the existential communicates directly with the elemental, with all other layers of significance stripped away."[15] For Shaviro, this explains why the film "doesn't take a stance on the Iraq war" and, "in the absence of critique . . . can only be read as ratifying the war."[16] According to Shaviro, the film's "harsh minimalism" undoes its antifeminist ideology in dissolving signification as such, reducing the "macho bravado of Renner's character" to his "routinized professionalism" and presenting the latter as "an inevitable quality of the element of sun and sand in which it is immersed." For Shaviro, both James's heroic subjectivity and that of the audience are overflowing in the "assemblage . . . of color, camera movement, and physical/elemental atmosphere" in the film's "(ultimately asubjective or more-than-subjective) atmosphere of affect."

Shaviro's Deleuzian approach thus foregrounds what I call the film's phenomenological aesthetics, an aesthetics he conceptualizes in terms of a "stripping away" of layers of signification through visual decontextualization.[17] This focus on the film's form presents a crucial counterpoint to Mirzoeff's political critique: it goes significantly further in explaining *The Hurt Locker*'s overwhelming critical success. Part of the rationale scholars have articulated for their turns to affect or a new phenomenology are precisely frustrations with wholesale critiques such as Mirzoeff's. As Rita Felski put it in the literary studies context, too much may have gotten lost in "the well-oiled machine of ideology critique."[18] At the same time, Shaviro's sand blocks that machine altogether, dissolving the visibility of war as a source of potential outrage into desert shades. The task of theorizing the in/visibility of contemporary wars therefore requires integrating the competing paradigms and accepting the methodological challenges posed by twenty-first-century turns to affect and phenomenology without discarding the moves of ideological, semiotic, or rhetorical critiques. Drawing on aspects of both Shaviro's and Mirzoeff's readings, I unfold a third, more complex interpretation attentive to the outlined layers of in/visibility.

My theoretical vehicle for developing this reading is an unconventional, postclassical notion of narrative worldmaking, which reconnects contemporary paradigms of phenomenology and affect to questions of signification and ideology.[19] Departing from common usages of *narrative* as a synonym for either plot or the process of ideological suture, I define *narrative* as a process and practice of affective(ly saturated) configuration: a worldmaking assemblage of heterogeneous, sometimes only tenuously connected affects, associations, bodies, gestures, images, memories, meanings, sounds, and words.[20] Thus defined, narrative is not affect's other: not a neatly sutured chain into which affect erupts as an opening counterforce. Rather, the multifaceted interplay of affect and ideological closure is to be located in the details of configuration: in how particular combinations of aesthetic technique effect specific narratives, within a multifaceted grid not exhausted by the polarity of "classical" versus "nonclassical" form.

"'Sticking' . . . signs to bodies," this process of narrative worldmaking shapes, and reshapes, audience orientations in their world through variously intertwined and foregrounded gestures of both decontextualization and recontextualization.[21] In other words, this notion of narrative can account for the phenomenological aesthetics of Bigelow's film, while acknowledging how its focus on the "elemental" remains embedded in the cultural: more or less bracketed signification does not entirely go inactive. As noticed by several critics, the sand in which the film immerses its audience is strewn with both explicit references and associative potentialities, which connect the Eastern desert to the frontier in the American West.[22] On the most explicit level of dialogue, the more rational and cautious teammate Sanborn provocatively asks the lead character James, "So you are a ranger, huh?" The backstory is that James has just joined the team as a replacement for the previous defusal specialist, whom the audience saw getting killed in the film's opening sequence. Both Sanborn and the third team member Eldridge are very distraught by James's all-too-heroic defiance vis-à-vis all safety regulations. Another western reference comes in the film's central desert scene, when Sanborn sarcastically reminds the British mercenaries they meet, "You know you can shoot people here." One of them joyfully applies that advice to their prisoners who try to flee during the subsequent enemy encounter: "It's 500,000, dead or alive."

Beyond dialogue, precisely the film's visual reductionism also contributes to the play of intertextual associations when, for example, an extreme close-up shows James lighting a cigarette after a particularly stressful bomb deactivation (fig. 8.1).

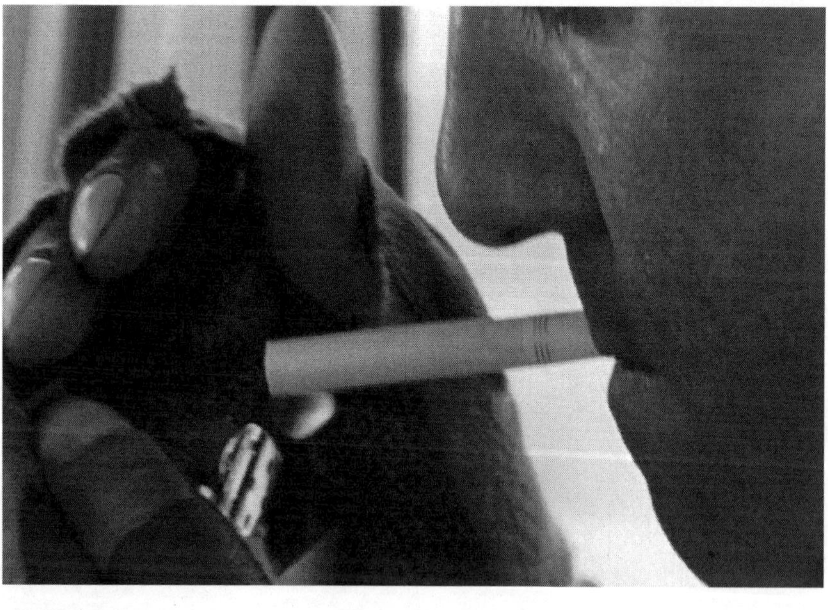

FIGURE 8.1

In momentarily bracketing the immediate diegetic context of the image, the decontextualization effect of the shot invites the surfacing of visual audience memories: the visual topos virtually reconnects to images ranging from the generic Hollywood 1950s to Marlboro "Wild West" advertising. Analogously, so does the (elemental) kitschy sunset at the end of the battle fought alongside the mercenaries in the desert, which adds an increasingly warm glow to the machine-man-dirt assemblages foregrounded through a series of close-ups in this tense sequence (fig. 8.2).

Although cultural intertextuality thus shapes one axis of virtual narrative connection, the second axis of contextualization is that of the film's diegesis. In other words, *The Hurt Locker* does have elements of a more classical narrative form. Even shots that seem designed to focus our attention primarily on the material, sensual, and affective qualities of the sight remain part of their action context. For example, when another close-up captures an empty cartridge falling to the ground against the beautiful background of desert stones (fig. 8.3), the onset of haunting electronic music in this very moment creates a narrative bond that ties the effect of aesthetic intensity back into the subsequently resurfacing, musically dramatized scenario of male battle comradeship.

Similarly, the elemental focus on the men's audible breathing and sweat finds its narrative role within this scenario as the desert shootout transforms Sanborn's preceding fantasy of killing James—because he is a threat to everyone's

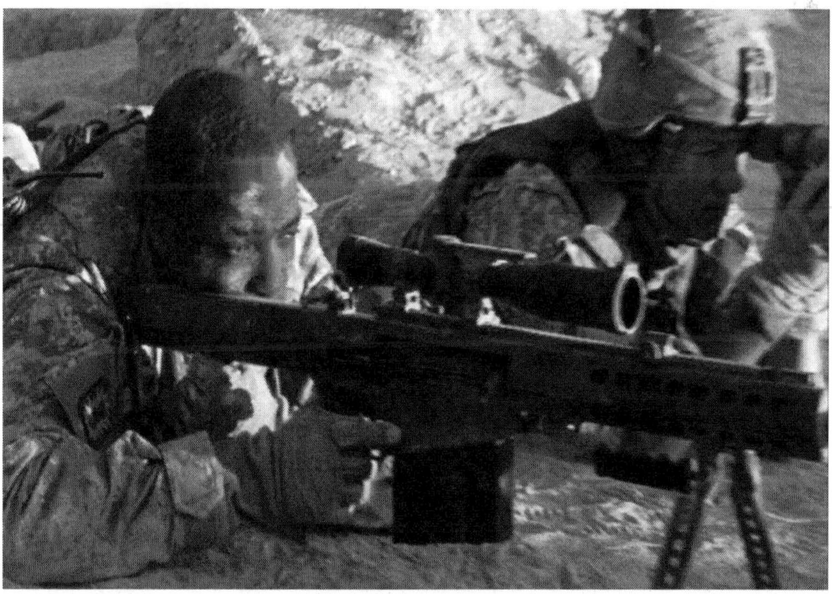

FIGURE 8.2

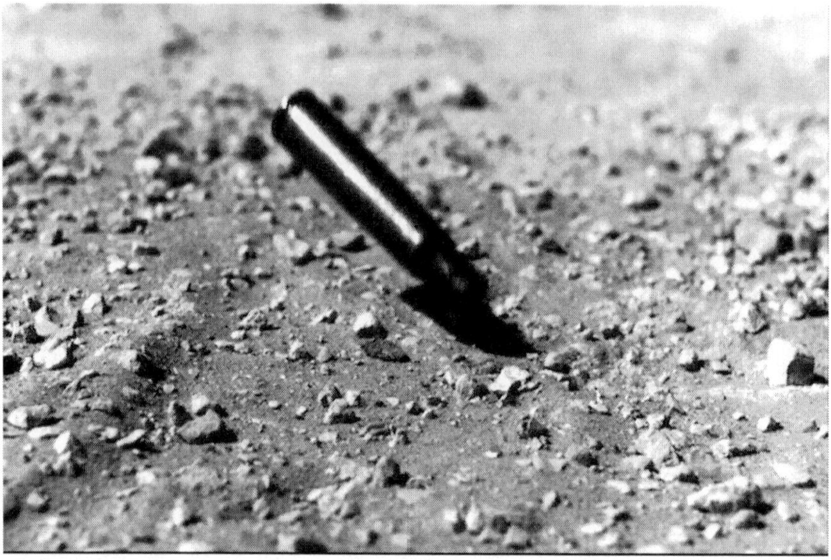

FIGURE 8.3

safety—into the solidarity of shared existential danger and sacrificial care: James feeds Sanborn the last sips of juice he was longing for himself.

The fact that decontextualization thus remains relative in *The Hurt Locker* does, of course, not yet answer the question of how to weigh and interpretatively organize the play of intertextual associations and emergence of diegetic connection against the force of the film's visual focus on the elemental. The play of frontier associations certainly does not make *The Hurt Locker* into a full-fledged western, and a traditional ideology critique may in fact fail to capture the experience it facilitates. Tracing this experience more fully requires engaging the concrete contours through which *The Hurt Locker* maps its cinematic encounter between citizen-soldier and Iraqi enemies in the sand in more detail. In the remainder of this essay, I undertake analytical close-ups at the filmic processes of de- and recontextualization. In doing so, I dissolve the apparent paradoxes of contemporary in/visibility into complex specifications, including the described layers of (non)critical visibility, but also the seemingly simple question of what and who exactly is in/visibilized, and how. These differential configurations of in/visibility reflect the persistence of gender and racialization in contemporary mediascapes and the crucial significance of these asymmetries for the project of critiquing contemporary wars, as foregrounded by Mirzoeff's focus on the histories of colonialism and slavery.[23]

PHENOMENOLOGICAL TAKES: CRITICAL VIRTUALITIES

Surprisingly perhaps, a closer look suggests that *The Hurt Locker* does have an antiwar framing. Among the film's most "visible" moments of explicit narration—here in the sense of authorial commentary—is its opening motto, a quote by the renowned left-wing critic Chris Hedges. The introductory title offers audience guidance in the form of an analytical perspective on the protagonist's fascination with the war: "The rush of battle is often a potent and lethal addiction, for war is a drug." Targeted by those conservative critics who found the film's apparent pro-war stance not sufficiently clear-cut,[24] this analytical narrative frame of addiction suggests that we would certainly be mistaken to identify *The Hurt Locker* as straightforward war propaganda. If we follow the opening guidance, does the film not dramatize its hyper-heroic protagonist's problematic story of "war abuse"?

As indicated also by the "ranger" interpellation quoted earlier, James is doubtlessly and amply marked as an ambivalent protagonist. Via dialogue once more, Colonel Reed admires him as "a wild man," whereas James's colleague Eldridge less appreciatively names him a "rowdy boy." For the context of the western (to which, again, I do not assimilate the film wholesale), Richard Dyer has explained such ambivalences with the narrative-generating "instability at the heart of the representation of whiteness" in the modern western imaginary.[25] At the heart of this imaginary is the tension that the claim to heroic masculinity depends on the "presence of [what is configured as] the dark" within the white man: sexuality and violence—here specifically the addictive pleasures of violence.[26] In that sense, it is precisely the transgression of the law—safety regulations and all—that constitutes James's heroism as an identity necessarily "tainted" by what can then be diagnosed as addiction. Toward the end of the film the audience, in this reading, follows James's failure to go clean: his difficulties with readjusting to civilian life back home and his halfway brutal, halfway melancholic monologue in front of his baby son about his "love" for only one thing, followed by his return into the war. The film's concluding scene shows him walking in his bomb deactivation suit once more. First, an increasingly closer shot captures his feet, body, and eventually face under the helmet, then, the film's final shot shows him as a small figure walking away from the camera toward the desert space indicated at the end of the road, while a title announces the "365 days" of his new rotation. If this configuration of camera work and movement remains ambiguous in its intertwining of closeness and distance, the music offers another moment of critical framing here in the end: the concluding scene and the following credits are accompanied by the soundtrack of Ministry's "Khyber Pass."[27] However, the song is stripped of its lyrics, and its anti-Bush stance is therefore decipherable only by those with the respective musical knowledge. A similar qualification can be made for Bigelow's dramatization of the opening Hedge motto, which visually underlines that the quote develops diverging vectors of emphasis: After a moment, the critical-analytic statement made by its first part is faded out, so that the motto is reduced to the phenomenological constative, "War is a drug." In this way, even the film's most explicit moments of critical commentary are assimilated into its phenomenological aesthetics.

About ten minutes into the film, the first shot of its protagonist captures his head and hands in a forward-bent pose as he listens to loud music. He is smoking a cigarette, onto which the camera then adjusts its focus (fig. 8.4) before panning back to capture his head more centrally.

Thus, the film's war hero is first introduced through a hand-drug assemblage. Leaning back in my desk chair (with the ability to stop the DVD in mid-action), I may analytically identify this introduction as a sign of James's addiction. But how does this diagnosis matter in the film's experiential world of sensual presence as prototypically projected for first-time viewers in the cinema, in which this hero is, first of all, visibly enjoying his smoke? In the course of the film analogous alignments similarly enable the audience to share his enjoyment of dangerous bomb activations and enemy encounters. Does the close, sensually overwhelming framing not in fact invite us to do what Deleuzian affect scholars recommend, namely let go of those norms of individual sovereignty that denounce James's pleasure as addiction?

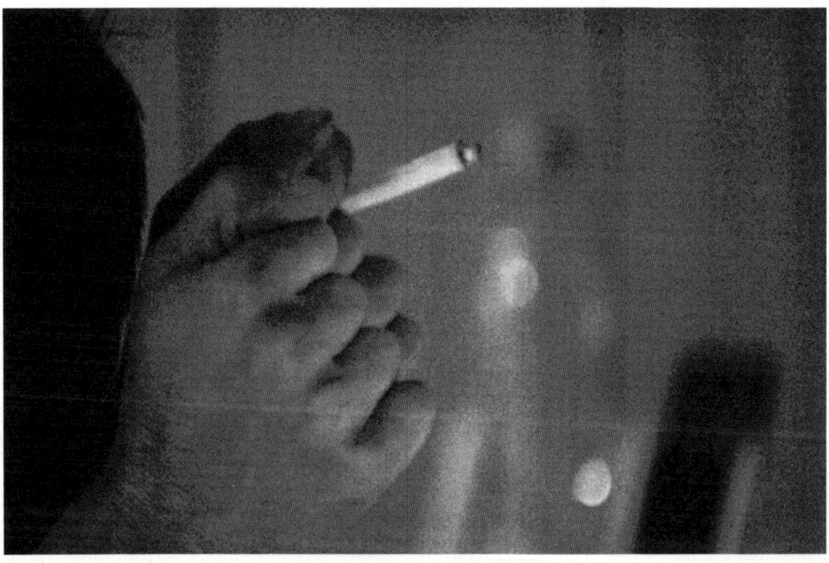

FIGURE 8.4

In other words, I argue that the film's phenomenological aesthetics encourage its audiences to put the analytical frameworks it introduces in parentheses. As discussed earlier, Shaviro's insistence on decontextualization does not hold up as a totalizing claim to a "stripping away" of all layers of significance. But the point can be resituated as one about the film's "phenomenological attitude" (to use Bert States's notion), that is, its aesthetic creation of "methodological solipsism" by way of bracketing context.[28] As States concedes, such bracketing does not erase meanings but merely creates "extremely ambiguous texts."[29] Rather than cutting off all analytical frameworks, *The Hurt Locker*'s phenomenological aesthetics create heightened ambiguity in not significantly unfolding, or foregrounding, a critical narrative. In that sense, the film's critique of the war as addiction remains virtual: it can, but likely will not be, fully "visibilized" (made intelligible) by the audience.

In addition to the addiction frame, this conclusion also holds for that of biographical trauma, which the film introduces as another layer of possible explanation for James's reckless heroism. After the tension between him and his colleagues has been momentarily resolved into solidarity during the desert shoot-out, it resurfaces at night in a game of drunk, eroticized wrestling and punching. In that scene, the third team member, Eldridge, discovers that James's chest is marked by scars and asks, "What happened?" James's answer, "My momma dropped me when I was a baby," is equivocal in tone, and deflected also by Eldridge's subsequent interpretation of the marks as "frag scars." Rather than sharing a moment of early trauma, James thus might be delivering an ironic response to an earlier comment by Sanborn. In the same scene that included the "ranger" interpellation, Sanborn had angrily proposed also a more contemporary framework for James's identity: "I am pretty sure I can figure out a redneck piece of trailer trash like you." Although thus introducing the interarticulations of race and class as further analytical virtualities, the film overall refrains from "figuring out" James: we never get any evidence, or further indications, about James's childhood or class positionality. Nor do we learn much about Sanborn's own background. How then do critical concepts of subjectivity, as a formation constituted in time at the intersection of positional markers and potentially shaped or unmade by trauma, actually matter in this film?

Short of stripping away all signification, the film's phenomenological aesthetics arguably bracket also the signifiers of race at play in its military trio. To avoid misunderstandings, Sanborn is "visibly" as unambiguously black as James and Eldridge are white, but the significance of these perception data in the film's world of war immersion is less clear. Like James, we first encounter Sanborn as a quasi-cyborgian assemblage, here with the machine of war: In the introductory sequence that shows the death of James's predecessor, we are on and off aligned with the mobile bomb deactivation device controlled by Sanborn. To be sure, this circumstance is established by a series of (more or less extreme) close-ups on the faces of Sanborn, and James's predecessor next to him, which fit perhaps less neatly with posthumanist Deleuzian insistences on the "dissemblage" of subjectivity. Although Deleuze himself discusses the potentially dehumanizing effects of the close-up as the "affection image," my sense is that such disturbing effects are curbed by dominant cultural codings of the face as the locus of individuality in most cinematic uses of facial close-ups.[30] In the introductory sequence of *The Hurt Locker,* the shots have a both contextualizing and decontextualizing function; they present first hints at the human being that the film narrative will construct.

As the film then unfolds Sanborn's character, the aesthetic politics of bracketing race in its military trio perhaps develops less as dehumanization than a move of humanist generalization. In Dyer's analytic categories, the trio receives its contours through the reversibility of racializations, namely the way in which James's "internal darkness" is dramatized through its contrast with the ways in which his African American colleague embodies norms associated with whiteness in the hegemonic imaginary: his anxiety about, and resulting anger at, James's reckless heroism seems to be based on his rational assessment of danger. On the other side of the spectrum, Sanborn's position is demarcated by its distance from the "unmanly" fear of the boyish Eldridge. In between James and Eldridge, Sanborn embodies the ostensibly unmarked norm of naturalized moderate masculinity notoriously identified with "the human" in Western modernity. In this way, the film's bracketing of symbolic markers and associated backstories also works in part through a branch of phenomenological investigation that is positioned at odds with Deleuzian approaches in contemporary theory: the return of humanist universalisms. In *Precarious Life: The Powers of Mourning and Violence,* for example, Judith Butler revisits her own earlier critique of humanism to the effect of reclaiming "a common human vulnerability" as a critical antidote to the differential symbolic regimes of war discourse.[31] In developing this argument, Butler also draws on Emmanuel Levinas's discussion of the face as conveying "the commandment, 'Thou shalt not kill.'"[32]

Crucially, Butler undertakes this humanist phenomenological intervention in response to the dehumanization of Muslims in the wars on terror, in which *The Hurt Locker* forcefully participates (as I detail following). On the domestic front of American racial relations presented through its diverse bomb deactivation team, however, part of the film's virtual critique of war is developed through such a humanist attitude of mourning rather than war enthusiasm. For the audience who is spatially, as well as narratively, mostly aligned with Sanborn in the first half of the film, his racially unmarked subjectivity presents a potential affective anchor that can facilitate a distancing from James's war lunacy. As Sanborn's initial anger then gives way to the solidarity facilitated by shared experience in the course of the film, this alignment might also foster a non-heroic (more acentral) approach to James in the mode of mourning.[33] At the very end of their deployment together, a closely shot car scene presents both of their faces with traces of blood from their last close call with death. In a state of openly displayed emotionality, Sanborn talks about not wanting to die. Throughout much of the dialogue, the slightly asymmetrical shot-countershot camera work keeps us extremely close to Sanborn, inviting empathy while also contrasting the vulnerability displayed on his face with James's composure, as he steers the car still armed in his helmet (figs. 8.5 and 8.6).

In this scene, Sanborn also articulates his desire for a son. Earlier, upon discovering that James has a son, he had projected all family desires on the "girl I like." Toward the end of the film, Sanborn thus affirms the civilian life to which James will fail to readjust.

If James cannot ultimately love more than "one" thing, the audience may, along with Sanborn, now have a better understanding of that failure. Clearly, his visible scars are evidence of some trauma. While speculations about his childhood are not supported by (audio)visual evidence, we have seen a moment of breakdown under the shower indicating that the war itself certainly has a traumatic effect on James. Helplessly, he performed gestures of self-aggression while rinsing off the blood on his body and clothes after a nightly raid—recklessly ordered by himself—during which Eldridge was injured. And for this incident, the film suggests a motivation for James's behavior: a motivation indicating

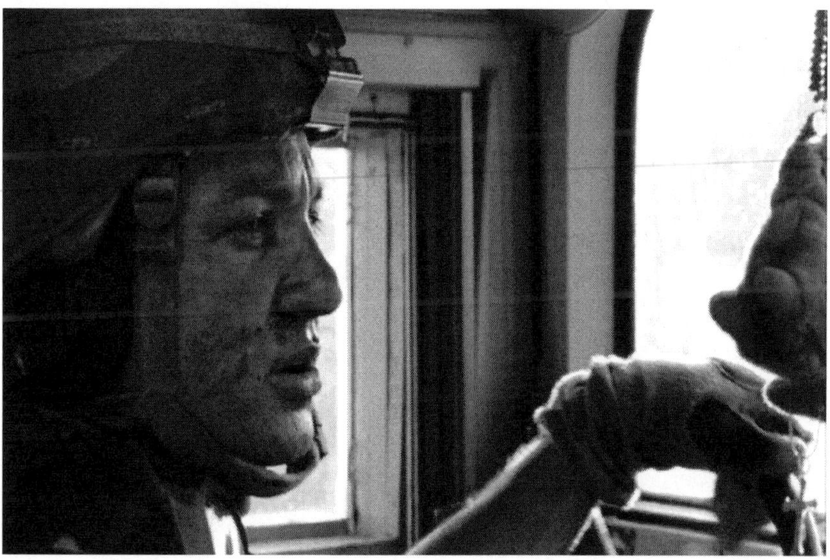

FIGURE 8.5

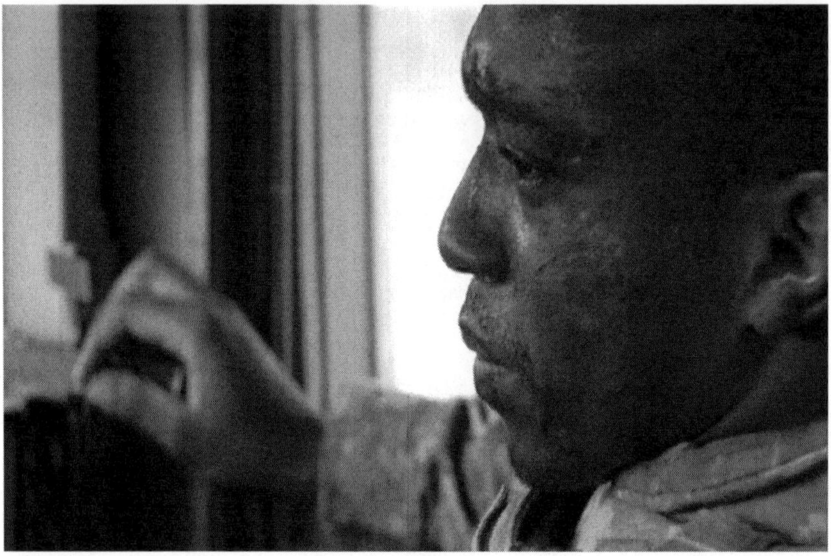

FIGURE 8.6

precisely his own vulnerability. Namely, he seeks retribution for the death of a child that has been transformed into a bloody body bomb, in which James believed he recognized the DVD-selling Iraqi boy with whom he had built a quasi-parental bond earlier. Visibly shaken by the bloody sight of this human-bomb assemblage, James calls his ex-wife at home, but then does not identify himself to her when she answers. Does James love more than one thing after all, even as his trauma prevents him from attending to these feelings?

FOREGROUNDED CONNECTIONS: VISIBILIZING POST-VIRTUOUS WAR

The film audience is certainly free, and arguably even invited, to answer these questions in the affirmative, which may allow us to respond to James's eventual return into the war in a continued mode of mourning. However, these critical virtualities are likely overpowered by the overwhelming, much more consistently foregrounded presence of other elements of the film's narrative configuration, specifically the threat posed by the Iraqis. The film's (equally phenomenological) visualization of this threat legitimates James's heroism and thereby makes it likely that *The Hurt Locker*'s narrative is consolidated by audiences as pro-war after all, despite the film's complexity and possibly against the director's intentions.

If the significance of race is relativized in the film's domestic variations on the themes of interracial war comradeship, *The Hurt Locker*'s new frontier encounter with the terrorist enemy is configured in aggressively racist terms whereby race operates not through skin color but a combination of cultural markings with a differentially dehumanizing fragmentation of subjectivity. The DVD-selling boy, who introduces himself as "Beckham" in an equivocally self-reflexive or simply stereotypical play on colonial histories, is the only Iraqi who gets significant individual contours.[34] Or does he? As the film plot has it, James misrecognized the body bomb (it was not "Beckham" after all), to the effect of confirming Sanborn's racist comment: "They all look alike."

And almost all of them are terrorists. In line with hegemonic Western constructions of gendered Islam, the film's exposition establishes "Bagdad 2004" (thus the explicating title) through shots of children and veiled women, characteristically in the mode of running from a bomb threat. Except for such in-passing stereotypical coverage, we see almost exclusively suspicious males from our varying angles of central and acentral alignment with the U.S. team in the process of doing their bomb defusal job. The film's tense atmosphere of virtually omnipresent threat is created through these quick glances at Iraqi men, be it on the surrounding roofs, peeking through windows or standing at the edges of the city space surveilled by the protagonists. *The Hurt Locker*'s aesthetics of paranoia thus work through the Iraqis threatening in/visibility, here in the sense of the camera's gestures at their limited visibility and possible hidden presence, as well as their ambiguous non/intelligibility as *potential* terrorists. Variously equipped with suspicious observation and communication devices, these Iraqi men are (de)figured by way of metonymy—as explicated again by dialogue: there are "a lot of eyes on us." In exhibiting the instability of surveillance from the perspective of the film's ground troops, the logic of paranoia thus contributes to partly reversing hegemonic structures of visuality—which, to be sure, were never quite as dichotomous as postulated by Laura Mulvey and others. Namely, the logic of paranoia posits "the enemy" as the main diegetic subject of the gaze, while the film's heroic man-machine assemblages assume center stage as a fully visible spectacle also for the audience, even while our gaze is (mostly) not ostensibly aligned with that of the Iraqis. Rather, *The Hurt Locker*'s aesthetics of immersion also invite the audience to get close to its heroic spectacle, and respond with anxious empathy or identification along with desire.

The filmic construction of the Iraqi threat is not dependent on classical narrative form. In some respects, it is precisely the film's episodic structure, that is, the unending series of action sequences inflected by video game aesthetics, that stabilizes the effect through relentless repetition. Much like the typical first-person shooter game, the film's city space attains its contours as a dusty wasteland full of hidden bombs. At the same time, *The Hurt Locker* does develop a fairly classical narrative framing through the configuration of its opening and closing episodes. The introductory sequence establishes the film's action pattern as a disruption of an initial state of equilibrium: the three initial members of the bomb defusal team are shown to cooperate effortlessly in an atmosphere of playful mutual teasing, until a bomb apparently triggered by an Iraqi on his cell phone kills Thompson, James's predecessor, making room for the tense dynamic in the new team as the film's major narrative conflict.

The qualifier *apparently* is appropriate in that the cause-and-effect relation is established exclusively by the film's editing pattern. As *The Hurt Locker*'s phenomenological aesthetics forgoes all conclusive evidence in the form of confessions, trials, or sentences, editing operates as our major source of "proof" (as well as suspense) throughout the film. In the introductory sequence, after Eldridge has spotted the suspect, we see a series of close-ups and extreme close-ups on the fingers operating the phone, Eldridge's gaze through the telescope in his gun, the face of the alarmed Thompson starting to run, the eyes of the apparent perpetrator, and a final click on the phone's call button followed by a long shot of the explosion. Could our cause-and-effect conclusion then not be a paranoid misconstruction merely indicating our experiential alignment with the American team? While the film's phenomenological aesthetics do not prevent such alternative readings, its techniques of foregrounding through sustained attention and repetition are likely to defuse respective doubts in the course of the film. Again and again, bombs do go off, and any suspicion seems justified as an adequate response to the narratively constituted reality of death. Indicatively, the Army psychologist who has tried to interact with language skills rather than guns and telescopes explodes before the end of the film.

In the introductory sequence, the extreme close-up on the apparent perpetrator's eyes (fig. 8.7) demands closer attention. Beyond experiential alignment with the U.S. team's telescope gazes, it functions as a narrative gesture of foregrounding, concretizing the metonymic portrayal of the enemy suggested previously.

In this particular narrative context, the extreme close-up does develop an erratic decontextualization effect operating as an instance of dehumanization along the lines of Deleuze's suggestion for the "affection image." In the play of de- and recontextualization developed by the explosion sequence, the eye shot fragments the Iraqi human into an "eye weapon," constituting "the enemy" as the agent of a delocalized gaze. Again, the film's phenomenological aesthetics do not foreclose alternative readings. In a later episode with a cab driver, who James stops at gun-point in another bomb suspicion scenario, we see a similar extreme close-up of the cab driver's eyes, this time in response to James's question, "what the f[. . .] are you doing?" (fig. 8.8).

Unlike the analogous shot in the introductory sequence, this one is not directed at "us" in angle, and the even closer take foregrounds the texture of aging skin surrounding the eye with its beautiful long lashes. Encouraged by this difference in detail, might we replace the Deleuzian framework with Laura

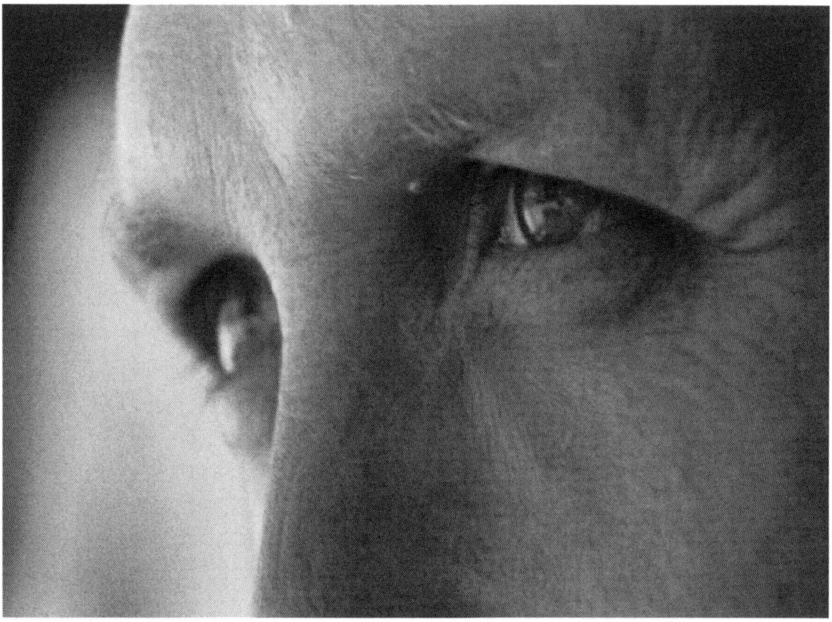

FIGURE 8.7

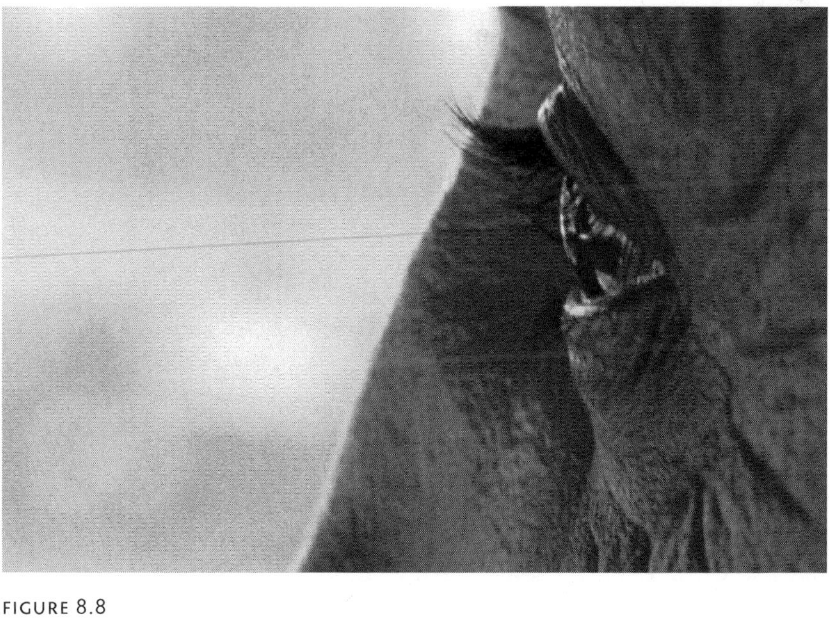

FIGURE 8.8

Marks's explorations of—tender rather than violent—haptic visuality in intercultural cinema and code this shot as a reverse shot onto a most likely innocent human targeted by racial profiling?[35] Does his nonresponsive stillness constitute an attempt at preserving his dignity? After his violent arrest, James inappropriately jokes, "If that wasn't an insurgent he sure as hell is now." The statement dramatizes the contingency of its friend/foe divisions, and the war's own dynamic of brutalization. As a cynical constative, however, the joke also summarizes the performative dynamic of this action moment and, by extension, the film's performance of ordering the world through its acts of insistent narrative foregrounding. Subsequent shots of the suspect and his car contextualize his "unknowable" eyes with his religious and nationalist paraphernalia. In retrospect, the impenetrability of his gaze will likely have signified his dehumanized "otherness" after all.

If contemporary necropolitics, as Mirzoeff suggests, insistently separates "the insurgent" from the "host population," with "no expectation of reforming or disciplining" the former, the film not merely reiterates this gesture, but performs a further, aggressively racist twist in phenomenologically identifying the insurgent with the (otherwise more or less invisible) host population.[36] In case any doubts have persisted throughout most of the film, its final action sequence—preceding James's return home and quick reenlistment—quite literally forecloses the space of Iraqi innocence. Once more, the team has to deal with a human-weapon assemblage, as an Iraqi man with a bomb strapped to his body is begging the U.S. team to take it off. While the translator pleas for his humanity ("Help this man. He is not a bad man"), Sanborn suspects a trap ("He's not a bad man? He got a bomb strapped to him"). James nonetheless heeds the call which, of course, provides a *mise-en-abyme* of the official—benign—ideological mission dramatized in the overall film ("He's a family man. . . . He's just asking for help"). Against the ticking of the bomb timer, this last operation once more showcases James's hyper-heroic performance, but at the very last second, he has to give up: the bomb is attached to the host population body with "too many locks." Praying, the man explodes.

If this concluding action episode does unfold a humanizing effect, it affects less the Iraqi "family" man—who is dehumanized as an indissoluble body-bomb assemblage—than the American hero who gives his very best, but eventually shows some judgment in the face of otherwise certain death. As he repeats three times, "I'm sorry!," the film sutures its construction of heroic masculinity. At the outset of this post–Abu Ghraib film, legitimacy had been highly questionable. ("Welcome to Camp Victory," the "rowdy boy" had been greeted upon joining the squad, followed by the explanation that the name sounded better than the original "Camp Liberty"). In the end, the film's overwhelming visual evidence for "Muslim" terrorist insurgency has established the necessity of this rowdy boy's post-virtuous heroism as an excess ultimately rooted in both rationality and humanist feeling. In narratively conferring this grounding to James, *The Hurt Locker* also solves his conflict with Sanborn. From that angle, the latter's decision in favor of a civilian life alternatively reads as his surrender. Sanborn disappears from the film after the car scene that established his respective choice: In whatever exact combination of mourning and celebration, the film's ending visibilizes only James.

To conclude, I hope to have demonstrated in this chapter that the question of the in/visibility of (U.S.) America's contemporary wars is usefully disentangled by breaking it down into layers and specific configurations. In *The Hurt Locker,* the violence and dirtiness of the war are highly visible, but this visibility has not translated into a critical stance—or, such a critical stance remains at best virtual so in the film itself, and has almost not at all materialized in its reception. I explained this puzzle with the film's phenomenological aesthetics, and the latter's fit with larger contemporary cinematic trends, habits of perception, and even influential scholarly concepts. Although the critics' dominant focus on affective experience has failed to visibilize the ways in which ideology continues to co-constitute *The Hurt Locker*'s filmic world, it does go some way toward explaining its reception. Intertwining twentieth-century approaches to ideology, discourse, or rhetoric with the new paradigms of affect and phenomenology, my own concept of narrative worldmaking allowed me to critically detail how *The Hurt Locker*'s phenomenological narrative form visibilizes the Iraq war as, ultimately, a dirty necessity. Namely, its aesthetics of decontextualization cooperate smoothly with the more classically narrative elements of its composition to a twofold effect. On the one hand, it brackets the critical frameworks of war addiction and trauma, which the film introduces as narrative virtualities, in favor of anxious audience pleasures in alignment with the American bomb defusal team. On the other hand, it persistently foregrounds the presumed terrorist threat in a logic of paranoia, which visibilizes the "enemy" as a dehumanized eye weapon and bomb assemblage.

Beyond attending to these configurations in detail, my reading suggests that the larger project of critiquing America's contemporary wars needs to facilitate the cultural foregrounding of different narratives. Such alternative narratives are entirely possible, and have even received some visibility, in the contemporary cultural circuit. Examples include Mira Nair's *The Reluctant Fundamentalist* (2012), which employs the form of a highly affective, arguably sensationalist thriller for the project of foregrounding U.S. racism, the post–September 11 politics of exclusion, and the fundamentalism inscribed in contemporary economic neoliberalism. A different path is explored in Asghar Farhadi's narratively much more reserved *A Separation* (2011), which indirectly displaces hegemonic narratives of Muslim fundamentalism through its phenomenological close-up of the affective complexities of everyday life at the intersections of class and gender, secularism and religion in contemporary Iranian society. As suggested by these examples and, more generally, the concept of narrative configuration unfolded in this essay, the call for "different narratives" does not imply a straightforward plea against (or for) phenomenological aesthetics as such, for third-person versus first-person approaches, or for categorically more (or categorically less) classical forms of narrative. Rather, different narratives come about as a result of different detail configurations of blood, sweat, and nonviolence, of variously (a)central alignments, of gender, race, and class. Disentangling the in/visibility of America's contemporary wars requires closer looks at specific configurations.

NOTES

1. Nonetheless, the reception of both films shows important parallels. Though many critics were outraged about what they perceived as *Zero Dark Thirty*'s political message, namely the implication that torture was effective in tracking down bin Laden, they still praised the film's aesthetics almost unanimously, resulting in a 93 percent rating at rottentomatoes.com, and making *Zero Dark Thirty* the best-reviewed film of the year according to metacritic.com (see Sven Von Reden, "Die Frau in der Fahne," *Die tageszeitung*, January 30, 2013). Meanwhile, the critical debate about whether the film actually claims the effectivity of torture, or rather invites audience deliberation in not establishing that connection (see, e.g., Andrea Köhler, "Was wirklich war: Debatte um Zero Dark Thirty," *Neue Züricher Zeitung*, January 3, 2013), resonates with my discussion of *The Hurt Locker*'s phenomenological aesthetics in this piece.
2. With 97 percent, based on 209 reviews, *The Hurt Locker* was the second-highest-rated film in 2009 on rottentomatoes.com. Despite somewhat lower audience ratings (83 percent), the film was also commercially successful and clearly outperformed all other Iraq War films ("The Hurt Locker," *Wikipedia*, Page last modified November 23, 2015. https://en.wikipedia.org/wiki/The_Hurt_Locker).
3. Tara MacKelvey, "The Hurt Locker as Propaganda," *The American Prospect*, July 17, 2009, http://prospect.org/article/hurt-locker-propaganda.
4. Conservative critics did in fact mostly like the film, notwithstanding discussion about "mistakes" in its representation of its Special Army unit. See, e.g., "Iraq Veterans Keep Sniping at 'The Hurt Locker,' Missing the Point," *The American Scene*, March 3, 2010, http://theamericanscene.com/2010/03/03/iraq-veterans-keep-sniping-at-the-hurt-locker-missing-the-point; Brandon Fibbs, "The Hurt Locker," *Christianity Today*, July 17, 2009, http://www.christianitytoday.com/ct/2009/julyweb-only/hurtlocker.html; Michael Medved, "Unexpected Hope—From Hollywood," *Townhall*, February 29, 2012, http://www.michaelmedved.com/column/unexpected-hope-from-hollywood/; Thomas E. Ricks, "The Hurt Locker: Recommended, but With Reservations," *Foreign Policy*, July 21, 2009, http://ricks.foreignpolicy.com/posts/2009/07/21/the_hurt_locker_recommended_but_with_reservations.
5. Nicholas Mirzoeff, *The Right to Look: A Counterhistory of Visuality* (Durham, NC: Duke University Press, 2011), xv.
6. Ibid., 3, see 6.
7. Ibid., 19, 21–22.
8. Ibid., 34, 282; see 284, 296, 302.
9. Roger Ebert, "The Hurt Locker," *Chicago Sun Times*, July 8, 2009; A. O. Scott, "Soldiers on a Live Wire between Peril and Protocol," *New York Times*, June 25, 2009; and Amy Taubin,

"The Hurt Locker Review," *Film Comment,* n.d., http://www.filmcomment.com/article/the-hurt-locker-review.

10. Roger Stahl, *Militainment, Inc.* (New York: Routledge, 2010), 21.

11. Ibid., 43–44; see Roger Stahl, "Becoming Bombs: 3D Animated Satellite Imagery and the Weaponization of the Civic Gaze," *Media Tropes* 2, no. 2 (2010): 65–93.

12. I cannot do justice to all layers of this larger argument in the frame of this essay. For a fuller discussion of different facets of this twenty-first-century *episteme,* see my recent work: Claudia Breger, *An Aesthetics of Narrative Performance: Transnational Theater, Literature, and Film in Contemporary Germany* (Columbus: Ohio State University Press, 2012) and Claudia Breger, "Configuring Affect: Complex Worldmaking in Fatih Akın's *Auf der anderen Seite (The Edge of Heaven),*" *Cinema Journal* 54, no. 1 (2014): 65–87.

13. See, e.g., Rita Felski, *Uses of Literature* (Malden, MA: Blackwell, 2008), 17, for use of this terminology; more generally also Eve Kosofsky Sedgwick, *Touching Feeling: Affect, Pedagogy, Performativity* (Durham, NC: Duke University Press, 2003); and Brian Massumi, *Parables for the Virtual: Movement, Affect, Sensation* (Durham, NC: Duke University Press, 2002).

14. Ebert, "The Hurt Locker"; Guy Westwell, "The Hurt Locker," *Sight and Sound,* September 2009, 67–68.

15. Steven Shaviro, "Kathryn Bigelow," *The Pinocchio Theory,* March 8, 2010, http://www.shaviro.com/Blog/?cat=3.

16. Having lost faith in the radical potential of critique as well as of cinema (see Steven Shaviro, "The Cinematic Body Redux," *Parallax* 14, no. 1 [2008]: 48–54, 52), Shaviro nonetheless expresses his preference for *The Hurt Locker* over all the "liberal hand-wringing films about the war, which for all their humanist anguish are not really any more radically critical of US imperialism" ("Kathryn Bigelow").

17. In his earlier *The Cinematic Body* (Minneapolis: University of Minnesota Press, 1993), Shaviro's argument relies in part on a mediaontological claim about images as "violently torn away from any external horizon or context" on the screen; as he asserts, "The immediacy of the image shortcircuits processes of signification" (28). This categorical reduction has, however, been widely criticized also in phenomenological film theory (see, e.g., Laura U. Marks, *The Skin of the Film: Intercultural Cinema, Embodiment, and the Senses* [Durham, NC: Duke University Press, 2000], 145; also Vivian Sobchack, *Carnal Thoughts: Embodiment and Moving Image Culture* [Berkeley: University of California Press, 2004]). More generally, scholars have convincingly insisted on the epistemological—as well as concrete technological—condition that "visual experience" is always already organized by "frames" (Judith Butler, *Frames of War: When Is Life Grievable?* [London: Verso, 2009], 3).

18. Felski, *Uses of Literature,* 1.

19. Drawing on phenomenology along with cognitive science, postclassical narratologies have defined *narrative* as a performative process of worldmaking (see, e.g., Marie-Laurie Ryan, "Introduction," in *Narrative Across Media: The Languages of Storytelling,* ed. Marie-Laurie Ryan [Lincoln: University of Nebraska Press, 2004], 8) situated in a "frame of embodied and evaluative experientiality" (Monika Fludernik, *Towards a "Natural" Narratology* [New York: Routledge, 1996], 322). While this emphasis on (bodily, not just "textual") worldmaking provides a link to affect studies (see, e.g., Gregory J. Seigworth and Melissa Gregg, "An Inventory of Shimmers," *The Affect Theory Reader* [Durham, NC: Duke University Press, 2010], 3; Sara Ahmed, *The Cultural Politics of Emotion* [Edinburgh: Edinburgh University Press, 2004], 10, 12), it can easily be combined with rhetorical approaches to narrative underlining how this process nonetheless unfolds in a realm of signification and—certainly in the case of cultural artifacts like film—communication, involving feedback loops between (nonsovereign) authors/artists/crews and their active audiences (see James Phelan, *Experiencing Fiction: Judgments, Progressions, and the Rhetorical Theory of Narrative* [Columbus: Ohio State University Press, 2007], 4). For film, David Bordwell has similarly described this feedback loop in his *Poetics of Cinema,* in a partial revision of his earlier accentuation of the spectator side. He still protests against a notion of communication as the transmission of messages from mind to mind, but accepts that cinema is an "experience of *representations*" (David Bordwell, *Poetics of Cinema* [New York: Routledge, 2007], 124).

20. Transcending problematic form-versus-content oppositions, this notion of narrative includes compositional elements as traditional as dialogue along with mise-en-scène, and editing and music, as well as audience response.

21. Ahmed, *Cultural Politics of Emotion,* 13.

22. Peter Rainer, "Review: The Hurt Locker," *Christian Science Monitor,* June 26, 2009, http://www.csmonitor.com/The-Culture/Movies/2009/0626/p17s07-almo.html; Denise Castillón, "Kathryn Bigelow's *The Hurt Locker*—Film Review," *Suite 101,* July 25, 2009; Peter Bradshaw, "The Hurt Locker," *The Guardian,* August 28, 2009, http://guardian.co.uk/film/2009/aug/28/the-hurt-locker-review.

23. See also Butler, *Frames of War.*

24. Andrew Klavan, "The *Hurt Locker* Question," *City Journal,* January 15, 2010. http://www.city-journal.org/html/hurt-locker-question-9602.html.

25. Richard Dyer, *White: Essays on Race and Culture* (New York: Routledge, 1997), 39.

26. Ibid., 28, 33.

27. Caetlin Benson-Allot, "Undoing Violence: Politics, Genre, and Duration in Kathryn Bigelow's Cinema," *Film Quarterly* 64, no. 2 (2010): 33–42.

28. Bert O. States, "The Phenomenological Attitude," in *Critical Theory and Performance,* ed. Janelle G. Reinelt and Joseph R. Roach (Ann Arbor: University of Michigan Press, 2007), 26 (States quotes Maurice Natanson here).

29. Ibid., 31 (States quotes Umberto Eco here).

30. Gilles Deleuze, *Cinema 1: The Movement-Image,* trans. Hugh Tomlinson (London: Athlone, 1986), 1, 99.

31. Judith Butler, *Precarious Life: The Powers of Mourning and Violence* (New York: Verso, 2004), 30.

32. Ibid., 132, with reference to Levinas (and the Bible).

33. See Murray Smith's breakdown of audience alignments, here specifically the distinction between empathy as a mode of (I would add: more or less) "central alignment," or "feeling with" and acentral sympathy, or "feeling for" (Murray Smith, "Altered States: Character and Emotional Response in the Cinema," *Cinema Journal* 33, no. 4 [1994]: 34–56).

34. See Robert Sklar, "The Hurt Locker," *Cineaste* 35, no. 1 (2009): 55–56.

35. Marks, *The Skin of the Film.*

36. Mirzoeff, *The Right to Look,* 279.

9 · THE CANINE-RESCUE NARRATIVE, CIVILIAN CASUALTIES, AND THE LONG GULF WAR

PURNIMA BOSE

In recent years, a new genre of memoirs of U.S. soldiers serving in Iraq has emerged that foregrounds a softer side of military intervention, which takes as its primary subject matter a soldier's strong attachment to a stray dog and the challenges of bringing this canine companion safely back to the United States. Sporting such titles as *From Baghdad, With Love: A Marine, the War, and a Dog Named Lava* and its sequel *From Baghdad to America: Life after War for a Marine and His Rescued Dog,* as well as *Welcome Home, Mama and Boris: How a Sister's Love Saved a Fallen Soldier's Beloved Dogs,* these memoirs represent a variant of the rescue narratives that have provided popular ideological justifications for the U.S. interventions in Afghanistan and Iraq.[1] In this essay, my focus is on the Iraq War. Consisting of a muddled assortment of explanations, the rationales for the U.S. invasion of Iraq included the false claim by the George W. Bush administration that Iraq had weapons of mass destruction, the erroneous assumption among some Americans that Saddam Hussein was responsible for the attacks of September 11, 2001, and the perception that Iraqis required saving from their president. This last rationale resulted in the widespread sense in the United States that Iraqis would welcome U.S. military intervention in their internal affairs and the toppling of their leader in a version of what we might call the Iraqi civilian-rescue narrative.

To this ideological justification, we can add the canine rescue narrative, a narrative that renders dogs as highly visible tropes for objects of U.S.

humanitarianism while simultaneously making invisible violence against Iraqi civilians. Containing parallel narratives in which canines are humanized and Iraqis are dehumanized, canine-rescue narratives function as a compensatory fantasy about the benign, indeed salutory, effects of U.S. military intervention on noncombatants. If the U.S. intervention in Iraq embodies a failed attempt to export American-style bourgeois democracy, the canine-rescue narrative misleadingly supplies a happy ending in which stray dogs are saved by virtue of their adoption by American families and thus given the opportunity to fully actualize their dogginess in the land of opportunity and the home of the free. In these accounts, the dogs' harrowing passage from Iraq to the United States signifies the divestment of their Iraqi citizenship and their investiture in American nationality. The logic underwriting these accounts substitutes for Iraqi civilians the canine subject's assimilation into the American polity as an index of the success of humanitarian intervention and the democratizing project.

In this essay, I chart the narrative strategies in one such memoir, Lieutenant Colonel Jay Kopelman and Melinda Roth's *From Baghdad, With Love: A Marine, the War, and a Dog Named Lava.* I begin by historicizing the larger cultural shifts toward pets in the United States, which involve the increasing anthropomorphism of canines, a trend that is visible in consumer practices, and the emergence of dogs as subjects in legal discourse. Turning to the memoir, I then provide a close reading of how it humanizes and nationalizes its tiny canine protagonist while simultaneously dehumanizing Iraqis. Finally, I contextulize the memoir in terms of its Iraq war palimpsest and consider how the blackout of visual representations of Iraqis in combination with the use of numerical means and the absence of official government body counts of civilians render them nearly invisible in the United States.

My interest is in what the conjuncture of nationality and canine subjectivity, which Lisa Uddin dubs "canine citizenship," reveals about the ideological legitimization of U.S. imperialism.[2] Understood less in conventional terms that define citizenship as a legal status with civic obligations to a larger polity, informed by ethical and moral dimensions, canine citizenship has more metaphoric resonances as elaborated by Uddin, connoting a "particular set of meanings about public participation" that have been invested in dogs.[3] For memoirs such as *From Baghdad, With Love,* those resonances include the nation, God, and family, and, ultimately, humanitarian intervention and gunboat democracy.

CANINE HUMANIZATION

The emergence of the canine-rescue narrative and its nationalization of dogs as U.S. citizens in the first decade of the twenty-first century is not surprising given the profound changes in American attitudes toward pets in the twentieth century, particularly at the century's end.[4] In her thoughtful history, *Pets in America,* Katherine C. Grier suggests that the anthropomorphization of pets is connected to developments in capitalism and dates to the rise of pet stores in the 1840s, which not only entailed the sale of animals, but also the marketing of products perceived as necessary for their well-being, including commercial pet food, toys, medicines, collars and leashes, and beds. In the first half of the twentieth century, according to Grier, "trade literature and advertisements" for pet supplies reveal "an ongoing conversation among manufacturers, store owners, and consumers," which "demonstrate[s] how changing perceptions of the needs of animals often paralleled a new understanding of human needs."[5] Various reform movements targeted at improving human health and comfort often had their corollaries in marketing campaigns for pet products. The development and marketing of commercial pet food, for example, echoed the themes of nutritional requirements and vitamin supplements that were a prominent part of reform efforts to improve human diets.[6]

For my purposes, the key point here is that the development of products such as dog food presaged the anthropomorphism of canines into sentient subjects of a special kind: family members, who, depending on the attitudes of particular families, occupied a status slightly below that of children or on par with them. By the advent of the big box pet store in the late 1980s, household animals were increasingly figured as family members. PetSmart, the largest retail chain for pet products in the country, has as its slogan "Where pets are family." According to the American Veterinary Medical Association, "In 2011, six-out-of-ten or 62.3% of American pet owners considered their pets to be family members."[7] The interpellation of domesticated dogs as members of the American family is legible in the vocabulary of dog ownership, which relies heavily on kinship terminology and vocabulary related to parenting children. Dogs that are acquired from animal shelters, for instance, are "adopted" by their owners. A 2013 advertising circular from Petco hails pet owners as "pet parents," advising that parental responsibilities entail "more than just play time, walk time, feeding time and all the other times in between," rather they are "about the daily commitment to helping your pet reach their full potential, and to having the best quality of life together." In advertising copy that could apply equally well to child raising, the circular identifies four areas for pet owners to attend: "It's important to keep your pet physically fit, mentally alert, socially engaged and emotionally happy." Petco, needless to say, has recommendations for products that can maximize the pets' well-being in all of these areas.

For such products, pet owners constitute a major market, which has expanded rapidly over the past two decades. In 1988, 56 percent of U.S. households owned a pet, a percentage that increased to 68 in 2014.[8] Americans are only too willing to shell out money for the dizzying array of products and services for their animals now available on the market. Whereas in 1994, consumers spent $17 billion on their household animals, that amount jumped to $58.04 billion in 2014.[9] To put these figures in perspective, in 2014, the top five recipients of U.S. foreign aid—Israel, Afghanistan, Egypt, Pakistan, and Nigeria—combined were allocated $8.79 billion in assistance.[10] Perhaps recognizing that there is money to be made from pet owners, companies such as Paul Mitchell, Omaha Steaks, Origins, Harley-Davidson, and Old Navy, which were traditionally oriented toward sales of commodities for human use, "are now offering lines of pet products ranging from dog shampoo, pet attire, and name-brand toys to gourmet treats and food."[11] Pet industry representatives view anthropomorphism as a market opportunity, which they name "humanization."[12] Their marketing logic involves building on the current ethos of considering pets as family members in order to sell more products to the animals' owners.

The humanization of pets has also been occurring linguistically with legal ramifications. Under U.S. and British law, household animals have been historically defined as the property of human individuals. Animal ethicists and animal rights advocates have argued for a change in vocabulary that does not characterize pets as personal property. In the 2011 inaugural issue of the *Journal of Animal Ethics,* the editors write that the vocabulary of "pets" and "ownership," "whilst technically correct in law, harks back to a previous age when animals were regarded as just that: property, machines or things to use without moral constraint." They urge replacing the "derogatory" terms "pets" with "companion animals," and "pet owners" with "animal caregivers" or "animal guardians."[13] The movement to alter the vocabulary of human–animal interactions not only has semantic consequences, but also legal ones, sufficiently alarming the American Veterinary Medical Association (AVMA) to result in the authoring of a 2005 "issue paper," "Ownership versus Guardianship."[14] The AVMA warns against the use of "guardian" to describe pet ownership because the legal status of "guardianship" entails "a fiduciary relationship (the highest legal civil duty owed by one person to another). The ward's interests are always to prevail over those of the guardian." Parsing out the potential legal ramifications of an embrace of the term "guardianship" for service providers, society, and animals, the AVMA emphasizes that such a semiotic change would grant legal status to animals and subject their relationships with their owners to outside intervention from third parties, who could bring civil lawsuits on behalf of the animals, and/or from the state.[15]

These changes in attitudes toward pets, namely, the symbolic incorporation of canines into the structure of the American family and the movement for pet personhood, in the ideological context of consumer capitalism, establish the groundwork for canine citizenship. Given how central the unit of the family has become to U.S. political discourse since the 1980s, it is not an imaginative leap to perceive dogs as possessing a nationality and American citizenship, the preferred ending of canine-rescue narratives such as *From Baghdad, With Love.*

THE CANINE-RESCUE NARRATIVE

Lieutenant Colonel Jay Kopelman and Melinda Roth's *From Baghdad, With Love* follows the basic plot of the canine-rescue narrative, consisting of a member of the U.S. armed forces saving a stray Iraqi dog by bringing it back to the United States, integrating it into a family, and nationalizing it as American. Almost always a puppy, the canine protagonist is constructed as a scrappy survivor who is extremely vulnerable to ill-intentioned Iraqis and an unfeeling American military that prohibits soldiers from having pets. Insofar as the preservation of the stray dog's life requires the intervention of a Marine or soldier, backed by the financial, logistical, and emotional support of U.S. civilians, the canine stands in for ordinary Iraqis, who, many American believe, needed U.S. military intervention to plant democracy and to save them from themselves. Unlike these puppies, most Iraqi civilians do not have the opportunity to leave Iraq, let alone do they have the financial and logistical support of American citizens to facilitate their emigration to the United States.

The book's cover visually emphasizes the vulnerable status of its canine protagonist by featuring a close-up of a sleeping puppy. The visual framing of Lava as unconscious and helpless encapsulates its narrative strategy: throughout the text he is represented as a passive agent whose fate hinges on the goodwill of Americans. Most of the plot involves Kopelman's attempts, at a distance, to secure the pup's safe passage to the United States. He bounces between different postings all over Iraq while Lava remains under the protection of fellow soldiers, various National Public Radio (NPR) reporters, and several Iraqis, with very few scenes in the memoir describing Kopelman and Lava interacting directly with one other. Yet if read against the grain, the cover image also hints at the more sinister subtext of this otherwise feel-good tale of canine rescue. The photograph of the slumbering puppy recalls the idiomatic expression "to let sleeping dogs lie," a prescription that the George W. Bush administration would have been well advised to heed prior to its 2003 ground invasion of Iraq. More ominously, in the very representation of Lava as inert, the image conjures associations with other states of unconsciousness such as the severe injury of being comatose and of being dead, thus, subtly insinuating the violence of war as its historical subtext.

Three quotations from Genesis introduce sections of the book, and the prologue makes the purpose of their presence in the text clear: "Iraq was considered by most biblical arachaeologists to be the location of the Garden of Eden," we are told, "God's only hard copy of Heaven, his Paradise on earth."[16] Several paragraphs later, we read, "If this country was Paradise, then the Marines weren't taking any bets on Hell."[17] In the first week of the U.S. assault on Falluja, in November 2004, the narrative stage is set for the entry of a small puppy discovered by the First Battalion, Third Marines, also called the Lava Dogs, who rescue the tiny dog and name him "Lava" after themselves. Evocative of the rhetoric of manifest destiny, the biblical opening of the memoir establishes Iraq within a Christian prelapsarian geography whose present circumstances reside in a postlapsarian temporality. This Edenic "paradise" has become a "hell," necessitating redemption for Marines and puppies alike in a teological plot that will culminate in Lava's successful rescue and his acquisition of American nationality.

Confronted with the puppy discovered by the men under his command, and with the knowledge that the military prohibits soldiers from fraternizing with native dogs, Kopelman faces a dilemna. Military regulations permit personnel at combat outposts or forward operating bases to interact only with military working dogs, and the Department of Defense (DoD) has hired contractors "to kill all nonmilitary dogs found on American bases in Iraq."[18] The lieutenant colonel has allowed his troops to care for Lava and promised he will help the puppy. He justifies his decision to violate military regulations and protect Lava by expressing a form of what we might call Marine exceptionalism: "I am a lieutenant colonel in the United States Marine Corps. I am an officer in a brotherhood that always goes in first, and that pretty much sums it up right there. We're brave to the point of insanity, so being a Marine takes a certain kind of mind-set to begin with. Which means you don't always follow orders."[19] Marine exceptionalism entails having "a primitive gene that requires some . . . to be the fittest and the bravest and the best-est there is," and also a stubborn aversion to authority: "We were Marines going in and Marines coming out. We don't *want* to take orders."[20] "I really like what I am—a Marine," Kopelman emphatically declares. "I like being strong. I like being brave. I like going in first. I *want* to go in first, and I'll be damned if I'm going to let anyone shoot my puppy."[21]

Lava quickly insinuates himself into Kopelman's heart and becomes part of the Marine fraternity. The first encounter between Marine and pup consists of Lava "licking and squirming and wiggling around" in the lieutenant colonel's hands. Soon the little dog is sharing Kopelman's sleeping bag. From the start, Kopelman engages in anthropomorphism, making Lava into an honorary soldier by referring to him variously as the "newest grunt,"[22] the "newest recruit," the "little warrior,"[23] and sometimes simply as the "little guy."[24] Moreover, he attributes emotions such as bravado, fear, and pride to the tiny canine and on occasion supplies him with dialogue such as the lines *"I-was-never-afraid-of-you,"*[25] *"I-didn't-mean-to-chew-up-the-only-porn-magazine-in-the-barrack,"*[26] and *"I am going to kick your ass."*[27]

As Kopelman becomes fonder and fonder of Lava, his contempt for Iraqis—both the soldiers whom he must train and civilians—becomes more and more visible in the memoir. His initial description of Iraqi troops is condescending, echoing colonial representational paradigms that liken natives to children, whom he must now "babysit."[28] The soldiers "are untrained, out of shape, and terrified," Kopelman writes, and most are so incompetent that they "haven't figured out how to keep their rifles safely locked."[29] His account of training the Iraqis—which appears to be a highly compressed version of boot camp—makes the U.S. military appear irresponsible and incompetent. Whereas basic training for American soldiers varies across different military branches from eight to twelve weeks, its duration for the Iraqi recruits only lasts a week, most likely because this is the final instruction before combat, following training by the Iraqi military.[30] The training regimen seems doomed to failure given its brevity and lack of cultural sensitivity: "The Iraqi soldiers endured both regular mortar shelling of their tents by insurgents and verbal bombardments from the Americans who only had one week to prepare them for their first-ever combat experience. So they were prone to the jitters and often woke up in the middle of the night shooting their unsafed rifles wildly. Thank God they didn't know how to aim."[31]

To the verbal abuse, the lieutenant colonel is only too happy to contribute; where Iraqis are concerned, Kopelman's favorite word is the unimaginative expletive "shit." His strategy to prevent a "freak out" by Iraqis on joint patrol with American troops is "to make them more afraid of [him] than they are of the streets."[32] Kopelman yells at them, several times, to "knock that shit off" until one of his fellow Marines advises him "to take it easy on them" because the Iraqis do not understand English.[33] In another scene, Kopelman berates Iraqi soldiers for looting candy bars and cigarettes, relying on an intepreter to translate his sentences. Jabbing a finger into one man's chest, he addresses the Iraqis as "pathetic excuses for soldiers" and lights into them: *"You are less than men for stealing," "You humiliate yourselves and the Iraqi forces," "You are no good as soldiers and I will abandon you here in Fallujah, where you will be beheaded by insurgents,"* and *"You are nothing but shit."*[34]

Iraqi civilians do not command much more respect than Iraqi soldiers either. Driving by Iraqi refugees from Fallujah, he reveals that "the four of us in the Humvee make jokes about the old men in dresses and the fat women behind veils and egg on Lava when he barks. '*Kill*,' we say and fall out laughing, because we think it's so damned funny. 'Kill, Lava, *kill*.'"[35]. When Lava responds by ratcheting up the volume with continuous barking, Kopelman screams at him, in an echo of his earlier verbal abuse of the Iraqi soldiers, *"Knock that shit off."*[36] At this moment, Lava and the Iraqis are aligned in their shared reaction to his yelling: "Lava stares at me. . . . The faces, the people outside, stare at me. And they've got that look, all of them, that look that says *Caught your cool off guard, did we?*"[37]

Repeated associations with the word *shit* and Iraqis in the text indicate that Kopelman despises the professionals he must train and the civilians on whose behalf the U.S. military intervention has ostensibly been launched. *Shit* has multiple and derogatory significations including feces, "a contemptible and worthless person" or thing, "garbage," "nonsense," "stuff," and "any psychoactive drug, especially marijuana."[38] How screaming the expletive "shit" at Iraqis figures into the strategy of winning hearts and minds is not clear. Kopelman frequently also uses a variation of this term more than any other as an endearment for Lava, who he repeatedly calls "little shit." The slang meaning of "little shit" encapsulates contradictory referents: a despicable person and also a small animal or child for whom one has affection.[39] While Kopelman clearly adores his puppy, the endearment "little shit" creates a chain of associations between Lava and Iraqis, functioning as a linguistic signifier of Iraqi national identity for the dog. (Given the devaluation of canines in the Muslim world, this association is not without its ironies.)

The linguistic parallel between Iraqis and Lava is echoed visually in the photographs, with a noticable difference that accentuates the relative material privilage vis-à-vis the occupation forces that accrues to the dog. Kopelman's memoir contains several photographs with a single subject, a few of Lava as a puppy and one of a young Iraqi boy. The photograph of the boy presents him as an isolated subject: apart from the step that he sits on, he has an inscrutable expression and appears without a visual context to understand his situation. Had the camera zoomed out, the little boy's location in a mosque that was serving as a refugee and work center would have been apparent.[40] Nor does the image contain any signifiers of sociality that connect him to other people. In contrast, the photographs of Lava hint at his embeddedness in a social matrix of care: he is pictured with toys, clothes, and food. On the one hand, the images draw a parallel between the puppy and the small boy insofar as they are both framed as the sole object of the photographic gaze, but, on the other hand, the presence of puppy paraphernalia implies the presence of caregivers for the canine which the boy sorely lacks. In this conflict zone, the photographs insinuate, it is better to be a puppy loved by American soldiers than an Iraqi child.

To be fair to Kopelman, his ill feelings are not directed solely at Iraqis, but at times at the U.S. military and government. Expressing no illusions about the function of a soldier, he comments that the military has "invested a lot of time and money into trashing your moral clarity, and they don't want anything like compassion messing things up. Your job is to shoot the enemy, period, and if anything close to compassion rears its ugly head, you better shoot that down, too, or you're in some deep, scary shit."[41] He identifies logical inconsistencies about military violence that inspire the ironic observation, "Seems word got out about the stray dogs eating dead bodies, and while it's perfectly okay for us to make the bodies dead in the first place, it's not quite cool to have dogs walking around eating them."[42] Kopelman also remarks on the failure of the U.S. government to account for Iraqi deaths: "While American deaths are meticulously accounted for by the U.S. government—by the end of that January, several thousand and counting—no credit columns are kept on how many Iraqis, whether insurgents or American-hired civilians, are killed or missing."[43] What distinguishes this criticism of the military from that leveled at the Iraqis, however, is that it lacks the tone of contempt that characterizes Kopelman's descriptions of his interactions with Iraqis. The one time he uses the word *shit* in relation to the military, it is not hurled as an invective against the U.S. armed forces but to describe a frightening situation.

Once the military bureaucratic hurdles are overcome, civilian material and logistical aid for Lava's transport secured, and harrowing experiences of attempted border crossings and movement in the Red Zone survived, Lava successfully arrives in the United States. Fervently hoping for a safe passage for his dog, Kopelman reflects, "I want [Lava] to be alive, because then there's still hope that he'll make it here to California and get to be an American dog who runs on the beach and chases the mailman instead of strangers with guns."[44] American identity for canines, in this quotation, means that they can actualize their nature as dogs, hurtling through the sand and water, and terrorizing familiar strangers. In the land of the free and home of the brave, dogs are free to be, well, dogs. On Lava's arrival at O'Hare, John Van Zante, a civilian with an animal rescue center that has assisted with Lava's transport, phones Kopelman to announce: "He's here, buddy. He's safe now. He's an *American* dog."[45] In a version of a performative speech act, Van Zante's naming of Lava as an American dog grants him canine citizenship, when he had previously been described as "the mangy little flea-bitten refugee."[46]

Canine citizenship, in Kopelman's memoir, metaphorically resonates with God, nation, and family. Like the U.S. military invasion of Iraq, with its overtones of manifest destiny and the moral certainty of George W. Bush that the United States had a divine mission to spread American-style democracy in Iraq through force, *From Baghdad, With Love* asserts the virtues of Americans and their institutions, particularly those geared toward dogs. A clear message of the text is that it is far better to be an American dog than an Iraqi one because Americans love dogs and Iraqis do not. The many Americans in the book, military and civilian, who make it their mission to rescue Lava, and the framing of the memoir with biblical verses imply that his arrival in the United States is divinely ordained. Indeed, the memoir ends with the revelation that Lieutenant Colonel Kopelman has married and that Lava has acquired both a canine and human sibling. Lava's acquisition of American identity and its solidification through his incorporation into the structure of the nuclear family illustrates Lauren Berlant's contention that one consequence of Reaganite conservatism has been that "nostalgic images" of a normative "familial America . . . define the utopian context for citizen aspiration."[47]

For Berlant, American citizenship has increasingly become "a condition of social membership produced by personal acts and values, especially acts originating in or directed toward the family sphere."[48] She astutely observes that "the American fetus" and "the American child," those subjects who themselves cannot enact the responsibilities of citizens, acquire a "supericonicity" and provide the grounds for politicized discourses of morality and for the formulation of reactionary legislative policies.[49] I follow Uddin in adding dogs to Berlant's categories of "infantile citizens."[50] But where Uddin explores what canines signify about "citizenship as a set of actions or inactions, as a definition of personhood, as a way of moving through and imagining the nation," my concern has been to consider how stray dogs displace Iraqi civilians as affective objects of identification in need of rescue by American soldiers. Military intervention becomes the means for stray dogs in conflict zones to acquire symbolic citizenship in the United States; in this sense, their incorporation into the national imaginary becomes one form of evidence for the success of the democratizing project. While the United States failed to export democracy to Iraq, individual soldiers working in tandem with American civilians are able to markedly improve the lives of the most abject subjects in Iraq, stray dogs, by importing them into the democratic space of the American nation. Such are the achievements of humanitarian intervention and gunboat democracy: canine citizenship and failed states.

THE DEHUMANIZATION OF IRAQIS AND THE LONG GULF WAR

Visual culture has an intimate relationship with the category of citizenship, which partially depends on which identities are visible and articulated with the nation-state. Modern democratic societies, Robert Hariman and John Louis Lucaites convincingly argue, rely on images to promulgate the proverbial imagined community of the nation and to encourage specific civic values. They note that photography represents "images of people acting together" in both mundane and exceptional situations "in the many different locales, subcultures, and preoccupations of a large, pluralistic society."[51] By viewing such images, citizens gain a sense of their commune with fellow citizens, thus helping to create the affective ties that mediate the abstract distance between the individual political subject and an impersonal state. "Because photojournalism consists of images of people one does not know personally," Hariman and Lucaites explain, "it creates its own deep rule of citizenship: the habit of being benignly attentive toward strangers."[52] Citizens, in other words, need to see and to be seen by each other. The power of images extends beyond mere sentiment into the realm of agency, motivating citizens to engage in public life sometimes in concert with the state and at other times in opposition to it.

Visual images become particularly meaning-laden during wartime when distinctions among different parties to the conflict are sharply drawn between an "us" and a "them."[53] Prior to the U.S. invasion of Iraq in 1991, a repertoire of stock images of Arabs, elucidated in Edward Said's magisterial *Orientalism,* circulated in mass culture: oil sheikhs, menacing Muslims, heavily veiled women, and erotic harem women. Once the George H. W. Bush administration started to beat the drums of war, these images were augmented with cartoonish respresentations of Arabs that rendered them as objects of technologized violence. The prosecution of the war largely through aerial bombardment lent itself to news coverage of the conflict as an impersonal spectacle of firework displays and video game–like visuals; very few images of individual Iraqis for whom one could develop empathy were visible.[54]

We can piece together the story of the impact of the invasion on Iraqis through numbers. Their invisibility in this conflict was partly constructed through the absence of photographic evidence of the ravages of war and through statistical means and the disappearance of any numerical tabulation for their wounded or dead. Indeed, the George H. W. Bush administration cultivated an image of Operation Desert Storm as "a war without death," and did not release "a single picture or video of anyone being killed." *Newsday* correspondent Pat Sloyan details the government restrictions placed on the press that made it difficult for journalists to provide independent coverage of the invasion and to document the effects of the war on civilians. "Under rules developed by Cheney and Powell, journalists were not allowed to move without military escorts," he writes. "All interviews had to be monitored by military public affairs escorts. Every line of copy, every still photograph, every strip of film had to be approved—censored—before being filed."[55]

Definitive casualty figures for Operation Desert Storm (with the exception of combat deaths for U.S. troops) are difficult to come by and estimates vary widely because of differences in how these numbers are calculated. Some estimates are restricted to people killed by direct violence, and others account for deaths caused by secondary causes such as an increase in disease as a result of damage to health care delivery systems. Depending on the source, the U.S. military killed between 1,000 and 6,000, or 10,000 and 20,000, or 56,000 Iraqi soldiers; the figures for Iraqi civilian deaths vary from fewer than 1,000 to 1,000–3,000 to 3,500. Particularly shocking are the estimates for indirect civilian deaths provided by Beth Daponte, a former demographer at the Commerce Department and now head of Social Science Consultants after being a research professor at both Carnegie Mellon and Yale Universities, who initially put the figure at 70,000. Together with the 13,000 direct civilian deaths, 40,000 Iraqi soldiers, and 35,000 people who died as a result of the Kurdish and Shiite rebellions, Daponte first estimated that the overall death count for Iraqis was 158,000; but, in 1993, she revised that figure to approximately 205,000 people.[56]

Yet whatever the tally of deaths from Operation Desert Storm itself, a sober appraisal of the effects of the Allied invasion must also acknowledge the devastating toll the U.S.-led UN sanctions regime has taken on ordinary Iraqis. In spite of his abysmal record on human rights, Hussein had done much to modernize Iraq, implementing free education, building up the electricity grid, increasing agricultural production, and creating a health care system that served about 93 percent of the population.[57] When the United States commenced its bombing campaign against Iraq in 1991, it deliberately targeted the country's water, sanitation, and electrical infrastructure to augment the effects of the UN economic sanctions that were levied against Iraq in August 1990.[58] The net effect was a humanitarian catastrophe, particularly for children whose mortality rates from malnutrition and preventable water-borne diseases such as cholera, typhoid, and dysentery skyrocketed. By 1999, UNICEF had estimated that 500,000 children under the age of five had perished as a result of preventable diseases and widespread malnutrition. The 1997 "Oil-for-food" UN-administered program, as a number of analysts have argued, did little to ameliorate the living conditions of Iraqis, and, paradoxically, strengthened Hussein's grip on domestic power.[59]

Although it has become commonplace in the United States to distinguish between the "First Gulf War" (Operation Desert Storm in 1991) and the "Second Gulf War" (Operation Iraqi Freedom in 2003), to my mind this terminology is misleading.[60] If the word *war* signifies open and sustained hostilities between nation-states, then the United States has been at continuous war with Iraq since the 1991 invasion; more careful terminology would refer to it as "the Long Gulf War." In addition to the brutal UN sanctions regime that it pushed through the Security Council over the objections of Russia, China, Argentina, and France, the United States has flown regular combat missions over two "no-fly zones," which it unilaterally established with Britain over 60 percent of Iraq's territory in 1992, initially to protect Kurds in northern Iraq and Shiites in the south from Hussein's forces. This prolonged bombing campaign has been variously named (in Orwellian fashion) "Operation Provide Comfort," "Operation Southern Watch," "Operation Northern Watch," and "Operation Desert Fox" (one wonders at the symbolic associations with this last designation and Nazi General Erwin Rommel's nickname) and has meant that between 1991 and 2002, the United States flew more than an average of 34,000 military sorties a year.[61] The Iraqi government claims that more than 1,400 civilians have been killed as a result of these attacks over a decade, but this figure cannot be independently verified.[62]

The strategic aims of these sorties were less humanitarian and geared at degrading Iraq's military capabilities in the event of an escalation of hostilities between the United States and Iraq, as General Tommy Franks admitted to Congress in 2001. The no-fly zones certainly proved a boon in terms of minimizing

Iraq's capacity to respond to attacks when the United States launched Operation Iraqi Freedom in March 2003, ostensibly because the George W. Bush administration had identified Iraq as a "rogue nation" that financed and trained terrorists and also claimed that Hussein was developing weapons of mass destruction. Both charges proved false and were based on massaged intelligence.

When President George W. Bush declared "mission accomplished" and an end to combat operations six weeks later, a resilient insurgency had emerged comprised of diverse and uncoordinated elements. Initially composed primarily of Sunni nationalists who were disenfranchised members of the Baathist party (ex-Iraqi military and Hussein loyalists), these groups were later augmented by moderate Sunni Islamists, Salafists such as Al-Qaeda in Iraq, and, more recently, what is variously called ISIS (Islamic State in Iraq and Syria), ISIL (Islamic State in Iraq and the Levant), IS (Islamic State), and *Daesh* (an acronym for "al-Dawla al-Islamiya fil Iraq wa al-Sham"). Complicating the insurgency landscape has been the presence of Shiite militias—themselves divided between the pro-Arab Shiites nationalists and the pro-Iranian Shiites—both of whom primarily target Sunnis for attack.[63] By invading and occupying Iraq, in effect, the United States created the conditions for an Islamist presence that it had trumpeted as a justification for its military offensive against a largely secular society in the first place.[64] As Noam Chomsky has noted, the United States often invokes the threat of "aggression" from states where none exists to ideologically legitimize military intervention as a form of "self-defense," which in turn results in those states becoming hostile and aggressive to the United States.[65]

Of the U.S. intervention in Afghanistan, General Franks emphatically declared that "we don't do body counts," a statement that "has been repeatedly quoted as more or less the final word on American policy" for both the Afghan and Iraq wars.[66] The U.S. government does not have an official accounting method to tally up civilian casualties from its incursions abroad, presumably because it fears that such numbers might ignite widespread public opposition to military interventions of the Vietnam-era kind. The most serious consequence of the U.S. government's refusal to conduct an audit of the effects of its military violence is to render civilian deaths nearly invisible. I qualify "invisible" with "nearly" because both Americans and Britons realize that Iraqi civilians have been killed in the conflict but they vastly underestimate the numbers. Forty-four percent of British respondents believe that only 5,000 or fewer Iraqi civilians have been killed from 2003 to 2013,[67] and in a separate poll of Americans, 24 percent thought that the death toll from 2003 to 2007 was between 1,001 and 5,000.[68]

Ascertaining how many Iraqi civilians have died since Operation Iraqi Freedom is not easy. Various studies, conducted over different time periods, provide a large range of figures from a low of 174,258 (Iraq Body Count) to a high of more than a million (Opinion Business Research and Just Foreign Policy).[69] The methodologies of all these studies have some limitations, and the precise number of dead remains ultimately unknown, though after perusing the studies and their analyses by Hannah Fischer, I am inclined to believe that the figures are in the high range.[70]

With the statistics of Iraqi casualties themselves a casualty of the American government's efforts to suppress knowledge about the impact of its intervention and no visual images of them in circulation, Iraqi civilians have been made nearly invisible in the United States. Not so with stray dogs in Iraq, such as Lava, who have become highly visible icons of U.S. humanitarianism, providing apparent evidence of one successful outcome of military intervention. Yet lest readers be lulled into a happily-ever-after-ending, the final pages of the memoir hint of the challenges ahead: Lava sometimes lapses into ferocious aggression, and he has failed several obedience classes. Dogs who have been in combat situations, as it turns out, can also suffer from posttraumatic stress disorder (PTSD), the subject of Kopelman's sequel to this memoir.[71]

Lava's PTSD is symptomatic of all that cannot in the end be suppressed utterly by the canine-resuce narrative. If Lava cannot be restored entirely to his full canine subjectivity, or embraced by U.S. familial-consumerist canine citizenship, the fantasy of his rescue cannot compensate totally for the complete failure of the Long Gulf War to democratize Iraq and turn its residents into citizens. The investment of empathy and resources by Americans in the tales of Iraqi dogs and their rescues, even if there is no happily-ever-after ending, means that they are barely interested in the fate of Iraqis. With eyes on Lava, what remain almost invisible in U.S. public culture are the deleterious effects of U.S. military violence on a population that has been ruthlessly bombed, had its infrastructure destroyed, had to contend with stringent sanctions, been subjected to ground invasion, and is now witnessing its country descend into chaos. For Iraqis, the Long Gulf War never ended, and no rescue has even been offered.

ACKNOWLEDGMENTS

I am grateful to Srimati Basu, Mona Bhan, Zhaleh Bose, Claudia Breger, Lessie Jo Frazier, John Lucaites, Jody Madeira, and, especially, Jon Simons for comments on drafts of this chapter. In addition, Jay Kopelman graciously read and responded to the final draft. Although he did not grant permission to reprint photographs from his memoir, I remain appreciative of his feedback and for his consideration of my request. Thanks to Saleem and Sona Bose for providing inspiration. All errors, of course, are mine.

NOTES

1. See Lieutenant Colonel Jay Kopelman and Melinda Roth's *From Baghdad, With Love* (Guilford, CT: Lyons Press, 2006), Lieutenant Colonel Jay Kopelman's *From Baghdad to America* (New York: Skyhorse, 2008), Terri Crisp and Cynthia Hurn's *No Buddy Left Behind* (Guilford, CT: Lyons Press, 2012), Carey Neesley and Michael Levin's *Welcome Home Mama & Boris* (White

Plains, NY: Reader's Digest Association, 2013). As numerous feminist scholars have noted, in the case of Afghanistan, the veiled woman became the iconic figure around whom sentiment was mobilized to drum up support for the U.S. military offensive. The key texts here are Lila Abu-Lughod's "Do Muslim Women Really Need Saving? Anthropological Reflections on Cultural Relativism and Its Others," *American Anthropologist* 104, no. 3 (2002): 783–790 and Miriam Cooke's "Saving Brown Women," *Signs: Journal of Women in Culture and Society* 28, no. 1 (2002): 468–470. For a critique of feminist interpretations of the U.S. invasion of Afghanistan as a case of white men saving brown women, see Purnima Bose, "From Humanitarian Intervention to the Beautifying Mission: Afghan Women and Beauty Without Borders," *Genders* 51 (2010), http://www.iiav.nl/ezines/IAV_606661/IAV_606661_2010_52/g51_bose.html.

2. Lisa Uddin, "Canine Citizenship and the Intimate Public Sphere," *Invisible Culture: An Electronic Journal for Visual Culture* 6 (2003), http://www.rochester.edu/in_visibleculture/Issue_6/uddin/uddin.html.

3. Ibid.

4. My focus is on the development of middle-class Anglo-American cultural attitudes toward dogs. I recognize that different cultural values attach to canines in ethnic and regional subcultures, where canines might be signifiers of masculinity as evident by the proclivity for pit bulls and dog fights in certain urban and rural communities.

5. Katherine C. Grier, *Pets in America: A History* (Chapel Hill: University of North Carolina Press, 2006), 275.

6. Ibid.

7. "US Pet Ownership and Demographics Sourcebook 2012," https://www.avma.org/KB/Resources/Statistics/Pages/Market-research-statistics-US-Pet-Ownership-Demographics-Sourcebook.aspx.

8. Insurance Information Institute, "Pet Statistics: Pet Ownership in the United States," n.d. http://www.iii.org/fact-statistic/pet-statistics.

9. See the American Pet Products Association fact sheet, "Pet Industry Market Size & Ownership Statistics," n.d., http://www.americanpetproducts.org/press_industrytrends.asp.

10. Daniel Wickham, "Top 10 US Aid Recipients All Practice Torture," *Left Foot Forward,* January 30, 2014, http://www.leftfootforward.org/2014/01/top-ten-us-aid-recipients-all-practice-torture/.

11. Groomer's Helper, "2011 Pet Products Trend Report," January 11, 2012, http://www.groomershelper.com/info/2011-pet-products-trend-report/.

12. James Vlahos, "Pill Popping Pets," *New York Times Magazine,* July 13, 2008, 40.

13. The Oxford Centre for Animal Ethics, "Animal Language Sends Wrong Message." News Release, April 26, 2011, http://www.oxfordanimalethics.com/2011/04/news-release-animal-language-sends-wrong-message/.

14. See the American Veterinary Medical Association's "Ownership versus Guardianship," June 2005, https://www.avma.org/Advocacy/StateAndLocal/Pages/ownership-vs-guardianship.aspx.

15. See the AVMA's "Ownership versus Guardianship" for a lengthy list and explanation of the potential legal ramifications of changing the vocabulary of ownership to guardianship. It is worth noting that existing state and municipal law permits the seizure of dogs under three categories: "the impoundment of loose or unlicensed dogs; the seizure of dangerous dogs; and the seizure of dogs that either appear rabid or as part of a rabies quarantine effort." For more information about these statutes, see Rebecca F. Wisch's "An Examination of State Dog Impound Laws" (2003), http://www.animallaw.info/articles/ddusdogimpound.htm.

16. Kopelman, *From Baghdad,* ix.
17. Ibid., x.
18. Ibid., 56.
19. Ibid., 58.
20. Ibid., 58 (original emphasis).
21. Ibid., 59 (original emphasis).
22. Ibid., 9.
23. Ibid., 69.
24. Ibid., 145.
25. Ibid., 6.
26. Ibid., 101.
27. Ibid., 173.
28. Ibid., 12.
29. Ibid., 11.
30. The U.S. military, in conjunction with the Iraqi military, developed a lengthier and more rigorous training program for recruits in 2005. Jay Kopelman, phone conversation with author, March 10, 2016.
31. Kopelman, *From Baghdad,* 12. See "Today's Military: Boot Camp," 2012, http://www.todaysmilitary.com/before-serving-in-the-military/boot-camp?campaign_id=SEM2012:on:google:basic_training-basic_training:broad.
32. Kopelman, *From Baghdad,* 13.
33. Ibid., 13.
34. Ibid., 35 (original emphasis).
35. Ibid., 46–47 (original emphasis).
36. Ibid., 48.
37. Ibid., 48.
38. Oxford Dictionaries, http://oxforddictionaries.com/us/definition/american_english/shit.
39. S.v. "little shit." Dictionary.com, *Dictionary of American Slang and Colloquial Expressions,* http://dictionary.reference.com/browse/littleshit. See also "little shit." Urban Dictionary, http://www.urbandictionary.com/define.php?term=little%20shit.
40. Jay Kopelman, phone conversation with author, March 10, 2016.
41. Kopelman, *From Baghdad,* 31.
42. Ibid., 56.
43. Ibid., 101.
44. Ibid., 161.
45. Ibid., 170 (original emphasis).
46. Ibid., 160.
47. Lauren Berlant, *The Queen of America Goes to Washington City* (Durham, NC: Duke University Press, 1997), 3.
48. Ibid., 5.
49. Ibid., 6.
50. Ibid., 21.
51. Robert Hariman and John Louis Lucaites, *No Caption Needed: Iconic Photographs, Public Culture, and Liberal Democracy* (Chicago: University of Chicago Press, 2007), 11.
52. Ibid., 17.
53. Ibid., 9.

54. The Allied forces flew more than 116,000 air sorties. "Fast Facts About Operations Desert Shield/Desert Storm," accessed July 31, 2013, http://www.gulflink.osd.mil/timeline/fast_facts.htm.

55. Pat Sloyan, "What Bodies?" 2002, Alicia Patterson Foundation, http://fair.org/media-beat-column/spinning-the-gulf-war-to-ignore-the-cost-in-lives/. See also his "Masking the Face of Battle" for an analysis of how Margaret Thatcher's managing of the media, and the sanitizing of violent images, became a model emulated by Ronald Reagan (Alicia Patterson Foundation, http://aliciapatterson.org/stories/masking-face-battle).

56. For the sources for these figures and the different methodologies used to calculate them, see Jack Kelly, "Estimates of Deaths in First War Still in Dispute," *Pittsburgh Post-Gazette,* February 16, 2003, http://old.post-gazette.com/nation/20030216casualty0216p5.asp. Kelly does not indicate when Daponte ended her study. Given that the death count from malnutrition and illness attributed to the effects of U.N. sanctions as of 1999, according to UNICEF, was 500,000, presumably Dapointe's study does not include the consequences of the military campaign beyond its official cessation.

57. Joy Gordon, "Cool War: Economic Sanctions as a Weapon of Mass Destruction," *Harper's,* November 2002, https://www.globalpolicy.org/component/content/article/170/41945.html.

58. See ibid. for chilling quotations by Pentagon officials about the intentional destruction of Iraq's infrastructure as a means to hasten the effects of economic sanctions.

59. See Joy Gordon and Denis Halliday's "The Impact of UN Sanctions on the People of Iraq," *Journal of Palestine Studies* 28, no. 2 (1999): 29–37, and David Rieff's "Were Sanctions Right," *New York Times,* July 27, 2003, https://www.globalpolicy.org/component/content/article/170/41951.html. Rieff's article includes appalling quotations from Clinton-era officials such as Madeleine Albright, Richard Holbrooke, and James Rubin, affirming their belief in the morality of the sanctions. It was Albright, of course, who answered Leslie Stahl's question on *60 Minutes* about whether the deaths of 500,000 Iraqi children justified the sanctions: "This is a very hard choice, but the price, we think the price is worth it" (qtd. in Rieff).

60. In the Arab world, the term "First [Persian] Gulf War" generally refers to the conflict between Iraq and Iran from 1980 to 1988.

61. The figure 34,000 sorties is taken from Phillip Gibbons's "US No-Fly Zones in Iraq: To What End?" The Washington Institute for Near East Policy, Policy no. 632, July 1, 2002, http://www.washingtoninstitute.org/policy-analysis/view/US-no-fly-zones-in-iraq-to-what-end.

62. Jeremy Skahill, "No Fly Zones Over Iraq: Washington's Undeclared War on 'Saddam's Victims,'" *Counterpunch,* December 4, 2002, http://www.counterpunch.org/2002/12/04/no-fly-zones-over-iraq/.

63. See Kevin Berger's interview with Evan Kohlmann, "The Iraq Insurgency for Beginners," *Salon,* March 2, 2007, http://www.salon.com/2007/03/02/insurgency_3/. For an earlier assessment of the strength of Sunni nationalists in the insurgency, see John Robb's "How Big Is the Iraqi Insurgency?" http://globalguerrillas.typepad.com/globalguerrillas//How%20Big%20is%20the%20Iraqi%20Insurgency.pdf. Although there are no dates on this webpage, Robb's data are taken from 2003 to 2005.

64. I recognize that secularism, in some parts of the world, is viewed with suspicion for its historical complicity with Western forms of imperialism, and, certainly, Saddam Hussein had the backing of consecutive U.S. administrations before he fell out of favor. However, I draw attention to the circular logic that Noam Chomsky identifies as a feature of U.S. foreign policy, which becomes a self-fulfilling prophecy in its pronouncements of national security threats.

65. Noam Chomsky, *On Power and Ideology: The Managua Lecture* (Boston: South End Press, 1987), 21.
66. Quoted in Peter Steinfels, "The Brutality of War, and the Innocents Lost in the Crossfire," *New York Times,* November 20, 2004, http://www.nytimes.com/2004/11/20/national/20beliefs.html?pagewanted=print&position=&_r=0.
67. David Edwards, "'Limited but Persuasive': Evidence: Syria, Sarin, Libya, Lies," *Media Lens,* June 13, 2013, http://www.medialens.org/index.php/alerts/alert-archive/alerts-2013/735-limited-but-persuasive-evidence-syria-sarin-libya-lies.html.
68. Rebecca Hellmich, "How Many Iraqis Died in the Iraq War?" *Fairness and Accuracy in Reporting,* June 7, 2013, http://www.fair.org/blog/2013/06/07/how-many-iraqis-died-in-the-iraq-war/. In the latter poll, conducted by Ipsos Public Affairs, 60 percent of respondents answered "feel upset" to the question "When you hear about the deaths of civilians in Iraq, do you personally tend to feel upset, or more that their deaths are unfortunate but part of what war is all about?" When asked the follow-up question, "Has there been an acceptable or unacceptable number of Iraqi civilian casualties in Iraq?" 77 percent of the same respondents answered "unacceptable." These responses suggest that Americans *are* concerned about the Iraqi civilian casualty count even though they remain woefully misinformed about the tally that this war has exacted. The U.S. government's refusal to conduct an official death count of Iraqi civilians might not so much indicate that Iraqi civilians do not matter as to affirm that they matter a great deal because of their potential to sway public opinion against the war.
69. See "Iraq Body Count" (http://www.iraqbodycount.org/) and "Death Counter Explanation Page" (*Just Foreign Policy,* http://www.justforeignpolicy.org/deathcount/explanation). The figure from *Just Foreign Policy* is based on the period between 2003 and 2008 and does not distinguish between civilian and combatant casualties.
70. For a convincing analysis of the limitations of various studies, see Hannah Fischer's "Iraq Casualties: US Military Forces and Iraqi Civilians, Police, and Security Forces," October 7, 2010, Congressional Research Service, 7–5700, R40824, http://www.fas.org/sgp/crs/mideast/R40824.pdf.
71. See his *From Baghdad to America: Life After War for a Marine and His Rescued Dog,* which tackles Kopelman's and Lava's PTSD and contains resources for veterans (New York: Skyhorse, 2008). For more on canine PTSD see Lisa Rogak's chapter, "Veterinary Care," in *The Dogs of War* (New York: Thomas Dunne Books, 2011) and Terri Crisp and Cynthia Hurn's "Afterword," in *No Buddy Left Behind.*

PART III THEORIZING THE IN/VISIBILITY OF WAR

10 · THE IN/VISIBILITY OF LIBERAL PEACE

Perpetual Peace and Enduring Freedom

JON SIMONS

In Episode 7 of the first season of *The Newsroom,* a TV drama created by Aaron Sorkin, the news breaks that Osama bin Laden has been killed.[1] *The Newsroom* is an enactment of the American liberal imaginary showing an idealized version of television journalism fit for liberal democracy.[2] The opening credits for Season 1 are "a montage of great moments in the history of TV journalism" that evokes a past, golden age.[3] Sorkin admits to portraying "a romanticized, idealized newsroom" in his script that delivers a message that "corporate concerns and ratings-chasings have left the US with an embarrassingly skewed, shallow, showbiz-centric news output."[4] The series stages the tension between the corporate boss of a fictional TV network and the *News Night* team, especially Charlie Skinner, president of the network's news division.[5] Yet for all its liberalism, Aaron Sorkin's *Newsroom* is unable to imagine anything other than a military response to 9/11.

At no point in the episode is there any questioning of the event, the unlawful killing of an alleged criminal, carried out on the sovereign territory of another state without its government's permission. Rather, bin Laden's death is the news that everyone in the studio wants to hear, says Charlie Skinner. The main anchor Will McAvoy (who happens to be stoned, having arrived in haste from a party) soberly reports the news moments before President Barack Obama makes his announcement. On his way to the studio, Will had run from his African American bodyguard Lonny when they found themselves caught in traffic. Two male police officers, one white, the other Hispanic, apprehended and searched Lonny, who was yelling in the street after McAvoy. Lonny told the nervous policemen that he was armed, with a permit, and then apologized for making them nervous by being simultaneously big and black. Before McAvoy's broadcast, an angry Lonny bursts into the newsroom, accompanied by the policemen. After a little joke, McAvoy vouches for Lonny who, he says, is a former military policeman. Will then whispers the news in Lonny's ear, and suggests that Lonny pass it on to the officers. Lonny's racial role as protector of the privileged white male is reinforced by privately informing the two officers about the nation's use of state violence, which another black male is about to publicly announce.

The team in the studio stands reverentially as McAvoy tells his audience that the world need no longer fear bin Laden, that 9/11 transformed America into "a different nation—more fearful, and so of course more hostile," and that "this [is the] victory the country has waited for." The camera slides behind McAvoy as the footage switches to the documented scene of Obama's announcement in the White House. McAvoy's fictional white authority in the democratic public sphere is visually preceded by and sutured to Obama's black authority, which comes to focus on the screen as if summoning a ghost, as civilian commander-in-chief. The episode is a festival of uncritical, racialized, gendered, liberal patriotism. If peace is imagined here, it is peace as victory, a liberal equivalent of "mission accomplished." *The Newsroom*'s hailing of victory echoes the liberal voices in the U.S. public sphere that have trumpeted the justness of America's twenty-first-century wars in Afghanistan and Iraq and against "terror."[6]

Why does liberalism, epitomized here by the imaginary *Newsroom,* find it so difficult to imagine peace without simultaneously invoking war, victory over nonliberals, and implicating itself in a context of inequality and injustice? What we see in *The Newsroom*'s liberal patriotism mirrors the distorted political imagination of liberal political theory, on which the rest of this chapter will focus. If we try to imagine peace, it tends to be along the lines of a bumper sticker, or Yoko Ono's "imagine peace" ad in the *New York Times,*[7] or a book of poems.[8] Yet the concept of peace emerged in English thought from the fourteenth century not only in theological and philosophical works, but also military handbooks, fiction, and popular ballads.[9] If political authority rests on the institutionalization of fictions, then perhaps the popular ballads of liberal democratic imaginaries take the form of broadcast televisual fictions.[10] Political conceptualization, then, is closely related to imagination. For Immanuel Kant, whose writing on peace is a focus of this chapter, imagination is a cognitive function that organizes the "schema" that the mind applies to empirical sense data in order to produce a unified image of the world in our minds. The mind's imaging capacity is a precondition for our perception of images of the world.[11] We do not literally see the image that we see with our imaginations, nor is such a (mental) image an object, but may rather be an idea, a concept such as "peace."[12] Yet at the same time, the imagined image requires a material support, a medium, whether that be a picture, a popular ballad, a TV show, or a work of political philosophy.[13] Thus if peace were entirely unimaginable it would also be inconceivable, invisible to thinking. Yet because peace *is* imagined in liberal public culture and political theory as "enduring freedom" forever shadowed by war, it is visible in a way that makes it even harder to see, to imagine, peace without war.

Peace is both visible and invisible in the liberal political imagination, but the sorts of liberal peace that are imaginable, conceivable, and practicable under liberalism are peace as pacification, as order, and ultimately as war. Liberalism is always in some sense at war with itself, and hence also with its others. By treating certain key texts as emblematic of liberal political theory, I argue, as Mark Neocleous does with reference to different texts, that "permanent war [is] normalized as peace" and that "civil society created in the name of peace and security remains for liberalism a space of war."[14] The critique of liberal peace theory leads toward an understanding of the sort of peace conceivable through liberalism as a policed peace, in which civil society ruled by coercive law is the correlate of disciplinary, biopolitical governmentality. The relationship of liberal regimes to its internal others is replicated in its enmity toward external nonliberal regimes, who also appear to threaten an international liberal peace zone. One upshot of this critique is that the regimes established in Iraq and Afghanistan as a consequence of America's twenty-first-century wars are themselves the continuation of war by other means, just as the War on Terror is but another manifestation of the "permanent or semi-permanent wars against the various 'enemies within,'" all the various "wars against. . . ."[15] An upshot of the argument here is that there is nothing new about the conflation of war and peace in contemporary American discursive practice, as liberalism in theory and practice has always presented war as peace keeping. It is no surprise, then, that "winning the peace" is a repeated trope in current discourse about the "postconflict" pacification of Iraq and Iran, or that the official name for the War on Terror was "Operation Enduring Freedom."[16]

KANT AND LIBERAL PEACE THEORY: "ON THE DISAGREEMENT BETWEEN MORALS AND POLITICS"

Kant's essay "To Perpetual Peace: A Philosophical Sketch"[17] is the keystone of liberal peace theory, a branch of liberal political theory that argues for the inherently pacific character of liberal politics. Broadly speaking, liberal political theory upholds that political authority rests on the consent of the governed, who are entitled to equality before the law and individual rights, especially to property. Civil society is conceived as a peaceful alternative to a warlike state of nature. According to Jonathan Schell, "The long march of liberal democracy is a 'peace movement'—possibly the most important and successful of them all."[18] Kant remarks that the "practical politician" may well disregard the impractical "political theorist" who fails to "detect some danger to the nation."[19] This observation indicates that there is a fault line within liberalism between its pacific ideals and its martial practices. Kant tries hard to overcome the gap between theory and practice, morals and politics, peace and war, but ultimately fails.

Commentators credit Kant's essay with "posthumous influence on the creation of the League of Nations and the United Nations."[20] According to the principles laid out in the essay: Each nation should have a republican constitution; nations' rights should be based in a gradually expanding federation of states or "league of peace"; and there is a cosmopolitan right of universal hospitality, which underlies rights to travel and trade. Kant conceives of peace as adherence to a set of moral-political prescriptions, establishing a clear liberal peace imaginary. Yet, Kant did not rest with these proposals, adding two supplements, the first explaining how "nature" guarantees peace; and the second underlining the special role of philosophers in advising about peace, thereby attempting to close the gap between the morality of peace and the politics of war. Kant's peace prescriptions are thus sandwiched between arguments that try to bridge practice and theory, politics and morality.

Kant's attempt to bridge between humans' natural aggression and their moral nature is central to his whole critical philosophical system—and I would suggest, to liberalism in general. The world appears to be governed by two different sets of laws. There are the scientifically discoverable laws of the "sensible" or empirical realm of nature and universal principles of autonomous human action, in the "suprasensible" (or transcendent) realm of freedom, that take the form of a moral law.[21] Yet how can humans be subject to both natural scientific laws that govern our self-interested, depraved, and bellicose behavior, and to the moral law, under which we are free? Kant admits that by the end of his first two *Critiques* there is a gulf between the sensible and suprasensible domain, "as if they were two different worlds."[22]

Kant has both a philosophical and a pragmatic strategy for bridging this gulf, which he never quite separates out, such that each appears to make up for the shortcomings of the other. His more pragmatic strategy looks to the role of law as a coercive mechanism through which moral conduct is induced. The key to the legal route to morality is that adherence to universally applicable law "can, along with the mechanism of nature, be the cause of the desired result."[23] The moral idea (duty, right, peace), Kant argues, becomes empirical through the actions of people who act according to the moral idea. Eventually people will learn to be good, to will what is right, but in the meantime law serves as an instantiation of morality. Kant's doctrine of perpetual peace among nations is an extension of the need to establish civil society with a lawful authority. Government of the behavior of the citizens of constitutional republics is replicated in international relations as the impulse to govern the "barbaric" conduct of nonrepublican nations, an impulse that is realized in U.S. (and other) "postconflict" regimes, as in Iraq and Afghanistan.

Although he has a "well-founded hope" that we can fulfill our duty nationally and internationally, thereby advancing toward perpetual peace, Kant underlines the empirical, natural, and depraved tendencies of humans to wage war against each other, especially in a "state of nature" whose lawlessness is overcome by the establishment of "civil society." Even "civilized" nations, who live under the rule of law, see their national "majesty" in unrestrained activity. So long as nations remain in a state of lawlessness in relation to each other, all lack the authority of the law. Kant thus requires that each nation become republican and for each nation to join in a federation that would serve as "a surrogate of the union in a civil society."[24] Law, national and international, is the constraint by which citizens in republics will correct their depraved tendencies, and by which republics will cease to wage war against each other.

In order to reconcile humans' bellicose nature with their transcendent moral nature, Kant advances a paradoxical argument whereby nature is endowed with a providential purpose that ensures perpetual peace, "permitting harmony to emerge among men through their discord."[25] Nature impels humans first to war and then to peace, according to the providential course of nature. As Kimberly Hutchings puts it, even war "comes to serve the ends of reason" as "Kant's account slips from the realm of ideas to the empirical realm and back again with bewildering consequences."[26] In his prohibition on standing armies, Kant switches quickly between the profoundly moral argument against treating soldiers as objects to kill and be killed and an empirical claim that armies are costlier to maintain than small wars.[27] Hutchings detects a "sleight of hand in mapping the relation of the real and ideal" as Kant variously figures the process of pacification as both a morally natural necessity and as empirically fragile. The ideal realm of peace and the real practice of international politics cannot be joined in Kant's philosophical constitution.

The most alarming consequence of Kant's sleight of hand is that his liberal peace theory is also a justification for war, in that he lays the ground for a less patient approach to the gradual achievement of perpetual peace. He argues that "a man (or a people) who is merely in a state of nature denies me . . . security and injures me *merely by being in this state*" (emphasis added). The nonrepublicans are not merely people and nations yet to be persuaded, but threats to security, and hence enemies. There is an "unwritten code of national and international rights," such that "a transgression of rights in *one* place is felt *everywhere*." Even as Kant accuses the European powers of "imbibing injustice like water," he also accuses the inhabitants of the Barbary Coast and Arab Bedouin of acting "contrary to natural right" by plundering aliens.[28] There is an irreconcilable tension between Kant's attitude to "barbarians" as threats to the security of civilized nations and his respect for their national rights to self-government.

Kant appears to rule out treating nonliberal states as enemies whose transgressions need to be corrected coercively: "No nation shall forcibly interfere with the constitution and government of another. For what can justify its doing so?"[29] Kant might answer himself: a people that threatens your security by being in a state of nature. He considers a punitive war inconceivable in the absence of an authoritative international tribunal, yet justifies an alliance against a nation that prepares for war.[30] The same reasoning that leads Kant to imagine an international federation of republics that upholds civic and national rights also envisages war against the nonrepublicans. In the same moment that liberal peace is imagined, so is the threat to its security in the form of its nonliberal enemies. Put differently, what mediates between morals and politics in liberalism is neither providential teleology nor social evolution, but the coercive power of sovereign law. More than that, liberal peace is a version of the peace of the victors, a police peace, or pacification, as in the "postconflict" pacification of Operation Enduring Freedom. Indeed, "post-conflict reconstruction" and "winning the peace" are synonymous in the discourse of twenty-first-century wars.[31]

CONTEMPORARY LIBERAL PEACE THEORY: MICHAEL DOYLE

The foundational essay for contemporary liberal peace theory by Michael Doyle is to a large extent a reflection on Kant's essay, thereby attesting to its continuing pertinence. In contrast to the Realist school in International Relations,[32] critiqued by James Der Derian in this volume, liberal peace theory insists that foreign policy must be consistent with liberal principles.[33] Yet Doyle is also critical of liberal foreign policy, finding in Kant both the "best guidance" on "the ever-widening pacification of the liberal pacific union" and why "liberal states are not pacific in their relations with nonliberal states."[34] Liberal states presume mutual amity at the same time as they "demarcate zones of enmity with nonliberal others."[35]

Doyle argues that the internal governance of liberal states makes a difference to their conduct of foreign affairs, because they do not behave as if in a state of nature. He lists chronologically in a table a growing number of liberal regimes according to historical periods, and in another he lists international wars, allowing for some exceptions and variations.[36] Doyle deduces his famous liberal peace thesis by comparing the growing number of liberal regimes to the occurrence of international wars: "*Even though liberal states have become involved in numerous wars with nonliberal states, constitutionally secure liberal states have yet to engage in a war with one another.*"[37]

Although openly critical of liberalism's external bellicosity, Doyle fails to follow through by questioning Kant's liberal doctrine of peace altogether. Kant's prescription becomes "a startling *prediction*" for Doyle,[38] who sees "a natural evolution" toward a situation in which "liberal wars are fought for popular, liberal purposes."[39] There is a tension in Kant's account of how this evolution occurs, between a "transnational" dynamic that pulls republican states to peace, and an "international" dynamic in which experiences of insecurity and war engender the formation of republican governments.[40] Doyle displaces the tension onto the empirical field of policy failure. "Even though liberalism has achieved striking success in creating a zone of peace . . . liberalism has been equally striking as a failure in guiding foreign policy outside the liberal world." Doyle does not flinch from referring to conflicts with weak nonliberal states as "imperial interventions . . . designed to create liberal societies." He sees that "the liberal dictum in favor of non-intervention does not hold" as it "requires ignoring the violations of rights they inflict on their own populations." Liberalism, he says, generates hostility to nonliberals: "We dislike what they are . . . public violators of human rights."[41]

However, Doyle does not see that the contradiction between interventionism and respecting national rights, between conceiving nonliberals as enemies and as bearers of rights, is inherent to Kant's liberal doctrine of peace. The problem is not that liberal principles are sidelined by Realpolitik, but that there is a gap between morals and politics, peace and war, that is internal to liberalism. Kant's and Doyle's unsatisfactory efforts to resolve these internal tensions are symptomatic of liberal wars against internal others, against "barbarians" at home who threaten the security of society. From this perspective, liberalism attempts to draw clear lines between its internal pacific zone and its external nonliberal zone. Liberalism's wars, including the twenty-first-century wars of the United States in Afghanistan and Iraq, are the structural corollary of its internal "peace." Wars are waged to enable "others to pursue that which U.S. citizens hold most dear—life, liberty, and the pursuit of happiness," to turn them into liberals like us.[42]

LIBERAL PEACE STUDIES AND PEACEBUILDING

In addition to Kant's essay and Doyle's liberal peace theory, the entire discipline of peace studies could be claimed as a conceptualization of peace. David Cortright's influential book, *Peace: A History of Movements and Ideas*,[43] can represent the liberal branch of peace studies. The book is a "synthesis among peacemaking traditions" that argues for a "pragmatic" or "realistic pacifism" that also draws on just war theory. Kant, says Cortright, "came closest to crafting a comprehensive peace philosophy," demonstrating the hold that Kant continues to have on contemporary thinking. Referring to Kant, Cortright declares that the triad of "mutual democracy, economic interdependence, and international cooperation" have been verified by current social science as the "*proven correlates of peace*" (emphasis added), so that "theory and empirical research have come together." Cortright thus exacerbates Kant's problematic relation between the empirical and the ideal, between politics and morals, by not acknowledging that there is a tension. Social scientific theory, according to which there are "natural tendencies towards both cooperation and competition" along a path of "social evolution,"[44] usurps Kant's failed yet telling effort to reconcile morals and politics.

By obscuring the gap, Cortright's version of liberal peace theory cannot imagine anything other than a police peace. He follows the usual move of peace studies in distinguishing between "negative peace" that is the mere absence of war, and "positive peace" that refers to the "maintenance of an orderly and just society," requiring the elimination of "structural violence." But if any version of order is reckoned to be more just than the absence of civil society, police become peace. Cortright envisages "peace" along the lines of the institutionalized UN-style peacebuilding and peacemaking that have proliferated since the end of the Cold War. Peace in his view is "fully compatible with the requirements of sound security policy," including an alternative strategy of "law enforcement" in the "war on terror." Although this strategy entails addressing legitimate social grievances that terrorists exploit, it rests also on an unsustainable distinction between war and policing.[45]

The "proven techniques of peace building" to which Cortright refers boil down to empirically measurable "good governance." Although committed to development and social justice, Cortright treats the clear line between the neoliberal "Washington consensus" and the global justice movement about the role of markets in fostering peace as a mere disagreement. It is as if we all know what peace looks like and we know how to get it, though we may have debates about precisely when self-defense and the "Responsibility to Protect" the innocent trumps "the presumption against violence."[46] If Kant implicitly argues and Doyle explicitly suggests that liberalism tends to wage war against its nonliberal others, Cortright points toward a new liberal interventionism according to which the "human security" and rights of people—especially the right to life—living under nonliberal regimes must be protected by the liberal peace zone. It is precisely such liberal interventionism that is at work in the U.S.-led liberation and "pacification" of Iraq and Afghanistan.

CRITICAL PEACE STUDIES

According to scholarship in critical peace studies, the practices of liberal peacebuilding and peacemaking in what are called postconflict societies are seriously wanting. Roger Mac Ginty notes how little "serious consideration of the meaning of peace" there is in such UN-style peacebuilding, arguing that peace studies has come to focus on "technocratic peacebuilding."[47] "Peace" is visible, but only as brought about by the "proven methods" discussed by Cortright. In most cases, Mac Ginty argues, the peace achieved is a state of "no peace, no war," such as a formal peace accord unmatched by transformation of the socio-cultural conditions of conflict. He explains that the frequency and longevity of these situations is a consequence of structural aspects of "liberal democratic peace" that follows a Western model and "set templates" of peace interventions and a "conveyor belt of programmes" that standardize the development sector of countries, co-opt NGOs, rely heavily on international financial institutions, and emphasize "civil society capacity building" and "good governance." Without denying that post–civil war peace orders have saved lives, Mac Ginty notes that "liberal democratic peace" does not live up to the vision of "positive peace" as it is "often characterized by poverty, insecurity, and a failure to deal with structural factors." Order and peace are confused.

Similarly, Oliver Richmond argues that the regimes established as a result of the United States' twenty-first-century wars in Iraq and Afghanistan are "parodies of the liberal state."[48] Postconflict states of peace "converge on a notion of *peace-as-governance*" that is "biopolitical and governmentalizing," entailing "a disciplinary framework that rests on coercion." According to Richmond, "really-existing liberal peace" sees peace instead only as "institutions" and "security." Whereas Kant and Doyle indicate liberalism's animosity toward its non-liberal others, Mac Ginty and Richmond suggest that in the era of liberal peacebuilding the trend is not simply to wage war against others, but to govern and pacify them. Peacemaking is a matter of imposing institutions that "emancipate the other from war, violence and unstable political, social and economic structures."[49] Liberal peacemaking is the contemporary form of liberal imperialist intervention. Peace is the white, liberal, Western man's burden.

In the related field of critical security studies, Michael Dillon and Julian Reid conceive of post–Cold War "liberal peace" as "a specific form of liberal governmental power." Contemporary liberal peace remains consistent with its predecessors by presenting itself as a system of law through the "pacifying effects of cosmopolitan law" obeyed by sovereign states. Global liberal governance, in the form of peacemaking and peacebuilding practices, is deployed not only economically and militarily but also morally, being war like in pursuit of "a combative and heavily armed peace."[50] Orwell would be proud, as peace and war are confused in a program of pacifying nonliberals through governmental order. The liberal zone does not "simply encounter" the barbarians on its boundaries, but constitutes the nations there as already in need of, amenable to, and programmable by global governance. Liberal peace makes its own enemies.

Critical security studies targets liberalism's very understanding of war through practices of the pacification of civil life.[51] As a form of governmentality, liberal peace is remarkably similar in its domestic as well as international relations. Following this insight, we can say that both in Kant's time and in ours, liberal civil society engenders the need to defend itself, often aggressively, against the abnormal, the nonliberals who do not follow the norms of civil peace either by maintaining nonrepublican government or by transgressing the norms of republican civil society. Liberalism sees itself as peaceful societies in federation with each other, but does not see that the sorts of liberal peace and peacebuilding it practices entail the governing of civil and international society through a form of policing that is not entirely distinct from war, even if it is not its equivalent. The liberal peace zone may be free of outright war, but not of forceful policing.[52] Referring back to Cortright's realist, pacifist endorsement of policing in place of the War on Terror, one should rather see continuity between policing and war, between liberalism's internal governmentalities and global governance. Hence our wars on drugs, and even poverty, as well as on terror.

MUST LIBERAL PEACE BE DEFENDED?

Liberalism's appeal to its moral-rational ideas, including its pacific principles, cannot defend it against its illiberal and bellicose practices. Michel Foucault's analysis of liberalism as governmental practices of police-war makes visible the war of liberal peace within states. The effort to limit political practice by means of political philosophy is misconceived from the start, argues Foucault in reference to Kant. Kant's thought mediates between an empirical, heteronomous, finite being governed by life, labor, and language, and an autonomous rational being governed by a universal law. The former is determined, the latter has free will, yet they are both Man.[53] There is not, says Foucault, a moral realm of human autonomy and freedom, and an empirical realm of human subjection to the laws of nature, but one world in which humans govern their conduct according to norms that are simultaneously empirical, moral and juridical.

Kant's resolution of the empirical-transcendental tension by means of the law as enforcement of morality amounts to a "contract of rational despotism with free reason."[54] According to Foucault, the liberal normative conceptions of modern power, such as sovereignty, rights, and social contracts, or in brief a juridico-discursive model of power, are at best unhelpful in understanding governmentality and at worst deceptive. Although "philosophers and jurists" had a "dream of a perfect society" based on a "primal social contract," there was also "a military dream of society" based on national discipline "as a fundamental means of preventing civil disorder" and as "a technique of internal peace and order."[55] Sovereign law does not instantiate "right," which sets limits to sovereign power. Rather, by determining what was within the rights of, and prohibited for, others, the sovereign's power appeared to be indispensable, judicial and fair in its settling of social disputes that endanger its order.[56] The supposedly neutral law of the monarchy is the inscription of the right of the victor. The sovereignty of rational law was established only when the din of battle was silenced, when "the blood . . . [had] dried on the codes of law."[57] "Civil peace" in the West emerged from historical struggles along the lines of race and class (and one should add, gender).[58] Reversing Clausewitz's proposition to say that "politics is the continuation of war by other means," Foucault proposes that the "civil peace" in which we live is a "sort of silent war."[59] We are all living in postconflict societies, all subject to the peace of the victor that is indistinguishable from domination, hierarchization, and differentiation.

The confusion of peace and order rests on normalization, that is, the colonization of "normative" juridical, philosophical norms by the "normalizing" norms of power/knowledge discourses and governmental practices. Juridical institutions, constitutions, and codes of law "were the forms that made an essentially normalizing power acceptable."[60] All those who are abnormal—delinquents, the insane, the sick, perverts—all those who find themselves on the wrong side of the "dividing practices" of normalization, find themselves "outside" the social contract of civil peace, which they inhabit because they endanger its security.[61] In modern, liberal governmentality, the abnormal are always a threat within the society against which it must defend itself. The civil life of liberalism is always insecure.[62] When the abnormal are racialized explicitly, normalization assumes the power to kill, waging war against them. "The other race (of abnormals) are not some external enemy that the society encounters but the result of a split within society." Modern governmentality creates its own enemies: "We have to defend society against . . . the other race . . . that we are, despite ourselves, bringing into existence."[63]

The relationship of liberal civil society to its internal others does not for the most part take the form of a "race war" in which the enemy may be killed (the death penalty being a notable exception). Liberalism does indeed reduce outright physical violence, even as it conceals structural violence. Nearly all liberal theory is oblivious to the conditions of possibility of civil society, namely, its governmental pacification along the model of police, whereby the abnormal are always perceived as a threat. Abnormals at home, nonliberals abroad: Foucault's account suggests that all must be variously fought or pacified by a liberal peace that cannot but envisage war against, or forceful policing of those who threaten its peace. The liberal way of life is preparation for war; it cannot imagine peace without simultaneously practicing war.[64]

ENDURING FREEDOM: THE PACIFICATION OF IRAQ AND AFGHANISTAN

Foucault is not alone in paraphrasing and reversing Clausewitz. "Full-spectrum operations are the continuation of major combat operations by other means," write Major General Chiarelli and Major Patrick Michaelis, commanders of the First Cavalry Division's campaign to win the peace in Baghdad. Full spectrum operations entail the simultaneous practice and coordination of combat operations, the training and employment of security forces, provision of essential services, promotion of governance, and economic pluralism (which means "creating the conditions for a true free market"). There could not be a clearer illustration of how establishing peace in postconflict Iraq meant not simply defeating the insurgency of 2004 but served as a military blueprint for governing the "populace." This disciplinary and biopolitical governmentality, this defense of society, "is built to create secure conditions," not only for the populace but "to keep our soldiers safe and our homeland sound." As if echoing Foucault's analysis of seventeenth- and eighteenth-century police discourse, the generals claim that "discontent erupts" when developing nations cannot provide services for the masses migrating to cities. They also give a nod to Foucault's notion of micropolitics by characterizing the pacification campaign as "the net effect of many microdecisive actions" concerning "sewage, water, electricity, and solid waste removal" and "the price of goods and services." All this had to be achieved with due recognition of the non-Westernness of the populace, "a firm grasp of . . . the value placed on extreme concepts of 'honor above all.'" Winning the peace in Baghdad entailed weaning the "barbarian" populace, as Kant might have put it, away from the "despised rule of law under Saddam Hussein" by "educating and mentoring the emerging Iraqi federalist-based, democratic system."[65]

In military terms, the "mission accomplished" moment is a "point of penetration," which was achieved on January 30, 2005 when Iraqis "proudly displayed" their "purple index finger," thereby proving "to the world their willingness to try democracy."[66] Having been educated by the U.S. military to dutifully and democratically achieve penetration with their own fingers, the pacified and policed Iraqis allegedly ceased to be a threat to western security by becoming liberals like us. At first blush, the tragedy seems to be that peace was not won, and that Iraq is still mired in a conflict that claims many lives, obstructs prosperity, and leaves its citizens insecure. Yet if peace in Baghdad could only be won by the U.S. military through "full-spectrum operations," it was doomed to remain the pursuit of democracy "by other means."

One could also argue that full-spectrum operations are not inherent to liberal peacemaking in the form of pacification and policing, as the United States had to learn the hard way in Afghanistan and Iraq that it could not leave a "light footprint" and avoid "nation-building" through reconstruction projects.[67] In the case of Afghanistan, U.S. and allied forces found themselves spending far more time combatting the Taliban than on civilian reconstruction. In the absence of a nation-building approach, the forces had only a patchwork of small Provincial Reconstruction Teams and the ISAF, whose jurisdiction was limited to

Kabul.[68] The United States was equally unprepared to ensure adequate security in Iraq that could lead to stable governance because basic services (for civilians) and resources to build democracy were lacking.[69] No doubt lessons had to be (re)learned, but these were simultaneously political and military lessons that did not divert U.S. liberalism from its regular course, but rather returned it to its role as "a successful world leader." The United States secures itself from the danger of failed states abroad by winning wars, then winning the peace, by creating "an environment in which freedom, democracy, and prosperity have a chance to flourish."[70] U.S. wars of the twenty-first century are wars for the security of liberal peace at home by enforcing liberal peace overseas.

LIBERALS LIKE U.S.

Liberal political theory consistently imagines peace as an idea that we can "see" as freedom and civil society. This chapter has traced the persistence of Kant's eighteenth-century conception of peace within contemporary liberal theory of international relations and liberal peace studies. On the face of it, liberal political theory enables us to imagine peace in each society and a global federation of states, in which social conflict is not addressed by recourse to armed violence. It is an attractive, reasonable and moral image of peace, of a world that permanently secures our rights, and hence our enduring freedom. Who could, reasonably, contest liberal peace?

They (those abroad who do not live by liberal theory) could, and do, which is why, with much regret, we invoke the need to intervene militarily in their countries so that they will become moral like us, pursuing the rights and freedoms which we hold most dear. They not only deny themselves civil peace but also threaten our security of rights by living in a barbaric state of nature. They are not normal like us, so it is our moral duty to normalize them. Ideally, we would not have to intervene and go to war to rescue them and bring them into the fold of liberal citizenship.[71] But empirically, it remains the case that they are aggressive, public violators of human rights, unwilling to comply with the moral law. For now, we need to impose the law coercively until they learn it themselves, and once they have, that will be our victory. We will have extended the liberal zone of peace. This ideal is not merely a hope, as we have solid empirical grounds for expecting evolution toward peace internationally and civilly to be the outcome of liberal interventionism. Admittedly, our effort to provide the non-liberals with security, rights, and good governance is not going so well, as armed violence rumbles on in Afghanistan and Iraq. But give it time and commitment (keeping boots on the ground and drones in the sky), and they will be peaceful like us.

Yet at the same time, as we see the liberal ideal of peace so clearly in our imaginations, we lack critical insight of the nature of that peace, the sleight of hand by which its ideal justifies its empirical implementation. The stage of pacification and moralization of the non-liberals abroad, which is the adjustment of their empirical belligerence into an ideal peacefulness, is not temporary but permanent. Civil society needs to be defended against sources of illiberal insecurity abroad and at home. Just as the post-conflict regimes of biopolitical governmentality in Iraq and Afghanistan institute situations of "no war, no peace," the normal state of affairs in U.S. civil society is one of disciplinary normalization, of coercive policing of the abnormal. And as in those twenty-first-century wars overseas, the U.S. wars against its domestic others are wars to make the abnormal be like us. In our fictional *Newsroom* and on our actual new screens we see that war, and we call it peace.

NOTES

1. *The Newsroom,* created by Aaron Sorkin, HBO, Season 1, June 24, 2012–August 26, 2012. Sorkin is well known for portraying idealized liberal politics in *The West Wing,* NBC, September 22, 1999–May 14, 2006 (Sorkin left *The West Wing* after its fourth season).
2. Dave Itzkoff, "This Just In," *New York Times,* June 6, 2012, http://www.nytimes.com/2012/06/10/arts/television/the-newsroom-aaron-sorkins-return-to-tv.html?_r=1&.
3. Alan Sepinwall, "Review: HBO's 'The Newsroom' Returns for Season 2," *Hitfix blog,* July 11, 2013, http://www.hitfix.com/whats-alan-watching/review-hbos-the-newsroom-returns-for-season-2#rpwpQAjVOFmGsiLY.99.
4. Jane Mulkerrins, "Aaron Sorkin, interview," *The Telegraph,* July 10, 2012, http://www.telegraph.co.uk/culture/tvandradio/9381606/Aaron-Sorkin-interview.html.
5. Ibid.
6. For a notable example, see Michael Walzer, *Just and Unjust Wars: A Moral Argument With Historical Illustrations,* 4th ed. (New York: Basic Book, 2006).
7. "Will Yoko Ono's *New York Times* Ad Help Bring World Peace?" *The Guardian,* January 1, 2013, http://www.theguardian.com/commentisfree/poll/2013/jan/01/yoko-ono-new-york-times-ad-peace-poll.
8. Philip Metres, Ann Smith, and Larry Smith, eds., *Come Together, Imagine Peace* (Huron, OH: Bottom Dog Press, 2008).
9. Ben Lowe, *Imagining Peace: A History of Early English Pacifist Ideas, 1340–1560* (University Park: Pennsylvania State University Press, 1997).
10. See Yaron Ezrahi, *Imagined Democracies: Necessary Political Fictions* (Cambridge: Cambridge University Press, 2012).
11. Sunil Manghani, Arthur Piper, and Jon Simons, eds., *Images Reader* (London: Sage 2006), 42.
12. W.J.T. Mitchell, *Iconology: Image, Text, Ideology* (Chicago: University of Chicago Press, 1986), 9–14.
13. W.J.T. Mitchell, "Four Fundamental Concepts of Image Science," in *Visual Literacy,* edited by J. Elkins (New York: Routledge, 2008), 14–30.
14. Mark Neocleous, "War as Peace, Peace as Pacification," *Radical Philosophy* 159 (2010): 13, 15–16. Because of his centrality to contemporary liberal peace theory, I focus on Kant rather than his many predecessors, from Francisco de Vitoria through Erasmus, Machiavelli, Hobbes, and Locke, whose thought Neocleous analyzes.

15. Ibid., 16.
16. United States Department of Defense (December 2014), "Obama, Hagel Mark End of Operation Enduring Freedom," *Defense,* http://www.defense.gov/News/Article/Article/603860/obama-hagel-mark-end-of-operation-enduring-freedom; Robert C. Orr, ed., *Winning the Peace: An American Strategy for Post-Conflict Reconstruction* (Washington, DC: Center for Strategic and International Studies Press, 2004).
17. Immanuel Kant, "To Perpetual Peace: A Philosophical Sketch," in *Perpetual Peace and Other Essays on Politics, History, and Morals,* trans. and intro. Ted Humphrey (Indianapolis: Hackett Publishing, 1983), 107–143.
18. Jonathan Schell, cited in David Cortright, *Peace: A History of Movements and Ideas* (Cambridge: Cambridge University Press, 2008), 233.
19. Kant, "Perpetual Peace," 107.
20. Pauline Kleingfeld, "Editor's Introduction: Kant on Politics, Peace and History," in *Towards Perpetual Peace and Other Writings on Politics, Peace, and History—Immanuel Kant* (New Haven, CT: Yale University Press, 2006), xv.
21. Immanuel Kant, *Critique of Practical Reason,* trans. Lewis White Beck (New York: Macmillan, 1956).
22. Immanuel Kant, *Critique of Judgment,* trans. Werner Pluhar (Indianapolis: Hackett, 1987), 14.
23. Kant, "Perpetual Peace," 133.
24. Ibid.,.
25. Ibid., 134, 139, 12, 111–11, 115, 117.
26. Kimberly Hutchings, *Kant, Critique and Politics* (London: Routledge, 1996), 49, 47.
27. Kant, "Perpetual Peace," 108.
28. Ibid., 118–119.
29. Ibid., 109.
30. Ibid., 110, 109.
31. Orr, *Winning the Peace.*
32. See the essay by James Der Derian in this volume for a critique of the Realist school.
33. Michael Doyle, "Kant, Liberal Legacies, and Foreign Affairs, Part 2," *Philosophy and Public Affairs* 12, no. 4 (1983): 345.
34. Michael Doyle, "Kant, Liberal Legacies, and Foreign Affairs, Part 1," in Michael Doyle, *Liberal Peace: Selected Essays* (Routledge: New York, 2011), 25. The essay was first published in *Philosophy and Public Affairs* 12, no. 3 (1983): 205–235.
35. Rosemary Shinko, "Agonistic Peace: A Postmodern Reading," *Millennium: Journal of International Studies* 36, no. 3 (2008): 481.
36. Doyle, "Kant, Liberal Legacies, and Foreign Affairs, Part 1," 17.
37. Ibid., 18.
38. Doyle, "Kant, Liberal Legacies, and Foreign Affairs, Part 2," 349.
39. Doyle, "Kant, Liberal Legacies, and Foreign Affairs, Part 1," 26, 28.
40. Doyle, "Kant, Liberal Legacies, and Foreign Affairs, Part 2," 351.
41. Ibid., 323, 324, 330.
42. Orr, *Winning the Peace,* ix.
43. David Cortright, *Peace: A History of Movements and Ideas* (Cambridge: Cambridge University Press, 2008).
44. Ibid., 20, 8, 14–16, Chapter 13, 2, 3, 335, 244.
45. Ibid., 6–7, 4–6, 176–178.
46. Ibid., 336, 252, 300, 334.

47. Roger Mac Ginty, "How Did Peace Become Order?" *Les Cahiers Paix et Citiyonneté* 1 (2006): 23–29, 24, 23, 27, 24.
48. Oliver Richmond, *A Post-Liberal Peace* (London: Routledge, 2011), 2.
49. Ibid., 6–7, 11, 15–16, 11.
50. Michael Dillon and Julian Reid, "Global Governance, Liberal Peace, and Complex Emergency," *Alternatives* 25, no. 1 (2000): 125–126.
51. Julian Reid, *The Biopolitics of the War on Terror* (Manchester, UK: Manchester University Press, 2006), 4–6.
52. Shinko, "Agonistic Peace."
53. Michel Foucault, *The Order of Things: An Archaeology of the Human Sciences,* trans. unidentified collective (New York: Vintage, 1973), 341–342.
54. Michel Foucault, "What Is Enlightenment?," in *The Foucault Reader,* ed. Paul Rabinow, trans. Catherine Porter (New York: Pantheon, 1984), 37.
55. Michel Foucault, *Discipline and Punish: The Birth of the Prison,* trans. Alan Sheridan (New York: Vintage, 1975), 168–169.
56. Michel Foucault, "Truth and Power," in *Power/Knowledge: Selected Interviews and Other Writings, 1972–1977,* ed. and trans. Colin Gordon (Brighton, UK: Harvester, 1980), 121.
57. Michel Foucault, "War in the Filigree of Peace: Course Summary," trans. Ian Mcleod, *Oxford Literary Review* 4, no. 2 (1979): 16–19.
58. Michel Foucault, *Society Must Be Defended: Lectures at the Collège de France, 1975–76,* ed. Mauro Bertani and Alessandro Fontana, trans. David Macey (London: Penguin, 2003), 8, 19.
59. Ibid., 15–16.
60. Foucault, *History of Sexuality I: An Introduction,* trans. Robert Hurley (Harmondsworth: Penguin, 1978), 144.
61. Foucault, "Subject and Power," afterword to *Michel Foucault: Beyond Structuralism and Hermeneutics,* ed. Hubert L. Dreyfus and Paul Rabinow (Brighton, UK: Harvester, 1982), 208. See also David Campbell, *Writing Security: United States Foreign Policy and the Politics of Identity* (Manchester, UK: Manchester University Press, 1992).
62. See Michael Dillon, *Politics of Security: Toward a Political Philosophy of Continental Thought* (London: Routledge, 1996).
63. Foucault, *Society Must Be Defended,* 256, 61.
64. Reid, *Biopolitics,* 10.
65. Peter Chiarelli and Patrick Michaelis, "Winning the Peace: The Requirement for Full-Spectrum Operations," *Military Review* (2005): 16, 13, 10, 17, 5, 16, 148.
66. Ibid., 4.
67. Orr, *Winning the Peace.*
68. Milan Vaishnav, "Afghanistan: The Chimera of the 'Light Footprint,'" in Orr, *Winning the Peace,* 244–262.
69. Bathsheba N. Crocker, "Iraq: Going It Alone, Gone Wrong," in Orr, *Winning the Peace,* 263–286.
70. Orr, *Winning the Peace,* 303–304.
71. See Purnima Bose's essay in this volume for an interpretation of the wars as rescue narratives.

11 • WHY WAR?

Derrida, Baudrillard, and the Absolute Televisual Image

DIANE RUBENSTEIN

On February 19, 2003, shortly before the start of the war in Iraq and immediately following mass antiwar demonstrations the prior weekend, French psychoanalyst René Major organized an impromptu roundtable discussion between Jacques Derrida and Jean Baudrillard concerning the likelihood and stakes of future hostilities in the Gulf[1] (fig. 11.1). The debate was structured around a series of questions, formulated by René Major, to serve as an introduction to each author's thought concerning war and its representation.[2] Would a war take place (*avoir lieu*)? What would such a taking place consist of in light of "live" television coverage? Was war an outdated concept? Is terrorism an ideology or a strategy? More significantly, this conversation exposed a crucial tension between Derrida's critical and Baudrillard's radical thought as two alternative metaphysics and modes of interpretation.

It should not be surprising that the 2003 exchange reenacted earlier responses to 9/11. But it also recalled former European and American politico-media events. The collapse of the Twin Towers on September 11, 2001, reiterated its hypervisual counterpart of the Berlin Wall. Baudrillard critiqued televised events in Romania (both "fake" such as Timisoara, or "real" as the trial and execution of Ceausescus), celebrity-humanitarian missions in Sarajevo, or the ongoing reality show of Le Pen's electoral impunity. Derrida queried transnational citizenship and its relation to political memory via artifacts such as the Rodney King tape. One can see in their shared objects of analysis (such as Le Pen or the television station *Arte*) differential interpretations—as a site of a robust democratic contestation to come (Derrida) or as a transpolitical "revenge of the mirror people" (Baudrillard).

One potential site of affinity was their respective thinking of the "event" as "unique, unforeseeable, without horizon and uncontrollable; that cannot be mastered by any *ipseity* or conventional and consensual performativity."[3] Whether September 11 could be qualified as an "event" remained a *différand* between both thinkers. Major's questions proffered potential common ground for this debate around Derrida's writings (on 9/11 and in *Rogues*) involving the conception of "war," "terror," "the event," "democracy," and "reason." In particular, he compared the idea of "autoimmunity" ("that strange illogical logic by which a living being spontaneously destroys in an autonomous fashion that which he has within him destined to protect him or to immunize against the intrusion of the other, of all others")[4] with Baudrillard's "evocation of the suicidal tendency of all unconditional power, without otherness or adversity."[5] The "auto-immune" thus links Derrida to Baudrillard as an "alternate biopolitical metaphor."[6] It is a bodily symptom of an earlier illness, "a Cold War in the head," "a global head cold" that had mutated in an autoimmune way.[7]

Were we to frame differences between these thinkers in relation to the theoretical concerns of this volume, they revolve around the relationship between televisuality and the concept, reality, and eventuality of war. What is the status of the media image in the "event" of war? In this essay I argue that the discussion of the Iraq War contrasts Baudrillard's "symbolic" depiction of an "absolute" and irrevocable event[8] with a Derridean account. Here "the turning point . . . lies in international law and the structure of the Security Council."[9] A hypervisual media regime obscures the event's stakes.[10]

Derrida places his hopes upon the way that a televisual image (of mass protestors or a vote within the United Nations, for example) can open a critical vantage point that might allow for democratic contestation of post–Cold War American hegemony. As with his writings on "democracy to come," the televisual image's potential is accompanied by a conditional affirmation of international organizations (here the Security Council; elsewhere the European Union).[11] Yet the televisual image also works in an autoimmune fashion; it offers the chance of new alignments or singular conditions (such as potential vetoes in the Security Council). At the same time, the image threatens to reveal these institutions or protests as forms of empty speech. Moreover, any futurity—an international law or organization "to come"—is held in tension with a keen appreciation of the originary *Gewalt* or force subtending all law.

Derrida's differential appreciation of the Iraq War's status (as event or nonevent) is affected by his reading of it as an iterative process. Thus it is never solely an effect of image transmission as such. Baudrillard's approach to the image would not allow for such a critical apprehension, yet he also directs us to

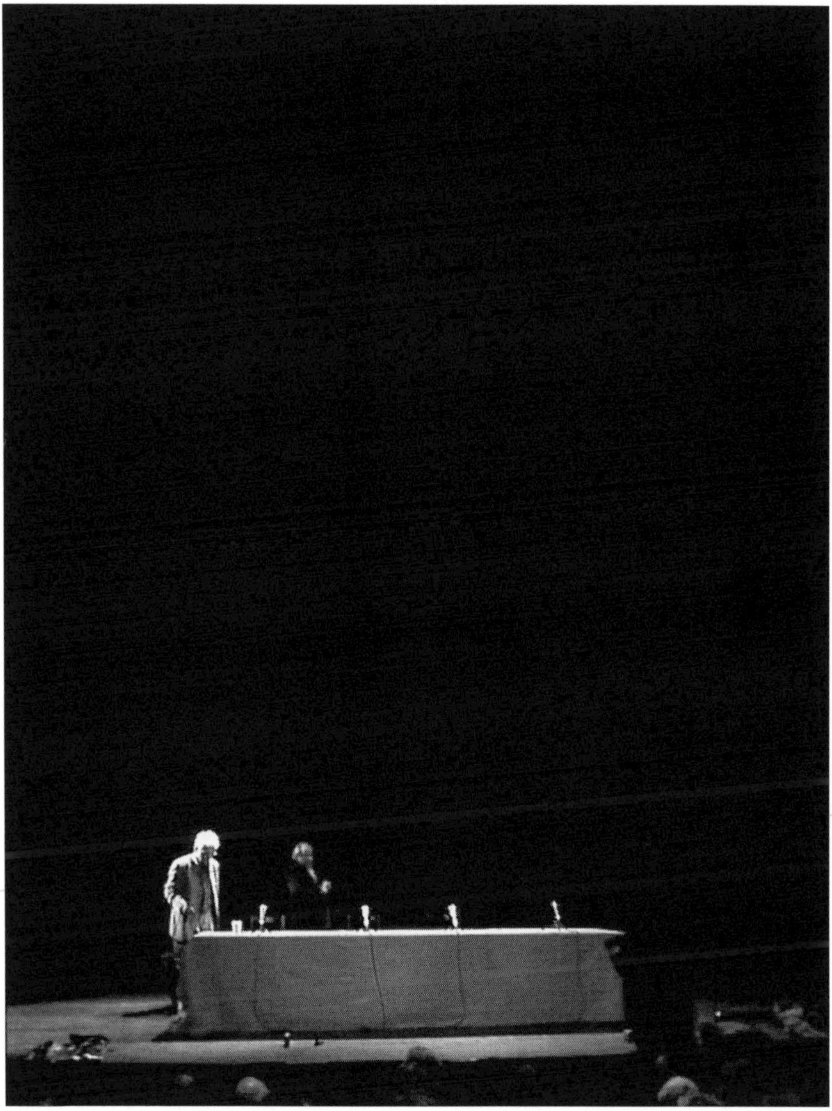

FIGURE 11.1

the challenge that mediated acts of terror pose for a unipolar global order. The "event-ness" of 9/11 finds its visual correlate in the "absolute televisual image," which displaces conventional spectatorship of war.

> Things no longer really take place, while nonetheless seeming to.
>
> —Baudrillard[12]

Major's initial query to Baudrillard addressed the *avoir lieu* of the war (the status and stakes of its eventuality) and its qualification as an event (or as a media "non-event"),[13] concepts tied to two of his most popularized essays. Both *The Gulf War Will Not Take Place* and *The Spirit of Terrorism* focus on the indeterminacy of historical events, epistemologically unknowable apart from mediated (televisual) consumption.[14] The Gulf War essay is but a latter moment of Baudrillard's semiotic critique. The media translates reality into equivalent and exchangeable signs that can substitute for "lived experience": "each signify each other reciprocally and mirror each other's content."[15] The Twin Towers are the architectural embodiment of this doubled circularity of signaling. "Perfect Parallelipeds. . . . The fact that there were two of them signifies the end of any original reference. . . . Only the doubling of the sign puts an end to what it designates."[16] Widely cited passages from the writings on simulation detail the mutual implosion of the real and the image or medium. In his reading of Coppola's *Apocalypse Now,* war and film mutually implode; film becomes war and vice versa in a dazzle of special effects.[17] This simulacral victory obliterates America's historic defeat.

The relation between history and events operates on a temporal logic that Baudrillard perceives as also informing the Iraq War. In *Why War Today,* he reverses the customary relation between Hollywood (disaster) films and their real-world enactment, claiming that such films did not provide a precedent nor an incitement to the terrorist act. These media were not 9/11's "cause": "Not at all. There was no reference. The event (9/11) was carried out *before* it was possible; its character is radically unforeseeable."[18] Following Henri Bergson's paradoxical temporal metaphysics, Baudrillard claims that "things are not possible, they become possible once they have taken place."[19] Events happen only retrospectively, *après coup.*[20]

Works contemporaneous with the Gulf War essays, such as *The Transparency of Evil* or *The Illusion of the End,* foreground a principle of uncertainty that results from the hyperbolic media saturation of everyday life—"events" now disappear: "There is no such thing as an act or an event which is not refracted into a technical image or onto a screen."[21] Political reality is transformed into an "empty *actualité*" (news) via its spectacularization and "speculative inflation."[22] Television as "the strategic site of the event" exacerbates the confusion of act and sign.[23]

Its real-time transmission provides high-definition images with low-definition meanings; its technological perfection effectively "exterminates" the event, both short-circuiting real life as well as leaving no time for history to take place.[24]

What Baudrillard identifies in the Gulf War essay is this over-proximity of an event and its mediation, which has perverse spatio-temporal consequences. This ambient televisuality portends simulacral predictability; "events happen with the strange aftertaste of something that has already happened before, something unfolding retrospectively."[25] At the same time, there is an anticipation of future minimal events, "so minimal that they might well not need to take place at all."[26] The anticipated Iraq War—in contrast to the unforeseeable attack of 9/11—is so overly programmed that its actual occurrence becomes unnecessary.[27]

Baudrillard is concerned with history receding into an acceleration of "vanishing events."[28] Their aim is preventative/dissuasive: "to arm us against the future with prophylactic memories." In *Why War Today* he returns to this "will to annul, efface, whitewash the initial event in some way which renders war *virtual.*" Events are now evacuated of their "finality" or "necessity."[29]

The Gulf War essay is also inscribed within a concept of deterrence, which refers to what causes something *not* to take place, by (its etymologically linked) *terreur* or dissuasion.[30] Simulation is presented as that which keeps events from happening; any meaning or possibility not included in its model is excluded a priori. In a manner that will take on added urgency after 9/11, deterrence now designates how anything revealed to be refractory to the dominant global order necessitates violent suppression. Reality must be predictable in order to remain credible. "In earlier times an event was something that happened—now it is something designed to happen. It occurs as a virtual artifact, as a reflection of preexisting media-defined forms."[31] What Baudrillard's thinking adheres to is a profound reversal of the Aristotelian logic concerning the actual and the potential (virtual).[32] In the old paradigm the virtual—what existed as potential—would become actual. Today, it is the virtual (potential) that *prevents* the occurrence of the actual due to the revolution in real-time technologies.

> What would "September 11" have been without television?
>
> —Derrida[33]

In *Why War Today,* Derrida sharply differs with Baudrillard concerning the status of 9/11 as an event—whether an Iraq War would have happened anyway without it as a pretext, or with a different electoral outcome (Al Gore not George W. Bush), and given oil interests in the Gulf and the Arab-Israeli conflict. He argued that the Iraqi chain of events had a relative autonomy.[34] But these are not two unrelated matters; they are at the heart of their respective readings of televisual coverage of 9/11 and its imbrication with the event.

As previously noted, both Derrida and Baudrillard address the singularity of American hegemony in the post–Cold War period. For Derrida, the looping of televisual images of 9/11 is a reassertion of its "virtually sovereign role among sovereign states." It assures a sort of faith and credit, through its "wealth and its techno-scientific and military power but also, at the same time, through its role as arbiter in all conflicts, through its dominant presence on the Security Council." These "looped" images reveal and multiply the suicidal paradoxes of the U.S. power: the "ground," that is, the literal figure of the founding or foundation of this "force of law" is "*seen to be exposed* to aggression." This aggression of which "it is the *object* (the *object exposed,* precisely to violence, but as also, 'in a loop,' to its own cameras in its own interests) comes as from the inside."[35] In other words, the forces that attack the United States receive their force in the form of high-tech knowledge sufficient to divert an airplane in a U.S. airport, to procure a weapon, to obtain a pilot's license on home turf, all via American training and hospitality.

Derrida's figure of the "loop" recalls Baudrillard on real-time transmission: "the re-productive re-transmission 'loops' . . . the same televised images of a 'live transmission' (the slashing open and then collapse of the two towers)."[36] It is a film running interminably on screens worldwide. The loop indicates "repetition compulsion" that both "confirms and neutralizes the effect of this reality." Fear and "terrified pain" are cathected to "unavowable *jouissance* . . . all the more uncontrollable, and irrepressible" in the distancing effect of neutralized reality. The loop designates a narcissistic specularity; "There is something we are elated about seeing here, terrified to find ourselves allaying our terror by our voyeurism."[37] Derrida here alludes to a Baudrillard provocation concerning the spectatorial identifications: "The (unwittingly) terroristic imagination which dwells in all of us. . . . At a pinch, we can say that they *did it,* but we *wished for* it."[38] Last, the loop figures a "vicious circle" of suicidal disavowal, self-witnessing, and, in a hyperbolic moment, "gets carried away in its own testament, that bears witness to what will remain, on the side of the 'suicides' (the hijackers and the 'missing' cadavers, *without witness*")."[39] While this exponential grieving and mimetic denegation of trauma can be read as a symptom of the new sentimental order in a virtual era, there is a pathos here that Baudrillard would refuse.

Derrida queries the inextricable tie between television and 9/11, noting how "maximum media coverage" worked in autoimmune fashion in the interests of both "perpetrators" and "victims" alike. He also avers that the "terror" was inseparable from the exposure and exploitation of the "image of terror by the target itself."[40] It was in the United States' "*interest* (the *same* interest it shares with its sworn enemies) to expose its vulnerability, to give the greatest possible coverage to the aggression against which it wishes to protect itself."[41] As with other "events" witnessed by Derrida, he followed "the first televised images" on CNN from his hotel room in Shanghai.

Derrida is quick to point out that there is "nothing purely modern" in this use of media; images or "rumors" have served to terrorize civilians in prior wars via radio and television.[42] In *Echographies of Television,* he observed that the event is never exterior to virtuality, which is "imprinted upon its very structure."[43] His quite elaborate presentation of television in *Above All, No Journalists!* prefigures the autoimmunity of 9/11: "When religion shows itself on television . . . it at the same time increases its power and its power to self-destroy."[44] Television's mediation of "September 11" reposes upon the suicidal autoimmunity of the event itself. This allows for the communication of a "new type of transgression" other than a violation of domestic territory.

> The concept of war did not take place.
>
> —Derrida[45]

Why War Today took place within the shadow of a build-up to the Iraq War. Derrida's first televisual example is the widely diffused, mass, antiwar demonstrations of the previous weekend. The political desires of these "physical" people—what one might "nickname . . . the *demos*"—are juxtaposed with the positions of their respective pro-war governments.[46] Derrida underlines not only the importance of their actual presence in the streets but also of their spectrality: "The possibility of these demonstrations to be televised, to be immediately . . . globalized, in such a way that one could hope to see . . . the quasi-unanimity of the world population represented by these demonstrations, opposing themselves like an immense public opinion to the war that is starting up."[47] The disenfranchised "have only the means of the poor in this age of globalization (which is, today, television, an instrument that is never neutral) to witness the spectacle of the offensive prosperity of others."[48] Yet television can also be credited for "recent movements towards democratization in Eastern Europe" that "owe a great deal, almost everything perhaps, to television, to the communication of models, norms, images, informational products and so on."[49] Teletechnological media is a post-Enlightenment heir, possibly enabling the "access to Reason in a certain public space."[50] Mediated televisual images matter; they display the divergence between popular and state sovereignty, where "a demonstration is not a vote and is not worth a vote," neither in one's country nor the United Nations.[51] The televised popular display of will is "heterogeneous" to legal sovereignty.

Derrida's examples are surprising in the relatively un-interrogated status of the televisual image itself. Although some attention is paid conceptually to the affects of terror, desire, and fear evoked in a spectator, little technical analysis is performed, analogous to his extensive work on the materiality of language—in particular to what is not verbal about language, either its imagistic properties or its sound. In *Above All, No Journalists!*, Derrida privileges the medium of television as the place where a kinaesthetic conversion of voice and image seems to "see what it touches."[52] The proximity of the televisual voice to the event conditions a stance of credulity toward the image; it is difficult not to believe what we see on television. For Derrida what is telegenic is the voice, not the image.[53] This counterintuitive insight might explain the conundrum that someone as "attuned" to "the ear" of the other paid little attention to what Jean-Louis Comolli noted as the first symptom of the terrifying images of 9/11—their silence: "It concerned the production of images without sound."[54]

> It seems that you place your hopes in the authority of international law.
>
> —Borridori[55]

Derrida signals that his response will be framed within the register of "authority, force of law, notably international law," an unsurprising gesture given Derrida's theoretical achievement in his rethinking of sovereignty and democracy.[56] As previously noted and in contrast to some of his other writings,[57] his discussion of televisual events in the debate privileges the relations among war, sovereignty, law, and image. In contrast to Baudrillard's reading of the 9/11 "televisual" image as spectacle, Derrida characterized the media storm as so much "noise" obscuring a "real" challenge to invisible or occluded ruptures in international law and organization. War would be the hyperbolic case of sovereignty. It figures as the disavowed violence of onto-theology and Enlightenment metaphysics that have informed Derrida's earliest essays in *Writing and Difference* (where war inheres in the philosophic *logos*) to his final interview where he declares to Jean Birnbaum that he is "at war with himself."[58]

Derrida mobilizes the arguments from *Force of Law* to foreground that there are conflicts of interest hidden underneath the debates in the United Nations and the media around legal violation. "Law does not break with force."[59] He invokes Kant to underline the synonymy between force and law: no law without force. He emphasizes the violence, force, and authority of law: "The legal (juridical) *Gewalt* is but a figure of a pre-juridical *Gewalt*."[60] Derrida's response to September 11 and the Iraq War only obliquely reference this theoretical apparatus. He emphasizes the relation to international law and organizations such as the United Nations and its "monstrous" Security Council, and to the rational antimonies of state power that make every sovereign state a *virtual* rogue state. His reading of terror/ism is situated in relation to the extant possibility of states (that is, revolutionary wars, colonial wars of independence, or partisan ones). The "present crisis 'should' lead to a profound transformation of the structures of international law."[61] Derrida hypothesizes an international law "to come" that will organize the given balance of forces and the "sovereignties in play." This hypothesis wagers on perfectibility and positions Derrida within critical Enlightenment thought, in contrast to Baudrillard.

The principal or the force of legal authority leads Derrida to consider the Iraq War as a reiteration of the Gulf War: "Before the Gulf War, there wasn't war. Before tomorrow's war, there was already war." Regarding the upcoming war in Iraq, there is ("at least virtually") a threat of a veto aligning France, China, and Russia "against the United States . . . against the global superpower determined to wage war." What is unprecedented is a possible confrontation between the United States and Europe. This possibility of an internal rift between superpowers may well impact the "constitution" of this international organization as well as its "structure and nature." Derrida concedes that he thinks "it is a good thing that there is the United Nations and even the Security Council, but I also think that . . . their incapacity to apply the law that they declare . . . just like the absence of an autonomous force for Europe . . . all of this evidently constitutes a deficiency that the current crisis or present upheaval must alter something, at some unforeseeable time." From the perspective of international law, the Gulf War (that "took place") and the Iraq War (that "has not yet taken place") are not the same. There is no longer the same "good conscience" of those representing the international community in 1991 as the invasion of Kuwait by Iraq was a clear violation of sovereignty: "There was a patent violation of international law, no problem."[62] This contrasts with the upcoming war, where it is not apparent that Iraq has committed a violation of law.

Derrida places "war" in quotation marks to signal that the legal requisites within European law concerning state sovereignty are inadequate to present conditions. Absent declarations of war between states or enemies in the form of state actors, it becomes unclear just whom one is waging war against. Thus "wars" cannot "take place" as the "concept of war no longer has a place."[63] Here he agrees with Baudrillard.

Derrida gives another televisual example as evidence for his position that what is at stake and elided is the revolution in international law. It concerns a UN debate presided over by Kofi Annan shortly after 9/11 involving a vote to condemn international terrorism. Kofi Annan honestly asserts that he could not define the concept of international terrorism or terrorism, which could apply to individuals or to rogue states. After the United Nations avowed that it did not know what it was talking about, it voted the resolution condemning international terrorism unanimously. Derrida reads this according to a devastating logic: the UN charter, having explicitly referenced as "democratic" states those being represented, such states then could not fail to condemn terrorism even if they didn't know what it meant. Television thus works in an autoimmune fashion here. It threatens to expose the surreal core of the United Nations' legitimacy, yet this potential of exposure creates the very conditions for "rescue." What must be saved ("vouchsafed") is the United Nations or its Security Council that risks self-destructing in such televised debates. It must be saved from its televisual self.[64]

Where Derrida most clearly disagrees with Baudrillard is on the terrain of the real. While one can virtualize war or wage virtual wars through the media (and television is directly mentioned as a site where this occurs),[65] "there are two names in the geopolitical, historico-political field *that resist virtualization.*" The first of these is "death"—the death of Iraqi victims as also those killed on September 11. The second "name" is oil—another word for "territorialization."[66] Oil is "linked to territory in an unmovable way."[67] Strategic oil interests impact international organizations and legal doctrines such as "self defense." And they qualify the opposition to the United States in this war by the French and German governments.

Thus the force that comes to represent, direct, and appease the conflict of forces is law. This reading of the political context of war and terrorism is predicated on a class-based model of poverty and exploitation where the "oil wealth" has not benefited Arab-Muslim populations in the Middle East, which could not help but impact terrorism. Derrida refers to an "elsewhere" to the Iraq War, which is the global war of market capitalism, "a permanent economic war" in which "we know the winners and the losers."[68] This war takes place or has its ambivalent place in the aporetic framework of "globalization." The task at hand is a critical one; new categories must be invented for these *real* and not *virtual* events, beyond the habitual images and semantics that obscure them at the same time that they offer us shelter. Signifiers matter: "Any politician who still says 'war' or 'terrorism' either does not know what he is talking about, or he is trying to make us believe something that isn't true."[69]

Terrorism is part of an economy of violence—of greater and lesser (formerly, "noble" and constitutive; today carried out as well by "rogue" states). For Derrida, it no longer plays the same role absent state sovereignty. Derrida situates the "noble" resonances of terrorism as associated with revolutionary terrorism in France. The concept is metonymically chained to other French historical wars of liberation and resistance under the Occupation or in Algeria. Terrorism is linked to moments of saving the state, constituting or otherwise recognizing it (for example, France, Algeria, Israel, Palestine).

Derrida aligns with Kant on the subject of terror. For Kant, the Terror was both a sign of the Revolution's failure and a sign of what had been attempted even where it failed. Derrida analogizes this event (the revolution and its terror) to his long-term hope in the transformation of international law, the United Nations and its Security Council: "The very fact that an attempt was made was a promising, commemorative sign and that this sign was an event."[70] The "unheard-of" fact that the United States went to the United Nations to get approval for the war instead of just declaring war is "an indisputable event" even if "one finally acts in a unilateral fashion." Like Kant, Derrida reads this as a "sign" of changing times, despite the obvious need to "perfect" the "structure of international decisions of the Security Council" and "change the world order." Only then would the concept of war have its place.

> We need a paradoxical way of thinking to meet this paradoxical state of things.
>
> —Baudrillard[71]

Baudrillard's writings in the decade between the Gulf War and 9/11 attest to political reality during an "event strike": "With the attacks on the World Trade Center in New York, we might even be said to have before us the absolute event, the 'mother' of all events, the pure event uniting within itself all the events that have never taken place."[72] Baudrillard is not saying that there have not been world events during this time: both hyper-mediated ones such as the death of Princess Diana, but also "violent, real events, from wars right through genocides."[73] Nor is he denying the suffering and death of victims of conflicts, contrary to the reception that met his essay on the Gulf War. Yet, a fixation on misery deflects from the politically more relevant terms of evil and the inhuman. "We have to come to terms with the inhuman. . . . The idea of the human can come only from elsewhere, not from itself. The inhuman alone can bear witness to it."[74] Baudrillard's writing is situated on a different plane where an authorial "right to indifference" vies with the more conventional "right to indignation."[75]

What Baudrillard designates as an event is of another order: a symbolic event. An event worthy of the name would be one that did not just receive "worldwide coverage" but one that could "represent a setback for globalization itself."[76] Sylvère Lotringer notes that while most philosophers were fortunate to have one idea informing their oeuvre, Baudrillard had two. The first is a "critical" one and it concerns the semiotic critique of the real: "That reality had disappeared and was replaced by simulacra."[77] The second idea concerning symbolic exchange was "agonistic": "to turn this disappearance into a challenge."[78]

The symbolic is a site opposing, possibly resisting, interrupting, and irrupting within the semiotic. Its principle of reversibility haunts the hegemonic exercise of sovereign power, whether in the survival of indigenous cultures (for example, Aboriginals) or in Islam as a singularity resisting integration into certain Enlightenment values. Baudrillard's diagnostic of present-day Western societies describes a passage from "the universal" to the "global." The universal is confronted by a unilateral global order without alternatives or by an "insurrection of singularities." The new global order is an inherently violent one "operating virally, by contagion and destroying our immunities."[79] However, there exist forces that are resistant to the global order's excessive "positivism, technical efficiency and the equivalence of all exchanges."[80] These can take collective (linguistic or ethnic) forms, or a form of singular individual. It can be nonviolent as well as violent. The existence of these potentialities within Baudrillard's thinking is the reason Major does not see him as a nihilist.

Rather than a clash of civilizations, Baudrillard sees the unipolarity and domination of the global system itself as responsible: "By seizing all the cards for itself, it forced the Other to change the rules. . . . Terrorism is the act that restores an irreducible singularity to the heart of a system of generalized exchange."[81] In other words, against the quite visible fractures of the exploited versus the dominant order, 9/11 was a case of "triumphant globalization battling against itself."[82] It did not occur via the machinations of an external enemy; it was an internal breach secreted at the heart of the culture combatting it and doubling the visible fracture along lines of inequality.

The global system can fight visible antagonisms but not the "silent reversion" of terrorism. Baudrillard's symbolic reading of terrorism contests Derrida's claim that terrorism is an "outdated" word for the structure of our present situation. Terrorism, for Baudrillard, is not only a mode of action but is a form of vision, which creates an irreversible situation from the standpoint of symbolic exchange. Using a language reminiscent of Marxist spectrality, after 9/11 "all the holy powers" (whether democratic, fascist, totalitarian, liberal) were coalesced into a single "apparition" on the same side—which was the side of "order."[83]

War cannot be the answer to terrorism; in the face of this impossible confrontation, the "idea" of war might attempt a rescue via "spectacular set pieces," but it does not respond to the symbolic challenge of the terrorist act.[84] Neither conventional war nor forms of bio- or nuclear terrorism, which annihilate without glory or risk, can adequately address the symbolic challenge of terrorists who directly wager their own deaths. A symbolic antagonist cannot be "impersonally eliminated" but must be humiliated, must be made to lose face, "targeted and wounded in a genuinely adversarial relation . . . the opposite of what the Americans did in the Gulf War (and . . . in Afghanistan) where the target is invisible and liquidated operationally."[85]

Nor did the show of force implicit in UN oversight and ongoing inspections in Iraq (with the resultant submission and humiliation inflicted) successfully compensate for 9/11's symbolic wound. *Au contraire!* According to Baudrillard's logic, they become "one more gift" that must be returned.[86] It is important to distinguish in this logic between "wounds" that are symbolic (and cannot be subject to an equivalent exchange or retaliation) and acts of war (which can exchange with other acts of retaliation). With Pearl Harbor, the United States suffered an act of war; in 9/11, it received a "wound."[87]

In *Why War Today,* Baudrillard elaborates upon the logic informing symbolic exchange as applied to American war. He inscribes America in the role of "slave" in the master–slave dialectic, as being incapable of putting his own death into play. The slave cannot sovereignly wager his own life; only the "master" can do that. Against "suicide bombers," America (as "allegoric" for Western superpowers) proffers a doctrine of "zero death," and "roughly, falls to the level of the slave."[88] Humiliation now passes to the American side.

Baudrillard underlines that he is giving a resolutely *symbolic* reading of the Iraq War's eventuality, not a political or economic one. He utters a provocative paradox: "It is absolutely indifferent if the war takes place or not." The Iraq War will be a "secondary event"—not in the sense of a lack of significance, but rather in the sense of "substituting" for or "buying back" or "laundering/face-lifting" the fundamental event of 9/11. Thus the war in Iraq, "whether or not it takes place, is a puppet (or phantom) event or non-event that only exists as an effect of substitution." Saddam Hussein is substituted for bin Laden, opening up a "work of interminable mourning" but also an "immense work of contraception" to ensure retroactively that 9/11 never would have existed. For Baudrillard, the Iraq War and 9/11 are radically opposed events, along the lines of "the virtual" and "the factual," respectively. The Iraq War is not, as Derrida suggests, a reiteration of the First Gulf War, but a double, a clone, just as George W. Bush is a "clone of his father."[89] The fact of being a clone, or of a double-ness, makes the Iraq War more virtual. Thus it will take place (or not) as a conjuration or exorcism of the singular event of 9/11.

In an interesting twist on the *avoir lieu* of the Iraq War, Baudrillard says that it will be "interminable, even before it has begun: opening up the eventuality of an infinite war that will never take place, that will never finish because it has never begun." This is a "preventative war . . . a retaliation or anticipated repression of an act of war that has not been committed—as . . . the virtual criminal act of Saddam has not taken place." War is then directed toward the prevention of a past event, that of 9/11. This principle of "security" and "prophylaxis" will be globally generalized, taking on an almost metaphysical dimension. War crimes and any possible singularity or event must be dissuaded in advance. Baudrillard refers to this as a *Minority Report*-ization of Western life: "singularity/the event will no longer have the right to take place."[90]

When all the powers ally unilaterally, the principles of legitimacy and representation become eroded, thus leading to the *end of sovereignty.* For sovereignty needs representation, manifested in a demonstration of popular will or public opinion. As noted previously, Derrida sees a dehiscence and heterogeneity between popular and state sovereignty (for example, a demonstration is not worth a vote) in the mass antiwar protests. Baudrillard reads the dissensus between populations and hegemonic power otherwise. As power is aligned with order and increasingly cut off from the populace, strange sorts of Stockholm syndromes occur where hostage and terrorist are complicit with one another. The absolute example here is the 2002 Moscow theatre incident, where Russian Special Forces killed 129 terrorists and hostages.

This planetary civil war is a new situation, as the division passes between powers and their populations. Baudrillard concurs with Françoise Gaillard's assessment of the massive demonstrations, either as a wild utopian sign of hope or as a more disquieting symptom of a democratic crisis, a harbinger of a Hobbesian world in which "absolute power," now "detached from any source of legitimacy" in the people, is "free to exercise itself in a pure state."[91] The terrorism of bin Laden was "the first to operate as a true process of globalization . . . not of markets and finances, creating a confrontation between two blocs—world powers and singularities."[92]

THE ABSOLUTE IMAGE

September 11, 2001, upped the media image ante. The absolute event had finally met up with its visual counterpart, what Jean-Marc Vernier calls the "absolute-image."[93] Hyperfocalization on the World Trade Center (to the exclusion of the Pentagon) was more congruent with a requisite of the codes of "attentat dramaturgy":[94] a unity of place, the site of the explosion; multiple witnesses and victims attesting to its cultural impact; rescuers to signify that "competent" authorities are at hand. It was not necessary to show the bodies of the victims in order to signify the horror of the event. Nor were the rescuers easily visible due to the clouds of dust resulting from the Towers' implosion. These particles also blanketed what could be seen of the victim's bodies, "the spectacle of an impossibility to see."[95]

The capacity to see what was going on in the televisual image was complicated by a "deceptive familiarity" with the visual regimes and special effects of Hollywood action films.[96] The bodies of abject victims, the visceral exposure of gruesome and bloody bodily injury, that are typically replayed in montage, underscored by an explosive soundtrack, were notably absent. Jean-Michel

Frodon saw these images as the very "opposite of a Hollywood spectacle" due to their "very high content of invisibility."[97] If it "felt" like a film we had already seen, this had more to do with the Hollywood codes we had ingested.

The visual distancing from the dead reversed the phenomenology of real-time transmission. But this effect was itself provoked by the event—by the collapse (or suicide) of the Towers. Thierry Jousse remarks that it is the fact of "seeing the Towers collapse—in live and global transmission—that is, from the point of view of the image, an event without equivalent."[98] This image becomes an icon.

The image has an ambivalent role, both exalting and hijacking the event—"taking it hostage." It diverts, consumes, neutralizes and can spiral the event exponentially. Baudrillard concedes that our fascination with the event of 9/11 is inextricably tied to the image. But here, "the real is superadded to the image like a bonus of terror, like an extra *frisson*," like something you might get with a DVD director's cut of a film. The advertising would read: "Not only is it terrifying, but what is more, it is real." It is subject to the paradoxical temporal logic: "Rather than the violence of the real being there first, and the *frisson* of the image being added to it, the image is there first, and the *frisson* of the real is added."[99]

Baudrillard's depiction of 9/11 as an absolute and irrevocable event has its visual correlate in the absolute televisual image. Vernier's earlier typology of televisual images was constructed according to criteria of belief or support, contracts of visibility linking spectators to images. Images are reposed on a "promise" of a type of spectatorship as well as an implicit outline of their expectations. Prior to 9/11, there were three types: "depth images," "surface images," and "fragmented images." 9/11 would combine them in an absolute image, without hierarchically ordering them or subtracting any aspect.

The depth image presupposes that there is something "real" to show and its promise with the spectator resides in its alleged "objectivity": the media takes itself for a transparent "window on the world." A naïve spectator watches the images unfold. This image register was operative during 9/11 in the incredulity of spectators; such disbelief made them forget that these were in fact mediated images. On 9/11, the incessant repetition of "depth images" reinforced their "high reality quotient." In repeated viewing, a spectator could pass from "It can't be true; it's not possible" to "But yes!" and thus constructs both a representation of and meaning to the event.[100]

The surface image is a meta-image; it plays on the media-savvy spectator already cognizant that reality is staged. Its criterion is not "truth" but "credibility" or "likeliness." Already in play in the viewer's projections of previous Hollywood blockbuster films, it was also at work in the impacted symbolism of the Twin Towers themselves. This surface image was troubled by the retransmission of the event, which ironically redoubled the schema of the Towers' duplication. The direct attack upon the second tower, having the first tower on fire as background, was reinscribed in a second, later viewing, which showed the image of the first Tower under attack. The repeated camera's-eye views confirm the image logic of the Gulf War as described by Baudrillard: the event does not exist outside of its televised images.

The "fragmented image" associates meaningless images with intensely visceral sensations. It is a collage made up of pieces of images spliced together and regularly recycled in a feedback loop, eroding their intensity only to recompose in a condensed fashion in one image, of the plane imminently striking one Tower.[101] The "absolute image" produces an effect of "self-ironization" of the global regime of images; it pushes credulity in the image to a paroxysm. The viewer's adherence to each type of image becomes too strong. Such excess triggers a process Vernier describes as "inverse fetishism." The formulaic disavowal, "I know very well but all the same" becomes "I can't stop myself from believing it, but I know very well that it is a belief." Inverse fetishism short-circuits demystifying or critical postures in relation to these images.

Baudrillard is aware of the potency of the terrorist's symbolic violence and its "singularity," combining in a "Manhattan disaster movie, the twentieth century's two elements of mass fascination . . . the white light of the image and the black light of terrorism." As such it is "the purest form of spectacle—and a sacrificial model." In demonstrating that both "white" and "black" lights are inextricably linked in the terrorist image, he offers a double bind at the extremes of Derridean undecidability. The event of 9/11 makes visible what was already apparent in the Gulf War: "There is no good use of the media; the media are part of the event, they are part of the terror and they work in both directions."[102]

Both Derrida and Baudrillard concede the uncertainty that conditions their utterances. Baudrillard's hypothesis from the perspective of Evil might be seen as a provocative bet or wager, a doubling down on virtuality's symbolic stakes, in his words, a "fatal strategy."[103] Derrida's statements concerning international organizations are also "bets" and like bets, they are virtual: "I hope for it, but I do not see it."[104] Derrida assumes his risk as "an act of faith" on the "basis of a number of signs" he can "interpret." As he says to Giovanna Borradori, "I decipher, I wager, I hope."[105] The bet is placed between a hermeneutic gesture and the act of faith. War is not a remedy to the image impasse, but as the terrorist attack of 9/11 demonstrated, it might be prudent to "wager" on evil, if only not to cede to the critical impotence of inverse fetishism.

ACKNOWLEDGMENTS

I express my gratitude to Marine Baudrillard, Marc Guillaume, and François Séguret for sharing their recollections of *Why War Today*, to Julie Webber's critical eye, and to the "three goddesses" at EDUCO—Monique Benesvy, Valérie Herbunot, and Giulia Squatriti—for their hospitality.

NOTES

1. René Major, ed., *Jean Baudrillard—Jacques Derrida: Pourquoi la guerre aujourd'hui?* (Paris: Lignes, 2015). All translations are my own.
2. My essay's exposition does not follow the order of the debate; it began with questions addressed to Jean Baudrillard.
3. Major, *Jean Baudrillard—Jacques Derrida,* 31–32.
4. See Michael Naas, *Miracle and Machine: Jacques Derrida and the Two Sources of Religion, Science and Media* (New York: Fordham University Press, 2012), in particular chapter 5, "The Telegenic Voice."
5. Major, *Jean Baudrillard—Jacques Derrida,* 30–31.
6. W.J.T. Mitchell, *Cloning Terror: The War of Images 9/11 to the Present* (Chicago: University of Chicago Press, 2011), 45. See also 30–31, 78–79, 179n7.
7. Giovanna Borridori, "Autoimmunity: Real and Symbolic Suicides," *Philosophy in a Time of Terror* (Chicago: University of Chicago Press, 2003), 92.
8. Jean Baudrillard, *The Spirit of Terrorism,* new rev. ed., trans. Chris Turner (London: Verso, 2003).
9. Major, *Jean Baudrillard—Jacques Derrida,* 38.
10. Borridori, "Autoimmunity," 111, 109.
11. Jacques Derrida, "A Europe of Hope" (trans. Pleshette DeArmitt, Justine Malle, and Kas Saghafi), *Epoche* 10, no. 2 (Spring 2006): 407–412.
12. Jean Baudrillard, *The Illusion of the End,* trans. Chris Turner (Stanford, CA: Stanford University Press, 1994), 16.
13. William Merrin, *Baudrillard and the Media* (Cambridge, UK: Polity, 2005), 63–80.
14. Jean Baudrillard, *The Gulf War Did Not Take Place,* trans. Paul Patton (Bloomington: Indiana University Press, 1995).
15. Jean Baudrillard, *Consumer Society: Myths and Structures,* trans. Chris Turner (London: Sage, 1998), 122.
16. Jean Baudrillard, *Symbolic Exchange and Death,* trans. Iain Hamilton Grant (London: Sage, 1993), 69–70 (as well as *Spirit of Terrorism,* 39). Concerning the Twin Towers' architecture, see Jean Baudrillard-Jean Nouvel, *Les objets singuliers: architecture et philosophie* (Paris: Calmann-Levy [Éditions de la Villette], 2002), 28–29, 61–62.
17. Jean Baudrillard, *Simulacra and Simulation,* trans. Sheila Faria Glaser (Ann Arbor: University of Michigan Press, 1994), 59–60.
18. Major, *Jean Baudrillard—Jacques Derrida,* 24.
19. Ibid.
20. Jean Baudrillard, *Paroxysm: Interviews With Philippe Petit,* trans. Chris Turner (London: Verso, 1998), 46.
21. Jean Baudrillard, *The Transparency of Evil: Essays on Extreme Phenomena,* trans. James Benedict (London: Verso, 2009), 79.
22. Jean Baudrillard, *The Illusion of the End,* trans. Chris Turner (London: Polity, 1994, 19).

23. Ibid., 56.
24. Jean Baudrillard, *The Perfect Crime,* trans. Chris Turner (London: Verso, 1996), 29–30.
25. Baudrillard, *Illusion,* 19.
26. Ibid.
27. Major, *Jean Baudrillard—Jacques Derrida,* 24–25.
28. Baudrillard, *Illusion,* 18.
29. Major, *Jean Baudrillard—Jacques Derrida,* 25–26.
30. Gary Genosko translates *avoir lieu* as "the Gulf War had not (a) place." The *avoir lieu* refers to temporality as well as space: "not here," the "non place" of the inscription of memory. See Genosko, "Virtual War," *Borderlines* 24/25 (1992): 52.
31. Baudrillard, *Transparency,* 41.
32. Jean Baudrillard, *The Vital Illusion,* ed. Julia Witmer (New York: Columbia University Press), 2000.
33. Borridori, "Autoimmunity," 108.
34. Major, *Jean Baudrillard—Jacques Derrida,* 61–62, 65.
35. Borridori, "Autoimmunity," 95.
36. Ibid., 188n8.
37. Ibid.
38. Baudrillard, *Spirit,* 5.
39. Borridori, "Autoimmunity," 188n8.
40. Ibid., 108.
41. Ibid.
42. Ibid., 109.
43. Jacques Derrida and Bernard Stiegler, *Echographies of Television: Filmed Interviews,* trans. Jennifer Bajorek (London: Polity, 2002), 24.
44. Jacques Derrida, "Above All, No Journalists!" trans. Samuel Weber, in Hent de Vries and Samuel Weber, *Religion and Media* (Stanford, CA: Stanford University Press, 2001), 56–93.
45. Major, *Jean Baudrillard—Jacques Derrida,* 49.
46. Ibid., 34.
47. Ibid., 36.
48. Borridori, "Autoimmunity," 122.
49. Ibid., 123.
50. Ibid., 125.
51. Major, *Jean Baudrillard—Jacques Derrida,* 36–37.
52. Naas, *Miracle and Machine,* 141–143.
53. Ibid., 151.
54. Jean-Louis Comolli, "Le silence des tours," *L'image, le monde* 2 (2001): 9.
55. Borridori, "Autoimmunity," 114.
56. Major, *Jean Baudrillard—Jacques Derrida,* 35. See also Simone Regazzoni, "Au-delà de la pulsion de pouvoir: Derrida et la deconstruction de la souverainété," *Lignes* 47, *Derrida Politique,* 2015, 72–86.
57. Derrida has written with great acuity on the image; for the photographic image, see *Copy, Archive Trace: A Conversation on Photography* (Stanford, CA: Stanford University Press, 2010); *Athens, Still Remains: The Photography of Jean-François Bonhomme* (New York: Fordham University Press, 2010); *Rights of Inspection: Photographs by Marie-Françoise Plissart* (New York: Monacelli, 1998); on painting and drawing, see *Memories of the Blind: The Self-Portrait and Other Ruins* (Chicago: University of Chicago Press, 1993).

58. Jacques Derrida, *Writing and Difference,* trans. Alan Bass (Chicago: University of Chicago Press, 1978); Jacques Derrida, *Learning to Live Finally: The Last Interview,* trans. Pascale-Anne Brault and Michael Naas (Hoboken, NJ: Melville House, 2007).
59. Major, *Jean Baudrillard-Jacques Derrida,* 44.
60. Jacques Derrida, "Force of Law," in *Acts of Religion,* trans. Mary Quaintance, ed. Gil Anidjar (New York: Routledge, 2002), 230–298.
61. Ibid., 45.
62. Ibid.
63. Ibid.
64. Ibid., 37, 40, 38–39, 39–40, 40, 49, 59–61.
65. Borridori, "Autoimmunity," 108–109, 121–123, 125.
66. Major, *Jean Baudrillard—Jacques Derrida,* 42.
67. Borridori, "Autoimmunity," 122. "Natural" resources such as South African gold or Algerian oil are also non-virtualizable.
68. Major, *Jean Baudrillard—Jacques Derrida,* 55.
69. Ibid., 50.
70. Ibid., 56.
71. Baudrillard, *Vital Illusion,* 46.
72. Baudrillard, *Spirit,* 4.
73. Ibid., 3.
74. Baudrillard, *Paroxysm,* 27.
75. Olivier Jacquemond, "Baudrillard ou le mystique du réel," *Lignes* 31 (2010): 80.
76. Jacquemond, "Baudrillard," 3.
77. Jean Baudrillard, *The Agony of Power,* trans. Ames Hodges (Los Angeles: semiotext[e], 2010), 9.
78. Baudrillard, *Power,* 9–10.
79. Major, *Jean Baudrillard–Jacques Derrida,* 19.
80. Ibid.
81. Baudrillard, *Spirit,* 8–9.
82. Ibid., 11.
83. Major, *Jean Baudrillard—Jacques Derrida,* 50–51.
84. Baudrillard, *Spirit,* 12.
85. Ibid., 25–26.
86. Major, *Jean Baudrillard—Jacques Derrida,* 20–21.
87. Baudrillard, *Spirit,* 61.
88. Major, *Jean Baudrillard—Jacques Derrida,* 21.
89. Ibid., 22, 25.
90. Ibid., 26, 28–29.
91. Ibid., 52–53.
92. Ibid., 54.
93. Jean-Marc Vernier, "*'l'image-absolu'* du 11 septembre 2001: une image télévisuelle pas comme les autres," *Quadreni* 48 (2002): 53–61.
94. Mésuline Harlé, *Attentats et television* (Paris-Brussels: De Boeck Université, 1998), 70.
95. Vernier, "*l'image absolu,*" 57.
96. Charles Tesson, "Retour à l'envoyeur," *Cahiers du Cinéma* 561 (2001).
97. Jean-Michel Frodon, "À Manhattan, la puissance abstraite des images," *Le Monde* 13 (2001).

98. Thierry Jousse, "L'envers du spectacle," *Cahiers du Cinéma* 561 (2001).
99. Baudrillard, *Spirit*, 27, 29.
100. Vernier, "*l'image absolu*," 58.
101. Ibid., 58–59.
102. Baudrillard, *Spirit*, 29–30, 30, 31.
103. Marc Guillaume, "Une approche ironique de figures transpolitique," *Critique* 442 (1984): 198–213.
104. Borridori, "Autoimmunity," 118.
105. Ibid.

12 • WAR IN THE TWENTY-FIRST CENTURY

Visible, Invisible, or Superpositional?

JAMES DER DERIAN

> You might not be interested in war but war is interested in you.
>
> —Leon Trotsky

Early in the twenty-first century, late one evening, war took an interest in me. The first feint came in an e-mail, an invitation to address a conference in Australia on "War 2.0." Unlike most numerically annotated wars signifying duration or repetition, "2.0" clearly intended a new, different, and possibly improved version of organized violence. Upon opening, however, the attached invitation disappeared in the blink of an eye behind a pop-up message of menace: "Warning: Security software updates are now available for your computer. Cancel or Accept."

The pair of messages triggered more than a few questions about wars visible and invisible. If I refused the update, would malware, spyware, or other worse-for-ware find a back door ajar and infect my deck? Were "invitation" and "warning" actually two parts of a single pharmacotic algorithm, a disease in the guise of a cure? (In)visible wars played a parenthetical game of hide and seek: Would I (and my network) be more (or less) secure with (or without) War 2.0 and Security Software? Knowledge of past wars as well as the outdated state of my antiviral software weighed like the dead upon the living; like a panchette on an Ouija board, my cursor slid toward "Accept."

But then I paused: Was there a CTRL-Z option? For War 2.0 and what might follow, I suspect not. Digitized and infinitely reproducible, without singular beginnings or ends or arrows of time to reverse, the new wars radiate outward across multiple platforms in near simultaneity. Conjured into existence as screened image events, not only their visibility but actuality is contingent upon the means by which they are (or are not) observed, recorded, measured, and transmitted. Now the power to make and unmake wars lies in acts of framing, projecting, and viewing, what Paul Virilio called the "logistics of perception." This means that the parenthetical (in)visibility of war is no longer discrete, hybrid or metaphorical but *superpositional,* in the sense of existing potentially and simultaneously in both states, not unlike Schrödinger's famous quantum feline that is dead and/or alive. Just as one must open the box to see for one's self, I must click on the warning to access the necessary information.

In a similar manner, when we click on the image of a drone attack, a terrorist beheading, or a suicide bombing, we no longer merely observe or witness war but become active (if noncombatant) participants. In this new form of warfare, full-spectrum violence phase-shifts from electromagnetic to kinetic code to image, invisible to visible, in the blink, literally, of an eye, producing what we might call, as the software and hardware of warfare converge, a new kind of *warware.* Perhaps the Greeks who thought sight came from fires in our head were not too far off the mark.

Warware is dependent upon *reconnaissance* and *surveillance,* whereby the technology and act of observation determines not only what we can see and know but also the actualization of war. Warware tracks the frequency and amplitudes of the spectral manifestations of war and peace that defy linear explanations or monocausal predictions. As war and the world grow weirder,[1] so too must our approach to contemporary global violence as it phase-shifts from War 1.0 to War 2.0 to something observable-dependent and numerical-indeterminate: in short, quantum war.[2]

WAR OF DISCIPLINES

> The unleashed power of the atom has changed everything save our modes of thinking and we thus drift toward unparalleled catastrophe.[3]
>
> —Albert Einstein

On one level, none of this is wholly new: the failure of conventional modes of thinking to respond to new forms of global violence recurs with a despairing regularity. Einstein's lament, prompted by the first use of the atomic bomb against Japan, finds a contemporary echo in Paul Virilio's warning of a new worst-case, the "information bomb."

As I pointed out some time ago, if *interactivity* is to information what *radioactivity* is to energy, then we are confronted with the fearsome emergence of the "accident to end all accidents," an accident that is no longer *local* and precisely situated, but *global* and generalized. We are faced, in other words, with a phenomenon that may occur everywhere simultaneously . . . this integral accident is the true detonator of the information bomb.[4]

Virilio deploys a critical inquiry that crosses and exceeds the traditional confines of war and security studies, making him a worthy theoretical companion for not just comprehending but getting the jump on contemporary transformations of war. Following his lead, this essay advocates: (1) a transdisciplinary approach to global conflicts amplified and in some cases created by information technologies, logistics of perception, and scientific innovations; (2) a transmedial perspective that recognizes the primacy of images over words in the organization, execution, justification, representation, and observation of global violence; and (3) a transnational response to global violence as image-enhanced terror, insurgency, and war evade and in many instances thwart efforts at state management and control. In Virilio's words:

> From now on everything passes through the image. The image has priority over the thing, the object, and sometimes even the physically-present being. Just as real time, instantaneousness, had priority over space. Therefore the image is invasive and ubiquitous. Its role is not to be in the domain of art, the military domain or the technical domain, it is to be everywhere, to be reality. . . . I believe that there is a war of images. . . . And I can tell you my feelings in another way: winning today, whether it's a market or a fight, is merely not losing sight of yourself.[5]

The largest and boldest headlines of the twenty-first century—technologically-enabled, media-amplified terror against the United States, a global financial crash, the coming of cyberwars, and the transformation of the Internet into a "systematic snooping operation"—had already been previewed by Virilio in the twentieth century.[6] Lines from a speech by General Ray Odierno, U.S. Army Chief of Staff, could have been lifted right out of Virilio's work:

> Throughout the course of history, world events have always presented militaries with both complexity and unpredictability. Today's environment sustains this norm, but adds the unprecedented speed at which events unfold and information travels. The pace of change is accelerating. There are emerging factors at work in today's strategic environment that we cannot ignore. The sheer number of connections between people and societies has increased exponentially. An ever-present global media can instantly elevate local actions to matters of strategic import. Technology and weapons once reserved to states can now find their way into the hands of disaffected individuals and disruptive groups. International tolerance for civilian casualties and collateral damage from military operations has

> decreased while the capabilities to inflict such damage have spread to a growing number of illicit actors.[7]

My view of war draws heavily from Virilio as well as fieldwork that encompasses a twenty-year-plus road trip into a virtual empire, the military-industrial-media-entertainment network. First recorded on Hi-8 videotapes as a kind of visual notebook, rediscovered in an Ecco shoebox, and transformed into a documentary film (co-produced with Phil Gara), *Project Z: The Final Global Event* is what I thought would be the last word on how images trump words, global media drives world politics, a war of spectacles displaces the spectacle of war, and zombies become the logical worst-case scenario.[8]

Now I am not so sure, as image and word contest for our attention and primacy in world politics. The premium placed on "live"-ness means War 2.0 will probably come and go before it can be captured by any kind of snapshot, linguistic or visual. As the modes of observation, representation, and execution of war become complexly entangled on multiple screens and platforms, we must venture even further afield from the social sciences.[9] One would think that International Relations (IR), an interdiscipline created from borrowed ideas, including history, philosophy, geography, economics, and psychology would have the intellectual adaptability to explain or at least accommodate transformations of warfare that defy extant models. The history of the discipline, however, tells a different story. The scientific turn in IR theory, adopted to add rigor, precision, and metrics to the discipline, for the most part added mortis to the rigor, pedantry to the precision, and fetishism to the metrics. This charge, first leveled in the 1960s by Hedley Bull, the preeminent Australian IR theorist, against the scientific-behavioralist turn in IR theory, was subsequently taken up by the post-positivist critique in the 1980s; together they helped keep the field open to more historical, philosophical, and critical approaches.

However, as often happens with mimetic rivalries, the critique by Bull and many of the post-positivists who followed threw the scientific baby out with the behavioralist bathwater, producing new blinders rather than new logistics of perception. This self-limiting gesture was reinforced by scientific purists intent on the maintenance of their own disciplinary boundaries (see the Sokal hoax for the most notorious example).[10] As a result, significant breakthroughs in post-Newtonian physics, post-Cartesian neuroscience, and post-Saussurean linguistics never really penetrated the palisades thrown up by all sides of the so-called Great Debates in international relations. With a few exceptions, new insights from chaos theory, complexity theory, and quantum theory were ignored, marginalized and slow to find acceptance in the social sciences.[11]

WAR OF WORDS

> I would hope that philosophers and all scientists will learn from this change which has occurred in quantum theory. We have learned that language is a dangerous instrument to use, and this fact will certainly have its repercussions in other fields, but this is a very long process which will last through many decades I should say.[12]
>
> —Werner Heisenberg

War has enjoyed a mimetic relationship to language that dates back at least to its linguistic origins, in the Greek *polemos* (a forceful dispute), Latin *bellum* (a duel among belligerents), and German-Frankish *werra* (a state of discord or confusion). Indeed, it probably goes back much further: fanciful or not, philosopher Walter Benjamin's interpretation highlights the enduring relationship between aesthetic representation and the earliest practices of corporal violence:

> It would be more emphatic than it ever has been up until now, to make fruitful for the early history of the arts the recognition, that the first material to which the mimetic faculty applied itself is the human body. . . . Perhaps the human from the stone-age sketches the elk so incomparably, only because the hand which leads the crayon still recalls the bow with which it shot the animal.[13]

War continues to be the bastard and often absent father of worthy as well as unworthy, of many if not all things (as Heraclitus decried), including many of the Ur-texts of Western civilization, like the Iliad, Bible, Declaration of Independence, Communist Manifesto, Treaty of Westphalia, and United Nations Charter.[14]

Indeed, the classic text of "War 1.0" was born from the Napoleonic wars. Its simple, declarative title, *On War,* is belied by a sophisticated account of the nature of war.[15] As a soldier and philosopher of war, Carl von Clausewitz links etymology and ontology, fact and interpretation, practice and theory in a dialectical manner. War might, in one of his more familiar, more straightforward definitions, be described as "an act of force to compel our enemy to do our will," or likened to "a duel on a larger scale."[16]

However, the interpretation of war that emerges from the multiple volumes is much more complicated, in a continual tension between the physical and metaphysical, simple and complex, literal and metaphorical. War is, as Clausewitz's favorite philosopher Immanuel Kant said of all things human, "crooked": even as a "continuation of political intercourse with an admixture of other means," it is planned "in a kind of twilight, which, like fog or moonlight, [which] often tends to make things seem grotesque and larger than they really are."[17] Potentially boundless, classical war like the concept of the sublime in Kant takes a "supersensible" faculty of mind; a human science is needed to make sense of war.

There is much—still—to learn from Clausewitz, but one lesson for all times stands out: War is a shape-shifter. War devolves as well as evolves, both analogically from the duel and formally from organized violence between states, making it difficult to extrapolate from particular acts of violence a general principle or universal concept of war. The lesson resonates: whereas sovereign nations once marched to mutually recognized wars on discrete battlefields, contemporary conflicts, like the "war on drugs," "war on terror," and "war for hearts and minds" or "infowar," "cyberwar," and "netwar" not only stretch across a global battlespace but now exceed the normal confines of time, place, and meaning. Wars continue to have, as in the time of Clausewitz, a wide range of intensity and duration. However, increasingly represented, observed, and executed through force fields of perception, information, and representation, war is no longer a mere continuation of politics (Clausewitz); nor, for that matter, is politics a continuation of war (Michel Foucault). In parallel (if you will) multiverses, wars that defy fixed definition (Syria: civil or international?), empirical verification (Yemen: open or secret?), and normal legal standing (drones: sub- or extra-judicial?), take on a multi-spectral, densely entangled, phase-shifting character. Marines I have interviewed on camera liken their experience in Fallujah to the videogame *Doom*, in Afghanistan to Isaac Asimov's sci-fi *Foundation* series, and in training exercises to that of the "Colonial Marines" in the movie *Aliens*.[18] This phenomenon goes beyond the intertextual.[19] When the battlefield becomes indistinguishable from the perceptual field, Clausewitz's famous fog pervades not just the planning and execution but also the representation and disinformation of war.

WAR OF NUMBERS

> So when we describe a system by writing down a few quantum numbers . . . this means that we know nothing except to say that this object is a representation of symmetries.[20]
>
> —Werner Heisenberg

Another sign of the devolution of war has been the decline, if not yet total disappearance, of the numerically sequential or accumulative signifier. To make sense and to assert some kind of order out of the historical disruptions of war, the naming of wars, from the "great" wars of the past or the speculative wars of the future, has usually been preceded, succeeded, or bracketed by numbers. More wars than one would care to count come with numbers: the First and Second Peloponnesian Wars, the Hundred Years' War, the Thirty Years' War, the Seven Years' War, ad infinitum, it would seem. The World Wars, from the actual First and Second to the worst-case scenarios and videogames of the imaginary Third and Fourth, have garnered more words in print and series on cable television than practically any other subject matter. And now we face War 2.0, which also assumes, albeit with a critical edge, that war continues to evolve in a fairly linear progression.

As previously mentioned, numbers attached to past wars usually signify continuity as well as duration, a sense of termination as well as repetition. *Signify* is the operative word here. In the battlefield of representation, the numbering process works to provide an ex post facto logic, a sequence of clear beginnings and endings in contrast to the indeterminate and contingent character of warfare.

Take one of the most famous examples, the First and Second Peloponnesian Wars between Athens and Sparta in the fifth century BCE, which are often cited for the foundational lessons they provide for the study of international relations. Frequently left out in the disciplinary accounts is the philosophical-historiographical battle that followed the temporal-geographical ones, resulting in the victory of Thucydides (and the "scientific" school) over Herodotus (and the mythopoeic way of storytelling). But here too, as metaphysical differences drive conflicts in the Middle East, Africa, and the United Sates, subnational phase-shifts rather than state-on-state conflicts continue to intrude and undermine that earlier victory.

Leaping forward, the Hundred Years' War that stretched across the fourteenth to the fifteenth century was a mix of feudal and dynastic conflicts, civil as well as chauvinist struggles, with privateers and mercenaries, and famine and pestilence claiming more victims and devastating more territory than the organized state-based violence that now enjoys the definition of "war."[21] When seventeenth-century religious hostilities between Catholics and Protestants in German principalities evolved into national wars between European monarchs of mixed or no religious affiliations, the multifarious conflict was subsequently rendered into the homogeneous Thirty Years' War. In similar fashion, the world war of the eighteenth century that stretched from North America to the Caribbean to Europe to India and beyond was known, in different times and locales, as the "French and Indian War," the "Third Silesian War," or "la guerre de la Conquête" (the name preferred by my Quebeçoise professor at McGill University). With the passage of time, it would earn the geographically opaque and ethnically cleansed sobriquet of the "Seven Years' War"[22]

Then there are the wars that appear to be beyond numbers, that seem, sui generis, to name themselves: as *Maclean's* magazine put it in October 1914, "This is the Great War." Illustrious others prophesied great things to come from it. "This is the war that will end war," wrote H. G. Wells; "this war will make the world safe for democracy," echoed (some say stole) U.S. President Woodrow Wilson (after running on a peace platform). However, doubts about both prospects were aired before the first pealing of church bells on Armistice Day, to mark the eleventh hour of the eleventh day of the eleventh month of the war's end. By the time of the 1919 Paris Peace Conference, David Lloyd George added a sardonic bite to the grandiose rhetoric, supposedly saying that "this war, like the next war, is a war to end war."[23] The Great War lost its grandeur and name in less than twenty years, becoming mere prequel (with an unprecedented 37 million casualties) to the Second World War (more than 60 million casualties). Contrary to what one might expect—a single history that follows a linear path in successive stages—the name change surfaces before the first belligerent act of the next war, the German invasion of Poland, when in a *Time* magazine article (June 12, 1939) titled, "War Machines," an anonymous author proved prescient in more ways than one: "In World War I, for example, command of the air changed hands several times, and the command changed not only when numbers varied but when one side introduced a superior new plane which could outfight the opposing machines. . . . In World War II it is possible that even nations who do not take sides may play a vital military part, for they may be invaded."[24]

WAR OF IMAGES

> When it comes to atoms, language can be used only as in poetry. The poet, too, is not nearly so concerned with describing facts as with creating images.[25]
>
> —Niels Bohr

At the risk of reopening a long-running theoretical dispute—what academic *polemos* lack in blood they make up in ink—I believe it can be said that the dominance of Realism in foreign and defense circles (if not international relations theory) is attributable to a special relationship between war and the representation of reality.[26] War serves as the reality principle of a theory in which international anarchy is a given, human nature is fixed, sovereign states are defined by the struggle for power, and the balance of power provides a modicum of order to the states-system. The conceit of this theory was aptly expressed in the motto of STRICOM (the U.S. Defense command in charge of simulations, modeling, training, and instrumentation): "All but war is simulation."

Indeed, when it comes to war, there is an incestuous relationship between the big *R* discipline and the small *r* philosophy that go by the name of realism. As the philosophical and physical evidence increasingly demonstrates that there is no reality independent of perception and observation, the greater the theoretical and metaphysical effort to assert—through violence if necessary—one's own as the universal reality. In a previous genealogy of realism I showed how the linear notion of causality, correspondence theory of truth, and the materiality of power failed to account for many of the transformative events of the past fifty years. I argued it was time—past time—for a "postclassical" or "virtual theory" of international relations to explain this phenomenon.[27] I believe that effort might have been untimely, perhaps overly ambitious but not, as images became the new currency of war, mistaken. I suggest a return to an earlier interwar, the twenty-year crisis when Realism reemerged after the failure of idealism and the League of Nations to stop Hitlerism, while simultaneously being repudiated in the continental philosophy and quantum physics.

Two interwar philosophers, Walter Benjamin and Ludwig Wittgenstein, offer the keenest insights on how realism has outlived its original raison d'être. To be sure, one (Benjamin) condemned while the other (the early Wittgenstein) endorsed the philosophical limits imposed by realism; but they were of one mind on the coexistence of other realities—in particular, immaterial realities—that words could not fully reflect, express, or capture: what Benjamin referred to as the "image" and Wittgenstein as the "picture." Benjamin remarked that "history decays into images, not into stories";[28] Wittgenstein that "what can be shown cannot be said";[29] or in the more famous closing remarks of the *Tractatus*, "Whereof one cannot speak, thereof one must remain silent."[30]

In the interwar period, Benjamin presented a withering critique of the faux realism that underwrites correspondence theories of the truth as well as geopolitical discourse. Quoting (but not citing) Leopold von Ranke, he wrote, "The history that showed things 'as they really were' was the strongest narcotic of the century."[31] Conversely, Wittgenstein constructed a correspondence theory of the truth based on the solipsism of realism. "I am my world," says Wittgenstein in the *Tractatus*, making the subject the limit of words that constitute the world: "*The limits of my language* mean the limits of my world."[32] For Wittgenstein, the only "I" existing outside the world is the eye itself, which can see the world but not itself. Here Wittgenstein saw fit to draw a crude diagram of the eye and its field of sight, words conveying what pictures cannot, pictures what words cannot: "Everything we see could also be otherwise."[33]

Benjamin and Wittgenstein are on the surface an improbable pairing of thinkers; but both responded to the mass violence of world war with a commitment to expose the irrational and barbarous potential of the word pictures generated by war. Although Benjamin was more radical in his subsequent dismissal of realism, deeming it bereft of the ethical reflexivity that might render it more responsible for reproducing the world it claims only to record, Wittgenstein was no less critical of realism's capacity to understand let alone translate the power and fluency of the picture.

But the ideas of these two leading thinkers pale in comparison to that of their interwar counterparts in physics. At the top of list of transformations that have failed to penetrate the realist model is not only how the image has superannuated the word as the dominant currency of global politics, but how realism as a philosophy has been debunked by new discoveries in the physical sciences. If we are to challenge the full spectrum dominance of realism in war, stretching from the epistemic (reality exists independent of our perceptions, observations, and theories) to the political (sovereign states enjoy a monopoly on legitimate violence) to the historical (only realism depicts the past as "it really was"), we must develop a fluency in postclassical physics as well as philosophy.

The realist hegemony is dependent upon a willful distancing from the radical innovations in both fields during the interwar period. The tensions between these two appraisals of realism are nowhere more apparent than in the simulacral re-territorialization of state violence after two devastating world wars. Taken hostage by the existential threat posed by nuclear weapons, the use-value of war—and the reality principle of world politics—became defined by its new model, the game theory of mutual assured destruction, flexible response, and, most recently, minimal deterrence. In spite of several close calls—Berlin in 1961, Cuba in 1962, Able Archer in 1983 (a less familiar crisis when the Soviets almost mistook a NATO wargame as the real thing)—the Cold War ended before the simulacrum generated a real war.[34]

However, the simulacrum of realism did not end, as one might have expected, with the end of the Cold War: even before the Berlin Wall became a tourist attraction, the race was on to imagine the next war, one that could actually be fought and won. There were many runners, but one, probably the least known outside the circles of strategic studies, outthought and outlasted them all: Andrew Marshall, officially known as the director of the Office of Net Assessment, but unofficially, the Yoda of the so-called Revolution in Military Affairs (RMA). I have previously recounted how Marshall was brought in by President Richard Nixon to help set up the Office of Net Assessment: "to weigh the military balance in specific areas, to determine what the important long-term trends are, and to highlight existing or emergent problem areas, or important opportunities that deserve top level management's attention to improve the future U.S. position in the continuing military-economic-political competition."[35] His most important memoranda, "Some Thoughts on Military Revolutions," first circulated in August 1993, has probably influenced U.S. national security strategy more than any other single writing, save George Kennan's famous "X" (1947) article. The memo focuses on, yes, the interwar period, and the ability of a defeated power (Germany) to operationalize the revolutions in military and information technology that helped produce the Blitzkrieg strategy. Marshall's fingerprints can be found on game changers that stretch from the decisions to provide Stinger missiles to the Afghan resistance to classify climate change as a security issue.

The name of Marshall—but not the person, who has a strong distaste for the glare of the media—briefly reappeared in the news when President Barack Obama decided to execute the "Pacific pivot." I was not surprised to see him attached to this significant shift in U.S. national security strategy. My final question to Marshall when I interviewed him in the early 1990s had been on the next threat to the United States. With unusual enthusiasm and a flutter of hands, he outlined the prospect of China emerging not as a peer competitor but as leap-frogging through the comparative advantage of new technologies—an "RMA by other means"—over and beyond the military capacities of the United States.

To punctuate the point, he invited me to a two-day workshop in 1997 on "Future War" that he was organizing at Science Applications International Corporation, the outsourced "shadow government" of the United States. He said surprisingly little during the proceedings, seemingly unimpressed by the presentations of the invitees, which included an ex-CIA futurist, a historian, a biogeneticist, an anthropologist, a science fiction writer, a computer scientist, and a bunch of military war gamers. But I distinctly remember him posing a series of pointed questions to the historian, Alan Beyerchen from Ohio State University. He seemed struck by Beyerchen's appraisal that future war would be "messy" and that new ways of thinking with new typologies were needed to understand the "amplifiers," which had been game changers of previous wars, from the First World War, or, as he put it, the "chemist's war," after the scientists who had innovated more powerful nitrates, gas, and rubber; to the Second World War, or the "physicist's war," which had introduced radio, radar, rocketry, and the atom bomb; to the Third World War, or the "information researcher's war," which had introduced simulations, war games, and game theory.

Ten years later, this revelatory moment returned as déjà vu (as all fans of *The Matrix* know, a symptom of a glitch in the simulacrum). Michael Bhatia, a visiting fellow and participant in our Military Cultural Awareness Project, had gone to the Air University in Mobile, Alabama, for a conference on cultural competency in the military, a pressing issue at a time when the United States was losing the wars in Iraq and Afghanistan. The keynote speaker was Major General Robert Scales, a former commandant of the Army War College. When Bhatia gave us his briefing on the conference, he began by singling out Scales's typologies of world wars: they were identical to Beyerchen's (to whom Scales gives credit), with one new addition.[36] The failure in Iraq of "shock and awe" (the bowdlerized version of the RMA) demonstrated the emergence of a new center of gravity—the "human terrain"—in what Scales referred to as "psychosocial warfare." The Fourth World War would be the "anthropologist's war." Although more imaginative, even the imaginary wars were linear and came neatly in sequence.

THE WARS OF THE FUTURE

> Predictions can be very difficult—especially about the future.[37]
>
> —Niels Bohr

It is not simply that our understanding of war lags behind innovations in other fields of knowledge. That too demonstrates an overly linear concept of the relationship between power and knowledge. Any attempt to comprehend the future of war must also consider how our very effort to understand, represent, and measure war will have a direct impact on the phenomenon under scrutiny. The lag-effect is easier to deduce: viewers once searched photographs for spectral evidence of dead loved ones; audience members rushed from a Paris theatre when the Lumière brothers first projected their cinematic image of an oncoming train. Old reality principles are continually challenged and then revised by new representational forms. It is more difficult to ascertain how new global media actually "produces" new global wars.

A few media theorists, perhaps most consistently Paul Virilio[38] and Friedrich Kittler,[39] have noted how cinema and film enjoyed a coeval development with modern warfare. Less chronicled has been the impact of video. Emerging from the Second World War innovation of radar, television provided the medium and the motive for a videographic revolution. By the First Gulf War, video—cheap to shoot, fast to edit, and easily broadcast—had become the medium of choice on, and even more critically, above the battlefield. As has been the case with preceding media, video conveys as well as exercises a spectral (in both senses of the word) power that often exceeds the analytical methods of the day. Now, when the electromagnetic and kinetic spectra converge, our perceptual fields and rational modes strain to keep up.

Networked, proliferated, and accelerated by multiplatform transmedia, the images of war are instantaneously Googled, wikied, and tweeted into branded identities and virtual realities.[40] We have seen, from the smart-bomb images of the Gulf War to the Wikileaked gun-camera images of the Iraq War, how images of violence, no matter how degraded, night-scoped, or pixelated, grab more eyeballs and engender more controversial interpretations than even the most well-crafted print story. We have seen how the shrink-sized video camera, made ubiquitous by the mobile phone, amplifies a local incident into a global crisis. And we have seen what happens when the same cameras shift focus to the next war; the crisis of the moment disappears into the blackest of news holes.

What we have not seen as war, as an upgrade from 1.0 to 2.0 and/or as a reiteration of past conflicts, is the end of global violence as a viable option in the face of intractable political differences, social injustices, and cultural struggles for recognition. The emergence of the nation-state and the concomitant spread of reason, rights, and prosperity might well have resulted in global decrease in the level of state-on-state violence. But these metrics, based on linear Enlightenment demarcations of space and time, fail to account for the displacement, acceleration, and perception of violent effects emanating from pre-, post-, and non-state actors that shift identities and addresses with every attempt to deter, disrupt, and destroy them.[41] This kind of random, reiterative, and emergent violence does not lend itself to the assumptions of rational action, methods of linear regression, or hopes for a progressivist future that drive much of contemporary international relations thinking today. States, democratic or not, might be inclined less to use violence to achieve political goals. However, a dozen individuals today, with access to networked technologies for the preparation, execution, and representation of violence, can do more damage to a system, be it state or corporate, organic or inorganic, physical or psychological, than at any time in history.

Following pathways worn by conditions of uneven development, war will continue to oscillate from 1.0 to 2.0 and back again. But networked global media, as the trigger and transmitter, catalyst and conveyor of global events, has produced a parallel universe, a virtual realm with all too real effects. In this infosphere, much of today's global violence increasingly resembles what Albert Einstein disparagingly called "spooky action at a distance," in which the parameters of cause and effect and linear demarcations of space appear to be exceeded not just by non-state but also by nonrational actions. As violence phase-shifts at light speed from states to substates, local to global, public to private, organized to chaotic, virtual to real—and back again—the transparent words, sequential numbers, and discrete images of war superposition into the wholly new phenomenon of quantum war.

ACKNOWLEDGMENTS

This essay is a revision of talks presented at the Australian National University's "War 2.0" conference (published in the *Australian Journal of International Affairs* 67, no. 5 [2013]) and the "In/visibility of America's 21st Century Wars" speaker series at Indiana University.

NOTES

1. In like manner, Freeman Dyson distinguished classical from quantum physics as "just plain weird" (Freeman Dyson, *New York Review of Books,* July 14, 2011), http://www.nybooks.com/articles/2011/07/14/dramatic-picture-richard-feynman/.

2. My interest in all things quantum was fueled regularly by a series of conversations with Hayward Alker Jr. that stretched over two decades; a year spent gate-crashing the physics seminars at the Institute of Advanced Study at Princeton in 2000–2001; and more recently, an extended stay at the Center for Advanced Security Studies in

Copenhagen, with trips across the bridge to the Niels Bohr Institute. An early effort to develop a "virtual theory" to understand quantum effects in war can be found in James Der Derian, "Virtuous War/Virtual Theory," *International Affairs* 76, no. 4 (2000): 771–788; James Der Derian, *Virtuous War: Mapping the Military-Industrial-Media-Entertainment Network* (New York: Routledge, 2009); on the emergence of a "quantum diplomacy," see James Der Derian, "Quantum Diplomacy, German-American Relations, and the Psychogeography of Berlin," *Hague Journal of Diplomacy* 6, no. 3–4 (2011): 373–392. A more systemic treatment of quantum theory and human consciousness can be found in Alex Wendt, *Quantum Mind and Social Science* (Cambridge: Cambridge University Press, 2015). And with the support of the Carnegie Corporation of New York and the University of Sydney, I have organized annual multidisciplinary symposia on quantum effects in global politics.

At these and other occasions I have found among younger colleagues a remarkably enthusiastic reaction to quantum theory as an interpretive tool for the social sciences. However, others in the field have reacted in ways that brought back memories of when continental philosophy first rolled up to the gates of the discipline in the 1980s, with responses that range in character from Niels Bohr's famous observation that "those who are not shocked when they first come across quantum theory cannot possibly have understood it" (Niels Bohr, *Essays 1932–1957 on Atomic Physics and Human Knowledge* [Oxford: Oxbow Press, 1987]) to James Gleick's "Ideas That Require People to Reorganize Their Picture of the World Provoke Hostility" (James Gleick, *Chaos: Making a New Science* [New York: Penguin, 2009]).

3. Albert Einstein, *Einstein on Peace,* ed. Otto Nathan and Heinz Norden with foreword by Bertrand Russell (New York: Random House, 1981), 546.

4. Paul Virilio, *The Information Bomb,* trans. Chris Turner (London: Verso, 2000), 134.

5. Paul Virilio, interview in *Block* 14, 4–7, 7.

6. Paul Virilio, *The Paul Virilio Reader,* ed. James Der Derian (Oxford: Blackwell, 1998); Virilio, *The Information Bomb.*

7. Ray Odierno, "The Force of Tomorrow," 2013, http://www.foreignpolicy.com/articles/2013/02/04/the_force_of_tomorrow.

8. The short video can be seen at thevisionmachine.com/2012/03/the-military-industrial-media-entertainment-network/. An earlier version of *Project Z: The Final Global Event,* premiered at the Leipzig DOK Film Festival in November 2012. A new educational version is now available at Bullfrog Films, http://www.bullfrogfilms.com/catalog/pz.html.

9. The first drafting of this essay coincided with the anti-Islamic video, "The Innocence of Muslims," which was broadcast on YouTube, picked up by Arab media, and became the catalyst for violent demonstrations in several major Middle Eastern cities, leading—*but not leading*—to the death of Ambassador Christopher Stevens in Libya as well as three other U.S. Department of State employees. This local incident escalated into a global event that attained media-induced quantum superpositionality as the "Benghazi effect."

10. Sokal's hoax article, "Transgressing the Boundaries: Towards a Transformative Hermeneutics of Quantum Gravity," published in the *Social Text* (Spring/Summer 1996) "Science War" issue (full disclosure: My first published article was in *Social Text*), put a chill on the science–arts dialogue. For a rigorous debunking of the debunker Sokal, see the response by mathematician Gabriel Stolzenberg (ath.bu.edu/people/nk/rr/).

11. There are some recent exceptions but they usually emanate from outside IR and when such approaches do penetrate the discipline, they are usually confined to the policy rather than the theory side of international relations. See, for example, Nassim Nicholas Taleb and Mark Blyth, "The Black Swan of Cairo," *Foreign Affairs* (May/June 2011), online edition,

https://www.foreignaffairs.com/articles/egypt/2011-04-15/black-swan-cairo; George Dyson, *Turing's Cathedral: The Origins of the Digital Universe* (New York: Pantheon, 2012); Gleick, *Chaos*; Hawking 2010; Ray Kurzweil, *The Singularity Is Near: When Humans Transcend Biology* (New York: Penguin, 2006); Nassim Nicholas Taleb, *The Black Swan: The Impact of the Highly Improbable* (London: Penguin, 2010).

12. Werner Heisenberg, *Physics and Beyond: Encounters and Conversations* (London: Unwin, 1971).

13. Walter Benjamin, "*Das Kustwek im Zeitalter seiner technischen Reproduzierbarkeit,*" in *Gesammelte Schriften* I.2, ed. Rolf Teidemann and Hermann Schweppenhauser (Frankfurt a/M: Suhrkam, 1974–1989), 6: 127, trans. by Jeneen Hobby, "Raising Consciousness in the Writings of Walter Benjamin" (PhD diss., University of Massachusetts at Amherst, 1996), 254n1.

14. Considering the singular contributions of great Eastern scholars of war, like Kautilya and Sun Tzu, the focus of this essay might appear to be, indeed is, overly Occidentalist; however, the reliance upon a Western canon is in recognition that most of the rules, rights, and institutions of modern warfare, whether by voluntary assimilation or violent imposition, have their origins in the West.

15. Carl von Clausewitz, *On War,* trans. and ed. Michael Howard and Peter Paret (Princeton, NJ: Princeton University Press, 1976).

16. Ibid., 75.

17. See ibid., 87, 140.

18. See James Der Derian and Phillip Gara, *Project Z: The Final Global Event,* film, 2012. Others have pushed the Asimov connection much further, attributing not only the origins of the name of Al-Qaida (Arabic for "base" or "foundation") but aspects of its strategy to the Foundation series. See Fred Halliday, *Two Hours That Shook the World. September 11, 2001: Causes and Consequences* (London: Saqi, 2002).

19. James Der Derian and Michael Shapiro, eds., *International/Intertextual Relations: Postmodern Readings of World Politics* (Lexington, MA: Lexington Press, 1989).

20. Heisenberg, *Physics and Beyond.*

21. James Der Derian, "War," in *Encyclopedia of Political Thought,* ed. Michael Gibbons et al. (London: Wiley-Blackwell, 2014).

22. See Fred Anderson, *Crucible of War: The Seven Years' War and the Fate of Empire in British North America, 1754–1766* (New York: Viking, 2001); David Kaiser, *Politics and War: European Conflict from Philip II to Hitler* (Cambridge: MA: Harvard University Press, 1990).

23. See "The War to End War," *Wikipedia,* https://en.wikipedia.org/wiki/The_war_to_end_war.

24. See "World War," *Wikipedia,* https://en.wikipedia.org/wiki/World_war.

25. Niels Bohr, quoted in Heisenberg, *Physics and Beyond,* 41.

26. This idea draws from conversations and collaborations with two former colleagues, Michael Bhatia (2005) on "Naming Terrorism" (see special issue of *Third World Quarterly* 26, no. 1 [2005]) and Nisha Shah on "The Art of Peace" (see http://www.artofpeaceconference.org).

27. James Der Derian, "A Reinterpretation of Realism: Genealogy, Semiology, Dromology," in *International Theory: Critical Investigations,* ed. James Der Derian (New York: Macmillan and New York University Press, 1995), 363–396; Der Derian, "Virtuous War/Virtual Theory."

28. Walter Benjamin, *The Arcades Project,* trans. Howard Eiland and Kevin McLaughlin (Cambridge, MA: Harvard University Press, 1999), 476.

29. Ludwig Wittgenstein, Tractatus Logico-Philosophicus (London: Routledge, 2001; originally published 1922, 4.1212).
30. Ibid., 7.
31. Benjamin, *The Arcades Project*, 463.
32. Ludwig Wittgenstein, *Tractatus Logico-Philosophicos,* trans. C. K. Ogden (1922; New York: Cosimo Classics, 2010), 5.63.
33. Ibid., 5.6331 and 5.634.
34. Der Derian, *Virtuous War,* 307.
35. Ibid., 28–33.
36. A partial version of Michael Bhatia's account can be seen in our documentary film, *Human Terrain* (directed and written by James Der Derian, David Udris, and Michael Udris, Bullfrog Films, 2010) as well as in the *Human Terrain: Teacher's Guide* (http://www.bullfrogfilms.com/guides/humtguide.pdf). The talk Bhatia recounted was the basis for Scales's influential article, "Clausewitz and World War IV," that appeared in *Armed Forces Journal* (July 2006), http://armedforcesjournal.com/clausewitz-and-world-war-iv/.
37. Niels Bohr, *Essays 1958–1962 on Atomic Physics and Human Knowledge* (Woodbridge, CT: Ox Bow Press, 1987).
38. Paul Virilio, *War and Cinema: The Logics of Perception,* trans. Patrick Camiller (London: Verso, 1989).
39. F. Kittler, *Literature, Media, Information Systems* (Amsterdam: G+B Arts, 1997).
40. The ascendance of images over words is born out by the numbers. While writing this essay, Instagram, the image-sharing social media website that first gained political attention for its role in the Arab Spring, announced that people were sharing 45 million images a day and 16 billion since its inception three years ago. The advantage of images as a universal language is also evidenced by Instagram's increased global base (now more than 50 percent of users are outside of North America) at a time when text messaging has peaked and multimedia messaging (MMS) increased by 41 percent in 2012 to 74.5 billion (*New York Times,* 2013).
41. Stephen Pinker (*The Better Angels of Our Nature: Why Violence Has Declined* [New York: Penguin, 2012]) being the most noteworthy example of late, but of a genre going back to Kant (Immanuel Kant, *Perpetual Peace* [New York: Liberal Arts Press, 1957]).

ACKNOWLEDGMENTS

This volume is the product of an ongoing collective project based at Indiana University Bloomington, and so we have a long list of people and funders to thank. The project evolved from the Images Forum, a faculty and graduate student interdisciplinary group for the study of images in the humanities. The forum was very grateful for the support of the Indiana University Patten Foundation, which funded a week-long visit to Bloomington by Professor W.J.T. Mitchell, and the Branigin Lectureship, which paid for a guest presentation by Professor Ariella Azoulay, both in the spring of 2010. We are thankful for our guests' lectures, which engaged productively with images of war, conflict, and peace, which gave the forum its focus for the academic year of 2010–11. The home-grown talents Jon Simons, Christiane Gruber, Ed Linnenthal, Josh Carney, and Jeff Wolin presented on the same theme that year, adding to the depth and breadth of the accumulative project.

By 2011–12 we settled on the seminar theme of the "In/visibility of America's Twenty-First-Century Wars" for an invited group of faculty and graduate students: Purnima Bose, Claudia Breger, Nick Cullather, Lessie Jo Frazier, Jeremy Gordon, De Witt Kilgore, Jody Madeira, James Paasche, Micol Seigel, and Jeff Wolin. Jeremy Gordon and James Paasche did double service as participants and graduate assistants to the seminar. That year we enjoyed generous support from Indiana University's Institute of Advanced Studies Remak New Knowledge Seminar Award, the College Arts and Humanities Institute Workshop Grant, the College of Arts and Sciences' Themester co-curricular program, and the Office of the Vice Provost for Faculty and Academic Affairs Multidisciplinary Ventures and Seminars Fund. During the year the seminar studied the work of esteemed scholars and photographers who came to the campus to present their work publicly and to participate in workshops: Professor Michael Shapiro, Professor Diane Rubenstein, Professor Wendy Kozol, Professor Roger Stahl, Professor David Campbell (whose visit was also supported by the Branigin Lectureship), Suzanne Opton, and Nina Berman. The Cultural Studies Program hosted and funded its annual conference in the same year on the project's topic.

As we moved into the writing and production stage of the project by editing the volume, we received further vital support from the Indiana University Institute of Advanced Studies Collaborative Fellowship. The fellowship funded the editorial assistance of Lisa Braverman, without whose careful, dedicated work and thoughtful insight the volume would never have been completed. We are also indebted to Elizabeth Gilmore-Kaszynski, whose proofreading proved to be invaluable. You would also not be reading this book without the encouragement and guidance of Leslie Mitchner at Rutgers University Press and the support of Daniel Bernardi, the editor of the War Culture series in which this book is published.

As editors we have a debt of gratitude to the former Department of Communication and Culture at Indiana University. The unique interdisciplinary configuration of what was always more of an intellectual experiment than an institutional unit enriched our collaboration and served as inspiration for the book as an interdisciplinary project.

Above all, as editors we are immensely grateful to all the contributors to this volume who have stuck with us through the years, kept their faith in the project and tolerated our persistent—but we hope productive—editorial demands.

John Louis Lucaites and Jon Simons, May 2016

NOTES ON CONTRIBUTORS

REBECCA A. ADELMAN is an associate professor in the Department of Media and Communication Studies at the University of Maryland, Baltimore County (UMBC). Her research focuses on the intersections of visual culture and militarized violence, with particular interest in questions of ethics, affect, and imagination. Her first book, *Beyond the Checkpoint: Visual Practices in America's Global War on Terror* (2014), maps the visual circuits linking the terrorized American nation-state, its citizens, and its enemies by exploring the practices of image creation, circulation, and consumption that animate these relationships. She is currently at work on two new book projects. She and Wendy Kozol are collaborating on a project about quotidian visual cultures of living, dying, and surviving in conditions of militarized violence, *The War In-Between*. Singly, she is working on a manuscript entitled *Figuring Violence: Affect, Imagination, and Contemporary American Militarism* that explores coalescences of fantasy, violence, and sentimentality around an array of militarized bodies.

NINA BERMAN is a documentary photographer, author of *Purple Hearts—Back from Iraq and Homeland*, an associate professor at the Columbia University Graduate School of Journalism, and a member of the NOOR photography collective. Her photography and video work have been exhibited at more than a hundred international venues, including the 2010 Whitney Museum Biennial.

PURNIMA BOSE is an associate professor of English and international studies at Indiana University. Bose is the author of *Organizing Empire*; along with Laura E. Lyons, she coedited *Cultural Critique and the Global Corporation* and a special issue of the journal Biography on "Corporate Personhood." She is currently working on a manuscript entitled *Intervention Narratives: Afghanistan, the US, and the War on Terror*.

CLAUDIA BREGER is a professor of Germanic Studies at Indiana University, Bloomington. Her research and teaching focus on the interrelations of gender, sexuality, and race in twentieth- and twenty-first-century culture, along with media and cultural theory. Her recent book publications include *An Aesthetics of Narrative Performance: Transnational Theater, Literature, and Film in Contemporary Germany* (2012).

DAVID CAMPBELL is a writer, professor, and producer, specializing in photography, multimedia, and politics. He is an honorary professor in the School of

Political Science and International Studies at the University of Queensland, Australia, and has been the A. Lindsay O'Connor Professor in the Peace and Conflict Studies Program at Colgate University. The author/editor of six books and some sixty articles and essays, he currently works for the World Press Photo Foundation in Amsterdam.

JAMES DER DERIAN is Michael Hintze Chair of International Security at the University of Sydney, where he directs the Centre for International Security Studies and Project Q: Peace and Security in a Quantum Age. He is author most recently of *Virtuous War: Mapping the Military-Industrial-Media-Entertainment Network* (2nd ed., 2009) and *Critical Practices in International Theory* (2009), and coeditor with Costas Constantinou of *Sustainable Diplomacies* (2010). He has produced three film documentaries with Udris Film, *Virtual Y2K* (MEF, 2000), *After 9/11* (Link TV, 2003), and *Human Terrain* (Bullfrog Films, 2010), which won the Audience Award at the 2009 Festival dei Popoli in Florence. His most recent documentary, *Project Z: The Final Global Event* (Bullfrog Films, 2015) was coproduced with Phillip Gara and premiered at the DOK Leipzig Film Festival.

CHRISTOPHER J. GILBERT is an assistant professor of English at Assumption College. His work is published across a number of leading journals, including the *Quarterly Journal of Speech, Rhetoric & Public Affairs, Philosophy & Rhetoric, Rhetoric Society Quarterly, Text & Performance Quarterly, Critical Studies in Media Communication*, and more. Gilbert's work traverses topics in rhetoric and cultural studies, but he has a particular interest in wartime caricatures of national character; past (including ancient) and present politics of comic artworks and performances; the phenomenon of satiric dictionaries and encyclopedias in the United States; circulations of the peculiar and the ugly in public culture; and combat logics that are embedded in armed conflicts as well as rhetorical contests. Currently, Gilbert is developing a handful of projects that variously look at returning soldiers who have turned to stand-up comedy to ease their transition home, the dynamics of pleasure and pain in portrayals of war trauma, and case studies of caricature and controversy.

JEREMY G. GORDON is a faculty member in the Department of Humanities & Cultural Studies and the Honors College at the University of South Florida, where he studies the layered relationships among visuality, myth, and public culture.

DE WITT DOUGLAS KILGORE is an associate professor of English and American Studies at Indiana University. He is the author of *Astrofuturism: Science, Race and Visions of Utopia in Space* (2003). His recent work includes "Seeking the Galactic Club: Fred Hoyle, Carl Sagan and the C/SETI Novel," in *The Palgrave Handbook of Society, Culture and Outer Space* (2016) and a review of *Past Futures: Science*

Fiction Space Travel, and Postwar Art of the Americas for the *Los Angeles Review of Books* (September 24, 2015).

WENDY KOZOL is professor of Comparative American Studies at Oberlin College and the author of *Distant Wars Visible: The Ambivalence of Witnessing* (2014).

JOHN LOUIS LUCAITES is Provost Professor of Rhetoric in the Department of English at Indiana University, Bloomington. He is the coauthor with Robert Hariman of *No Caption Needed: Photojournalism, Public Culture, and Liberal Democracy* (2007) and *The Public Image: Photography and Civic Spectatorship* (2016). He and Hariman co-host the blog www.nocaptionneeded.com. He is the senior editor for a book series on Rhetoric, Culture, and Social Critique at the University of Alabama Press and currently serves as the associate dean for Arts and Humanities in the College of Arts and Sciences at IU.

JODY LYNEÉ MADEIRA is an associate professor of law at the Indiana University Maurer School of Law and the author of *Killing McVeigh: The Death Penalty and the Myth of Closure.* Her scholarly interests primarily involve the intersection of law and emotion in criminal and family law.

DIANE RUBENSTEIN is a professor of government and American studies and a member of the French Graduate Field at Cornell University. Her more recent books include *This Is Not a President: Sense and Nonsense in the American Political Imaginary* (2008), and, as coeditor, *Michael A. Weinstein: Action, Contemplation, Vitalism* (2015). She is presently completing a book entitled *(In)hospitality: Derrida at Work in Law, Politics, and the University* and a coedited volume with Marine Baudrillard, *From the Archives: Baudrillard's Women.* She is at work on a coauthored (with Julie Webber) study of Hillary Clinton and feminine leadership.

JON SIMONS was an associate professor of media and political science at Indiana University, Bloomington, when this volume was edited. He is now Reader in Media at Leeds Trinity University, U.K. He has edited three volumes about critical theory: *From Kant to Lévi-Strauss* (2002), *Contemporary Critical Theorists* (2004), and *From Agamben to Žižek* (2010). He serves on the editorial board of the interdisciplinary journal *Culture, Theory, and Critique.* He has published books, chapters, and journal articles across the fields of political theory, cultural and visual studies, and media analysis. His work now focuses on political imagery, in particular images of peace in the Israeli peace movement, about which he writes a blog *Picturing Peace.*

ROGER STAHL is an associate professor of communication studies at the University of Georgia, where he studies and writes about rhetoric, media, popular culture, and conflict. He is the author of *Militainment Inc.: War, Media, and Popular Culture* (2010).

PHOTO CREDITS

Figure I.1: Michael Conroy/AP
Figure I.2: Art © Vik Muniz/Licensed by VAGA, New York, NY
Figure 1.1: David Guttenfelder/AP
Figure 1.2: Damon Winter/The New York Times/Redux
Figure 2.1: © Craig F. Walker/AFP/Getty Images
Figure 2.2: © Craig F. Walker/AFP/Getty Images
Figure 2.3: © Craig F. Walker/AFP/Getty Images
Figure 3.1: Steven Hensel
Figure 3.2: John Kipp
Figure 3.3: Steven Lopinto
Color plates: © Nina Berman
Figure 11.1: © Compagnie des Phares et Balises

INDEX

Page numbers in bold refer to figures.